BUILDING SUSTAINABLE PEACE

Building Sustainable Peace

Edited by Tom Keating & W. Andy Knight

United Nations
University Press
TOKYO • NEW YORK • PARIS

Academic Foundation
New Delhi

Cover photograph: Two Haitians peer through a gate on a bridge over the Massacre River at the Dominican-Haitian border. Miguel Gomez/Associated Press. Used by permission.

Title page and back cover photograph: The Gun Sculpture, by Sandra Bromley and Wallis Kendal. © i human 2000, photograph by Roth and Ramberg. Used by permission.

Book Design by Alan Brownoff

This edition is published in India in 2006

by : ACADEMIC FOUNDATION
4772-73 / 23 Bharat Ram Road, (23 Ansari Road),
Darya Ganj, New Delhi - 110 002 (India).
Phones : 23245001 / 02 / 03 / 04.
Fax : +91-11-23245005.
E-mail : academic@vsnl.com
www.academicfoundation.com

First published in 2004 by the United Nations University Press,
The United Nations University, 53-70 Jingumae 5-chome,
Shibuya-ku, Tokyo 150-8925
(ISBN 92-808-1101-0)
and
The University of Alberta Press
Ring House 2, Edmonton, Alberta, Canada T6G 2E1
(ISBN 0-88864-414-0)

Building Sustainable Peace
Edited by Tom Keating and W. Andy Knight

ISBN 81-7188-500-4
(South Asian Edition)

Printed and bound in India.

In Memory of

SERGIO VIEIRA DE MELLO

(1948–2003)

UN Special Representative for the Secretary-General in Iraq and

UN High Commissioner for Human Rights

Contents

Foreword

LEARNING TO BUILD PEACE

Senator
Douglas Roche, O.C.

THE TRAGIC EVENTS of 11 September 2001 did not change the world so much as remind us that it has been changing drastically for some time. Now that the veil of superpower rivalry has been lifted, we can better see how advances in technology with regard to the movement of people, materials, and information are transforming our world. The last decade has seen the devolution of power from governments to groups and individuals and, as violently demonstrated by the terrorists of 9-11, not all of these actors have peaceful intentions.

Based on the violent showdowns that dominate international conferences, one might be left with the impression that globalization is something to be resisted and rejected. However, globalization is not a decision or policy that some government or international organization is forcing the world into; it is the new international system into which policies now must fit. As such, it must be the point of reference for any discussion on peacebuilding.

To be sure, globalization has produced much that is good. From an economic point of view, the technologies that fuel the new international system have enabled more countries to produce more products more cheaply and to participate in markets they were effectively excluded from in the past. It is certainly true that globalization has made a welcome contribution to reducing poverty in some of the largest and strongest economies. More than simply facilitating trade and investment, new technologies have also been the driving force behind advances in communication and information services, and advances in the sciences.

Still, the world we live in is still very much a violent one—both physically and structurally. The lesson of 9-11 is that the same forces that drive economic prosperity, civil society and scientific advance also drive inequality, injustice and conflict. To date, globalization has been a very unequal process and has done nothing to narrow the gap between the world's haves and have-nots. According to the 2002 United Nations Development Programme (UNDP) Human Development Report, the number of people living in extreme poverty remained unchanged in the 1990s.[1] Based on current trends, this disparity will widen in the future.

The prospects for a peaceful and constructive civil society mirror the bleakness of this economic disparity. The lowering of economic barriers along with the declining cost of transportation and information technologies has been a boon for illicit arms merchants, drug traffickers, warlords and terrorists alike. Promoting ideologies of hate, these suddenly stronger actors have the power to not only threaten state sovereignty, but also disrupt the lives and sense of security of ordinary citizens. The economic successes of globalization have served to hide this legacy of day-to-day individual suffering. The social decay caused by grinding poverty, human rights violations, communal violence and the arms trade—to name just a few—is a legacy that reproduces itself as new generations learn from the violence of generations past. In short, just as with economic injustice, globalization has done little to address the culture of violence that permeates the world today.

The world is confronted by a major dilemma. The official international order—represented by the United Nations system—is one of peace, whereas the parallel unofficial system is one based on militarism and war. Both of these international orders claim the loyalty and dedication of humankind. The official order sees human rights, cooperation and toleration as the main instruments, while the rival system reaches for power and subjugation to maintain order. Although social and political injustice do not by themselves lead to terrorism, terrorists and other extremists exploit these factors for their own violent ends; as disparity widens and technology progresses, it will become increasingly difficult for these two systems to coexist. It is a sad fact that in this era touted as the most prosperous and advanced, violence continues to claim 1.6 million lives each year and hinders many millions more.[2] This harm is not inevitable. Violence is a complex problem related to attitudes and behavior and is shaped by forces within our communities and families. Put simply, if we can learn differently, we can act differently.

Of course, violence remains a widely accepted means to achieve national interests. It is legally based and controlled and this legitimacy serves as an invitation to those seeking to challenge state power to acquire and use weapons to promote violent extremism. This war culture has been glorified throughout history. Poets have praised it, painters have dramatized it, clergymen, rabbis and imams have reassured warring factions that God is on their side and youth have been encouraged to sacrifice their lives in the name of racial and national patriotism. The disastrous consequences of this culture of violence over the past century are obvious and easily obtained from history books and the daily news—yet this system is allowed to persist.

Despite the end of the Cold War, governments continue to pursue an elusive peace through militarism. In 2001 alone, global military expenditure was estimated at US$800 billion[3] and this amount was expected to rise by another $50 billion in 2002.[4] Close to 70 percent of these weapons will be imported by developing countries, many of which are trying to lift themselves up from conflict. In an interconnected world, both developed and developing countries bear the consequences of this enormous expense through grinding poverty, disease, a despoiled environment, and terrorism to name only a few. Little attention is given to the effect of continuing high military expenditures on the ability of governments to devote sufficient resources to economic and social development. Yet, according to the 2002 UNDP's Human Development Report, all of the UN Millennium Development Goals could be achieved if official development assistance (ODA) was increased by only $50 billion.[5]

The continued development, production, distribution and use of increasingly sophisticated and destructive weaponry is the lynchpin that keeps the culture of war in place. However, in a world of widening disparity and rapid technological progress, a system based on suppression and force is untenable. The terror attacks of 11 September 2001 are the most obvious example of what lie ahead if this archaic system is allowed to persist and, with the suddenly very real possibility that nonstate actors may acquire weapons of mass destruction (WMD), worse may be in store.

Judging by the coverage in our media, the policies of our governments, and the curricula in our schools, one might assume that violence is inherent to the human condition. This could not be further from the truth. Violence can be prevented and the culture of violence can be transformed into one of peace. Recent peace agreements in El Salvador, Namibia, Mozambique, Angola, South Africa, Ireland and East Timor demonstrate that there is a strong desire for peace. But there is little comfort in this progress when one considers the countless lives sacrificed and curtailed on the long road to peace and the highly combustible animosity that remains in post-conflict societies.

The war culture must be addressed through education. Just as minds can be programmed for violence and prejudice, they can be programmed for peace and tolerance. To date, education systems have been very successful at increasing literacy and numeracy and thus increasing overall wealth. With economic success measured by the number of university degrees per capita and with education ranked alongside corporate tax policy and other economic indicators, education policy is considered just another competitive advantage for those Western countries at the forefront of globalization. This approach has done little to widen the prospects for peace or sustainable development and has instead served to harden national feeling and competitive individualism. Consequently, the present generation has been left ill prepared to adapt peaceably to a globalized world that demands precisely the opposite qualities.

The reality of globalization demands that the current generation, and those who come after, acquire more knowledge and understanding of the world than their elders now (and certainly did) possess. In a world where our fate is held in common, simply learning to manage conflict within the current war system—through arms control, peacekeeping and humanitarian assistance to name a few examples—is not enough. Something more profound must be done.

While nothing less than a revolutionary transformation of the status quo is required, the first step is enabling the coming generation to understand that in a globalized world security can no longer come from the barrel of a gun. Although threats to security are at the global scale, our answers and solutions are anchored in an old nation-state system that finds it increasingly difficult to predict or respond to the new security environment. A security defined in terms of human and ecological needs must replace the prevailing definition based on armaments, violent conflict and war. Adjusting to the new security paradigm will not be easy since the strategic interests of the major powers—fed by the military-industrial-scientific complex—are still the driving force in international relations.

Peace education offers a concrete strategy that goes beyond the current management approach to violent conflict. More than the simple advocacy of the avoidance of war, it seeks to create something more systemic and lasting from the bottom up. The foundation of peacebuilding and peace education goes beyond the science of conflict that preoccupies the current curricula and aims to create the knowledge, skills and attitudes that will allow people of all ages and levels to develop the behavioral changes needed to prevent the occurrence of conflict, to resolve it peacefully and to create the social conditions conducive to peace. Certainly, there are many actions that can be taken to make postconflict societies more peaceful; most of them are detailed in the pages of this book. To cement peace into place, there must be a much deeper and sustained effort to educate present and future generations to use nonviolent means to resolve conflict.

Education has been an underutilized peacebuilding tool. For too long, the business of conflict resolution and peacebuilding has been left to the experts and assumed to be too technical for the average citizen, let alone the world's youth. However, today's security dilemmas are too multifaceted to be left in the hands of a few. In order to make the transition to a culture of peace, there must be a demystifying of the technicalities that obscure the fundamental security issues. People at all levels should be empowered to assess and evaluate the possibilities for change.

Peace education makes the necessary investment in the coming generation and helps to activate its potential free from outside interference. Essentially, this requires a massive educational effort that seeks to better shape our children's consciousness by injecting values of tolerance and respect for cultural, religious and political diversity. This challenge is so broad that it must become the sustained priority of all levels of organization and can only be accomplished if governments, communities and individuals take the culture of peace to heart and mind. Only in this way can humanity move beyond the kind of calamity that has engulfed past and current generations.

The UN is at the cutting edge of this effort. The new UN study on disarmament and nonproliferation education provides specific measures for opening up current curricula to address the complexity of international conflict issues.[6] Specifically, the study recognizes the crucial link between disarmament and other international issues and seeks to raise the level of public engagement through education. For too long, disarmament has been an issue monopolized by experts and high-level government discussions. Recognizing this, the UN study recommends establishing close collaboration between experts in the field and civil society—especially educators and academic institutions. Through education and training, individuals can become empowered to make a contribution to achieving concrete disarmament and nonproliferation measures. The study realizes that the knowledge required by a school-age child in a refugee camp will be different from that needed by a diplomat, but understands that the most effective way to inspire activism, and thus change, is through learning.

Time is running out before the confluence of sustainable development problems and the proliferation of weapons produces a massive conflagration. Governments will have to put to rest old mentalities and open up education systems to reflect the new global environment. The challenge then is to ensure that the vision and requirements for peace education are not sublimated by the daily grind of politics that perpetuates the culture of violence. The agenda for peace must transcend the daily marketplace of politics and confront the war mentality head-on. In teaching coming generations "how" and not "what" to think we will open up the political process to include those it claims to encompass, move beyond the prevailing violence and cynicism, and put peace on the agenda.

Notes

1 United Nations Development Programme, *Human Development Report 2002: Deepening Democracy in a Fragmented World* (New York: Oxford University Press, 2002), 18. http://hdr.undp.org/reports/global/2002/en/pdf/chapterone.pdf (accessed November 24, 2003).

2 World Health Organization, *World Report on Violence and Health* (Geneva: World Health Organization, 2002), 9. http://www5.who.int/violence_injury_prevention/download.cfm?id=0000000582 (accessed November 30, 2003).

3 Jayantha Dhanapala, *Statement before the First Committee of the General Assembly* (New York: United Nations, 8 October 2002), 3. http://disarmament.un.org/speech/08oct2001.htm modified (accessed November 24, 2003).

4 Dhanapala, *Statement*, 1.

5 United Nations Development Programme, *Human Development Report 2002: Deepening Democracy in a Fragmented World*, 30.

http://hdr.undp.org/reports/global/2002/en/pdf/complete.pdf (accessed November 24, 2003).

6 United Nations, *United Nations Study on Disarmament and Non-proliferation Education* (New York: United Nations, 30 August 2002). http://disarmament.un.org/education/study.html (accessed November 24, 2003).

Preface

Tom Keating &
W. Andy Knight

THE DEBACLE of the US-led coalition intervention in Iraq reminds us of the difficulties involved in building peace. For the world's sole superpower, winning the war against the inferior Iraqi army was relatively easy. However, winning the peace is proving to be much more complex than the occupying power had anticipated. This book is about more than winning the peace. It is about making peace sustainable.

In order to explore the potential and pitfalls of peacebuilding and pre- and postconflict reconciliation, a symposium was held at the University of Alberta on 10 March 2000 to coincide with the visit of Madam Justice Louise Arbour to the University of Alberta to deliver the Second Annual Visiting Lectureship in Human Rights. Madam Arbour's participation in the symposium provided a focal point for examining the different instruments and actors involved in peacebuilding operations—ranging from the work of international criminal tribunals through to truth commissions to the work of NGOs at the level of civil society and the militaries of national governments.

The symposium brought together academics, policy advisors, practitioners and members of the general public to examine and discuss various dimensions of the peacebuilding and postconflict reconciliation process. The essays in this collection were inspired by this symposium and address, *inter alia*, the following issues: the factors that have encouraged foreign governments and international institutions that intervene in an effort to contribute to the process of resolving civil wars and reconciling divided societies; the different techniques that have been used in the peacebuilding process; the role of various nongovernmental actors and regional organizations; and the experiences of peacebuilding efforts in different parts of the world. Many of the essays collected here were first presented at this symposium. Others have been included in an effort to examine particular issues more extensively. While not all of the presentations delivered at the symposium could have been included here, this collection was certainly inspired and guided by the comments, questions and discussions of all of those who participated in the symposium. The event was generously supported by the Human Rights Education Foundation (now known as the John Humphrey Centre for Peace and Human Rights), the University of Alberta, the Canadian Centre for Foreign Policy Development and the Security and Defence Forum of the Department of National Defence.

Acknowledgments

THE EDITORS wish to acknowledge first and foremost the financial assistance of the Canadian Centre for Foreign Policy Development (CCFPD), the Security and Defence Forum of the Department of National Defence, the University of Alberta's Faculties of Arts and Law, the Department of Political Science, the Office of the Vice-President (Academic), and the Provost. This collection would not have been possible without their support. We would also like to acknowledge the support of the University of Alberta International and the Human Rights Education Foundation (now known as the John Humphrey Centre for Peace and Human Rights).

A number of individuals were instrumental in planning and organizing the Symposium out of which the idea for this edited volume emerged. The advisory committee for the Symposium consisted of Nancy Hannemann (Symposium Coordinator), Tom Keating, W. Andy Knight, Patrick Bendin, Gurcharan S. Bhatia, Gerald Gall, J.S. (Jack) O'Neill, Satya Das and Madhvi Russell. The following students made a significant contribution to the smooth running of the Symposium: Vladimir Gomez, Kim Hiller and Sean McMahon. Senator Roche chaired the Symposium.

A special note of gratitude also goes to Tanya Narozhna for her research assistance on the book manuscript, Monique Carley, Anna

Lund and Megan Murphy for providing the index. At the University of Alberta Press we would like to thank Leslie Vermeer for shepherding this manuscript through the initial process; Michael Luski, who, as Aquisitions Editor, picked up where Leslie left off; Peter Midgley for his meticulous copy editing; Alethea Adair, for her editorial assistance; Alan Brownoff for book design; Denise Ahlefeldt for text formatting; and Mary Mahoney-Robson for her advice on style.

Sandra Bromley and Wallis Kendal, the two artists who created the inspired and provocative sculpture portrayed on the titlepage and back cover, generously donated the photograph for the book. The 5-tonne gun sculpture was created in 1999 as a Millennium Project against violence. It has now been exhibited around the world, including at the United Nations headquarters in New York during the 2001 Conference on the Illicit Trade in Small Arms and Light Weapons that was attended by representatives from more than 120 UN Member States and about 177 nongovernmental organizations (NGOs). This gun sculpture is symbolic of one of the planks necessary for building sustainable peace, i.e. the need to address the issue of the proliferation of small arms, especially in conflict-ridden developing countries.

Finally, we acknowledge with thanks the United Nations Department of Public Information for providing the photograph of Sergio Vieira de Mello, UN Special Representative for the Secretary-General in Iraq and UN High Commissioner for Human Rights, who in our opinion was the quintessential peacebuilder. Sergio was unfortunately killed in Bagdad, Iraq, while on a UN mission to build sustainable peace in that troubled country.

Acronyms

ACRI	African Crisis Response Initiative
AFRC	Armed Forces Revolutionary Council
AMM	ASEAN Ministerial Meeting
APDOVE	Association of Protestant Development Organizations in Europe
APEC	Asia Pacific Economic Cooperation
ARF	ASEAN Regional Forum
ASEAN	Association of South East Asian Nations
ATU	Anti-Terrorist Unit
BICC	Bonn International Center for Conversion
BRJ	Bureau de Renseignement Judiciare
CDC	Community Development Committee
CEP	Community Empowerment and Local Government Project
CGDK	Coalition Government of Democratic Kampuchea
CIDA	Canadian International Development Agency
CIDSE	Cooperation Internationale pour le développment et la solidarité
CIVPOL	Civilian Police
CMG	Conflict Management Group
CPAS	Politico-Administrative Committees

CRC	Central Revolutionary Front
CRDP	Community Reintegration Development Project
CSCE	Council of Security Cooperation in Europe
CSDP	Common Security and Defence Policy
DEA	Drug Enforcement Administration
DFAIT	Department of Foreign Affairs and International Trade, Canada
DND	Department of National Defence
DOP	Declaration of Principles
DRC	Democratic Republic of Congo
ECOMOG	ECOWAS Ceasefire Monitoring Group
ECOWAS	The Economic Community of West African States
EPLF	Eritrean Peoples' Liberation Front
EPRDF	Ethiopian Peoples' Revolutionary Democratic Front
EU	European Union
FEWER	Forum on Early Warning and Early Response
GTZ	Gesellschaft für Technische Zusammenarbeit
IANSA	International Action Network on Small Arms
ICC	International Criminal Court
ICG	International Crisis Group
ICISS	International Commission on Intervention and State Sovereignty
ICITAP	International Criminal Investigative Training Assistance Program
ICRC	International Committee of the Red Cross
ICTR	International Criminal Tribunal for Rwanda
ICTY	International Criminal Tribunal for the former Yugoslavia
ICVA	International Council of Voluntary Agencies
IDA	International Development Association
IDPS	Internally Displaced Persons
IGADD	Intergovernmental Authority for Drought and Development
IGOS	Intergovernmental Organizations

IMETP	International Military Education and Training Program
INGHAS	International Nongovernmental Humanitarian Actors
INGOS	International Nongovernmental Organizations
INTERFET	International Force for East Timor
IPM	International Police Monitors
ISS	Institute for Security Studies
IUHEI	Institute Universitaire de Hautes Études Internationales
EU	European Union
JICC	Joint Intelligence Coordination Centre
JIMS	Jakarta Informal Meetings
G 7/8	Group of 7 or 8 (Russia added)
KFOR	Kosovo Force (NATO)
KLA	Kosovo Liberation Army
LDCS	Less developed countries
LDF	Lofa Defence Force
LNGOS	Local Nongovernmental Organizations
LPC	Liberia Peace Council
LURD	Liberians United for Reconciliation and Democracy
MCPMR	Mechanism for Conflict Prevention, Management and Resolution
MNF	Multinational Force
MSF	Médecins Sans Frontières
MTCR	Missile Technology Control Regime
NATO	North Atlantic Treaty Organization
NGOS	Nongovernmental Organizations
NFD	Northern Frontier District (Kenya)
NIF	National Islamic Front
NISAT	Norwegian Initiative on Small Arms Transfers
NPFL	National Patriotic Front of Liberia
NRP	National Reconstruction Program
OAS	Organization of American States
OAU	Organization of African Unity (now the African Union)
ODA	Official Development Assistance

OECD	Organization for Economic Cooperation and Development
OSCE	Organization for Security Cooperation in Europe
PCIA	Peace and Conflict Impact Assessment
PRIO	Peace Research Institute
RCMP	Royal Canadian Mounted Police
RS	Republika Srpska
RUF	Revolutionary United Front
SALF	Somali Abo Liberation Front
SALW	Small Arms and Light Weapons
SFOR	Stabilization Force
SLA	Sierra Leone Army
SNM	Somali National Movement
SRV	Socialist Republic of Vietnam
SWAT	Special Weapons and Tactics
TAC	Treaty of Amity and Cooperation
TFET	Trust Fund for East Timor
ULIMO-J	United Liberation Movement of Liberia for Democracy—Kraun Branch
ULIMO-K	United Liberation Movement of Liberia for Democracy—Madingo Branch
UN	United Nations
UNAMIR	United Nations Assistance Mission in Rwanda
UNAMSIL	United Nations Mission in Sierra Leone
UNDP	United Nations Development Programme
UN-Habitat	United Nations Human Settlement Programme
UNHCR	United Nations High Commissioner for Refugees
UNICEF	United Nations Children's Education Fund
UNMIH	United Nations Mission in Haiti
UNMIK	United Nations Mission in Kosovo
UNOMIL	United Nations Observer Mission in Liberia
UNTAET	United Nations Transitional Administration in East Timor
US	United States

USIP	United States Institute for Peace
WFP	World Food Program
WMD	Weapons of Mass Destruction
WSLF	Western Somali Liberation Front

Contributors

FRANCIS KOFI ABIEW teaches in the Political Science Department at Kwantlen University College, Surrey, British Columbia. He is the author of *The Evolution of the Doctrine and Practice of Humanitarian Intervention* (1999), and has published articles on humanitarian intervention, NGOs, and peacekeeping.

ADEKEYE ADEBAJO is Executive Director of the Centre for Conflict Resolution (CCR) at the University of Cape Town. Between 2001 and 2004, he was Director of the Africa Programme at the International Peace Academy (IPA) and Adjunct Professor at Columbia University's School of International and Public Affairs (SIPA), both in New York. He is the author of *Building Peace in West Africa: Liberia, Sierra Leone, and Guinea-Bissau* (2002); *Liberia's Civil War: Nigeria, ECOMOG, and Regional Security in West Africa* (2002); and co-editor of *Managing Armed Conflicts in the Twenty-First Century* (2001), as well as the forthcoming *West Africa's Security Challenges: Building Peace in a Troubled Region.*

HOWARD ADELMAN was Professor of Philosophy at York University in Toronto from 1966–2003 where he founded and was the first Director of the Centre for Refugee Studies, and Editor of *Refuge* until 1993. He has written well over one hundred academic articles and chapters in books as well as authored or co-edited 21 books. In addition to his numerous writings on refugees, he has written on the Middle East, humanitarian intervention, membership rights, ethics, early warning and conflict management. He co-edited *The Path of a Genocide: The Rwanda Crisis from Uganda to Zaire* (1999). His latest volume *Humanitarian Intervention in Zaire* appeared in January of 2004.

CHRISTOPHER P. ANKERSEN is Dahrendorf Scholar at London School of Economics and Political Science's Centre for Civil Society. He spent twelve years as an infantry officer in the Canadian Forces, including duty on peace support missions in Croatia (1992–1993) and Kosovo (1999). He has written and consulted extensively in the fields of international conflict, security, and defense, receiving awards from the US, the UK, and Canada for his work. He is completing a PhD in International Relations at the LSE. He lives in London with his wife and three children.

DAVID BEER is a Superintendent in the Royal Canadian Mounted Police. He has been seconded to the Canadian International Development Agency and the Department of Foreign Affairs and has worked in Haiti, the Central African Republic, and most recently Iraq. He was primarily responsible for creation of the five year Canadian plan for bilateral policing development assistance offered to Haiti from 1996–2001. He is a recipient of the Canadian Peacekeeping medal, among other awards, for his work abroad.

KENNETH BUSH is Assistant Professor in the Conflict Studies Programme at St. Paul University, Ottawa. He has worked extensively with governmental, inter-governmental, and non-governmental actors on the challenges of peacebuilding. He received his PhD in International Relations and Comparative Politics from Cornell University.

JARAT CHOPRA is Chief Monitor of the Palestinian Monitoring Group (PMG) and previously served as Head of the Office of District Administration for the United Nations Transitional Administration in East Timor (UNTAET). He is also Professor of International Law and directed the International Relations Program at Brown University. He authored *Peace-Maintenance: The Evolution of International Political Authority* (1999) and edited *The Politics of Peace-Maintenance* (1998).

SATYA BRATA DAS is an experienced opinion leader, a noted policy advisor and analyst, and most recently, the author of the best selling *The Best Country: Why Canada Will Lead the Future* (2002). With more than 25 years of public policy experience as an award-winning editorialist, foreign affairs specialist and national commentator, Das is now a principal in Cambridge Strategies Inc., a Canadian public policy consultancy. His volunteer time is committed to human rights, community building and a host of cultural endeavors.

JEAN DAUDELIN is Assistant Professor at the Norman Paterson School of International Affairs, where he teaches on conflict and development. His research now deals mainly with land and resource conflicts and with Brazilian and Canadian foreign policy. He has published, among other journals, in *International Peacekeeping, Third World Quarterly* and the *Journal of Church and State*.

KASSU GEBREMARIAM holds a PhD in Political Science from York University, Toronto. Over the years he has taught a wide assortment of courses at various American universities, and for the past two years has taught at Southeastern University, Washington, DC. He is a coordinator of Social Sciences at the Department of Liberal Studies. Currently, he is working on a book project with W. Andy Knight on Somalia, and another on conflict resolution in the countries on the Horn of Africa.

TANJA HOHE is a social anthropologist who served for two-and-a-half years in East Timor, as a District Electoral Officer for UNAMET, and also as Political Affairs Officer for UNTAET. She co-authored the 2001 Final Report on *Traditional Power Structures and the*

Community Empowerment and Local Governance Project for the World Bank. She is currently a Visiting Fellow at the Thomas J. Watson, Jr. Institute for International Studies, Brown University.

TOM KEATING is Professor of Political Science at the University of Alberta where he teaches in the areas of Canadian foreign and defense policy, international relations, international institutions and ethics in international relations. He has authored or co-authored many essays and four books, the most recent of which is *Canada and World Order: The Multilateralist Tradition in Canadian Foreign Policy* (2003).

W. ANDY KNIGHT is Professor of International Relations and McCalla Research Professor in the Department of Political Science at the University of Alberta. He is past Vice Chair of the Academic Council on the UN System and currently editor of *Global Governance Journal*. His recent books include: *Adapting the United Nations to a Postmodern Era: Lessons Learned,* (2001) and *A Changing United Nations: Multilateral Evolution and the Quest for Global Governance* (2000). He was recently awarded a major three-year research grant by the Social Sciences and Humanities Research Council of Canada (SSHRCC) to study "Children and Armed Conflict."

MELISSA LABONTE's research and teaching focuses on international and national nongovernmental organizations, international organizations, humanitarian crises, multilateral peace operations and the politics of humanitarian intervention. She has served as a researcher for the Governance in War-torn Societies project of the Watson Institute for International Studies, Executive Director of the United Nations Association of Greater Boston, and Program Director for the Academic Council on the United Nations System. Her recent publications include "Dimensions of Post-Conflict Peacebuilding and Democratization" in *Global Governance* (2003), and "The Case of Sierra Leone" in *Twenty-first Century Peace Operations: The Critical Cases* (2004) edited by William Durch and Paul Stares. During 2003–2004, she was awarded the Belfer Family Fellowship and is presently completing her PhD in Political Science/International Relations at Brown University in Providence, Rhode Island.

CAROLYN ELIZABETH LLOYD is a PhD candidate in Political Science at the Université de Montréal. Her dissertation is titled "Controlling the Light Weapons of the World." She was recently the Norman Robertson Fellow at the Department of Foreign Affairs and International Trade and has previously co-authored an article in the *Third World Quarterly*.

JOSEPH MASCIULLI is Assistant Professor of Political Science at St. Thomas University, Fredericton, New Brunswick. He teaches international relations, US Politics, and human rights.

SUMIE NAKAYA is a doctoral candidate in Political Science at the Graduate Center, The City University of New York. Currently she works with the Conflict Prevention and Peace Forum at the Social Science Research Council. At the time of writing, Ms. Nakaya was Program Specialist at the United Nations Development Fund for Women (UNIFEM), focusing on the impact of conflict on women and women's role in peacebuilding.

SHAUN NARINE is Assistant Professor of Political Science at St. Thomas University, Fredericton, New Brunswick. He has published extensively on issues related to institutional development in the Asia Pacific. His book, *Explaining ASEAN: Regionalism in Southeast Asia* was published in 2002. His current work includes research on regional financial institutionalism in the Asia Pacific and great power relations.

SENATOR DOUGLAS ROCHE, O.C., author, parliamentarian and diplomat, he was appointed to the Senate of Canada in 1998. He served as Canada's Ambassador for Disarmament from 1984-1989 and was elected Chairman of the United Nations Disarmament Committee, the main UN body dealing with political and security issues, at the 43rd General Assembly in 1988. Douglas Roche was elected to the Canadian Parliament four times, serving from 1972-1984, specializing in the subjects of development and disarmament. He is an Officer of the Order of Canada, Chairman of Canadian Pugwash, and Chairman, Middle Powers Initiative, a network of eight international nongovernmental organizations specializing in nuclear disarmament. He is the author of over fifteen books. His most recent publications include *Bread Not Bombs: A Political Agenda for Social Justice* (1999) and *The Human Right to Peace* (2003).

Introduction

Tom Keating & W. Andy Knight

RECENT DEVELOPMENTS IN POSTCONFLICT STUDIES—PEACEBUILDING AND GOVERNANCE

PEACEBUILDING has emerged as one of the most critically important, albeit vexing, aspects of international involvement in conflict and postconflict situations. Peacebuilding, as a concept and strategy, has been adopted by national governments, nongovernmental organizations (NGOs) and regional and international intergovernmental institutions (IGOs) as a means by which the outside world can contribute to the resolution of intrastate [or societal] conflict and to the reconstruction, or construction, of a culture of peace in postconflict situations. Persisting conflicts in places such as Afghanistan, Bosnia, Chechnya, the Democratic Republic of the Congo, Eritrea, Haiti, Israel/Palestine, Kosovo, Rwanda and Sierra Leone demonstrate both the overwhelming need for and significant difficulties in building sustainable conditions for peace in postconflict societies.

Peacebuilding operations in these and other settings have confronted many barriers and have achieved varying degrees of success. Yet the very attempt on the part of outsiders to undertake such measures reflects an acknowledgment of international humanitarian and human rights law and a significant shift in international attitudes and practices towards civil conflicts.

The years since the end of the Cold War in 1989 have been marked by two distinct but interrelated trends in the arena of global politics. The first has been the persistence of violent conflict, much of it in the form of civil wars or internal repression where the overwhelming majority of the victims are civilians. Civil wars and repressive governments are not exceptional phenomena, and have been a part of the history of many nations; yet their prevalence in the post–Cold War period and the level of violence committed against civilian populations have become matters of increased international concern. They have also become a significant source of regional and international instability in the post–Cold War system. Civil wars are often more brutal than interstate wars in the extent to which they endanger civilians or result in attacks on civilian property.[1] Thus, civil wars and other forms of intrastate conflict present a difficult set of problems for outside actors.

A second, more promising, feature of the post–Cold War years has been the concern that individuals, groups, governments, and international organizations have displayed for human rights, individual security and good governance, alongside an increased willingness among the international community and regional organizations to intervene in the internal affairs of countries in support of these concerns. There has been a significant increase in the number, variety, scope, and prominence of these interventions for overtly humanitarian purposes. These interventions have, with great frequency, adopted peacebuilding as one of their main objectives. The increased prominence and critical importance of peacebuilding are the primary reasons for undertaking this volume that brings together analysts and practitioners to assess the merits of peacebuilding.

Peacebuilding, as it has been practiced to date, involves a number of diverse instruments and players, and much like an orchestra, the instruments must be finely tuned and the players must work in concert in order to produce anything resembling a coherent approach to postconflict reconciliation and sustainable peace. As a multidimensional exercise, peacebuilding encompasses a variety of tasks such as disarming warring parties, decommissioning and destroying weapons, de-mining, repatriating refugees, restoring law and order, creating or rebuilding justice systems, training police forces and customs agents, providing technical assistance, advancing efforts to protect human rights, strengthening civil society institutions, and reforming and strengthening institutions of governance—including assistance in monitoring and supervising electoral processes and promoting formal and informal participation in the political process.

The players involved in peacebuilding are equally diverse—ranging from civil society and NGOs, governments, international and regional organizations, ad hoc criminal tribunals (and potentially the International Criminal Court (ICC)), to truth and reconciliation commissions and prominent individuals like the Special Representatives of the UN Secretary-General. The complex character of peacebuilding reflects an acknowledgment of the multidimensional and integrated causes of civil war and of the need to address the economic, social and political aspects of reconstruction and reconciliation.

Much of the literature that has examined postconflict reconstruction mirrors the complex, multidimensional character of peacebuilding. This literature has examined, *inter alia*, the factors that have encouraged foreign governments and international and regional institutions to intervene in support of the process of resolving civil wars and reconciling divided societies; the different techniques and mechanisms that have been used in the peacebuilding process; the role of various nongovernmental actors; the relationship between the military and civil society groups in the process of peacebuilding; and the experiences of peacebuilding efforts in different parts of the world. One can discern a number of themes in the literature on peacebuilding, indicating the range of issues involved and the extent to which the discourse on and practice of peacebuilding has been evolving. For our purposes, these themes can be listed as follows: conceptualizing peacebuilding; relocating peacebuilding from postconflict to preventive strategies; deconstructing the culture of war and constructing an indigenous culture of peace; broadening the scope and scale of peacebuilding; assessing the international architecture in support of peacebuilding; examining civil-military relations and the tensions between order and justice; positioning peacebuilding within the broader concept of human security; and balancing demands for reconciliation and retributive justice.

The first theme in the literature addresses the conceptualization of peacebuilding. The genealogy of peacebuilding suggests rather radical origins found in the peace research writings of Johan Galtung and Kenneth and Elsie Boulding.[2] From this perspective, peacebuilding involves addressing underlying structural causes of conflict. It emphasizes bottom up approaches and the decentering of social and economic structures. In short, it calls for a radical transformation of society away from structures of coercion and violence to an embedded culture of peace. These ideas, although generally trumped by band-aid and sometimes shortsighted approaches to building peace, continue to resonate in the contemporary period.[3]

Many others have taken a less radical approach, while maintaining a holistic framework for peacebuilding. Lederach, for example, writes of marshalling all sectors of society in support of sustainable peace.[4] Oliver Richmond elaborates on the model:

> In Ledarach's model, the problem-solving approach to conflict resolution is combined with a public, process-oriented approach in order to address the multidimensional nature of protracted social conflicts in the context of a nonlinear peace-building process. This emphasizes the need for a multisectoral approach to conflict transformation that brings in grassroots, local, and NGO actors in order to create a sustainable process.[5]

The objective of such holistic approaches is to bring about a fundamental transformation of conflict-ridden societies. While the roots of peacebuilding can be traced to more radical peace studies literature (some appearing in the 1960s), the pervasive interest in peacebuilding in the contemporary period can be found in the search for specific programs, policies and practices that can be employed to resolve civil conflicts in various regions of the world and restore conditions to the point where peace can be sustained.

Peacebuilding became part of the official discourse in the 1990s when former UN Secretary-General Boutros Boutros-Ghali used the term in *An Agenda for Peace*.[6] Initially, the concept was linked specifically with postconflict societies. Boutros-Ghali defined postconflict peacebuilding as "action to identify and support structures which will tend to strengthen and solidify peace in order to avoid a relapse into conflict."[7] He saw peacebuilding as an integral part of the UN's work. For him, preventive diplomacy, peacemaking and peacekeeping ought to be linked to peacebuilding so as to provide a seamless and comprehensive strategy for dealing with violent conflicts. The precise elements involved in peacebuilding, as envisioned by Boutros-Ghali, included disarming warring parties, restoring order, decommissioning and destroying weapons, repatriating refugees, providing advisory and training support for security personnel, monitoring elections, de-mining and other forms of demilitarization, providing technical assistance, advancing efforts to protect human rights, reforming and strengthening institutions of governance—including assistance in monitoring and supervising electoral processes—and promoting formal and informal participation in the political process.

In the aftermath of war, postconflict peacebuilding might also take the form of concrete cooperative projects that link formerly warring parties together. These projects would be designed to be mutually beneficial and ideally would contribute to socio-economic development for all parties and to confidence building between former combatants. Other projects might include educational exchanges and curriculum reform designed to reduce hostile perceptions of the "other" and forestall the renewal of hostilities between the factions. In essence, peacebuilding has been conceived as the construction of a new environment in many areas—political, economic, social, security—and can be viewed as a direct counterpart to preventive diplomacy "which seeks to avoid the breakdown of peaceful conditions."[8]

The challenge, according to Kenneth Bush, is "to encourage the creation of the political, economic, and social space, within which indigenous actors can identify, develop, and employ the resources necessary to build a peaceful, prosperous, and just society."[9] Boutros-Ghali's view was premised on the notion that the UN (and other would-be peacebuilders), as a global governance institution, has an obligation to provide support for the transformation of deficient national structures and capabilities and to work towards the strengthening of democratic institutions. Furthermore, social peace is as important as strategic or political peace.[10] Most discussions of peacebuilding thus accept that it involves a multilayered approach, involving participants from many sectors who attempt to reconstruct deficient practices and institutions in support of sustainable peace. Kenneth Bush considers that,

> In the broadest terms, peacebuilding refers to those initiatives which foster and support sustainable structures and processes, which strengthen the prospects for peaceful coexistence and decrease the likelihood of the outbreak, reoccurrence, or continuation, of violent conflict. The process entails both short- and long-term objectives, for example, short-term humanitarian operations, and longer-term developmental, political, economic, and social objectives.[11]

A second theme in the peacebuilding discourse focuses on repositioning peacebuilding from simply being a response in the aftermath of conflict or crisis to being a preventive strategy that is initiated before the conflict erupts. One sees this theme in studies that call for a shift from the "culture of reaction" to a "culture of prevention."[12] Initially there was a tendency among scholars and practitioners of peacebuilding to focus on postconflict reconstruction and band-aid solutions to crises. The authors in this volume by and large reject this and argue that a different approach is needed and that a broadened time perspective for peacebuilding has begun. There is an attempt in a number of quarters to move back and focus first on conflict prevention. At their summit in Cologne, the G-8 raised the significance of conflict prevention and dedicated a meeting to this issue in Berlin in 1999. The G-8 subsequently adopted the Miyazaki Initiatives for conflict prevention.[13] The Organization for Economic Cooperation and Development (OECD) has conducted a study on the effectiveness of aid for the prevention of conflict.[14] The Swedish government has commissioned several studies developing the concept of a culture of prevention.[15] The current UN Secretary-General, Kofi Annan, has devoted much time and energy to the issue of conflict prevention.[16]

Although Boutros-Ghali's use of peacebuilding was conceived as a postconflict activity, peacebuilding can, conceptually, be practiced at a "preconflict" stage; the purpose being to forestall the outbreak of violent conflict. The Carnegie Commission on the Prevention of Deadly Conflict viewed peacebuilding as either "structural prevention" (strategies designed to address the root causes of deadly conflict) or "operational prevention" (those strategies and tactics taken in the midst of a crisis or immediately thereafter to reconstruct the peace and thereby prevent a recurrence of violent conflict).[17] So we can speak of structural peacebuilding and operational peacebuilding (to replace the notion of pre- and postconflict peacebuilding). Used in this way, peacebuilding is tied closely to preventive diplomacy and other chapter VI measures in the UN Charter that aim to address the underlying economic, social, cultural and humanitarian obstacles to sustainable peace. Peacebuilding is therefore concerned not just with postconflict situations, but also with the broad spectrum of conflict and its main aim is to generate and sustain conditions of peace while managing differences without recourse to violence.

Regarding the shift in attention to conflict prevention, there are observers who acknowledge that the most desirable solution to the problems we have witnessed since the end of the Cold War is to prevent violent conflict through policies aimed at reconciling divided societies and constructing a stable peace—thus moving beyond a culture of war to a culture of peace.[18] As Senator Roche notes in his foreword, just as the mind can be programmed for violence and prejudice, it can also be programmed for peace and tolerance. There is a need for people at all levels of society to work toward the establishment and entrenchment of a culture of peace and especially to advance it through supporting participatory and people-centered processes. Some authors, like James Scott, advocate tapping into society and indigenous knowledge that exists within societies, such as the wisdom of the elders. Scott makes a distinction between the use of abstract knowledge (*techne*) on the part of outsiders and the potential benefits of practical knowledge (*metis*) provided by locals.[19] The pattern of intervention in the post–Cold War international system has tended not only to undermine the war-torn state, but also to ignore local actors and thus overlook the indigenous capacity of these local actors who in turn must assume greater responsibility for many aspects of sustainable peacebuilding, including security. This has sparked authors like Jarat Chopra to introduce the concept of participatory interventions, particularly in cases where international administrations are introduced in a country to govern temporarily:

> The idea of "participatory intervention" stands in contrasts to the practice of state-(re)building processes of relying on only international appointees or elites self-appointed as representatives of the people. Instead the aim would be to include direct involvement of the local population from the very beginning of an international intervention, in order to ensure justice for the parts and that new governing structures resonate with local social reality.[20]

He argues further that in these kinds of peacebuilding exercises, "participation has become a minimum standard and a moral imperative."[21]

Other analysts have called attention to the significant progress that has been made when groups in civil society collaborate with governments to improve the tools of peacebuilding—citing, *inter alia*, the Ottawa Treaty banning antipersonnel land mines, the Treaty of Rome establishing the ICC, and the recent conclusion of a convention banning the use of child soldiers.[22]

Others, like Roland Paris, have warned against the "single-paradigm," or liberal internationalist, approach to peacebuilding that has guided the work of many international agencies engaged in efforts to strengthen civil society in war-torn states. Part of the difficulty here is the assumption that the surest foundation for peace, both within and between states, is market democracy (a liberal democratic polity and a market economy). Such an assumption does not address other forces that have shaped the culture of these communities: "Peacebuilding in effect [becomes] an enormous experiment in social engineering—an experiment that involves transplanting Western models of social, political, and economic organization into war-shattered states in order to control civil conflict: in other words, pacification through political and economic liberalization."[23] From this perspective, peacebuilding becomes a method for imposing particular solutions on other societies and ignoring more viable alternatives.

Ronnie Lipschutz maintains that such practices fail to address the underlying justice issues present in most contemporary conflicts. Lipschutz argues that too often the role of outside governments has been to support the formal institutions of democracy in an effort to restore political stability and, not coincidentally, viable economic activity. Agreements are signed, constitutions are drafted, elections are held, and a deeply divided society appears restored to a level of civility. Yet in almost all-important respects, the underlying fissures that have divided the society remain intact and are merely papered over through these cosmetic changes. Underlying issues are not addressed and unjust structures and practices continue and, in some cases, are exacerbated. One of the problems that confronts any attempt to reconcile societies divided by years of bitter conflict is that the institutional and procedural devices for addressing social problems—the foundational political culture that sustains societies—are often destroyed or so severely corrupted that they are effectively inoperable. Peacebuilding should necessarily raise "fundamental questions not only about what to reconstruct but also about how to do so in order not to recreate the unsustainable institutions and structures that originally contributed to the conflict."[24]

A fourth theme emerging from the literature on peacebuilding addresses the broadening scale and scope of peacebuilding. This includes an effort to encompass a wider array of development issues, as reflected, for example, in Bernard Wood's work for the UN Development Programme that examines the contribution that economic and sustainable development efforts can make to the peacebuilding objectives.[25] It also reflects a view that the approach of treating peacebuilding as a concentrated operation in an insular and isolated state is *passé*. Practitioners, policymakers, and analysts are now aware of the extent to which peacebuilding operations have expanded in scale and scope, involving in some cases nonfunctioning states, neighboring states and regional agencies. We have had to scale up to deal with these more complex issues. Due to the spillover effect, it has become necessary to examine civil conflict as a part of regional conflict and to develop appropriate peacebuilding strategies that involve roles for the neighbors of the target state. Regional actors and organizations in Africa, Latin America, and Asia have not only taken an interest, but also a more active level of intervention in support of peacebuilding operations in their respective regions.

Additionally, peacebuilding demands the support of an international environment and critically important international and/or regional actors. In this respect, the practice of peacebuilding must include strategies at two levels: (1) the level of regional and international regimes and (2) in-country peacebuilding measures. Regional and international regimes refer to those principles, norms, rules and practices with respect to peacebuilding that are developed mostly in and around regional and international organizations and form a framework for action in societies that are moving away from violent conflict. In-country peacebuilding refers to national and local level efforts, involving both governmental and civil society actors, that are aimed at economic development, institution building and, more generally, the creation or restoration within countries of the conditions necessary to bring about stability and sustain peace.

A related aspect to this theme involves the North-South dimension of peacebuilding operations. What is the place of the South in peacebuilding? Interventions to date have tended to reflect asymmetrical distributions of power in which Northern states have determined where, when and how such interventions will occur. Many southern countries have taken on peacebuilding roles, especially in Africa. Yet the big Southern countries are often not even at the table when proposals for deploying peacebuilding operations are discussed at the UN. Some analysts have advocated that measures be undertaken to ensure the involvement of key Southern countries such as Brazil, Mexico, China, India, Pakistan, and Indonesia in developing peacebuilding strategies. If they were more integrally involved, the colonial overtones surrounding intervention would be reduced and the legitimacy of these operations would be strengthened. It may also be possible that these countries will have some familiarity with the sorts of problems being confronted by postconflict societies in the South and thus make an effective contribution to the content of peacebuilding operations.

A final issue regarding the broadening of the scope of the concept is that of national interests and the extent to which these guide interventions. At one level, interventions in support of peacebuilding challenge the whole concept of national interest as the norms of human or individual rights and security are strengthened. Yet national interests are also crucial to the whole process of intervention and peacebuilding. Such interests are necessary for the mobilization of resources in support of peacebuilding operations. They are particularly important in securing the attention of the principal governments that initiate these operations. At the same time, interests color and distort peacebuilding activities and undermine efforts to retain impartiality and to give primary attention to the needs of the people in postconflict settings. One cannot swim against the current of national interests and therefore one must harness national interests to serve peacebuilding objectives.

Another critically important theme in the discourse on peacebuilding has been a focus on the design and capacity of the international architecture in support of peacebuilding. As indicated above, successful peacebuilding does not take place in a vacuum. Indeed, international and regional organizations have been the principal sponsors of peacebuilding operations. In Cambodia, Eastern Slovenia, Baranja and Western Sirmium, East Timor and Kosovo, the UN was given full responsibility for implementing the peacebuilding operation. These transitional administrative operations were decided on, designed within, and resourced through the UN. Organizations have also developed specialized instruments in support of peacebuilding, such as the Secretary-General's Special representative in Afghanistan, Kosovo, and Iraq or the more permanent UN Office for the High Commissioner for Human Rights.

It is surprising that despite the growing pool of knowledge about the experience of international transitional administrations, particularly since the end of the Cold War, there are still major problems with these postwar reconstruction projects and not all of them are viewed as legitimate. Especially problematic are those operations controlled by a single state or small coalition of states as the US/UK-led coalition efforts in Iraq. Even those that are approved and sanctioned by the UN are sometimes seen as attempts at bringing back trusteeships and protectorates. There is a general sense, especially within the developing countries, to view these operations with suspicion. Mohammed Ayoob points out that developing states, being new states that have only recently "acquired the formal trappings of juridical sovereignty," are rather "apprehensive of the new international activism" associated with the emerging norm of humanitarian intervention.[26] They tend to place international administration in the same category, viewing it as a major constraint on sovereignty. It is therefore essential to assess these interventionary measures critically rather than to allow them to be inserted into countries on a purely ad hoc and uncritical basis. As Edward Mortimer succinctly put it: "the only possible justification for international intervention and administration is the need to rescue people from the effects of arbitrary or ineffective government, and to help them acquire the skills needed for stable and enlightened self-rule."[27]

International and regional financial institutions are also becoming integrally involved in peacebuilding efforts. The World Bank, for instance, has been heavily involved in the peacebuilding efforts in East Timor. The International Development Association (IDA) of the World Bank was designated the trustee of the reconstruction Trust Fund for East Timor (TFET) and played a major role in community empowerment and local governance there. But here again, we need to assess whether these external financial administrative interventions are actually contributing to sustainable peace or not. At times these institutions attempt to conduct practices as usual in the midst of major peacebuilding operations. The most often cited criticisms in this regard are the strict conditions imposed by international financial institutions that may impede reconstruction efforts in post-conflict countries.

Disarmament at all levels is another part of this international architecture: nuclear, small arms, landmines, etc. Yet there are many concerns about the capacity of disarmament treaties and conventions to support peacebuilding.[28] There have also been very significant concerns expressed about the coordination of the activities of the many organizations that are involved in peacebuilding operations. Authors have noted that one set of international institutions may be supporting a peacebuilding process at the same time as another has sought to enforce policies that directly or indirectly undermine such efforts. Most often cited in this regard are the strict conditionalities imposed by international financial institutions that may impede reconstruction efforts in postconflict situations. Many other issues, including concerns about the coherence and coordination of institutional responses, have also been discussed widely—yet solutions are often difficult to implement.[29]

A fifth theme has been the recognition of the tensions involved in civil-military relations during peacebuilding operations. Since the initial stage of peacebuilding will generally involve attempts at stabilizing a country that has been undergoing violent conflict, it is expected that military forces will be involved in some capacity during a peacebuilding operation. There has been a significant change in the military's role in what is now commonly described in Canada's Department of National Defence as peace support operations. This change makes it necessary to determine the proper role for the military in peacebuilding. Moreover, given the multidimensional nature of peacebuilding, the military must necessarily interact more extensively with the civilian population and with a variety of civil society entities. Part of the problem in discerning a clear division of labor between the military and civilian operations lies in the inherent difficulty in generating a clear definition of conflict and, more specifically, determining when a conflict begins and ends—a difficulty confounded by the nature of many contemporary conflicts and the nature of peacebuilding itself.

Since peacebuilding looks at ensuring a lasting peace, it is expected to involve much more than a cessation of hostilities. It must include such essentials as economic development, human rights, the rule of law, democracy, social equity, and environmental sustainability. Many of these tasks require the capacity of nonmilitary (civilian) actors and it therefore becomes essential for the military to work with civilians in support of peacebuilding. Yet the military also possesses some important tools that are not available to others. It provides an essential element of force and the application of this force to create a secure environment in which others can work to build the peace. The military can also be commanded into the field and be required to participate in these operations, unlike NGOs or even other public servants.

One of the critically important issues emerging in postconflict societies is finding the proper balance between military forces and civilian policing activities. While the military is particularly important during the crisis phase, helping to ensure that the other actors have a stable environment in which to work, there is a need to hand over responsibilities to others as the situation moves from crisis to longer-term development. In the interim, there is a need to reconcile the two approaches. Some of the postconflict literature reveals the tensions that result from the intersection of these two entities (civil/military) that have different value systems and *modi operandi*. Yet there is also some indication in the literature of attempts at developing a cooperative civil-military approach to peacebuilding.[30]

A related issue is the pressing need in most postconflict situations to develop and support in a sustainable fashion a civilian policing component to maintain internal order in a peaceful and just manner. Civilian policing, or civ-pol as it is commonly known, has become one of the more important, yet problematic, aspects of postconflict reconstruction.[31] This is particularly difficult in societies that have experienced the coercive hand of an oppressive state. In these circumstances there has been little to distinguish between the forces of oppression and domestic policing activities. Maintaining civil order is also complicated by the proliferation of small arms and the economic dislocations that usually occur in postconflict settings. Such conditions are conducive for a dramatic growth in criminal activity that might leave the local civilian population even more insecure than it was during the conflict. The lack of effective regional and international resources to support reconstruction and the activities of civ-pol operations adds a further complication to this difficult situation.

A sixth theme examines the relationship between peacebuilding and human security. Peacebuilding has emerged as a significant international practice alongside a growing concern about human security. Originating in the UNDP reports of the early 1990s, human security has been identified by a number of governments, including Canada, Chile, Norway and South Africa as a foreign policy priority. These governments have advocated for a more profound understanding of what is needed for personal security and have warned that not only conflict but also postconflict conditions disrupt personal security for people who lack protection under international law.

For governments like Canada, the commitment to peacebuilding emerged from this shift in focus on the part of certain policy officials. As a result of this commitment, security guarantees that touch the lives of individuals have been built into the Canadian conception of international peacebuilding missions. There is also a growing recognition of the differing security needs of men, women and children. Ending the fighting and restoring calm does not necessarily increase security in all cases. For example, many postconflict societies experience a significant increase in violent crime and personal insecurity after the war. Crime, for many individuals, can be as pervasive a source of insecurity as civil conflict. Alternatively, securing a safe environment for men or for one ethnic group does not necessarily reduce the security threats to other segments of the population. This is one of the primary reasons for the recent emphasis on security sector reform. It is also an important reason to consider the effects of peacebuilding practices on gender and ethnicity. This also indicates a need to shift from looking at peacebuilding as a discrete activity to viewing it within the broader conception of human security governance; a need to put individuals, and not just sovereign states, at the heart of international relations.[32]

A final theme identified in the postconflict literature tackles the tensions between reconciliation and retributive justice and the mechanisms by which these are to be achieved. Internal wars tend to be devastating for individuals within war-torn societies and such wars are often marked by an extensive array of crimes against innocent and vulnerable populations. Trying to establish a sustainable peace for these societies after the shooting or oppression has ended has, in some cases, been stymied by the perception or reality of impunity. Yet many efforts have been undertaken to address underlying injustices that marked the period of conflict. Such situations often demand an element of retributive justice as part of the process of reconciliation.

Dealing with the past is one of the unavoidable issues that peacebuilding has to confront. The society coming out of conflict must find a way to address the fact that gross violations of human rights (genocide, ethnic cleansing, forced displacement, torture, rape and assassinations) may have occurred during the conflict. Impunity is a grave practical problem for peacebuilding. Amnesties for gross violators of human rights or refusal to prosecute perpetrators of past abuses may indicate lack of justice, which is why the horrors of the past must be confronted, recognized, and addressed. One mechanism for this is a truth commission. Sometimes accompanied by amnesty for some perpetrators of abuse, the intent of these commissions is to bring about reconciliation through a public accounting of abuses. However, they may also inadvertently keep alive the memory of the atrocities, which may be a good or bad thing, depending on the particular circumstances. In some cases, truth commissions simply accentuate cleavages in the society. However, on the positive side, they could act as a deterrent and remind people that such atrocities should never again be allowed to occur.

Truth commissions have been varied in mandate, composition, objectives, legitimacy and results, as the examples of the differences in Argentina (1983–84), Chile (1991), El Salvador (1993), Haiti (1995), South Africa (1995), and Guatemala (1996) indicate. The Truth and Reconciliation Commission (TRC) in South Africa, composed entirely of South Africans and given a mandate to carry out an exhaustive analysis of the weaknesses of truth commissions elsewhere, has been considered an important contribution to the peacebuilding process in that country. The objectives of the TRC were to examine each case of human rights and power abuse, identify the perpetrators, and bring to justice the intellectual authors of the abuses, and to promote truth and forgiveness through direct confrontation between victims and perpetrators.

Despite local demands for justice by victims and families of victims, at the international level there remains some resistance to the idea that retributive justice can contribute to the peacebuilding process. This resistance has been combined with a great deal of controversy with respect to the implementation of formal justice or Western-imposed forms of justice, still in its infancy at the international level. The *ad hoc* International Criminal Tribunals for the former Yugoslavia (ICTY) and Rwanda (ICTR) have served as important laboratories for the application of international criminal justice in postconflict (or ongoing conflict) situations. They have, however, operated in very different circumstances and under different mandates.

The ICTY operated in the middle of ongoing conflict, amidst an array of IGOs and NGOs, including the NATO peace support operations—the NATO-led Implementation Force (IFOR) and the NATO-led Stabilization Force (SFOR). In contrast, the ICTR operated after the conflict had ended and in a virtual political vacuum, as only a handful of IGOs and NGOs continued to operate in the region. The ICTR itself worked from a small office for the prosecutor in Kigali and the Tribunal conducted its hearings in Arusha, Tanzania. The ICTR worked under a very restricted mandate that was bound in terms of time and territory. The ICTY's mandate, in contrast, was more open ended. This allowed the ICTY to continue its work in Kosovo, whereas the ICTR could not investigate any activities that took place before or after 1994 or outside of Rwanda.

One of the difficulties that the Tribunals have encountered in their work has been a strong resistance on the part of the military to support the enforcement of proper conduct by combatants. The ICTY was given a chapter VII mandate from the UN Security Council, but, as former Chief Prosecutor Louise Arbour pointed out,[33] there was an initial reluctance on the part of military units to work with the ICTY in the field. The ICTY, for its part, relied on the military rather extensively for logistical support in conducting its on site investigations of war crimes. This was necessitated by the need to operate in high-risk areas where the conflict was often ongoing, as well as the need to keep the "scene of the crime" secure while the prosecutors completed their investigation. The military eventually became more cooperative and IFOR was subsequently tasked to aid in the apprehension of indicted war criminals.

A second difficulty encountered by the Tribunals and the more general effort to pursue justice at the international level has been the strong commitment on the part of the UN, other IGOs, and most NGOs to a culture of neutrality. A culture of neutrality does not favor the production of evidence to support the prosecution of war criminals. While adopted in good faith, a culture of neutrality limits the willingness of these actors to support the work of the Tribunals for fear that the actors will be tainted with being on one side or the other during the conflict, or in its aftermath. The prosecutor's office of the International Tribunals took great pains to explain that they were pursuing criminals not Serbs or Croats or Hutus and that the only side they took was the side of justice and truth. They refused to participate in the discourse of ethnic communities and instead stood firm on the discourse of justice and criminals. The culture of neutrality is, however, pervasive throughout most international institutions and remains one of the more significant challenges confronting future efforts in this area such as the work of the ICC.

The international community's intervention in the postconflict search for justice has been the cause of resentment for different reasons. For some it interferes with local efforts and undermines the development of domestic judicial capacities to pursue justice. This has, for example, been a concern in Rwanda where a government that holds considerable resentment towards the international community and its tribunals has adopted its own methods for distributing justice in the aftermath of the 1994 genocide. In addition to the more formal but excruciatingly slow legal methods, there are attempts to turn to a more traditional method, known as *gacaca*, in the hope that this will not only expedite the process of reconciliation, but also secure a greater degree of legitimacy and thereby contribute more directly to the peacebuilding process in that country.[34]

IN SOME FORM or another, the issues noted here are represented in this collection of essays. Jean Daudelin tackles one of the first hurdles that any international peacebuilding effort will have to overcome—the fundamental dilemmas surrounding "humanitarian intervention." Daudelin notes that there are certain circumstances that ought to trigger humanitarian and moral calls for intervention by the international community. Using Rwanda as an example, he argues that apathy is not an option in the face of massive human rights abuse and humanitarian tragedies. As long as such instances continue to persist, it is best to have, up front, a full and frank discussion of the pros and cons of such interventions and to assess honestly the concrete requirements of such actions in terms of scope, timeframe, resources and political sustainability. According to Daudelin, such criteria and mechanisms for international interventions are sorely missing, and this presents a real obstacle to the proper initiation of peacebuilding missions.

Daudelin identifies four key issue areas or problems that need to be addressed urgently. First, there is the scope and duration of peacebuilding operations. Peacebuilding should not be viewed as a short-term exercise. Indeed, with attendant intervention, peacebuilding missions will inevitably be long and protracted because they have to deal with significant problems such as massive human abuse and, in some cases, the complete breakdown of government and societal order. Interveners must therefore be committed to long-term involvement. One approach suggested by Daudelin is for peacebuilders to think in terms of tasks, not time. The second important issue raised by the author is funding. Peacebuilding can be very costly. While there is currently a commendable willingness on the part of the international community to invest in the process, the resources are not always forthcoming or sufficient for the task. As the author points out, inadequate funding can threaten the credibility, consistency, and effectiveness of interventions. The third issue raised is the North-South dimension of these operations. The author is particularly concerned here with the place of the South in peacebuilding and with the reality that it is difficult to avoid colonialist/imperialist overtones of externally imposed peacebuilding operations. Finally, Daudelin discusses the place of national interests and the extent to which these guide interventions. He notes that national interests will inevitably be a crucial part of the peacebuilding process, and argues that if we cannot link peacebuilding to the national interest (with all the support, commitment, and resources that this would imply), it is better to "stay home and shut up."

Kenneth Bush expands the conceptual discussion of the interventionary aspects of peacebuilding. He first provides an overview of the different instruments used by the international community in pursuit of peacebuilding, but cautions against overemphasizing certain peacebuilding instruments to the exclusion of others. Bush maintains that too little attention is devoted to certain instruments not commonly associated with peacebuilding and that may in fact actually contribute more than the frequently discussed ones to establishing a sustainable peace. He raises the following important questions: do the so-called instruments of peacebuilding serve to undermine or enhance prospects for a truly sustainable peace? How do we determine if peacebuilding instruments work? Bush stresses the importance of not ghettoizing, or compartmentalizing, peacebuilding. Rather, he calls for a closer integration of peacebuilding and development activities and recommends that scholars and practitioners examine carefully how development work can contribute to peacebuilding, and vice versa.

This kind of intersecting analysis should cause one to consider the tensions that exist between the instruments of peacebuilding, particularly those that involve military or security forces, and the desired outcomes. In cautioning against the "commodification" and militarization of peacebuilding, Bush is critical of the conflict-nurturing aspects of some Western-designed peacebuilding activities and of attempts to suppress and undermine indigenous capacity for recovery. He advocates the delegitimization of gun-based structures of power and a search for other means of establishing and exercising authority in the administration of international peacebuilding efforts.

In contrast to Bush's analysis, Melissa Labonte begins with the assumption that in the foreseeable future, the development of robust norms of peace and prevention in the global community will necessarily have to include the use of force. Ankersen and others echo this theme. Noting that a necessary precondition for the establishment of a peacebuilding mission in a war-torn state is the restoration of political stability, Labonte maintains that armed force will most likely be needed to end military hostilities and enforce weapons disarmament of local conflicting parties. Labonte's concern is with preventive value of external military forces to diffuse situations of unfolding and incipient violent conflict that could negatively affect peacebuilding and humanitarian activity if left unchecked.

Labonte is particularly interested in the outcomes resulting from interactions between various actors involved in peacebuilding: international nongovernmental humanitarian actors (INGHAs), governments, and intergovernmental organizations (IGOs). These actors help define and influence policymakers with respect to the operational preventive strategies of peacebuilding. The author is interested in understanding why such strategies are rare and why the decision to undertake preventive humanitarian responses that include a military component varies so much among complex emergencies and conflicts that share similar characteristics.

Chris Ankersen agrees with Labonte and argues that force continues to play a significant role in peacebuilding in his discussion of the military's role in the peacebuilding operation in Kosovo. However, his case study demonstrates a significant change in the military's role in what are now commonly described as peace support operations. Such operations make it necessary to determine the proper role for the military, and perhaps even more importantly, to determine the relationship between the military and other actors involved in peacebuilding. Part of the difficulty confronting the military in peacebuilding is generating a clear definition of conflict and, more specifically, determining when a conflict begins and ends. If peacebuilding is about ensuring a lasting peace, then it must involve much more than a cessation of hostilities. It needs to include such essential building blocks as economic development, human rights, the rule of law, democracy, social equity, and environmental sustainability. Many of these are dependent on the capacity of non-military actors and it therefore becomes essential for the military to work with civilian players such as NGOs in support of peacebuilding. As the author suggests, an enduring peace requires more than the military alone can provide and it also obliges all actors (military and civilian) to cooperate and to overcome their institutional prejudices.

Francis Abiew and Tom Keating examine the role of NGOs in peacebuilding missions and consider both the reasons for and the effects of NGO involvement in these operations. They demonstrate the extent to which the direction and outcome of peacebuilding processes have been strongly influenced by the participation of local and transnational NGOs. Abiew and Keating point out that the military's partnership with civil society is, in most instances, not an option these days, but a necessity. The importance of an active NGO presence in peacebuilding situations is supported by examples from the point of view of operations on the ground. For example, the authors argue that NGOs have a wealth of experience in relief and recovery operations. These groups know who can be rapidly and economically deployed and are generally aware of the importance of linking relief efforts to longer-term sustainability and capacity building. We learn from Abiew and Keating that sustainable peacebuilding concepts seem to be more readily understood by NGOs than by the military establishment or even some governments.

Issues such as people-centered development, the significance of women and gender issues (such as the education of girls), and more generally, the importance of ensuring that educational structures do not replicate past injustices, are generally familiar terrain to NGOs. As Abiew and Keating suggest, these nonstate actors are at the forefront of efforts to reintegrate combatants, refugees, and displaced persons into postconflict society. Yet NGOs are not free from problems and may need codes of conduct that are publicly enunciated and enforced. In building local capacity, outsiders, including international NGOs, must recognize that they are not neutral actors and that their involvement will have political consequences—some negative, some positive.

David Beer demonstrates some of the political consequences that can befall some of the most laudable international peacebuilding efforts. His study focuses on the efforts to return the legitimately elected leader of Haiti, Jean-Bertrand Aristide, to power and to strengthen the institutions of justice and policing that were systematically corrupted during the decades under the country's former Duvalier and Cédras dictatorships. Beer shows that while these were worthy peacebuilding goals, the process was tainted by the blatant self-interest of the US, the lack of coordination between the many external players, and the reluctance of the Haitian government to embrace the need for radical change in the justice and police sectors. This case points to the need for peacebuilding efforts to have clear and attainable goals, to be better coordinated in order to avoid the overlapping of projects by the multiple players involved, thus wasting time and resources. Beer also clearly indicates that the local (recipient) government must be a responsible and reliable partner in the peacebuilding process if that process is to reap success.

Sumie Nakaya examines the role of women in peacebuilding, drawing on evidence from some peacebuilding strategies applied in Mozambique and Somalia. Nakaya highlights the importance of enhancing gender equality in postconflict governance and in the process of structural and social transformation, noting that women's commitment to peace is crucial if any postconflict society is to be able to sustain peace agreements. In her opinion, the often-ignored discriminatory effects of peacebuilding operations on women, such as continued violence, discrimination, and poverty, encompass political, security, social and economic aspects. It is important therefore to examine these areas in the search for building a sustainable peace based on the platform of gender equity. If Nakaya is right, then conflict resolution and peacebuilding will provide a window of opportunity for social transformation and the integration of gender equality into emerging state and social structures. But this will mean gender mainstreaming both within institutions and at the center of the structural base of power in postconflict societies.

Adekeye Adebajo concentrates on the role that regional and international actors played in attempts at building peace in Liberia and Sierra Leone during the last decade of the twentieth century. He labels these two countries "West Africa's tragic twins" and describes the interlocking relationships that existed between them. Both countries were plunged into a decade-long civil war by warlords Charles Taylor (Liberia) and Foday Sankoh (Sierra Leone), who used revenue from blood diamonds and other raw materials to fuel the conflicts. In discussing the peacebuilding tools that were used, Adebajo notes that interventions must be provided with timely resources if they are to achieve their goals. He also notes that the role of regional hegemons, like Nigeria, is important, and that international efforts to contribute to peacebuilding could be built around pillars of regional hegemons, with the UN helping to share the burdens and costs of the operations. In such cases, the author emphasizes the importance of funding for the reintegration of ex-combatants into society, for the stabilization of the security sector, and for the rebuilding of state and societal structures and institutions. In addition, donor conferences, such as have been held for the Balkans, should be replicated for other regions (like Africa) if peacebuilding operations are to be successful. Adebajo also notes the importance of putting a stop to illicit activities. In addressing all of these concerns, it will be essential for the international community to dig deeper to provide resources.

Kassu Gebremariam reviews the peacebuilding process in the Horn of Africa (Ethiopia, Sudan, Somalia, Djibouti, Eritrea, Kenya, and Egypt) and the role of outside agents, especially that of the Organization of African Unity (OAU) and the Intergovernmental Authority for Drought and Development (IGADD). He argues that the existing approach to peacebuilding will not alleviate the crisis in the region. The current approach is, in his view, overly deterministic and inadequate, for it fails to address critical values such as the influence of the international factor, especially in an historical context. He questions the commitment to human rights in the region. He also argues that with the emergence of the neoliberal world order there has been a disintegration of the state and a decline in individual security. Thus an international order that sought to protect national borders might provide a more effective structure of security than one that adopted a more permissive view of intervention in the name of human security.

Gebremariam strongly suggests that it is necessary for peacebuilders to tap into the local society and to benefit from its indigenous knowledge, particularly that of the elders. The pattern of intervention that has marked the post–Cold War international system has tended to undermine African states and overlooked the indigenous capacity of local actors who are expected to assume the responsibility of state and societal rebuilding once the international actors withdraw from their territory.

Shaun Narine is even less sanguine about peacebuilding in Southeast Asia in his insightful examination into nontraditional forms of intervention and peace support currently being considered by members of ASEAN. He argues that insofar as "peacebuilding" requires physical intervention within postconflict societies, ASEAN can be considered more of an impediment to regional peacebuilding than a help because peacebuilding norms are generally at odds with most ASEAN members' view that external intervention in the affairs of the regional states should be avoided as much as possible. Yet, insofar as peacebuilding is concentrated on preventing the outbreak and escalation of conflict, Narine suggests that ASEAN may have a meaningful, albeit limited, role to play in laying the foundations for a "culture of conflict prevention" in Southeast Asia. A move into this area provides a critically important point of departure for this regional institution. However, developing a culture of conflict prevention is very much contingent upon how well the values embodied in that peacebuilding concept corresponds with the narrower political and economic self-interest of the states in this region.

Jarat Chopra and Tanja Hohe suggest that peacebuilding can overcome the powerful norms of nonintervention and the preservation of sovereignty. However, the authors are quick to point out that for peace to be sustainable, the external actors and transitional administrations must give more thought to the nature of "participatory governance." Chopra and Hohe are highly critical of Western-imposed paradigms of state building which seem mostly preoccupied with instituting national elections and building western style forms of governance. There is a noticeable tendency to exclude local people from the intervention and peacebuilding processes. This "asocial" form of alienation may have been tenable for limited types of intervention, but they are disastrous when intervention for longer-term peacebuilding is contemplated. Given that the notion of participation amongst the peacebuilding cognoscenti appears to lack clarity at the levels of concept and strategy, the authors, drawing on lessons from Afghanistan and East Timor, offer a number of steps to ensure that local people are properly included in every stage and aspect of the state-building engineered by external actors.

Following on from the policy prescriptions of Chopra and Hohe, Satya Das proposes a number of recommendations for improving prospects for sustainable peace. Learning lessons from the culture of violence that seems to have pervaded the latter half of the twentieth century in such places as Central Africa, Rwanda, Sierra Leone, and the Balkans, Das suggests that to build the peace may require violating the sovereignty of states, ignoring territorial integrity, and acting aggressively against states that blatantly violate human rights standards. He argues that investing in peacebuilding is tantamount to taking out an insurance policy. Das is concerned with the question of who should pay for that insurance plan, how the money should be collected and who should control the collected funds. He offers a number of solutions to this problem, including the highly controversial suggestion of a global tax on defense spending and the arms trade, and a novel idea of creating a new post—the UN High Commissioner for Peacebuilding and Postconflict Reconstruction.

Carolyn Lloyd tackles another issue that is a major stumbling block to the development of sustainable peace. Her analysis of the prospects for constructing an effective small arms regulatory regime is significant in that it demonstrates how the excessive flow and indiscriminate use of small arms and light weapons, if left unchecked, can undermine attempts at building sustainable peace. Yet establishing international norms in this area has been difficult for a variety of reasons. Lloyd poses the question: what are the prospects of developing an international regime that will bring small arms and light weapons under control when major states like the US appear not to be interested in establishing such a regime? She addresses her question by exploring the conditions under which states decide to abide, or not, by emerging international norms and rules. Lloyd arrives at a central hypothesis that posits that three variables (knowledge, power, and interest) are indispensable for such regime formation. These variables are present during the creation of other arms control regimes but are not yet in place for small arms and light weapons (SALW). Few measures exist to govern the flow of SALW. They have been, in essence, the "forgotten" weapons in international arms control. However, with increased knowledge of the problems small arms pose, we may be witnessing significant movement towards the creation of a set of global controls. Beyond the immediate interest in focusing on a matter foremost amongst the issues that have frustrated the envisioned "agenda for peace" of the post-Cold War era, Lloyd contributes as well to the broader debate about how and when we can expect global actors to cooperate in sustainable peace projects.

Howard Adelman and Joseph Masciulli provide critical reflections on the importance of moving beyond the norms that result in a culture of war to those that support a culture of peace. Adelman examines the work of scholars who analyze cultures of violence and offers a particular vision of how peace can be constructed as well as an antidote lest we think that we have definitive answers. For as critical as we must be of those processes that have already been developed in the search of better and more comprehensive solutions, we must remain wary of the solutions we propose and be aware of the importance of being self-critical. Adelman's contribution is akin to the story Sören Kierkegaard tells in his *Journals* of a man who sees a sign in a store window that says, "Pants Pressed Here" and then takes in his trousers to be pressed—only to discover that the store sells signs. Adelman does not offer to press the pants of those concerned with peacebuilding but rather to "sell the signs" that urge us to be more critical when we are analyzing cultures of violence and offering lessons on how to develop a better peacebuilding model.

Masciulli's cosmopolitan and ethical position does not allow him to hold out too much hope for a complete elimination of violent conflict. As far as he is concerned, war cannot be "uninvented" because the ability and knowledge to make war persist in the minds of human beings. Nevertheless, he suggests that partial peace is possible if it is built on decent politics that are inspired by a global cosmopolitan culture and world polity. Unlike breathing, eating and sex, war is not a requirement of the human condition. Thus, there is a chance that human beings might at some point eliminate it as a prominent practice in the same way that slavery and human sacrifice are no longer widespread.

On the hopeful note that building a sustainable peace is possible, we now turn to the critical analyses offered by our contributors.

Notes

1 Michael Ignatieff, *The Warrior's Honor* (New York: Henry Holt and Company, 1998).

2 See for example Johan Galtung et al., *Searching for Peace: The Road to TRANSCEND*, (London: Pluto Press, 2000); E. Boulding and K. Boulding, *The Future: Images and Processes* (Thousand Oaks, CA: Sage Publications, 1995).

3 Oliver P. Richmond, "A Genealogy of Peacemaking: The Creation and Re-creation of Order," *Alternatives* 26, no. 3 (July–September 2001): 317–48.

4 John P. Lederach, *Building Peace: Sustainable Reconciliation in Divided Societies* (Tokyo: United Nations University Press, 1997), 60–1.

5 Richmond, "Genealogy of Peacemaking," 330.

6 It should be noted, however, that Javier Perez de Cuellar, from the time when he represented the UN on the Cyprus issue in the late 1970s to his work as Secretary-General after succeeding Kurt Waldheim in 1982, laid the foundation for the development of the concept of peacebuilding. Certainly his strong advocacy of assertive peacekeeping and his involvement in negotiating the ceasefire in the Iran-Iraq war, in facilitating the Soviet withdrawal from Afghanistan, in negotiating a peace pact between the El Salvadorian government and rebels, and in brokering the 1991 Cambodian peace accord, laid the foundations for the doctrine of peace-building. One might say he prepared the soil for, and planted the seeds of, UN peacebuilding. The actual document under Boutros-Ghali's name that advocated peacebuilding was written largely by a Finnish acolyte of de Cuellar's—Tapio Kanninen—when he was Chief of the Policy Planning Unit in the Department of Political Affairs at the United Nations.

7 Boutros Boutros-Ghali, *An Agenda for Peace* (New York: United Nations, 1992), 11.

8 Boutros-Ghali, *Agenda*, 33.

9 Kenneth D. Bush, "Beyond Bungee Cord Humanitarianism: Towards a Democratic Agenda for Peacebuilding," *Canadian Journal of Development Studies*, Special Issue on Governance, Democracy & Human Rights (1996): 75–92.

10 Boutros-Ghali, *Agenda*, 34.

11 Bush, "Bungee Cord Humanitarianism," 76.

12 Annika Björkdahl, *From Idea to Norm: Promoting Conflict Prevention* (Lund: Lund University, 2002).

13 "G8 Miyazaki Initiatives for Conflict Prevention," http://www.auswaertiges-amt.de/www/en/infoservice/download/pdf/friedenspolitik/miyazaki_konfl.pdf (accessed 24 November, 2003).

14 Organization for Economic Co-operation and Development, *Helping Prevent Conflict: Orientations for External Partners. Supplement to the DAC Guidelines on Conflict, Peace and Development Co-operation on the Threshold of the 21st Centruy*, (Paris: OECD, 2001). http://www.oecd.org/dac/htm/g-gom.htm (accessed December 10, 2003).

15 Peter Wallensteen, "Global Development Strategies for Conflict Prevention," Report to the Parliamentary Committee on Swedish Politics for Global Development (Globkom), August 2001.

16 United Nations, Report of the Secretary-General on the work of the Organization to the 55th General Assembly Session, *Prevention of Armed Conflict*, 7 June 2001, A/55/985-S/2001/574.

17 Carnegie Commission on Preventing Deadly Conflict. *Preventing Deadly Conflict, Final Report* (New York: Carnegie Corporation, 1997).

18 E. Boulding, *Cultures of Peace: The Hidden Side of History* (New York: Syracuse University Press, 2000).

19 James Scott, *Seeing Like a State: How Certain Schemes to Improve the Human Condition have Failed* (New Haven: Yale University Press, 1998).

20 Jarat Chopra, "Building State Failure in East Timor," *Development and Change* 33, no. 5 (2002): 999.

21 Jarat Chopra, "Building State Failure," 999.

22 W. Andy Knight, "Soft Power and Moral Suasion in Establishing the International Criminal Court: Canadian Contributions," in Rosalind Irwin, ed., *Ethics and Security in Canadian Foreign Policy* (Vancouver: University of British Columbia Press, 2001), 113–37; Andrew Latham, "Theorizing the Landmine Campaign: Ethics, Global Cultural Scripts, and the Laws of War," in Rosalind Irwin, ed., *Ethics and Security in Canadian Foreign Policy*, 160–80; and, Deirdre Van der Merwe and Mark Malan, "Codes of Conduct and Children in Armed Conflicts," in Andrew Cooper, John English and Ramesh Thakur, eds., *Enhancing Global Governance: Towards a New Diplomacy?* (Tokyo: United Nations University, 2002), 229–47.

23 Roland Paris, "Peacebuilding and the Limits of Liberal Internationalism," *International Security* 22, no. 2 (Fall 1997): 55.

24 Reginald H. Green, and Ismail I. Ahmed, "Rehabilitation, Sustainable Peace and Development: Towards Reconceputalisation," *Third World Quarterly* 20, no. 1 (1999): 189–206.

25 United Nations Development Programme, *Development Dimensions of Conflict Prevention and Peace-Building*, An Independent Study prepared by Bernard Wood for the Emergency Response Division (New York: United Nations Development Programme, 2001).

26 Mohammed Ayoob, "Third World Perspectives on Humanitarian Intervention and International Administration," *Global Governance* 10, no. 1 (Jan.–Mar. 2004): 99–118.

27 Edward Mortimer, "International Administration of War-Torn Societies," *Global Governance* 10, no. 1 (Jan.–Mar. 2004): 7–14.

28 Alvaro de Soto and Graciana del Castillo, "Obstacles to Peacebuilding," *Foreign Policy* (Spring 1994): 69–83.

29 Wilton Park, "Strengthening the United Nations in Conflict Prevention and Peace-Building," Wilton Park Conference WP667 (Wilton Park, UK, 2002).

30 Danford W. Middlemiss, "Civil-Military Relations and Democracy", in Ann L. Griffiths, ed., *Building Peace and Democracy in Post-Conflict Societies* (Halifax: Centre for Foreign Policy Studies, 1998), 71–82.

31 Chuck Call and Michael Barnett, "Looking for a few good Cops: Peacekeeping, Peacebuilding and CIVPOL," in Tor Tanke Holm and Espen Barthe Eide, eds., *Peacebuilding and Police Reform* (London: Frank Cass, 2000): 43–68.

32 Lloyd Axworthy, "Human Security and Global Governance: Putting People First," *Global Governance* 7, no. 1 (January–March 2001): 19–23.

33 Louise Arbour, "Opening Comments to the Symposium on Peacebuilding," University of Alberta, March 2000.

34 Peter Uvin and Charles Mironoko, "Western and Local Approaches to Justice in Rwanda," *Global Governance* 9, no. 2 (2003): 226–28.

1 Rethinking Humanitarian Intervention

Jean Daudelin

ON 21 APRIL 1994, at the height of the Rwandan genocide, the UN force commander, General Romeo Dallaire, declared that he could stop the genocide with 5,000 men.[1] The UN Security Council responded the same day by reducing his contingent from 2,548[2] to 270 men.[3] Dallaire was thus condemned to absolute impotence in the face of one of the worst slaughters of human beings since World War II: in three months, over 800,000 men, women and children were killed.[4]

In the face of such disasters, a growing body of opinion argues that there are times when the international community has the responsibility to move in by force to stop massive human rights violations.[5] International irresponsibility provides a shield behind which these kinds of abuses occur.[6] Prevention of such crimes should be pursued by all means and when such crimes occur, prosecution is a necessity. However, a soft consensus now exists on the need to do something more. In fact, on 7 September 2000, during the UN Millennium Summit, Canada's Prime Minister, Jean Chrétien, announced the formation of an International Commission on Intervention and State Sovereignty (ICISS) to identify "the appropriate international reaction to massive violations of human rights and crimes against humanity."[7] A year later, the Commission's Report recognized the "responsibility to protect" as a central duty of the international community.[8]

Humanitarian intervention, in sum, has become not only a "hot" topic, but a very real policy option.

Or has it? The discussion has certainly intensified since the end of the Cold War as broadly supported, well-meaning and so-called "nonideological" operations have multiplied: Bosnia, East Timor, Haiti, Kosovo, Northern Iraq and Somalia. However, interventions that were meant to be decisive and short have turned into hurried retreats from countries left on the brink of chaos, or into a continued presence with unclear mandates, growing unease, fast rising bills and doubtful sustainability. Even the rhetoric has been toned down. Well before the end of the US Democratic administration, little was left of the "Clinton Doctrine" as the Somalia debacle was followed by the US's prominence in the global inaction against the Rwanda genocide, and by the increasingly dirty and deepening mess in Kosovo.[9]

Tony Blair's "ethical foreign policy" also went through hard times in the wake of arms sales to Zimbabwe and Indonesia,[10] and Canada's "Human Security" agenda has taken the backseat to the interests of Canadian oil companies in Southern Sudan.[11] Among activists and practitioners, the complexities of the field and disasters such as the debacle in Western Zaire, where the estimated number of victims among Rwandan refugees is at 200,000 (60 percent of whom are children), have produced a sense of crisis: "In the modern history of humanitarian action dating from civilian relief during the Second World War, never before has the legitimacy of the enterprise been so pro-foundly and publicly challenged."[12] As push comes to shove, the dream and reality of interventionist regimes driven by humanitarian norms appear to be receding.

Here, I examine the dilemmas confronting humanitarian interventions and identify ways of resolving and/or circumventing them. My starting point is straightforward: humanitarian tragedies and massive human rights violations will happen again, and apathy is not an option. However, the current discussion in policy and academic circles is caught in a box. I take a peek outwards and argue that a more effective interventionist regime must be centered on the regional powers of the South, that it must be largely self-sustaining economically, and that it must necessarily be built on mixed motives. First, I examine the box in which current thinking on humanitarian interventions is caught before exploring potential ways of thinking outside that box.

Current thinking about humanitarian intervention is premised on three "conclusions:" (1) humanitarian interventions are likely to involve very significant investments in resources and personnel, for extensive periods of time; (2) the choice and fate of intervention depends on a few rich countries in the "West"; and (3) intervention is best implemented by neutral parties. These assumptions have important consequences for the ways in which humanitarian interventions are devised, and they also determine very narrow avenues for resolving the problems that plague the budding interventionist regime. It need not be so, for only one of those assumptions—which pertains to cost, personnel, and time—really looks credible.

We need to admit that short-term, limited operations will be the exceptions and that the rule will be long, protracted endeavors. The reason is simple: humanitarian interventions are only contemplated in cases of massive human rights violations or total absence of a governance structure. Typically, these involve either a collapsed state that cannot regain what Max Weber called "a monopoly of legitimate violence"[13] (Haiti, Guinea Bissau, Liberia, Somalia, and the Democratic Republic of the Congo, come to mind here), or a well-functioning state that devotes its capacity to expelling, abusing, torturing and slaughtering people (Rwanda, Sudan and Yugoslavia are obvious recent examples; Nazi Germany, Leninist and Stalinist Russia barely older ones).

The implications for intervening parties are quite obvious: they need a significant number of soldiers and administrators, as well as lots of money. Moreover, if they are to fulfill their mandates properly, these missions must be prepared to remain for an extended period of time. This issue has recently dawned on a number of commentators with different political orientations—from Edward Luttwak to David Rieff and the International Crisis Group (ICG). Luttwak puts it most bluntly:

> ... UN interventions in Sub-Saharan Africa to disarm all comers and establish law and order cannot be mere raids or visitations à la Somalia.... They must instead lead to the establishment of UN protectorates that can build infrastructures, provide education, and administer all the necessary functions of civil government. Of necessity the duration of these protectorates is more likely to be measured in decades rather than years.[14]

People like Ali Mazrui and Michael Waltzer, who are not typically in agreement with "hawks" such as Luttwak, have echoed these views. In fact, a whole movement (termed "re-colonialism" by Tim Shaw and Clement Adibe) has emerged that calls for a reconsideration of international trusteeship arrangements.[15]

Such thinking, however, is by no means limited to observers of Africa. The recent involvement of the international community in the Balkans, and now in Afghanistan and Iraq, brought home to Europe and North America the material implications of such endeavors. It is becoming clear that the West's involvement in Bosnia, Kabul and Kosovo is unlikely to be wrapped up quickly.[16]

While there is a growing consensus that humane interventionism will be protracted and costly, there is also a growing admission that the political and material resources needed are unlikely to be available. "Triage" as Thomas Weiss put it, is shaping up as the emerging rule[17] that simply cannot be reconciled with a legitimate regime[18] and, hence, severely weakens the political sustainability of interventionism.

The "triage" problem is further aggravated by the absolute prominence of the richest and most powerful countries in current interventions. There appears to be unanimous agreement on the fact that if the problems to be dealt with are concentrated in the South, the "solution" or "non-solution" that intervention might represent can only come from the West (or the North).

When Edward Luttwak talks of the need for "neocolonialism"[19]; when David Rieff calls for a "new age of liberal imperialism"[20] and Michael Ignatieff for "heavy" nation-building and a well-meaning imperialism;[21] or when Ali Mazrui recommends a "benign colonization" of Africa, the agent, explicitly or not, is the West—primarily the United States.[22] Critics, however ferocious, work within the very same parameters, denouncing the West's arrogance in thinking only it could govern (Zartman), its "new colonialism" (Adibe), or its new "military humanism" (Chomsky).[23]

There are obvious reasons for such "single-mindedness." The players *in most cases discussed* are Western countries, their common institutions, or the more inclusive ones that they dominate: the Security Council, NATO, the CSCE, the EU and the G-7/8. Critical recent interventions have been enabled or disabled by the West, in particular by the United States or US-led coalitions: Bosnia, East Timor, Eastern Zaire, Haiti, Iraq, Kosovo, Rwanda, and Somalia, to name a few.

As matters are currently framed, the fate of any interventionist regime is in the hands of the West. Yet the West does not seem particularly keen on intervention. Even in Kosovo, Europe and the United States now appear unwilling to support and finance the administration of the *de facto* protectorate established after the war. In January 2001, the entire UN mission established to administer Kosovo after the war ran out of money—in 2001 it required $325 million to pay workers, teachers and doctors, manage utilities and traffic lights, and pay police officers and prosecutors. The French came up with an emergency transfusion of $3 million, and the Americans helped. By 4 March 2001, with some $16 million in the bank, the bankruptcy date shifted slightly to March 23.[24]

Beyond the ridicule evoked by this situation looms the clear incapacity or unwillingness of the West to sustain a serious interventionist endeavor, even in the best political conditions—*i.e.* with massive press and TV coverage. If this is the case in the "heart of Europe," what becomes of Sudan, Angola, or the Democratic Republic of Congo (DRC)?

Even with the current degree of Western commitment, continuing reliance on the United States and Europe further damages prospects for a broad humanitarian regime as these countries inevitably tie their interventions to their interests, values and media-driven humanitarian frenzies. The West, in other words, would do the "triage," and the resulting regime would inevitably be liable to bear the accusations of inconsistency, bias and unfairness. As a result, the legitimacy and ultimate political sustainability of such regimes cannot but suffer.

An underlying assumption of the current discussion is that interested parties cannot be relied upon. Humanitarian motives are felt to be exclusive and their pursuit must be tainted by no aim other than the will to do good. That view is further bolstered by the perception that no intervention can be considered legitimate by the affected populations unless it is as strictly principled as possible.

A bureaucratic expression of such an outlook is the UN peacekeeping system, which makes use of mixed contingents of people from diverse and faraway places. The quest for a disinterested regime logically aims at setting up a force that does not have to answer to state parties, but only to a neutral, principled, and an unbiased international organ. Suspicion about mixed motives in humanitarian intervention is such that suggestions of their presence are a central component of any attempt at delegitimizing a player, be it a country or an organization, or a whole operation. Examples can be found in many analyses that present Nigeria's involvement in Liberia and Sierra Leone as a quest for regional hegemony; or of Syria's intervention in Lebanon as being for the sake of its absorption into Greater Syria; or of France's *Opération Turquoise* in Rwanda as a poorly disguised attempt at sustaining the remnants of its African influence. Similarly, it has been suggested that Canada's leading role in documenting and denouncing the embargo violations that sustain UNITA's war effort in Angola could be motivated by its hopes of gaining ground in diamond production there.[25]

Mixed motives are indeed difficult to discard and they have possibly played a role in many cases. The problem, however, is precisely that it is difficult to imagine significant support for a regime involving important expenses and potential losses of life without some kind of interest being at stake. Disinterested parties seem unable to find the resolve and support needed to sustain costly long-term humanitarian interventions.

This constrained discussion leaves open few avenues for action: doing nothing, however cruel; doing something, however insufficient; or changing minds on interest and "national" allegiance, however daunting the challenge.

The "attentist" school—from the French verb *attendre*, to wait—has its degrees of radicalism. Edward Luttwak asks us to "Give War a Chance," because "although war is a great evil, it does have a great virtue: it can resolve political conflicts and lead to peace."[26] Charles Krauthammer is less sanguine and simply argues: "Humanitarian war requires means that are inherently inadequate to its end."[27] On the left, there is a feeling that interventionism is so inextricably mired in the West's interests that just about any military operation would do more harm than good.[28] In Noam Chomsky's words, "one choice, always available, is to follow the Hippocratic principle: 'First, do no harm;' if you can think of no way to adhere to that elementary principle, then do nothing; at least that is preferable to causing harm."[29]

By contrast, the activist outlook insists on the need to act, however insufficient the means, however limited the mandates, and however biased the selection, for some good will come out of it. This is the line pursued by humanitarian diplomacies, such as that advocated by Canada: if Sudan is a lost cause, but something can be done in Angola, then let us go there; if at the very least 10,000 troops are needed in the DRC, but only 5,000 can be obtained, well let us go anyway, for we could not—or would not—do anything in Rwanda. However, let us at least do something for the Rwandan refugees in Eastern Zaire, and so on.[30] The activist line, however, is quickly losing ground to the attentists: resources are tied up and problems are multiplying where we have already acted. The ambiguities of improvised operations, such as in Kosovo, are coming back to haunt the interventionists as they confront the human consequences of their action.

A second strand of activists reach the same conclusion, but argue that it is national interest rather than narrowly humanitarian motives that justify humanitarian interventions. This line of thinking, propounded recently by Chester Crocker,[31] has noble roots in the moral realism of Reihnold Niebuhr, but it is very difficult to see how it could escape from the "triage" problem: can one really conceive that every humanitarian disaster is a matter of national interest for the United States?

Finally, there are the new idealists who are working hard at convincing skeptical elites and electorates that national interest is a thing of the past, that global governance is a public good, and that a fair interventionist regime is in everybody's interest. Andy Knight succinctly describes a representative variant of this outlook:

> [Peace-maintenance] is a concept that recognizes the need for the exercise of political authority by the international community in the quest for global governance (....) As such, peace-maintenance is explicitly designed to transcend the parochial interest of nation-state politics and is aimed at developing forms of political action based on the notion of cosmopolitan interests.[32]

The same neo-idealistic energy appears to drive what one could call the "blue-think" that dominates UN discourse and that, in Canada for instance, includes the neo-Pearsonians.[33] From this standpoint, the slightly pathetic appeal of the Brahimi Report is paradigmatic:

> [UN Member States] must summon the political will to support the United Nations politically, financially, and operationally once they have decided to act as the United Nations if the Organization is to be credible as a force for peace.[34]

The recent ICISS report adopts a similar outlook as it intends to goad states into acting by defining an abstract obligation to intervene whenever massive human rights violations are committed. Without clear and concrete interests and in the absence of political will, this "responsibility to protect" would lead—*legis ex machina*—to the mobilization of humanitarian armies and to their deployment on the other side of the planet.

It is difficult not to agree with the judgment made implicitly by the Brahimi report, and explicitly by the ICISS, on the UN's humanitarian intervention regime. Yet nothing suggests that calls for "political will" and "responsibility to protect" would contribute in any significant manner to the establishment of a fair humanitarian intervention regime. Doing nothing in the face of future Rwandas similarly cannot be an option and intervening without the required means ends up being little more than rhetoric. Given the lukewarm attitude of Western elites and electorates toward intervention, and the unease of Southern elites about challenges to their national sovereignty, it appears that a fairer interventionist regime is either doomed or that its basic needs are to be sought elsewhere.

Few analysts or policymakers would challenge the suggestion that humanitarian interventions are and will be long-term, costly and complex endeavors. Yet this consensus has not yet affected the ways in which interventions are planned and implemented. A case in point is the 24 February 2000 UN Security Council decision to expand its mission in the war-torn DRC (with a population of 50 million) to 5,537 soldiers until 31 August 2000 to "protect civilians under imminent threat of physical violence."[35] Very few Congolese civilians ended up being protected by the UN.

The surreal nature of this mission notwithstanding, to even think that a defined time frame could be established in advance is utopian. One needs in fact to think along the lines proposed by the ICG, and to define mandates not in terms of time but in terms of tasks.[36]

At a more abstract level, Jarat Chopra neatly sums up what is needed:

> ... the UN must deploy decisively and establish a center of gravity around which local individuals and institutions can coalesce until a new authority structure is established and transferred to a legitimately determined, indigenous leadership. In the interim period, the UN needs to counterbalance or even displace the oppressors or warlords. This implies that the UN claims jurisdiction over the entire territory and ought to deploy throughout if it can.[37]

At the very least, the time horizon of intervention planners should be extended to 3–5 years, and the size of the missions systematically improved. Only such moves could give credibility to these endeavors.

There is a comforting circularity to the West's self-centered discussion of its responsibilities and motives in humanitarian interventions: the only cases discussed are those where the role of the West is critical. The idea that Southern countries could also have such responsibilities or motives is simply foreign to the debate: the South is generally thought of as the "theater" and at best its soldiers play figurative roles.

Recent history, however, is replete with interventions of the South in the South.[38] Examples are many: Syria in Lebanon, Cuba in Angola and Ethiopia, Tanzania in Uganda, Nigeria and ECOMOG in Liberia and Sierra Leone, and—stretching the South—Australia in East Timor.[39] Even *Opération Turquoise*, France's belated and supremely ambiguous intervention in Rwanda, is said to have been precipitated by South Africa's announced intention to do something.

The point here is that the South also has a moral responsibility as well as a demonstrated capacity to intervene militarily in conflict situations in that region. Therefore, it should also have a primary place in the design and implementation of broadly agreed humanitarian interventions. In fact, such a more central role is critical if there is to be any hope of global legitimacy for interventionist regimes. This is especially true as humanitarian intervention involves the suspension of sovereignty, respect for which is the ultimate retrenchment of weaker states against great power diktats. The problem is recognized by some, but just as quickly dismissed once the gravity of the situations to be dealt with is brought to bear. A recent statement by Lloyd Axworthy is typical:

> Those who have suffered under colonialism and other outside involvement in their countries might well be skeptical. However, preventing abuse, stopping atrocities and dealing with the impact of war are also their issues, pertaining to their realities and clearly affecting stability in their backyards.[40]

If this is the case, then why should they not be parties to the decision to intervene, and central players in its design and implementation?

To which the easy answer is: it cannot be done without major reforms to UN institutions or substantial changes to the way in which "Southern" regional organizations operate. Yet, the Gulf War, Kosovo, and *Opération Turquoise* demonstrated that the *de facto* decision-making process in these operations is not at all prisoner of Byzantium on the Hudson. When the political will is there, mandates can be circumvented, obtained *ex-post facto,* or avoided altogether. More pragmatic decision-making mechanisms other than the formal Security Council would have to be devised in order to allow key countries of the South to be systematically included in discussions of intervention affecting their region. However, this does not require a revolution.

For the sake of the political sustainability of the emerging regime, a number of Southern powers need to join in. The countries to be brought onboard, right now, in the discussion of a Southernflavored interventionist regime are Brazil, Mexico, Nigeria, South Africa, Egypt, Turkey, China, India, probably Pakistan, as well as Indonesia. With them, the anticolonialist/anti-imperialist argument would lose much of its force, and the truly global meaning of intervention would be emphasized. Without them, the legitimacy of interventionary regimes would be flimsy and their ultimate sustainability doubtful.

A major stumbling block appears to derive from the South's sheer lack of the material means necessary to claim a role in the play. For in spite of the many Southern interventions mentioned, there is indeed a capability gap when poorer countries confront such massive endeavors. Is there not, however, a way around this problem too?

The problem of resources is typically understood as the difficulty in finding money and personnel to wage operations. There is much more to the resource issue, though, than simply the unwillingness of rich countries to support financially their formal commitments to human rights. The cost of humanitarian interventions makes them totally dependent on the will and interests of a few countries, namely the United States and those in the European Union (EU). This is massively damaging to a crucial component of any credible regime of intervention: its consistency. Need should determine intervention, i.e. genocide and massive human rights violations must be met by forceful interventions—whomever they affect and wherever they occur. Yet we know that this is NOT happening, that tens of thousands of Western soldiers went to the Balkans, that General Dallaire had to manage with only a few hundred in Rwanda, and that at the moment nobody in the West is sending soldiers to South Sudan.

The key requirement for consistency, fairness and ultimately legitimacy is to delink humanitarian interventions from their financing by the North. A UN compulsory tax, however, cannot do the trick, as the still running story of unpaid contribution shows. The dream of a globally financed UN-controlled international force, in other words, will likely remain a dream. The only realistic way to achieve such a delinking is to make the operations as self-sustaining as possible.

To many, the use of local resources by armed foreigners is the very mark of colonialism and imperialism, precisely what any kind of humanitarian intervention is meant NOT to be. What happens, though, is that the international authority does not direct many resources to the nations in need—thus giving genocide and ethnic cleansing a chance. Which is the point: either the rich decide, as in Rwanda or Sudan, or the rest of the international community, most of whose members are poor, use what is available to stop massive human rights violations.

Beyond this founding argument, at least two others merit consideration. Many of the countries currently in need of intervention are being disemboweled by forces devoted to exploiting key resources, such as diamonds (Angola, Liberia, Sierra Leone and the Democratic Republic of Congo), emeralds (Afghanistan) and oil (Sudan).[41] These resources are stakes in these wars but they also fuel them, engendering massive human suffering. Why could they not be used to stem what they have made possible? Why could the economic logic of war not be harnessed to end war?[42]

A third argument has to do with another taboo: current interventions already live off the land or contemplate ways to do so. According to the Report of the UN Secretary General on the UN administration in Kosovo, the budget for the year 2000 has among its guiding principles "to strengthen the domestic revenue base, with an expected drop of dependence on donors from 70 per cent in 1999 to 46 per cent in 2000."[43] Similar arrangements also exist in East Timor,[44] where "royalties from production in the [Timor Sea] Zone of Cooperation were equally split between Australia and the United Nations Transitional Administration in East Timor (UNTAET)."[45] In addition to such clear cases, the logic that underlies the various proposals for "trust funds" in which diamonds or oil revenues would be put, as well as that of the "oil for food" program that the

UN managed in Iraq, can also be likened to attempts to control local resources for internationally imposed purposes.[46]

In all those cases the use of local resources does not serve a broadening of the intervention coalition: it only reinforces the grip that the West has over global peace enforcement. What I am proposing here is to use this logic to break the currently exclusive grip that the West has over humanitarian interventions. The mechanics needs to be thought through. A modicum of international participation would for instance facilitate control and monitoring and contribute to avoiding the subordination of a given intervention to the interest of the parties involved. In the end, moreover, it might not be feasible everywhere or even anywhere, but the core issue remains: as long as intervention depends on the money, interests and changing media focus of Northern countries, consistency will be unattainable.

While a reliable resource base is certainly a necessary condition to creating a fair interventionist regime, it is not sufficient. The willingness of countries to put their soldiers in harm's way is also required. Unless one contemplates the use of mercenaries, which Kenneth Bush rules out,[47] interventions in failed states or civil wars will call for the commitment of countries to risk the lives of the men and women serving in their armed forces. And this is where national interest comes into play.

Intuitively, the notion of national interest is inimical to the internationalist logic of humanitarian intervention. At the core of the interventionist logic is a challenge to sovereignty and an attempt to establish a rule of law that transcends national states to better protect their citizens. Hence the tendency to prefer a diverse UN mission to a more narrowly constituted coalition force led by a regional middle power. Hence the discomfort felt by many at seeing NATO take the lead in the Balkans, at France playing such a prominent role in Rwanda, at the US acting alone in Afghanistan, or the US and UK dominating the intervention in Iraq.

In theory, the multilateralist bias looks just fine: disinterested players are most likely to uphold universalist moral principles. In practice, however, it is a different story. For the amount of resources and the risks involved are such that there needs to be something significant at stake for a country to support seriously humanitarian interventions. In fact, the poor record of disinterested (in)action demonstrates the critical importance of national interests to an interventionist regime. Michael Mandelbaum, for instance, makes a strong case that it is the absence of a clearly defined national interest that forced the Clinton administration to opt for the lame air war, no-troop casualty strategy in Kosovo—at significant cost to indigenous civilian human lives[48]—both there and in Serbia.[49]

National interest needs not be defined in the positivistic terms of traditional realist thought. Rather, it needs to be understood as what a significant portion of a country's population consider important enough to risk the lives of their sons and daughters, jobs and profits perhaps, as well as significant amounts of their tax money. National interest gives staying power to interventions and it greatly facilitates the mobilization of resources. As David Rieff put it recently:

> Where politics and, above all, in the conduct of international relations that can result in war are concerned, however, the picture is much more mixed. States must wage war, and only the state's inherent legitimacy can make it plausible both for young soldiers to kill and die and for their fellow citizens to support or at least tolerate such tragedy.[50]

A sad example of the power of national interest is the speed and effectiveness with which France was able to set up, deploy, and effectively use in combat, for *Opération Turquoise* in Rwanda, a force that dwarfed anything the UN had been able to muster.[51] Mitterand took the decision to move on 16 June 1994[52] and the Security Council approved France's plan on 22 June.[53] In a few days, 2,924 French soldiers and 510 from other countries—mostly from Senegal—were mobilized, [54] along with important amounts of military material.[55] On 23 June, the force was already able to take control of the

Nyarushishi camp in Southwestern Rwanda.[56] In a few days, France realized what the UN typically requires weeks and sometimes months to do.[57] France's behavior and motives were highly questionable, but the events rest my case: France was ready to invest and risk a lot, and it did so because its political establishment felt that the intervention was justified in terms of national interest.

The policy implications are clear: an interventionist regime still cannot swim against the current of national interest because, as William DeMars put it, "all classes of potential interveners—superpower, former colonial power, or regional power—when acting for humanitarian goals rather than national interests, lack either the political determination or the military capacity to accomplish the task."[58] The regime can thus only be effective by harnessing national interest for its purposes. Multilateral forces, regional "coalitions of the willing" and key regional powers might in other words be much better instruments of the new regime than "disinterested" UN-managed international forces. There has to be a lesson learned from the supremely ineffective 2,500-strong mission in Rwanda, which had soldiers from 24 countries, none of them (except Belgium) with any stake, however symbolic, in the conflict.[59] The UN Rapid Reaction Force, an old dream of the UN Secretary-General which has been promoted by Canada for quite a while now, would from that perspective be a questionable idea, for in all likelihood it would never be adequately financed, or be allowed by participating countries to put their soldiers at risk.

To put things a different way, an interventionist regime *needs* mixed motives. The point Joseph Nye makes about the United States applies to all: "We should generally avoid the use of force except in cases where our humanitarian interests are reinforced by the existence of other strong national interests."[60] This also means that the role currently claimed by players such as Canada, Denmark, the Netherlands and Norway in the global peace regime is likely to shrink, for the scope and danger of the operations needed are clearly beyond the *political* capabilities of such disinterested parties.

"Bringing national interest back in" for the sake of a global humanitarian regime runs against much of the internationalist grain and is not a little counterintuitive. The dangers involved in relying on interested parties cannot be underestimated either. The dilemma lies between two questions. On the one hand: how can an effective regime be established that would not rely on bad old national interest? On the other: How Faustian a bargain would harnessing national interest be?

Given the state of the world, the establishment of a fair and sustainable regime of intervention must be seriously contemplated. Current practice is more than disappointing. Moreover, much of the current thinking is caught in a box made up of mostly wrong assumptions. We need to go beyond our fixation with neutrality, disinterested funding and cosmopolitan outlook to consider less righteous and more pragmatic stances.

The construction of a humane international order calls for the establishment of some kind of regime under which massive human rights violation would quickly be met by force mandated by the international community. Humanitarian intervention must be thought through, its concrete requirements in terms of scope, time frame, resources and political sustainability must be honestly assessed for a workable mechanism to emerge. Such a mechanism is sorely needed and noble-sounding internationalism should not be an obstacle to the endeavor.[61]

Acknowledgement

This final version owes a lot to Lee Seymour and Ken Bush. Thanks to both.

Notes

1 Philip Gourevitch, *We Wish to Inform You That Tomorrow We Will Be Killed with Our Families* (New York: Picador, 1999), 150; Alan J. Kuperman, "Rwanda in Retrospect," *Foreign Affairs* 79, no. 1 (January/February 2000): 106. Kuperman, who argues that

intervening in April—even a full division, with 13,500 troops and 27,000 tons of material—could only have saved 125,000 people, has challenged this assessment very systematically. However, he admits that "[m]ore troops with the proper equipment, a broad mandate, and robust rules of engagement could have deterred the outbreak of killing or at least snuffed it out early. Such reinforcement would have required about 3,500 additional high-quality troops in Kigali (...) this would have been the 5,000-troop force that Dallaire envisioned—but one deployed prior to the genocide." The basic issue remains the same, in other words: the West could have done something.

2 United Nations, *Report of the Independent Inquiry into the Actions of the United Nations During the 1994 Genocide in Rwanda* (New York, 15 December 1999), Section III–2, 24.

3 United Nations Security Council, Resolution #912, April 21, 1994; Gourevitch, *We Wish to Inform You*, 150.

4 After reviewing a number of estimates, French expert Gérard Prunier settles on 800,000–850,000, which is the number most used now. Some estimates, which cannot be discarded out of hand, reach one million or more (Gérard Prunier, *The Rwanda Crisis: History of a Genocide* [New York: Columbia University Press, 1997], 261–65).

5 For an early call to action, see M. Bettati and Bernard Kouchner, eds., *Le devoir d'ingérence* (Paris: Denoël, 1987). For a review of much recent discussion, Tonya Langford, "Things Fall Apart: State Failure and the Politics of Intervention," *International Studies Review*, 1, no. 1 (Spring 1999): 59–83. For more recent favorable views, see also Edward N. Luttwak, "Kofi's Rule: Humanitarian Intervention and Neocolonialism," *The National Interest* 58 (Winter 1999/2000): 57–63; and David Rieff, "A New Age of Liberal Imperialism," *World Policy Journal* 16, no. 2 (Summer 1999): 1–11. On the political side, see Lloyd Axworthy, "Notes for an Address by the Honourable Lloyd Axworthy, Minister of Foreign Affairs, at the New York University School of Law," *The Hauser Lecture on International Humanitarian Law: Humanitarian Interventions and Humanitarian Constraints*, New York, February 10, 2000 (Ottawa: Department of Foreign Affairs and International Trade, 2000), http://www.un.int/canada/html/s-10feb2000axworthy.htm (accessed 10 December 2003).

6 Estimates of the number of killings by the new Rwandese government number in the tens of thousands, and "the likelihood that the figure could indeed be up to 100,000 is high...." Yet, the international community is groping for a moral ground from which to condemn those atrocities: "Western neglect of the genocide has been turned by the present regime in Rwanda into internationally useful political capital" (Prunier, *The Rwanda Crisis*, 360, 366).

7 "Axworthy Launches International Commission on Intervention and State Sovereignty," News Release No. 233, September 14, 2000 (Ottawa: Department of Foreign Affairs and International Trade, 2000).

8 International Commission on Intervention and State Sovereignty, *The Responsibility to Protect. Report of the International Commission on Intervention and Sovereignty* (Ottawa: International Development Research Centre, 2001).

9 For pessimistic views on the "Clinton Doctrine," see David Rieff, *Slaughterhouse, Bosnia and the Failure of the West* (New York: Touchstone, 1996), 255; Charles Krauthammer, "The Short, Unhappy Life of Humanitarian War," *The National Interest* 57 (Fall 1999):

5–9; Joseph Nye, "Redefining the National Interest," *Foreign Affairs* 78, no. 4 (July/August 1999): 32; Michael J. Glennon, "The New Interventionism: The Search for a Just International Law," *Foreign Affairs* 78, no. 3 (May/June 1999): 2–8; Ivo Daalder and Michael O'Hanlon, "Unlearning the Lessons of Kosovo," *Foreign Policy* 116 (Fall 1999): 128–41, especially 129.

10 See the web editions of *The Guardian* for the following dates: January 12, 19, 25, 26, 2000; and of *The Financial Times* for the following dates: January 21, 24, 2000.

11 Madeleine Drohan, "Why Axworthy stopped talking tough," *The Globe and Mail*, February 15, 2000, A–1; Roger Winter, "Canada's appalling hypocrisy," *The Globe and Mail*, March 23, 2000, A–13; Jean Daudelin, "Canada must stick to its guns," *The Globe and Mail*, February 28, 2000, A–13.

12 William DeMars, "War and Mercy in Africa," *World Policy Journal* 17, no. 2 (Summer 2000), 1.

13 Max Weber, *Economy and Society, An Outline of Interpretive Sociology*, ed. Guenther Roth and Claus Wittich (Berkeley: University of California Press, 1978), 54.

14 Luttwak "Kofi's Rule," 62.

15 Tim Shaw and Clement E. Adibe, "Africa and Global Issues in the Twenty-First Century," *International Journal* 51, no. 1 (Winter 1995–6): 9.

16 To measure up the size and complexity of the endeavor with regard to Bosnia, see: International Crisis Group, *Is Dayton Failing? Bosnia four years after the peace agreement*, ICG Balkans Report no 880, Sarajevo, 28 October 1999; with regard to Kosovo, see: United Nations Security Council, *Report of the Secretary-General on the United Nations Interim Administration in Kosovo*, S/2000/177, 3 March 2000, especially sections VI and up. For a more critical assessment, see: International Crisis Group, *Starting from Scratch in Kosovo, The Honeymoon is Over*, ICG Balkans Report No 83, Pristina, 10 December 1999.

17 Thomas Weiss, "Triage: Humanitarian Interventions in a New Era," *World Policy Journal* 11, no. 1 (Spring 1994): 59–69.

18 This is admitted openly by advocates of intervention such as Canada's Lloyd Axworthy, for whom "consistency" is a key condition, for "all civilians are inherently worthy of protection" (Axworthy, *The Hauser Lecture*), http://www.un.int/canada/html/s-10feb2000axworthy.htm (accessed 10 December 2003).

19 Luttwak, "Kofi's Rule."

20 Rieff, "A New Age of Liberal Imperialism."

21 Michael Ignatieff, "Nation-Building Lite," *The New York Times Magazine*, July 28, 2002, 1–10.

22 Ali Mazrui, "Decaying Parts of Africa Need Benign Colonization," *International Herald Tribune*, August 4, 1994, 6.

23 I. William Zartman, "Putting Things Back Together," in I. William Zartman, ed., *Collapsed States: The Disintegration and Restoration of Legitimate Authority* (Boulder, Lynne Rienner Publishers, 1995), 272; Clement E. Adibe, "Accepting External Authority in Peace-Maintenance," in *Global Governance* 4, no. 1 (January–March 1998): 116–17; Noam Chomsky, *The New Military Humanism, Lessons from Kosovo* (Vancouver: New Star Books, 1999).

24 "UN Chief in Kosovo Says Lack of Money Imperils Mission," *New York Times*, March 4, 2000, A7, column 1.

25 "Mr. Fowler [Canada's Ambassador to the UN and the chairman of the UN Security Council Committee on Angola] spent part of his time this week rejecting allegations that Canada was using the Angola panel as a lever to win a bigger share of the global diamond market" (Paul Knox, "Finding the will for UN sanctions," *The Globe and Mail*, March 17, 2000, A-13).

26 Luttwak, Edward N., "Give War a Chance," *Foreign Affairs* 78, no. 4 (July/August 1999): 36.

27 Krauthammer, "The Short, Unhappy Life," 6.

28 Along the latter lines, see *Le Monde Diplomatique*, which waged a war on NATO in May and June 1999. For the general outlook see Ignacio Ramonnet, "Nouvel ordre global," *Le Monde Diplomatique* (Paris), June 1999, 1, 4, 5.

29 Chomsky, *The New Military Humanism*, 156.

30 See Axworthy, *The Hauser Lecture* for the Minister's views. For a general outline of Canada's policy in this area, see Department of Foreign Affairs and International Trade, *Human Security: Safety for People in a Changing World* (Ottawa: Department of Foreign Affairs and International Trade, April 1999). For an interesting case study of the modalities of such a policy, see Donald Smith and John Hay, "Canada and the Crisis in Eastern Zaire," in Chester Crocker, Fen Hampson and Pamela Aal, eds., *Herding Cats* (Washington: United States Institute for Peace, 1999), 85–107.

31 "Like the British empire in the nineteenth century, the United States has an interest in stronger international institutions and strengthened norms for advancing—with no apologies—its national interests" (Chester Crocker, "A Poor Case for Quitting. Mistaking Incompetence for Interventionism," *Foreign Affairs* 79, no. 1 [January/February 2000]: 185).

32 W. Andy Knight, "Establishing Political Authority in Peace-Maintenance," in *Global Governance* 4, no. 1 (Jan–Mar. 1998), 35. I leave aside those who, even in the face of the world's apathy before the one million deaths of Rwanda and its aftermath, find a way to see norms of humanitarian interventions emerging in the world. Such constructions of unreality (unwittingly one hopes) border on the obscene. See Martha Finnemore, "Emerging Norms of Humanitarian Interventions," in Peter Katzenstein, ed., *The Culture of National Security* (New York: Columbia University Press, 1996), 153–86.

33 See Fen Osler Hampson and Maureen Molot, eds., *The Axworthy legacy: Canada Among Nations 2001* (Toronto: Oxford University Press, 2001) for various chapters analyzing of that movement. Note that Axworthy and his followers chose to forget the extreme sensitivity of Pearson to Canadian national interests and to the requirements of its North American and north Atlantic "embeddedness."

34 United Nations, *Report of the Panel on UN Peace Operations*, A/55/305–S/2000/809, 21 August 2000, para. 5.

35 United Nations Security Council, Resolution #1291, 24 February 2000, para. 8.

36 International Crisis Group, *Is Dayton Failing?*, 70.

37 Jarat Chopra, "Introducing Peace-Maintenance," *Global Governance* 4, no. 1 (Jan–Mar. 1998): 8.

38 The "South" is used here in reference to developing or less developed countries.

39 For comments along those lines on some of these cases, see Weiss, "Triage," 65.

40 Lloyd Axworthy, *The Hauser Lecture*.

41 On Angola, see: United Nations Security Council, *Report of the Panel of Experts on Violations of Security Council Sanctions Against UNITA*, S/2000/203, New York, 10 March 2000; on Sierra Leone, see: Ian Smillie, Lansana Gberie and Ralph Hazleton, *The Heart of the Matter. Sierra Leone: Diamonds and Human Security* (Ottawa: Partnership Africa Canada, January 2000), 39–48; on sub-Saharan Africa—with a special emphasis on the Democratic Republic of Congo—see: Samia Kazi Aoul, Emilie Revil et. al., *Vers une spirale de la violence? "Les dangers de la privatisation de la gestion du risque des investissements en Afrique," Les activités minières det l'emploi de compagnies privées de sécurité*, (Montréal: Table de concertation sur les droits humains au Congo/Kinshasa, Organisation Catholique Canadienne pour le développement et la paix, février 2000); on Sudan, see: John Harker, *Human Security in Sudan: The Report of a Canadian Assessment Mission* (Ottawa: Department of Foreign Affairs and International Trade, January 2000). The reference to Afghanistan is to a remark made by Mats Berdal of the "Economic Agendas in Civil Wars" program of the International Peace Academy at a workshop in Ottawa in January 2000.

42 See Adeke Adebajo, Rapporteur, *Economic Agendas in Civil Wars. A Conference Summary* (New York: International Peace Academy, 1999).

43 United Nations Security Council, *Report of the Secretary-General on the United Nations Interim Administration Mission in Kosovo*, chapter X, section A. par. 141, 30–31.

44 See Jarat Chopra and Tanja Hohe in this volume (chapter 11).

45 Factiva, "West Oil says Timor Gap drilling starts," *Reuters News*, 6 October 2000.

46 Harker, *Human Security in Sudan*, 16, 67.

47 See Kenneth Bush in this volume (chapter 2).

48 An exceedingly careful assessment by Human Rights Watch has concluded that "500 Yugoslav civilians" have been killed by NATO (Human Rights Watch, *Civilian Deaths in the NATO Air Campaign* [New York: Human Rights Watch, February 8, 2000]).

49 Michael Mandelbaum, "A Perfect Failure, NATO's War Against Yugoslavia," *Foreign Affairs* 78, no. 5 (September/October 1999): 5. For converging views, see Nye, "Redefining National Interest," 32; Krauthammer, "The Short, Unhappy Life," 6; David Rieff, "A New Age of Liberal Imperialism," *World Policy Journal* 16, no. 2 (Summer 1999): 1–11; Richard K. Betts, "The Delusion of Impartial Intervention," in Chester A. Crocker and Fen Osler Hampson with Pamela Aall, eds., *Managing Global Chaos* (Washington, D.C.: United States Institute of Peace Press, 1996), 340.

50 David Rieff, "A New Age of Liberal Imperialism," 6.

51 "While the United States still had not managed to deliver the armoured personnel carriers promised to UNAMIR's African volunteers, the French had arrived in Zaire decked for battle, with an awesome array of artillery and armour, and a fleet of twenty military aircraft that was instantly the most imposing flying power in central Africa" (Gourevitch, *We wish to inform you*, 158). See n.28 for further references to *Opération Turquoise*.

52 France, Assemblée Nationale, *Rapport d'information déposé par la Mission d'information de la Commission de la défense nationale et des forces armées et de la Commission des affaires étrangères, sur les opérations militaires menées par la France, d'autres pays et l'ONU au Rwanda entre 1990 et 1994*, Paris, 15 décembre 1998, 319.

53 United Nations Security Council, Resolution #929, 22 June 1994.

54 France, Assemblée Nationale, *Rapport d'information déposé*, 326.

55 "... more than 100 armoured vehicles, a battery of heavy 120mm. Marine mortars, two light Gazelle and eight heavy Super Puma helicopters and air cover provided by four Jaguar fighter-bombers, four Mirage F1CT ground-attack planes, and four Mirage F1CRs for reconnaissance. To deploy this armada ... one Airbus, one Boeing 747 and two Antonov An-124s to supplement a squadron of six French Air Force Lockheed C-130 and nine Transalls" (Prunier, *The Rwanda Crisis*, 291). This information is very reliable: the author joined as an outside expert the commission set up by the French government to devise the operation. See pp. 282–91 for references to his involvement with the mission.

56 France, Assemblée Nationale, *Rapport d'information déposé*, 328.

57 In fact the Brahimi report on peace operations recommends that the delay be *reduced* to 30 days. United Nations, *Report of the Panel on United Nations Peace Operations*, par. 91, 6.

58 DeMars, "War and Mercy in Africa," 5.

59 France, Assemblée Nationale, *Rapport d'information déposé*, 213.

60 Joseph Nye, "Redefining the National Interest," 32.

61 For, as Philip Gourevitch wrote in his recent book on Rwanda: "Denouncing evil is a far cry from doing good" (Gourevitch, *We wish to inform you*, 170).

2

Kenneth Bush

Commodification, Compartmentalization, and Militarization of Peacebuilding

You have to relinquish a lot until the reckoning comes, you snap off a twig, examine it and realize it's just the relationship between yourself, killers and victims that counts. Look some more and you see there is not much gulf at all between the three. Close your eyes, open your fingers and discover you are a hybrid. Open your eyes again, look in the mirror and someone else looks back: someone older and degraded. People call it wisdom but it is just a substitute for hope.[1]

THIS ESSAY IS A PART OF A PROJECT that critically examines the "instruments of reconciliation, retribution [*sic*], and peacebuilding."[2] More specifically, the project seeks to reflect upon our peacebuilding experiences and capacities, and to assess the effectiveness of our instruments, leading to the development of recommendations. In its effort to be genuinely critical, I do not take "peacebuilding" initiatives at their self-described face value. Indeed, my starting point is the observation that there are instances where so-called peacebuilding initiatives have had negative peacebuilding consequences; and where other activities—which are not conventionally understood within the rubric of peacebuilding—have had positive peacebuilding impacts. This alone should be sufficient to evoke a much more self-critical examination of so-called peacebuilding projects. However, this has not been the case.

An explanation of the absence of such an examination may be related to what we find when we probe the various activities that have positive and negative peacebuilding impacts. It is argued here that we are beginning to see the rise of a phenomenon that could be called "the commodification of peacebuilding"—initiatives that are mass-produced according to blueprints that meet Northern specifications and (short-term) interests, but that appear to be only marginally relevant to or appropriate for the political, social, and economic realities of war-prone societies. Indeed, as peacebuilding is commodified, there is a decreasing interest among increasingly "professionalized" peacebuilders to engage in a truly critical examination of the impact of their work.

The current discussion is meant to be an invitation into a *critical* discussion of the practice and politics of peacebuilding. If we ignore the phenomenon of the commodification of peacebuilding, then the best we can hope for is incidental positive impacts or no impact at all. At worst, we will continue to see conflict exacerbation in the name of peacebuilding.

An honest answer to the question concerning the "efficacy" of our peacebuilding instruments is: "we haven't got a clue." The current study proposes a number of conceptual, technical, and political reasons for this state of ignorance and suggests that it may be linked to the rise of the commodification of peacebuilding. More importantly, it offers a way of overcoming it by calling for the acceptance of a straightforward understanding of peacebuilding as an *impact* rather than a taxonomic set of activities. Only then will we be able to recognize and measure when, why, and how Northern activities or Northern-supported initiatives can have peacebuilding or conflict-nurturing impacts. While the eventual development of tools for

"Peace and Conflict Impact Assessment" (PCIA)[3] may help us to identify instances where peacebuilding has been commodified, ameliorative action will require many more political resources than analytical and technical ones.

To address these issues, discussion is structured around analyses of the concept of (1) "peacebuilding"; (2) a number of conflict-nurturing peacebuilding initiatives; (3) the militarization of peacebuilding; (4) the peacebuilding impacts of some nonpeacebuilding initiatives; and (5) the underpinnings of the commodification of peacebuilding.

Any critical discussion of peacebuilding must begin by revisiting our vocabulary. Thus, it is useful to begin with a brief discussion of the term "peacebuilding"—particularly in light of the intentional and unintentional fuzziness in its current use.[4]

Here, "peacebuilding" is used in its broadest sense to refer to those initiatives which foster and support sustainable structures and processes which strengthen the prospects for peaceful coexistence and decrease the likelihood of the outbreak, reoccurrence, or continuation of violent conflict.[5] This process entails both short- and long-term objectives, for example, short-term humanitarian operations and longer-term developmental, political, economic, and social objectives. Peacebuilding is therefore a twofold process of *deconstructing* the structures of violence, and *constructing* the structures of peace. These are two interrelated *but separate* sets of activities that *must be undertaken simultaneously*. Any intervention that includes one without the other is guaranteed not to have a net positive peacebuilding impact. Clearly, the instruments required for peace construction are different from those required for violence deconstruction.

Peacebuilding is not about the imposition of "solutions," it is about the creation of opportunities. The challenge is to identify and nurture the political, economic, and social space, within which *indigenous* actors can identify, develop, and employ the resources necessary to build a peaceful, prosperous, and just society. Ultimately, peacebuilding entails strengthening or creating democratic structures and processes that are fair and responsive to the needs of an entire population—*e.g.*, institutions which protect and advance the political rights and responsibilities of state and civil society, and which strengthen human security through the promotion of robust and sustainable economic, judicial and social practices.

It cannot be overemphasized that at its essence, peacebuilding—like reconciliation—is an *impact* or *outcome* more so than a type of activity. Over the last few years, peacebuilding instruments have typically focused on such activities as human rights projects, security sector reform, democratic institution strengthening, public sector reform, and more nebulously, "good governance" projects. It is essential that we consider the peacebuilding and peace-destroying impacts of those *development* activities that are not conventionally framed or analyzed in this context—for example, activities and initiatives in agriculture, irrigation, health, or education. If we understand peacebuilding as an impact, then it is necessary to delineate the "peacebuilding impact" of an initiative from its developmental impact, economic impact, environmental impact, or gender impact. When we do so, we see that positive humanitarian or developmental impacts are, at times, coincident with producing a positive peacebuilding impact; however, disturbingly, sometimes they are not.

When we understand peacebuilding as an impact, we are compelled to reassess Northern-supported activities in war-prone regions regardless of whether they are labeled developmental, humanitarian, "peacebuilding," commercial, or cultural. We then begin to unearth some unsettling instances where so-called peacebuilding initiatives (and other kinds of initiatives) have had conflict-nurturing impacts.

Some preliminary thinking on this phenomenon has been undertaken by the well-marketed work of Mary Anderson, who points out that the economic and political resources bundled into International Assistance may affect conflict in many ways, such as (1) aid resources are often stolen by warriors and used to support armies and to buy weapons; (2) aid affects markets by reinforcing either the war economy or the peace economy; (3) the distributional impacts of aid affect intergroup relationships, either feeding tensions or reinforcing connections; (4) aid substitutes for local resources required to meet civilian needs, freeing them to support the conflict; and (5) aid legitimizes people and their actions or agendas, supporting the pursuit of either war or peace. [6]

While Anderson is concerned largely with humanitarian assistance in conflict-prone regions, the examples below illustrate two self-described peacebuilding initiatives that appear to have had negative impacts. One is a large scale, high profile "operation." The other is a small scale, low profile project. Following these two cases, discussion turns to a related phenomenon: the militarization of peacebuilding.

Iain Guest of the Overseas Development Council outlines the first example in an editorial entitled "Misplaced Charity Undermines Kosovo's Self-Reliance."[7] He develops the contentious argument that the $456-million UN Mission in Kosovo (UNMIK) operation "was squandered on a foreign-driven emergency relief operation that has undermined Kosovo's [significant] indigenous capacity for recovery." According to Guest, International aid officials brought a profound misconception to their work in Kosovo. They viewed the returning Kosovar refugees as victims in need rather than survivors with strengths.

In some respects, Kosovo's civil society emerged tougher and more mature from the ordeal. Yet, this was not the way it looked to Geneva and New York. From the start, the international agencies assumed they were dealing with a "humanitarian emergency." At first sight this was not surprising. Sixty thousand houses were destroyed. Heating, water, and electricity had stopped functioning. Over 10,000 Kosovars were missing. Mass graves were being found. Kosovo's minorities—the Gypsies (Roma) and Serbs—were isolated and frightened. It is easy to see why governments (and multilateral agencies) threw humanitarian aid at Kosovo, and why so many seasoned international nongovernmental organizations (NGOs) responded. As of the beginning of December, 285 NGOs were registered in Pristina.

Throughout the second half of 1999, UNMIK, NATO, and their NGO partners mounted a classic relief operation. They delivered food aid, handed out shelter kits, and dispatched patrols to guard Orthodox churches and rescue individual families. Yet, by December, there was little to show for the effort. Garbage was still piled high in the streets of Pristina. Electricity, water, and heating were intermittent. Only one class of Kosovar police had graduated from UNMIK's police training academy. Most Serbs and Roma had fled or were in hiding.

None of this is to underestimate the difficulty of rebuilding Kosovo. But it is to argue that reconstruction would have been put on a more solid footing if it had been built around civil society instead of humanitarian commodities and services. The massive concentration of international aid in such a tiny country has had a devastating impact. By December 1999, car accidents had overtaken landmines as a source of injuries. Less visible, but equally damaging, was the inflation caused by agencies snapping up houses at prices way beyond the means of Kosovars. Unable to pay rents, and with their families on welfare, many students were forced to sleep in classrooms. But nothing caused more distortions than UNMIK's policy on salaries. Kosovar teachers, doctors, and police officials receive between $100 and $150 a month. But a Kosovar could earn over ten times as much by working for an international agency as a driver, watchman, or interpreter. Guest mentions one of Kosovo's most experienced human rights activists who had helped to establish a women's legal aid center and had attended lengthy human rights training courses in Norway and Geneva during the 1990s. But as a "local employee" of the Organisation for Security and Cooperation in Europe (OSCE), she now translates for international staff with a fraction of her experience. Officially, she is unable even to take testimony from victims. It is a "scandalous misuse of local talent." This reservoir of local talent should have been the centerpiece of UNMIK's reconstruction strategy. The ultimate net impact was a contribution to the incapacity—rather than capacity—of civil society to rebuild itself upon a foundation of tolerance and respect.

In June 2000, I had the opportunity to review a number of youth programs in the Republika Srpska ("RS"), many of which included "conflict resolution" workshops. I left Bosnia Herzegovina asking what, if any, positive peacebuilding impacts are being generated by the hundreds of internationally supported workshops in the ethnically cleansed post-/prewar reality of Serbian Bosnia Herzegovina.

What would peacebuilding look like in postwar Germany if the Nazis had won? In the shadow of some of the dirtiest ethnicized violence of the 20th Century—which included the butchering of 200,000 to 250,000 children, women and men—one cannot but be struck by the realization that this question is no longer hypothetical.[8] In many cases, the willingness of internationally supported projects to work within "the givens" on the ground, effectively accepts, excuses, and ultimately legitimizes the atrocities that created the current political dispensation. The subtlety with which some project officers achieved this was impressive. One informed me that his conflict resolution workshops worked within what he called "geographical communities"—which, when translated from English to English, meant the Serb areas in RS. This sleight of hand avoided the question of whether in fact the Canadian-funded project worked to build bridges between ethnic communities. Without mentioning the fact of ethnic cleansing, the impression is created that they were working in the intergroup arena, whereas this was not the case. The workshops themselves did not create a multiethnic space within which youth and young adults from all communities could begin to address the many unburied issues of such conflicts. When pushed on this issue, he argued that the distance was necessary "in light of the intergroup hyper-violence."

As a result, workshops of homogenous groups of Serbian youth dealt largely with various interpersonal problems universal to adolescents and youth around the world. When their wartime experiences were addressed, it appeared to reinforce a sense of common victimhood and a need to maintain ethnically cleansed geographies—rather than initiate contacts across the interethnic divide.[9] The memories of close friendships with kids from other ethnic groups were fading with time, allowing those personal linkages and opportunities for peacebuilding to fade also. The foundation of peacebuilding was being allowed to crumble in the same way as the burnt out houses on the Bosnian landscape. Sadly, biographical borders were being reshaped along with ethnicized geographical borders—with the help of internationally supported peacebuilding projects.

How can there be any semblance of genuine peacebuilding if there is no contact with members of other ethnic groups? The result of conflict resolution workshops in RS is not peacebuilding, but the reinforcement of apartheid geographies sought and achieved by the Balkan génocidiers.[10] Interestingly, and disturbingly, despite the fact that every male in the region over the age of 22 would have been directly involved in the militarized cleansing campaigns, to my knowledge there is not a single project addressing the individual and collective pathologies that must inevitably have accumulated during the war on civilians.

While there are often clear military security tasks in "post"-conflict settings that are best undertaken by military actors, it is an increasingly common mistake to cast military activities as the cardinal referent from which all other activities take their bearing. International intervention in Somalia, where ten dollars were spent on the military-security requirements for every one dollar spent on humanitarian assistance, demonstrates how this may jeopardize peace and reconstruction efforts.[11] Peacebuilding is essentially a developmental initiative with a crucial security component, rather than the other way around. While the military security dimension should not be neglected, the prospects for longer-term development are compromised to the extent that it is dominated by military security logic. It needs to be emphasized that the militarization of peacebuilding does not simply refer to the use of military personnel in nonmilitary self-described peacebuilding or humanitarian roles. It refers to the application of a militarized logic and approach to the peacebuilding problematic.

In many ways, the *modus operandi* of military organizations runs contrary to most approaches to a sustainable developmental approach to peacebuilding. Military-led approaches minimize local inputs and place a priority on self-sufficiency; development approaches tend to maximize local inputs and build on local resources. Military-led approaches bring with them the material and human resources for their anticipated job; development actors attempt to develop state and community capacities to identify problems and formulate solutions. A military-led approach is task-oriented, short-term and dependent on high institutional support; a development approach is process-oriented, long-term, and minimally dependent on institutional support.

In an already militarized situation, a trained and disciplined military force is essential for some tasks in the first stages of demilitarization—for example the decommissioning of arms, demobilization of soldiers, and de-mining. Also, the contributions of military engineers in the areas of logistics and infrastructural construction in the immediate postconflict setting are sometimes invaluable, as Ankersen notes.[12] This is where the military's talents are best used. However, the military does not possess the necessary skill set to play effective nonmilitary roles.

A fine example of a study advocating the militarization of humanitarianism and peacebuilding is the CARE Canada-sponsored study entitled *Mean Times: Humanitarian Action in Complex Political Emergency* that makes the recommendation that NGOs should "consider the privatization of security for humanitarian purposes."[13]

The expanded use of "professional security/military private companies" is an especially dangerous path to follow. Notwithstanding the very real and serious human rights, humanitarian law, accountability, transparency and funding problems inherent in these companies (KMS, Sandlines, Executive Outcomes, MPRI, etc.), an approach which increases the "privatization of security" at the international level further erodes the legitimacy of the state as an institution and the very idea of the state as the sole actor with legitimate recourse to the use of armed force. Unfortunately, the checks and balances which allow private security instruments at the sub-national level are not present internationally to a degree which would ensure that legal, humanitarian and human rights abuses do not take place.

Such "privatization" would allow for the further militarization of an already difficult, complicated and violent situation in a variety of ways. For peacebuilding initiatives, the extent to which actors work through and adopt a "culture of violence,"[14] determines whether they are legitimizing and subsidizing the further militarization of the conflict. This approach includes treating warring factions as if they were the legitimate representatives of a terrorized population and includes the use of militarized forces to "protect" the delivery of humanitarian assistance, often with no thought as to the "safety" of the civilian recipients.

In particular, such an approach would serve to legitimize gun-based authority structures, undermining attempts to identify and strengthen the often voiceless masses who were silenced through policies of intimidation and terror during a conflict. Surely, the real challenge we are called upon to answer is how to deligitimize violent gun-based authority structures and to religitimize traditional and/or alternative authority structures based on the constructive conflict management techniques of discussion and compromise.

The militarization of society takes on many forms. There is the increasing prevalence and influence of military and paramilitary actors in the political-economic and social decision-making apparatus of the communities engulfed in the conflict. There is also a shift of priorities and resources from civilian, humanitarian and human rights needs to warfighting. Then there is the large influx of small arms into the hands of civilians, especially children, on the streets and fields of conflict.[15] Most importantly, it refers to the tendency for intergroup relations and conflict management to be defined solely in narrow military-security terms. Hence, social and political problems come to be represented as "military-security" problems that justify and require military-security solutions. The fact that the political, economic and social root causes of these violent conflicts require appropriate corresponding political, economic and social strategies and instruments seem to be largely ignored. Military instruments alone cannot provide sustainable solutions to deep-rooted sociopolitical conflicts. Indeed, it is a well-known lesson of fieldwork that when humanitarian actors arm themselves, the local dynamics escalate and further polarize an already extremely difficult situation.

If armed forces are employed by so-called "humanitarian" actors, and are to be used for something more than window dressing, then at some point they will have to pull their triggers. In crude terms, the following questions must be addressed: what is an acceptable ratio of "locals" killed to assistance delivered? Perhaps both "humanitarians" and peacebuilders would be better served by following strategies which support community-level constructive conflict management rather than hiring mercenaries (directly or indirectly) to fight their way into situations. This would be one way of shifting from a culture of violence to one of sustainable peace.

If the examples above illustrate the conflict-nurturing impact of self-described peacebuilding activities, the next two examples focus on less glamorous types of "instruments" which have had significant and positive peacebuilding impacts but are not usually identified as "peacebuilding instruments" *per se*. As peacebuilding is commodified, these are the types of projects that are likely marginalized from peacebuilding discussions.

The first example is the national immunization days project in war zones that, in addition to having measurable health impacts, has also created the space within which health benefits led to the recognition of common interests and the measurable expansion of peacebuilding space. In active war zones around the world, ceasefires have been arranged to enable the mass immunization of children inside and outside war zones as part of the massive effort to eradicate polio from the face of the planet.[16]

There can be little doubt that the health impact of the polio eradication initiative has been profound in both war and non-war zones—having succeeded in eliminating polio from large parts of the planet. The access that has been achieved under difficult circumstances has exceeded all expectations. For example, the "National Immunization Days" in the DRC from 13 to 15 August 1999 reached an estimated 80 percent of the approximately ten million children in that country. Despite fighting in the northeastern city of Kisangani, 91 percent of the children there were immunized.[17] Similarly, in Sri Lanka, in September and October 1999, "Days of Tranquility" were established to permit the immunization of all children in the country— for the fifth time since the conflict spiraled into violence in 1983. According to some experts, Sri Lanka may now be free of polio.[18] The success of this initiative illustrates that children's health can become a superordinate goal around which interests can converge across battle lines to induce the cooperation necessary for immunization campaigns. Cambodia, El Salvador, Lebanon, and the Philippines provide important instances from which lessons can be learned.

The challenge for health workers is to monitor the impact of the conflict environment on immunization initiatives. However, it is equally important to consider the impact such initiatives may have on the peace and conflict environment, because this may be the critical factor in explaining how interventions of this kind are possible in the midst of brutalizing wars.

There is a growing understanding among development workers on the ground that immunization days may have a positive impact on efforts to end conflicts. For example, in the Batticaloa District of Sri Lanka, the process of organizing Days of Tranquility in the war zone cultivated important informal channels of communication and cooperation across political and ethnic divides. These channels appear to have been central to the negotiations that finally brought electricity back to the region.[19] They have also been essential in defusing local level tensions following the formal ceasefire in February 2002.[20] In Somalia, the demand from the local population that their children be immunized led local leaders to de-mine roads to permit access for vaccination teams. Decrees were issued that no weapons were to be displayed on the days of the immunization campaigns.[21] Such events have contributed both directly and indirectly to peacebuilding.

The second example is the USAID-supported Gal Oya water management project in Sri Lanka, which provides an excellent example of a project that generated both developmental and peacebuilding benefits.[22] Interestingly, its peacebuilding function was entirely incidental to the project. By cultivating the mutual interests of members from different ethnic and socioeconomic groups, the project managed to thrive even in the midst of severe communal conflict. And perhaps more importantly, it resulted in the construction of ad hoc institutions of intercommunal cooperation beyond the scope of water management. In other words, it had a significant, positive impact on the incentives for peace within a particular area of Sri Lanka.

The Gal Oya Water project was one of the largest and most complex water schemes in Sri Lanka. It faced daunting obstacles—physical, infrastructural, bureaucratic, and political. To top it all off, the project was confronted with an over-arching ethnic dimension: the Tamil-Sinhalese divide, which constitutes the main battle line in the ethnic violence at the national level, was paralleled at the local level of the project. In the context of ethnic tensions, if water did not reach the Tamil "tail-enders," there would be good chance that this would be attributed to the "maliciousness" of the Sinhalese "head-enders" rather than to geographical or other factors. In other words, the incentive structure was not especially conducive to cooperation between the communities.

The specific impact on the incentive structures for peace is most evident in the detailed studies of the Gal Oya project undertaken by Norman Uphoff, who, in the midst of a project set in the context of escalating intergroup violence, expressed surprise at seeing "demonstrations of co-operation and generosity—within farming communities, between ethnic groups, on the part of officials, and between officials and farmers."[23] He recounts incidents during communal riots when Sinhalese farmer representatives took it upon themselves to guard the homes of the Work Supervisor and Technical Assistant (Tamil) in Gongagolla. Uphoff explains the interest-based component of why this was so as follows:

> Water distribution creates foreseeable incentives for co-operation among users. There is likely to be some competition, even conflict, among users within any given command area if the supply of water from a common source is inadequate to meet all the demand. At the same time, there are incentives for co-operation to increase that supply, if possible, thereby reducing conflict and enhancing productivity, converting a zero-sum situation to a positive-sum one by collective action. Farmers on different field channels who may clash over the distribution of their water among their channels have reason to co-operate when it comes to getting more water supply into the distributary channel that serves their respective field channels.[24]

Gradually however, there evolved not only a common set of interests, but a shared common identity among Tamils and Sinhalese.[25] Mutually exclusive ethnic identities gradually gave way to a shared identity as farmers. The combination of contact, interest, and participation helped to forge strong bonds of friendship that "took on practical meaning with the emergence of co-operation and energization in Gal Oya."[26]

What does the Gal Oya project teach us about successful peacebuilding? It appears that some of the factors that contributed to its success as a development project also contributed to its success in peacebuilding. The fact that it is a thoroughly participatory development project may be an important factor in explaining its success in both areas. The emphasis on promoting participation generated a number of operating principles which have clear peacebuilding implications: (1) ensuring continuity of personnel to make a learning process more feasible; (2) having a network of supportive, committed persons in a variety of positions; (3) avoiding partisan political involvement; (4) attracting and retaining the right kind of community leadership; and (5) going beyond narrow conceptions of self-interest. Particularly relevant to the argument that peacebuilding requires a strong participatory dimension is Uphoff's observation that "more important than knowing *how much* participation is occurring is knowing *who* is or is not involved in different kinds of participation."[27]

It is possible to identify other lessons from Gal Oya that may be generalized and applied to the explicit cultivation of a peacebuilding dimension in development projects. There was an emphasis on local capacity building in self-management and self-reliance in both resource use and communal relations. The project steered away from too much government involvement and, perhaps most importantly, it

> accept[ed], genuinely and fully, that intended beneficiaries have intelligence and social skills, not just labour and funds, that can be useful for project design and implementation. The poor can even usefully comment on technical design questions, but more important, they can help to plan and carry out the management of project activities.[28]

Although some of the factors that contributed to the development success of the project may also have contributed to its peacebuilding success, there is still a need for a different set of criteria to assess the peacebuilding impact of the project.

Within the spatial constraints of this current study, the empirical discussion above sets the context for a more explicitly political analysis of the commodification of peacebuilding.

There are many possible approaches to the examination of peacebuilding. One approach has been the development of taxonomies of instruments that are sometimes accompanied by case studies claiming to assess the efficacy of different instruments in different settings.[29] The comparison of different instruments in different contexts is meant to provide the basis for determining more systematically how and why certain instruments are more or less suitable and effective in particular settings. In other words, it might help to match instruments to the operational environment. Thus, for example, it might enable us to better understand the sociopolitical postconflict conditions that make South African style Truth Commissions a better bet than International Criminal Tribunals—or *vice versa*.

Taxonomic approaches work when they increase our understanding of a phenomenon by highlighting its elemental features while muting extraneous or tertiary features. Such approaches might be seen as methodologically prudent, even elegant. However, I confess to being wary about adopting them in the current examination of peacebuilding—*not* because they unavoidably exclude more than they include, but because of competing inflationary and deflationary tendencies by practitioners and policymakers in the application of the label "peacebuilding" to their initiatives. On the one hand, it seems that from a field perspective almost any project set in a region of militarized violence can be labeled a "peacebuilding project." On the other hand, from a donor and policy perspective, the label is typically applied to a narrow set of activities such as human rights projects, security sector reform, democratic institution strengthening, public sector reform, and more nebulously, "good governance" projects (typically focusing on government rather than civil society or the private sector or the relationships between the three entities).

In the worst case scenario, this leads to the commodification of peacebuilding: a process in which peacebuilding as an idea and as a set of practices is simply stuffed into the standard operating systems of the standard international actors who do the same old song and dance. When "new monies" are found, or existing monies are reallocated to support "peacebuilding activities," the old wine-new bottle syndrome is as prevalent as the faces at the funding trough. Nowhere is this more evident than in the continued militarization of peacebuilding interventions.

Integral to the commodification of peacebuilding is its compartmentalization and perhaps, eventually, its ghettoization—not unlike the less-than-effective mainstreaming of gender and the environment into our development thinking and programming. Discussions of peacebuilding have so far excluded the vast majority of activities supported or undertaken by international actors that directly affect the dynamics of peace and violent conflict, such as "conventional" development and humanitarian initiatives by aid agencies (health, education, agriculture, and so on); the business practices of multinational corporations; or foreign economic policies of states that often subsidize corrupt, human rights-abusing regimes in the South.

Without the compartmentalization of our peacebuilding thinking and programming, we would have to confront the big, and uncomfortable, contradictions between peacebuilding rhetoric and standard international practices. How, for example, can we take seriously the peacebuilding rhetoric of the permanent members of the UN Security Council when they are also the world's largest arms traffickers?[30] Or how can we take seriously the US concerns about East Timor when it supported training programs for the Indonesian military forces (following in the US tradition of the School of the Americas in the United States that trained the military and paramilitary arms of human rights abusing regimes throughout Latin America) implicated in the atrocities that preceded East Timor's independence?[31] Or how can we take seriously the US's concern for Palestinians in the Fall 2000, when it sat mute as the Israeli State used its helicopter gunships, tanks, and full military force against Palestinian children, women and men? Or how can we take seriously the rhetoric of the UK, when its so-called "Ethical Foreign Policy" allowed for the sale of military equipment to Pakistan (only ten months after it condemned the military regime that overthrew the elected government) and to the Mugabe Regime in Zimbabwe while it is embroiled in military adventurism in the DRC—not to mention its vicious attacks on internal political opponents and white farmers?[32]

It is for this reason that this study is prefaced by the quote from Anthony Loyd, which is meant to underscore the moral and political ambiguity of the motives and impact of the Northern-driven Peacebuilding Project. The quote would fit perfectly if the final sentence read, "People call it *peacebuilding* but it is just a substitute for hope."

How do we know that any self-described peacebuilding instrument/initiative even works, aside from anecdotal stories shared over warm beer in generic bars in war-prone regions around the world? An unsettling characteristic of the proliferating self-described peacebuilding projects has been the failure to evaluate them systematically—a situation not unique to this particular set of international activities, by any means. There are many reasons for this, but three in particular need to be highlighted in the current context. One is political; the other two are technical.

The political reason is tied directly to the need for Northern donors to show their domestic constituencies that they are programming in the area of peacebuilding—a need heightened by (1) the public nature and scale of post–Cold War massacres of civilians (epitomized in the hyper-violence of Rwanda and the Balkans) and (2) the conspicuous failure of Northern States to intervene effectively in such dirty militarized violence—or worse, to fuel it implicitly through acts of commission and omission. For this reason, in the mid- and late 1990s, Northern donors became quite desperate to be seen as funding anything that could plausibly be construed as peacebuilding in intention. In such circumstances, the profile of an initiative was more important than the potential impact. Accordingly, we saw the rise of high profile, media-savvy, low-impact-on-the-ground projects like the War-Torn Societies Project and the Carnegie Commission on Preventing Deadly Conflict. In some of these projects, a bizarre funding dynamic appeared to set in whereby the very lack of substantive impact by the project encouraged some donors to continue funding it just to avoid being seen as having backed a loser—classic cases of good money following bad. The absence of independent audits and evaluations of these projects, in effect, served the interests of both donors and recipients.

The technical obstacles to the evaluation of self-described peacebuilding projects are twofold. The first is simply the absence of appropriate methodological tools and the means to apply them. The second is the application of inappropriate existing programming and evaluation tools. Thus, some efforts to examine peacebuilding-related programs (such as governance programs) that use conventional evaluation methods have generated rather bizarre indicators—such as the World Bank's use of "length of time it takes to have a telephone line installed" as a governance indicator.[33]

It is becoming increasingly clear that there is a fundamental mismatch—not a "gap"—between the planning, implementation and evaluation tools at the disposal of international actors in conflict settings and the types of challenges they are ostensibly meant to address.[34] The current focus on so-called "gaps" by many within the academic, policy and operational communities[35] may inhibit us from critically assessing the structures, processes, and standard operating procedures that currently define and limit bilateral and multilateral developmental humanitarian "institutions"/organizations. The logic and rules of the conventional humanitarian, development, and peacebuilding "game" often undercut peacebuilding impacts/outcomes. The conventional programming logic of efficiency, product-over-process, linearity, and "results-based management" inherent in Northern-control projects (under the guise of monitoring and accountability) is at odds with what is often required for sustainable, effective, humanitarian/developmental peacebuilding initiatives, *e.g.*, approaches that are organic, process-oriented, community-controlled, responsive, and nonlinear. If our current approaches—our standard operating procedures—are at odds with our peacebuilding objectives, then we require a new and different approach to our work in conflict-prone regions—an approach that is very different from our standard operating procedures; an approach that may be antithetical to our current methodologies and tools.

One starting point for the casting of a new approach/instrument is to subvert/reverse the principles that, so far, have been guiding our work, as suggested in Table 2.1:

TABLE 2.1

Principles Guiding Present Approach	Principles to Guide Future Approaches
Structured/mechanistic	Less Structured/organic
Control obsessed (externally)	Locally controlled
Ostensibly predictable	Patently unpredictable
Product-obsessed	Process-oriented
Time limited (bungee cord interventions)	Open-ended
Absence	Presence
Rigidly Planned	Responsive
Routine	Creative

Despite the increasing momentum of the commodification of peacebuilding, there is still the space within which to challenge and resist this process. It requires us constantly to ask the following question of all self-described peacebuilding initiatives: "Will/did the activity foster or support sustainable structures and processes which strengthen the prospects for peaceful coexistence and decrease the likelihood of the outbreak, reoccurrence, or continuation of violent conflict?" And it requires us to ask the same question of almost any activity in conflict-prone areas.

The development of the instruments necessary to answer this question is a relatively straightforward technical exercise that will respond to the application of intellectual resources, community participation, and appropriate levels of funding. However, the biggest challenges to answering this question are political not technical.[36] Nonetheless, we should recognize that the very posing of this question is an essential part of the process of nurturing activities that have genuine, just, and lasting peacebuilding consequences.

We find ourselves at a unique moment in this peacebuilding discussion. There are many allies within gatekeeper organizations that are committed to genuine peacebuilding, but they frequently find themselves stymied by rigid and unhelpful bureaucratic structures and internal political feuding. One colleague at the World Bank explained that his biggest battles in the area of postconflict reconstruction are the daily fights within his organization—leading him to describe himself as a "bureaucratic guerrilla." However, despite the obstacles, there are the opportunities to work both within and outside the "peacebuilding establishment" to move this question to the center of our work.

Notes

1 Anthony Loyd, *My War Gone By, I miss it So* (London: Doubleday, 1999), 7.

2 Personal correspondence with Nancy Hannemann concerning the University of Alberta Peacebuilding and Human Rights Symposium, January 2000.

3 See Kenneth Bush, "A Measure of Peace: Peace and Conflict Impact Assessment (PCIA) of Development Projects in Conflict Zones," *Working Paper #1* (Ottawa: International Development Research Centre, 1998), http://www.idrc.ca/peace/p1/working_paper1.html (accessed 27 November 2003).

4 I recall a former military officer claiming that peacebuilding was simply subset of peacekeeping. He simply replaced "peacekeeping" with "peacebuilding" in his presentations and funding applications. This is a fine example of the way in which institutional interests define terms to suit their existing resources and skill sets.

5 This definition is first introduced in Kenneth Bush, "Towards a Balanced Approach to Rebuilding War-Torn Societies," *Canadian Foreign Policy* 3, no. 3 (Winter 1996): 49–69.

6 Mary Anderson, *Do No Harm: How Aid can Support Peace—or War* (Boulder, CO: Lynne Reinner, 1999), 39.

7 Iain Guest, "Misplaced Charity Undermines Kosovo's Self-Reliance," The Overseas Development Council, http://www.odc.org/commentary/vpfeboo.html (Password protected site. Accessed 20 March 2000). This section draws directly from the above piece.

8 For ground level details, see: Anthony Loyd, *My War Gone By*; Roy Gutman, *A Witness to Genocide* (New York: Macmillan, 1993); Peter Maass, *Love Thy Neighbor: A Story of War*

(New York: Vintage Books, 1996); Nader Mousavizadeh, ed., *The Black Book of Bosnia: The Consequences of Appeasement* (New York: Basic Books, 1996).

9 This should in no way suggest that Serbian youth have not also been affected profoundly by the wars. However, the experience of the violence varied significantly across "ethnic" groups. In an exhaustive report to the UN, a Special Commission of Experts chaired by Cherif Bassiouni of De Paul University in Chicago, concluded that 90 percent of the crimes in Bosnia Herzegovina were the responsibility of Serb extremists, 6 percent of Croat extremists, and 4 percent of Muslim extremists. The death toll follows similar proportions. See Florence Hartmann, "Bosnia," in Roy Gutman and David Rieff, eds., *Crimes of War: What the Public Should Know* (New York: WW Norton & Co., 1999), 56.

10 This harsh assessment is drawn directly from discussions with children and adults in Bosnia in June 2000. I welcome a critical and honest discussion of this unasked question among donors, "practitioners," and researchers.

11 Jan Eliasson, former UN Under-Secretary-General for Humanitarian Affairs quoted in Samuel Makinda, *Seeking Peace from Chaos: Humanitarian Intervention in Somalia*, International Peace Academy Occasional Paper Series (Boulder, CO: Lynne Reinner, 1993), 185.

12 See Christopher P. Ankerson in this volume (chapter 4).

13 Michael Bryans, Bruce D. Jones, and Janice Gross Stein, *Mean Times: Humanitarian Action in Complex Political Emergencies—Stark Choices, Cruel Dilemmas* (University of Toronto: Program on Conflict Management and Negotiation Centre for International Studies, 1999). I am indebted to colleagues at DFAIT and CIDA for sharing their ideas with me concerning this study. I would particularly like to thank Chris Cushing for his keen insights.

14 See Howard Adelman in this volume (chapter 14).

15 See Carolyn Elizabeth Lloyd in this volume (chapter 13).

16 See R. Tangermann et al., "Eradication of poliomyelitis in countries affected by conflict" *Bulletin of the World Health Organization* 78, no. 3 (2000): 330–38; and F. Valente, et al., "Massive Outbreak of Poliomyelitis caused by type-3 wild polio virus in Angola in 1999," *Bulletin of the World Health Organization* 78, no. 3 (2000): 339–46, http://www.who.int/bulletin/ (accessed 27 November 2003).

17 R. Tangermann et al., "Eradication," 332.

18 H.F. Hull, "Fighting stops for polio immunization," World Health Organisation, http://www.who.int/docstore/bulletin/pdf/2000/issue3/bu0424.pdf (accessed 27 November 2003).

19 Personal interviews in Batticaloa, January and February 1998.

20 Kenneth Bush, *From Putty to Stone: Report of a Mission Investigating Human Rights Programming Opportunities in Sri Lanka* (Colombo, Sri Lanka: UK Department for International Development [DFID] Sri Lanka, April 2002).

21 Hull, "Fighting stops for polio immunization."

22 This section draws from: Norman Uphoff, *Learning from Gal Oya: Possibilities for Participatory Development and Post-Newtonian Social Science* (Ithaca: Cornell University Press, 1992); and Norman Uphoff, "Monitoring and Evaluating Popular Participation in World Bank-Assisted Projects" in Bhuvan Bhatnagar and Aubrey C. Williams, eds.,

Participatory Development and the World Bank: Potential Directions for Change. World Bank Discussion Paper 183 (Washington: World Bank, 1992), 135–53.

23 Uphoff, *Learning from Gal Oya*, 104.

24 Uphoff, *Learning from Gal Oya*, 331–32.

25 Uphoff, *Learning from Gal Oya*, 109.

26 Uphoff, *Learning from Gal Oya*, 365.

27 Uphoff, "Monitoring and Evaluating," 143.

28 Uphoff, "Monitoring and Evaluating," 143.

29 See for example Elizabeth M. Cousens and Chetan Kumar, eds., *Peacebuilding as Politics: Cultivating Peace in Fragile Societies* (Boulder, CO: Lynne Reinner, 2000); and Luc Reychler & Thanian Paffenholz, *Peacebuilding: A Field Guide* (Boulder, CO: Lynne Reinner, 2000).

30 A recent study from the International Institute for Strategic Studies reports that the West's three permanent members of the UN Security Council (US, UK, France) account for 80 percent of the World's weapons sales, with the US increasing its share of the international arms market to almost 50 percent. See: "US Takes Lion's Share of World's Arms Exports," *Guardian Weekly*, Oct. 26–Nov. 1, 2000, p.7.

31 "US Trained Butchers of East Timor, *The Guardian Weekly*, 23–29 September 1999, 2.

32 "Call for Tighter Arms Control," *The Guardian Weekly*, 17–23 Feb. 2000, 8.

33 See The World Bank Group, Public Sector Governance, "Institutional and Governance Reviews (IGRs)", http://www1.worldbank.org/publicsector/igrs.htm (accessed 27 November, 2003).

34 This is a conclusion drawn from interviews conducted from 1998 to 2000 with development workers in war zones in Sri Lanka, Bosnia, and Russia, with policymakers in Ottawa, New York, and Geneva, and with Northern donors in various forums.

35 For example, the Brookings Process in 1999 which focused specifically "on the gap between humanitarian assistance and development cooperation" (Jeff Crisp, "Mind the Gap! UNHCR, Humanitarian Assistance and the Development Process," *Journal of Humantiarian Assistance*, Working Paper 43, http://www.jha.ac/articles/u043.htm, 11 November 2001 [accessed 20 December 2003]) by convening an action group leading up to high level meeting at the Brookings Institute convened by High Commission of Refugees and the President of the World Bank.

36 This was a fascinating point of discussion in an electronic exchange of ideas on Peace and Conflict Impact Assessment sponsored by the Breghof Research Centre for Constructive Conflict Management. See A. Austin, M. Fischer and N.Ropers, eds. *Berghof Hand Book for Conflict Transformation* (Berlin: Berghof research Centre for Constructive Conflict management, 2003), http://www.berghof-handbook.net/ (accessed on 27 November 2003). Contributors are: Mark Hoffman, Kenneth Bush, Manuela Leonhardt, Christoph Feyen, Hans Gsaenger, Marc Howard Ross and Jay Rothman.

3 Humanitarian Actors and the Politics of Preventive Action

Melissa Labonte

THE FOLLOWING CONCEPTUAL NARRATIVE represents research in progress that explores and explains a select aspect of the processes that lead to strategic policymaking and decisions about humanitarian intervention in complex emergencies. It focuses on outcomes resulting from interactions between international nongovernmental humanitarian actors (INGHAs),[1] governments, and intergovernmental organizations (IGOs) in defining agendas and influencing policymaking concerning operational prevention and peacebuilding strategies.[2]

The discussion begins with this key assumption: In the foreseeable future, the development of robust norms of peace and conflict prevention in the global community of state and nonstate actors will have to include the possibility of the use of force. Even in the most forward-looking operational frameworks of conflict prevention and peacebuilding, the option to employ preventive action in the form of military or armed humanitarian intervention will inevitably be featured.[3] To paraphrase one scholar, "[a] necessary condition for successful peace-building is the restoration of political stability.... [A]t a minimum, this calls for the termination of military hostilities and the control of weapons."[4] While this statement does not necessarily mean that force should always be used to end violence, the linkage of political stability to the cessation of military hostilities leaves open the use of armed force as an option in pursuit of that goal. From the perspective of theory and practice, frameworks that disregard options of coercion or use of force will likely not be effective operationally, nor will they alter the behavior of would-be perpetrators of civil unrest and internal violence.

The use of force, when employed in a discriminate, selective, and proportionate fashion, can contribute to the development of norms of peace and conflict prevention. Its preventive value resides in the potential it has to halt further spirals of violence that, in extreme cases, can lead to protracted social conflict or "low intensity" civil conflict—conditions that perhaps are best equated to a culture of violence.[5] These conditions have befallen far too many states in the recent past—among them Afghanistan, Angola, Burundi, Congo (Zaire), Iraq, Lebanon, Liberia, Sierra Leone, Somalia, and Sudan—and the international community has only just begun to address the special needs of such societies.

Operational prevention in the form of armed humanitarian intervention is designed primarily to defuse situations of unfolding, imminent, widespread conflict and/or complex emergencies; positively influence the local conflict dynamics so as to enhance the effectiveness of humanitarian operations; and help create the necessary conditions under which parallel efforts to restore peace and stability, most notably diplomatic and peacebuilding endeavors, can be carried out with a greater chance of success.[6] It should be noted that the concept of humanitarian intervention used here differs from that of humanitarian assistance or humanitarian operations with a military component, as the latter two center mainly around the partnering of military and civilian efforts to manage a conflict environment. The goals of these undertakings include creating humanitarian access zones (*cordons sanitairès*), providing military escorts to humanitarian relief convoys and shipments, or offering protection alongside humanitarian workers in refugee camps.[7]

There is evidence to suggest that INGHAs do play an important role in helping to explain part of the variance in these outcomes. The proposed logic that underlies this claim can be presented in the following way: (1) Following the end of the Cold War, governments and IGOs recognized the logic of including preventive action strategies as part of an overall conflict prevention framework. However, states and IGOs have been unwilling and/or unable, in many cases, to undertake preventive action strategies that involve forcible intervention for humanitarian purposes; (2) States instead rely on other actors, especially INGHAs, to act where they cannot or will not. This devolution can be attributed to the perception by states (and IGOs) that INGHAs are responsive, flexible, and effective agents of good governance. In turn, INGHAs have experienced rapid growth in the post–Cold War era, as well as tremendous changes in the scope and nature of their operations in zones of conflict; (3) Ultimately, this combination of increased state and IGO reliance on INGHAs, as well as changes in INGHA attitudes on how to manage more effectively the intersection of politics and their own expanded activities in complex humanitarian emergencies, has led to the development of new sets of relationships between these actors, IGOs, and states; (4) Characteristic of these new relationships are: increases in the perceived legitimacy and credibility of INGHAs as information providers to policymakers; increased access by INGHAs to individuals and institutions that are key players in policymaking circles and significant advances in the organizational sophistication of INGHAs, such that they are capable of advancing an advocacy and/or campaigning dimension to their work; (5) A growing number of INGHAs have sought and gained access to key policy arenas and their activities are challenging traditional notions of nonpartisanship, impartiality, and neutrality that once governed their operations in the field;[8] and (6) One posited outcome of this evolving, interdependent relationship between states, IGOs, and INGHAs, and the maturing capacity of INGHAs to advocate and/or campaign effectively, is that these organizations can influence state and IGO decision-making to conduct or not conduct humanitarian interventions in complex emergencies.

A rigorous examination of the explanatory value of INGHAs as intervening actors in the process of shaping political perceptions, interests, and outcomes as they relate to decisions regarding preventive humanitarian intervention should yield useful results for academics, practitioners, and policymakers. It also represents an important component in an overall research program that focuses on the concept of peacebuilding—which contains at its very core a fundamental transformation of the way that conflict is viewed within society.[9]

Given that the Westphalian system is one that has been structured around and dominated by states, what would compel a scholarly examination of the role of units other than the state—NGOs in general and INGHAs in particular—in order to help explain actions taken by states? Following on from the actors and relationships that comprise what James Rosenau has termed a "multicentric world," the answer in part has to do with the fact that INGHAs constitute more than a negligible actor in the contemporary global system.[10]

Certainly, traditional approaches that explain variance in state or IGO decisions to launch armed humanitarian interventions emphasize sovereignty and non-use of force, mandates, resources, and political interest. These elucidations generally discount the role of nonstate actors as having causal significance in foreign policymaking processes, particularly concerning matters of high politics. Even in the literature on just war, which provides for the criteria and circumstances under which intervention and the use of force by one state against another can be considered legitimate, the major actors and centers of decision-making authority are states.[11]

Yet a number of contributions to the literature in various subfields of the social sciences posit that actors other than states are important variables in formulating correlative and causal explanatory frameworks of international politics. For example, in the field of environmental studies, a number of compelling and analytically rigorous arguments have been produced that focus on the effect that nonstate actors, networks, and institutions have in influencing state behavior.[12] In the field of human rights, Keck and Sikkink and Sikkink and Finnemore have demonstrated that transnational and international nonstate actors have to be factored into explanations of state behavior pertaining to the protection and advance of international human rights.[13] The success of the International Campaign to Ban Landmines demonstrated the critical influence of international and national NGOs over state behavior. Even in the realm of international diplomacy, there is evidence to suggest that NGOs are penetrating into those domains previously reserved for states only.[14] Moreover, critical reassessments of key assumptions (*e.g.* sovereignty and anarchy) that have comprised most of the dominant theoretical scholarship in international relations theory have made it possible to reconceptualize the relationship between states, international organizations, and nonstate actors, and the outcomes resulting from their interactions with one another over time.[15]

A corollary question may also be asked: is it antithetical to use force in the name of humanitarian objectives? As one scholar has noted, "the use of force in humanitarian interventions signal[s] a new idealism in humankind's use of war."[16] Another source recognizes that "genuinely preventive efforts (in responding to humanitarian crises) are both attractive and repellent."[17] In addition to the normative grounds on which humanitarian intervention might be rationalized, Lund's "spectrum" of conflict is illustrative of the potential pragmatic utility of early action. Using limited force early on in a conflict or complex emergency may preclude the necessity of using large-scale force later on.[18] Along this spectrum, which runs from "durable peace" to "stable peace" to "unstable peace" to "crisis" to "war," early action that includes a military component can come anywhere between the stages of an unstable peace, crisis, or war. In some conflict settings, the use of force may be more effective than diplomatic efforts or economic sanctions in creating *rapidly* an environment in which other tools of conflict prevention and peacebuilding can be employed with greater probability of success. These efforts would then address the underlying or structural causes of violence, and would increase the chances of creating conditions for a more stable and peaceful society.

That is not to say that the implications of the use of force are insignificant or marginal. Because it is likely to be met with an in-kind response, using force can create unanticipated military, political, social, and humanitarian dilemmas. There are serious considerations that must be resolved before determining whether, when, how, and why force should be part of a conflict prevention and peacebuilding strategy.[19]

In attempting to provide direction to answer some of the abovementioned questions concerning what factors shape decisions by states and IGOs to launch a military humanitarian intervention, an argument will be made that there is a need for greater systematic study of INGHAs and their role in the process of formulating and implementing operational prevention strategies. At first glance, this would appear to be counterintuitive. The traditional view of NGOs in general, and INGHAs in particular, is that their work is, and should be, characterized by the avoidance of becoming parties to activities that are coercive and appear to violate operational codes of conduct that stress impartiality and neutrality.[20]

The prevention of deadly conflict, be it interstate or intrastate, is accepted as one of many principal goals of the global community. Indeed, as pointed out by Keating and Knight,[21] prevention itself is central to the peacebuilding concept.[22] In academia, the literature abounds with studies that attempt to explore the seemingly limitless range of factors and conditions that give rise to conflict and those that contribute to its resolution.[23]

Governments and IGOs, too, have begun to examine seriously the possibilities of how to strengthen or integrate prevention into their security strategies. Proposals for multilateral preventive deployment and other preventive efforts that are linked to humanitarian objectives have gained momentum as viable responses to deal effectively with contemporary conflict. According to one UN report (1995), there is a "full gamut of rapid deployment teams, stand-by arrangements with donor governments, and stockpiles of equipment and relief supplies" to respond to complex emergencies.[24] In addition, the US has been involved in the development of the African Crisis Response Initiative (ACRI); the African Union (formerly the Organization for African Unity) has established its own Mechanism for Conflict Prevention, Management, and Resolution (MCPMR); the European Union (EU) has publicly stated that it is readying a sizeable, 60,000-plus member rapid reaction force as part of its evolving Common Security and Defence Policy (CSDP); and a coalition of NGOs has established the Forum on Early Warning and Early Response (FEWER), a coalition of academic institutions and international organizations that share and disseminate information on complex emergencies.[25]

The first three examples could be described as representing the institutional incorporation of norms of prevention, including coercive measures, although they remain relatively untested. They reflect a broader pattern of changing attitudes about humanitarian action that has been prompted by the very nature of contemporary civil conflict itself, the use of foreign aid to fuel conflict, and the targeting of civilians and relief personnel in direct defiance of the Geneva Conventions.[26] The latter example is demonstrative of how nonstate actors build networks that are normatively driven. The potential role for INGHAs in early warning is not without its skeptics.[27] However, taken collectively, these illustrations could be an indication that a growing number of state actors in the international community are increasingly viewing the world in multilateral terms, and that efforts designed to mitigate conflict in its earliest stages are emerging at a variety of levels, even if in fits and starts.

Indeed, the rationale behind conflict prevention is both intuitive and logical. Complex humanitarian and political emergencies associated with civil strife and interstate aggression have a degenerative effect on all segments of the societies in which they occur. Increasingly, failure of the state apparatus to ensure basic social provisions to its citizens serves to fuel a spiral of deprivation and volatility that, in turn, can perpetuate protracted social conflict and regional instability.[28] And yet, while the development of operational prevention strategies has gained currency as a viable response to complex emergencies, the actual implementation of such strategies, especially those involving the use of force, remains rare. For example, in the past decade members of the international community wrestled with at least eleven situations in which the ample early warning evidence that signaled imminent internal crisis legitimated, if not warranted, strong consideration by states and intergovernmental organizations to take some form of preventive intervention. These include the complex emergencies that unfolded (and, in many cases, continue at the time of this writing) in Burundi, Bosnia-Herzegovina, Chechnya, Congo (Zaire), Croatia, Kosovo, Liberia, Northern Iraq, Rwanda, Sierra Leone, and Somalia.

Despite sharing similar characteristics—rapid escalation of human rights violations, organized violence aimed at vulnerable groups, destruction of national social, political, and economic infrastructures, the inability of the recognized governmental authority to meet its sovereign responsibilities toward its populace, and the potential for regional and/or international destabilization—only three (Northern Iraq, Somalia, and Kosovo) resulted in armed preventive humanitarian intervention. Postemergency humanitarian action by the international community—that is, action taken well after the violence had escalated dramatically in intensity, scope, and magnitude—occurred in Bosnia-Herzegovina, Croatia, and Liberia. No appreciable preventive humanitarian action was taken in the case of Rwanda; in fact, as Daudelin has noted,[29] the multinational peacekeeping force (the UN Assistance Mission in Rwanda—UNAMIR) that was deployed to the area in 1993–94 was downsized at nearly the same time that the most intense period of violence was unfolding.[30] Consensus with reference to the need for external intervention in Sierra Leone has been characterized by a resounding "pass" by the US and instead resulted in Britain taking a unilateral lead with UN backing and the regional leadership of Nigeria; multilateral intervention in Congo (Zaire) cannot be described as preventive in nature; and there appears to be no real probability of launching humanitarian interventions in either Burundi or Chechnya.[31]

Why is operational prevention in the form of humanitarian intervention so rare? Moreover, why does the decision to undertake a preventive humanitarian response that includes a military component vary among conflicts that share similar characteristics? Researchers, practitioners, and policymakers have elucidated a plethora of practical and theoretical obstacles.[32] Likewise, the literature is replete with questions that are linked to the theoretical and empirical effectiveness of operational prevention, such as under what conditions action is most likely to succeed; should actions be taken in incremental stages or should specific types of early warning correlate with specific types of action; how are the decisions to take (or not take) early action made, and which groups are critical to the process; and should action and/or intervention be unilateral or multilateral?[32] A range of factors can help explain why state actors fail to take preventive action, including structural and cognitive factors, but state actors are especially constrained by considerations of resources, mandates, norms of sovereignty and nonintervention, and political interest, as Abiew and Keating remind us.[34]

The interactive effect of the above-listed factors influences decisions that states and IGOs make regarding preventive action in general. However, these factors have also led to changes in the relationships between states, IGOs, and INGHAs. When interpreted from this perspective, it is possible to develop a series of questions designed to analyze the role that INGHAs play in mitigating these constraints. Whether, how, and to what degree INGHAs affect the process of decision-making concerning preventive humanitarian intervention may illustrate better their role in the broader framework of peacebuilding.

Indeed, recasting some of the commonly held perceptions of INGHAs to include the possibility that they are relevant and effective organizational actors within such a framework may also lead to the development of more holistic and compelling explanations of how norms of prevention and peacebuilding are transmitted into policy arenas and affect state behavior.[35]

The very nature of these kinds of contemporary interdependencies has led a number of scholars to question the usefulness of viewing the global system from a purely Westphalian view.[36] Rosenau even claims that NGOs in general are "changing societal norms, challenging national governments, and linking up with counterparts in powerful transnational alliances...and they are muscling their way into high politics...that were previously dominated by the state."[37] A multiplicity of interactions is now bypassing the governments of states and act directly on their domestic environments and "[i]n the transnational view, nonstate actors (especially NGOs) are much more important than previously thought."[38]

In situations where states and IGOs are pressed by a moral imperative to respond to internal conflict or complex humanitarian emergencies but cannot or will not, they continue to rely on INGHAs to at least provide some level of relief to vulnerable populations. Whether humanitarian operations are being used as a cover for political action by states (also termed the "fig leaf theory") is less important than formulating inquiries that focus on how this relationship has evolved in the past decade and where it is headed in the future.[39] It is even possible that the norms and principles espoused by humanitarian actors are now finding their way into the policy circles of governments.[40]

Complex humanitarian emergencies, particularly those that coincide with civil strife, have been the hallmark of 1990s conflict. Geographically, the regions that have experienced the greatest internal strife are Africa, the Middle East and Central Asia, Southeastern Europe, and the former Soviet Union. From 1990 to the present, civil unrest and/or outright civil war has broken out in at least eleven states in Africa; five in the Middle East and Central Asia; three in Southeastern Europe; and six in the former Soviet Union.[41] The duration and intensity of these conflicts has varied widely, but the collective scope of instability produced by them has included the creation of some 40 million refugees and internally displaced persons (IDPs), as well as the destruction of national infrastructures and governmental, economic, and civil society institutions.[42]

Despite numerous scholarly critiques that provide evidence to the contrary,[43] the activity of nonstate actors continues to be equated with good governance and these actors are perceived as having greater response flexibility in responding to complex emergencies. INGHAs are also perceived by states and IGOs as having a unique capacity and credibility to strengthen civil society groups and organizations—a precursor to democratization—which has also emerged in the 1990s as a desideratum of IGOs and many Western governments.[44]

Running parallel to these trends, the traditional pattern of allocating emergency relief and development aid on a strictly bilateral basis has been transformed over the past decade. Donor states have become increasingly disillusioned with gross mismanagement and corrupt practices by states in administering humanitarian relief and development resources. Thus, not only have states continued to rely on nonstate actors as operational alternatives to state action, they have actually deepened their relationships with these organizations by channeling sizeable portions of aid through NGOs and INGHAs.[45] In addition, IGOs have recently begun to emulate and institutionalize this practice through "subcontracting" operational arrangements with NGOs and INGHAs. Indeed, NGOs in general and INGHAs in particular are valued by states and IGOs as vehicles for dispersal of humanitarian resources *precisely because they are not states*. In turn, the presence and level of operations in intrastate conflict by INGHAs have intensified, and a veritable cottage industry of humanitarian operations has developed as a result.

As with any industry, there exists within this one a continuum of organizational types ranging from the advocacy or "whistle-blower/

information providing" organizations, to those that specialize in operational activities only (and avoid whistle-blowing), to those that undertake both advocacy and operational activities (*see* Table 3.1).[46]

Examples of whistle-blowers include Human Rights Watch and International Alert. Operations specialists who avoid whistle-blowing include the International Committee of the Red Cross (ICRC), and examples of dual or multi-mandate organizations include Save the Children, Médecins sans Frontières, the American Council for International Voluntary Action (InterAction), the International Council of Voluntary Agencies (ICVA), CARE, and the Community of Sant'Egidio. There are even quasi-humanitarian NGOs, such as Search for Common Ground and the Conflict Management Group (CMG), whose operations focus on conflict management and resolution in complex crisis situations.

Traditionally, nearly all of these actors have operated under a broadly defined humanitarian framework and code of conduct that places emphasis on impartial "provisions" of humanitarian goods/ assistance to vulnerable populations. The form of "provisions" varies with the mandate of the organization and the operational environment. For example, advocacy groups provide a voice and often protection; operational groups provide shelter, access to medical care, food, and clothing.

Still other groups provide longer-term provisions, such as education, community building, and/or development of infrastructure. As would be expected, many organizations are engaged in providing more than one type of provision, particularly as the complexity of need drives aid expansion, and leads to changes in mandates and missions as organizations develop expertise in more than one area.

However, the recent past has witnessed a change in the way that INGHAs themselves operate. Many have experienced exponential growth and have become quite sophisticated organizationally and professionally. Strict adherence to depoliticization of aid by humanitarian organizations has, in some cases, given way to various other

TABLE 3.1 INGHA Dimensions[47]

Structural Features

- Single headquarter
- Multiple, autonomous chapters or independent field organizations
- Multiple national fundraising offices, pooled centrally via a single, worldwide field organization that is indigenously staffed and managed
- Central organization subcontracting out to indigenous NGOs not part of their organizational structure
- Hybrid of any of the above

Geographic Range

- International or transnational
- Regional
- National
- Sub-national
- Community

Support Base

- Intergovernmental
- Popular membership base
- Quasi-governmental or national
- Other organizations
- Mixture of above

Operational Range

- Information gathering and research
- Early warning
- Aid/relief delivery
- Protection
- Whistle-blowing
- Advocacy or campaigning
- Education
- Conflict management and/or resolution
- Mixture of above

Mandate Objectives

- Single issue
- Multisectoral
- Broad social
- Church/faith related
- Social ideology

activities that cannot be construed as non-neutral, but are also highly political.[48]

Moreover, the operational demands on INGHAs have changed in recent years; it is no longer the norm that these groups restrict their activities to refugee camps across the border from conflict zones. For many INGHAs, having a "permanent presence on the ground" now means setting up operational bases in the middle of a war zone. This proximity to conflict complicates the delivery of relief and, even more importantly, raises issues about the need for protection from combatants. Both of these considerations are humanitarian—but they are also very much political.

Indeed, there is also a growing recognition that humanitarian activity is not neutral and cannot be apolitical. Complex humanitarian emergencies are usually manmade acts—they involve political means and objectives. Thus, humanitarian assistance activities, by their very nature, interfere with these political acts and become enmeshed in a political environment. Any significant action on the ground by outsiders in such a "highly charged" political arena will affect political outcomes—even if that action is humanitarian in nature. For example, a number of INGHAs regularly participate as information providers in the early warning process, despite the risks and potential moral hazard that such activities present for them and their operations on the ground in conflict zones.

However, opinion regarding whether such a shift represents a net positive or negative for the humanitarian industry is, not surprisingly, mixed and the motives for embracing or resisting such a shift are complex and contested. They include endogenous and exogenous variables such as the imperative for organizational self-preservation and the desire to be effective, and the compromise of morally and normatively-based traditions of neutral and/or impartial "relief." In the realm of academia, the ongoing dialogue among and between humanitarian practitioners and scholars about whether to broaden humanitarian efforts that cross into the *politics* of relief and conflict management, or to return to a "back-to-basics" or minimalist model of provision based on the principle of strict operational neutrality or impartiality, further illustrates this point.[49]

It is commonly assumed that humanitarian operations in complex emergencies have a greater chance of success when they are integrated with initiatives aimed at resolving political differences among belligerents. Efforts to promote peacebuilding and peace maintenance, in their present and nascent stage of development, need constructive input from a wide range of actors and institutions, including INGHAs. As governments and IGOs continue to grapple with and respond to the imperatives of early warning and strategies of operational conflict prevention, changes will be required in the nature of (1) the reliance of IGOs and governments on INGHAs to provide large-scale relief and protection to vulnerable populations during unfolding complex humanitarian emergencies and strengthening civil societies damaged by civil conflict; and (2) the humanitarian actor perception of their mandates and role(s) in complex humanitarian emergencies and broader frameworks of conflict prevention and peacebuilding.

The end result may be placing INGHAs in a position whereby their ability to influence state behavior may be undergoing dramatic change, both in terms of their partnership in policy creation and in terms of policy implementation regarding operational prevention and peacebuilding strategies, including armed humanitarian intervention (Table 3.2). What is of central concern analytically is the relevance and effectiveness of these actors in the politicized realms of conflict prevention and peacebuilding; a related concern would be issues of accountability and responsibility that are likely to arise, depending upon levels of relevance.

Which humanitarian actors are in the best/worst position to influence policy on early humanitarian action and why? How do these groups attempt to influence the political process leading to decisions concerning preventive-style humanitarian intervention? What variables and cases best explain this influence (or lack thereof)? As these groups attempt to bring influence to bear, what are the

TABLE 3.2 Components of the Humanitarian Intervention Calculus

	Cold War	Post–Cold War
Nature of conflict	Peripheral Proxy wars	Intrastate Protracted civil violence Targeting of civilians
Factors affecting decisions to intervene	Geopolitics Strategic interest/value Sovereignty Nonintervention norm Ideology Political will	Strategic interest/value Sovereignty Nonintervention norm Political will Human rights norms Destabilization potential Transboundary effects
Actors affecting decisions to intervene	States	States IGOs (e.g. UN system) IOs (e.g. ICRC) NGOs (e.g. INGHAs, epistemic communities, transnational advocacy networks)

potential consequences of overstepping the boundaries of "neutrality" and "impartiality" in the corridors of governments, at the UN, and on the ground in complex emergencies? What dilemmas do we create by attempting to reinforce norms of prevention and peacebuilding if the former includes the possibility of using force to create the conditions for the latter?

This discussion has raised more questions than it can possibly answer about conflict prevention, response, peacebuilding, and humanitarian assistance and action. The focus was on the question of why states and IGOs respond differently to complex humanitarian emergencies that share similar characteristics. Traditional explanations emphasize concepts like political interest, sovereignty, and resources. Absent from these explanations is one variable that is important for explaining differences in outcomes concerning military humanitarian intervention strategies: INGHAs. An important factor in addressing whether and how INGHAs fit into this analysis is how they also fit into a broader framework of peacebuilding and conflict prevention.

The social science literature does not offer much in the way of systematic analysis of these issues, which makes the search for answers even more problematic. Future research that might take a small step in remedying this should address the above-listed questions with a view to understanding how they relate to a number of the broader conceptual issues of conflict prevention, peacebuilding, and humanitarian assistance and action. In turn, some of the factors that may be analytically useful to test the relevance of INGHAs in defining agendas and influencing decisions regarding conflict prevention strategies that include humanitarian intervention might include organizational resources and access to decision-making forums, the range and scope of organizational mandates, experience, funding, and legitimacy and credibility.

Attempting to explain operational humanitarian prevention policy outcomes through an analysis of the influence of INGHAs poses a difficult falsification test. As opposed to the use of good offices, preventive diplomacy, or the leveling of economic sanctions, operational prevention in the form of military humanitarian intervention is not a widespread phenomenon and, as outlined above, must pass several very large conceptual and practical hurdles before being undertaken. Moreover, there is much theoretical debate regarding the structural constraints on actors other than states in the contemporary global system.

Such operations are important elements in broader frameworks of peacebuilding, and a rigorous examination of the explanatory strength of INGHAs as a variable in the process of shaping political perceptions, norms, interests, and outcomes (in the form of operational humanitarian prevention strategies) should yield results that are useful to academics, practitioners, and policymakers.

Notes

1 At the risk of introducing yet another acronym in a field of study that is quite overrun with them, the convenience of using five letters to describe the type of organization under study could not be resisted. INGHA is defined as a nongovernmental organization that operates mainly within the field of humanitarian affairs and that may or may not be headquartered in one country but whose operations are global in scope. For the purposes of the other acronyms used in this abstract, an NGO is defined generally as a nonstate actor (the term, used in this broad sense, covers those organizations that are local or indigenous, quasi-governmental, and international, operating in any field), and an IGO is defined as a global organization comprised of governments/states, the United Nations being the most common example.

2 Recent work by the Carnegie Commission on Preventing Deadly Conflict (1997) separates strategies of prevention into two main types: *operational prevention* and *structural prevention*. The former focuses on strategies that are used "in the face of crisis," while the latter focuses on strategies that address the "root causes of conflict" (Carnegie Commission on Preventing Deadly Conflict, "Executive Summary," *Preventing Deadly Conflict, Final Report* [New York: Carnegie Corporation, 1997], 3, http:///www.wilsoncentre.org/subtitles/frpub.htm [accessed 20 December 2003]).

3 Kofi Annan, *Facing the Humanitarian Challenge: Towards a Culture of Prevention* (New York: United Nations, 1999); Robert J. Art & Kenneth N. Waltz, eds., *The Use of Force: Military Power and International Politics*, 3rd edition (Lanham, MD: Rowman & Littlefield, 1999); Boutros Boutros-Ghali, *An Agenda for Peace*, 2nd edition (New York: United Nations, 1995); Jarat Chopra, ed., *The Politics of Peace Maintenance* (Boulder, CO: Lynne Reinner, 1998); and Michael S. Lund, *Preventing Violent Conflicts: A Strategy for Preventive Diplomacy* (Washington, DC: United States Institute for Peace, 1996).

4 Raimo Väyrynen "More Questions Than Answers: Dilemmas of Humanitarian Action." *Peace & Change* 24, no. 2 (1999): 172–97.

5 See Howard Adelman in this volume (chapter 14).

6 Adam Garfinkle, "Strategy and Preventive Diplomacy," *Orbis* 45, no. 4 (2001): 503–18 (special issue on humanitarian intervention); Katrina West, *Agents of Altruism: The expansion of humanitarian NGOs in Rwanda and Afghanistan* (Aldershot, UK: Ashgate, 2001); James Kurth, "Lessons from the Past Decade," *Orbis* 45, no. 4 (2001): 569–79; International Peace Academy, *Humanitarian Action: A Symposium Summary* (New York: International Peace Academy, 2000); Advisory Council on International Affairs, *Humanitarian Intervention* (The Hague: Advisory Committee on Issues of Public International Law, 2000); and Hugo Slim, "Military Humanitarianism and the New Peacekeeping: An Agenda for Peace?" *Journal of Humanitarian Assistance* (22 September 1995), http://www.jha.ac/articles/a033.htm (accessed 27 November 2003).

7 West, *Agents*; International Peace Academy, *Humanitarian Action*.

8 Thomas G Weiss, ed., *Beyond UN Subcontracting: Task-Sharing with Regional Organizations and Service-Providing NGOs* (London: Macmillan Press, 1998).

9 United Nations, *Report of the Panel on United Nations Peace Operations*, A/55/305, S/2000/809 (New York: United Nations, 2000); United Nations Development

Programme, *Development Dimensions of Conflict Prevention and Peace Building*, An Independent Study Prepared by Bernard Wood for the Emergency Response Division, UNDP (New York: United Nations Development Programme, 2001); and Federico Mayor, "A new beginning," *UNESCO Courier* 48, no. 11 (1995): 6–8.

10 James N. Rosenau, *Turbulence in World Politics: A Theory of Change and Continuity* (Princeton: Princeton University Press, 1990); James N. Rosenau, *The United Nations in a Turbulent World* (Boulder, CO: Lynne Reinner, 1992).

11 Michael Walzer, *Just and Unjust Wars: A Moral Argument with Historical Illustrations* (New York: Basic Books, 1977); Richard J. Regan, *Just War: Principles and Cases* (Washington, DC: Catholic University Press of America, 1996); and William V. O'Brien, *The Conduct of Just and Limited War* (New York: Praeger, 1991).

12 Paul Wapner, *Environmental Activism and World Civic Politics* (Albany: State University of New York Press, 1996); Shanna Halpern, *The United Nations Conference on Environment and Development: Process and Documentation* (Providence, RI: Academic Council on the United Nations System, 1993); Elizabeth R. DeSombre, *Domestic Sources of International Environmental Policy: Industry, Environmentalists, and U.S. Power* (Cambridge: MIT Press, 2000); Lisa L. Martin and Liliana Botcheva, "Institutional Effects on State Behavior: Convergence and Divergence," *International Studies Quarterly* 45, no. 1 (2001): 1–26.

13 Margaret E. Keck and Kathryn Sikkink, *Activists Beyond Borders: Advocacy Networks in International Politics* (Ithaca, NY: Cornell University Press, 1998); Margaret E. Keck and Kathryn Sikkink, "Transnational Advocacy Networks in International and Regional Politics," *International Social Science Journal* 51, no. 1 (1999): 89–102; Kathryn Sikkink, "Principled-Issue Networks, Human Rights, and Sovereignty in Latin America," *International Organization* 47, no. 3 (1993): 411–42; and Martha Finnemore, *National Interests in International Society* (Ithaca, NY: Cornell University Press, 1996).

14 Peter Willetts, "From 'Consultative Arrangements' to 'Partnership': The Changing Status of NGOs in Diplomacy at the UN," *Global Governance* 6, no. 2 (2000): 191–212; and Chadwick F. Alger, "The Emerging Role of NGOs in the UN System: From Article 71 to a People's Millennium Assembly," *Global Governance* 8, no. 1 (2002): 93–118.

15 Stephen D Krasner, *Sovereignty: Organized Hypocrisy* (Princeton: Princeton University Press, 1999); Stephen D. Krasner, "Sovereignty," *Foreign Policy* 122 (Jan./Feb., 2001): 20–27; Alexander Wendt, "Anarchy is What States Make of It: The Social Construction of Power Politics," *International Organization* 46, no. 2 (1992): 391–426; Alexander Wendt, *Social Theory of International Politics* (Cambridge: Cambridge University Press, 1999); Thomas J. Biersteker and Cynthia Weber, *State Sovereignty as Social Construct* (Cambridge: Cambridge University Press, 1996); Paul Wapner and Lester Edwin J. Ruiz, eds., *Principled World Politics: The Challenge of Normative International Relations* (Lanham, MD: Rowman & Littlefield, 2000); Judith Goldstein and Robert O. Keohane, eds., *Ideas and Foreign Policy: Beliefs, Institutions, and Political Change* (Ithaca: Cornell University Press, 1993); Jackie Smith, Charles Chatfield and Ron Pagnucco, *Transnational Social Movements and Global Politics: Solidarity Beyond the State* (Syracuse: Syracuse University Press, 1997); and Michael Barnett and Martha Finnemore, "The Politics, Power, and Pathologies of International Organizations," *International Organization* 53 (Autumn 1999): 699–732.

16 Hugo Slim, "International Humanitarianism's Engagement with Civil Wars in the 1990s: A Glance at Evolving Practice and Theory," *Journal of Humanitarian Assistance* (19 December 1997), http://www.jha.ac/articles/a033.htm (accessed 28 November, 2003).

17 International Commission on Intervention and State Sovereignty (ICISS), *The Responsibility to Protect: Report of the International Commission on Intervention and State Sovereignty* (Ottawa: International Development Research Centre, 2001), 43.

18 For an in-depth discussion, see ICISS, *The Responsibility to Protect*, chapter 3; see also the Carnegie Commission on Preventing Deadly Conflict, *Preventing Deadly Conflict, Final Report* (New York: Carnegie Corporation, 1997).

19 International Peace Academy, *Humanitarian Action*, 6; ICISS, *The Responsibility to Protect*, 57–58.

20 Mary B. Anderson, "Humanitarian NGOs in conflict intervention" in Chester Crocker, Fen Osler Hampson and Pamela Aall, eds., *Managing Global Chaos: Sources and Responses in International Conflict* (Washington, DC: USIP Press, 1996), 347–351; Mary B. Anderson, *Do No Harm: How Aid Can Support Peace—or War* (Boulder, CO: Lynne Reinner, 1999); and Barbara Harrell-Bond, *Imposing Aid: Emergency Assistance to Refugees* (Oxford: Oxford University Press, 1986).

21 Keating and Knight in this volume (Introduction).

22 Michael Pugh, *The Challenge of Peacebuilding: The Disaster Relief Model*, Plymouth International Papers No. 3 (Halifax: Centre for Foreign Policy Studies, Dalhousie University / Plymouth: University of Plymouth, 1995); and Boutros-Ghali, *Agenda*, 1995.

23 Kevin M. Cahill, *Preventive Diplomacy: Stopping Wars Before They Start* (New York: Basic Books, 1996); David Cortright, ed., *The Price of Peace: Incentives and International Conflict Prevention* (Lanham, MD: Rowman & Littlefield, 1997); Elizabeth Cousens and Chetan Kumar, *Peacebuilding as Politics: Cultivating Peace in Fragile Societies* (Boulder, CO: Lynne Reinner, 2000); Crocker, Hampson and Aall, *Managing Global Chaos*; John L. Davies and Ted Robert Gurr, eds., *Preventive Measures: Building Risk Assessment and Crisis Early Warning Systems* (Lanham, MD: Rowman & Littlefield, 1998); Francis Deng and I. William Zartman, eds., *Conflict Resolution in Africa* (Washington, DC: Brookings Institution Press, 1991); Alexander George, *Forceful Persuasion: Coercive Diplomacy as an Alternative to War* (Washington, DC: USIP Press, 1992); Alexander George and Jane E. Holl, *The Warning-Response Problem and Missed Opportunities* (Washington, DC: Carnegie Commission on Preventing Deadly Conflict, 1997); Bruce Jentleson, ed., *Opportunities Missed, Opportunities Seized: Preventive Diplomacy in the Post–Cold War World* (Lanham, MD: Rowman & Littlefield, 1999); Michael S. Lund, *Preventing Violent Conflicts: A Strategy for Preventive Diplomacy* (Washington, DC: USIP Press, 1996); Connie Peck, *Sustainable Peace: The Role of the UN and Regional Organizations in Preventing Conflict* (Lanham, MD: Rowman & Littlefield, 1998); Kumar Rupesinghe, *Civil Wars, Civil Peace: An Introduction to Conflict Resolution* (London: Pluto Press, 1998); Kumar Rupesinghe and Michiko Kuroda, eds., *Early Warning and Conflict Resolution* (New York: St. Martin's Press, 1992); Harvey Starr, ed., *The Understanding and Management of Global Violence: New Approaches to Theory and Research on Protracted Conflict* (New York: St. Martin's Press, 1999); John Tessitore and Susan Woolfson, eds., *A Global Agenda: Issues Before the 55th General Assembly* (Lanham, MD: Rowman & Littlefield, 2000); Raimo Väyrynen, *New Directions in Conflict Theory: Conflict Resolution and Conflict Transformation* (Newbury Park,

California: Sage Publications, 1991); William Zartman, *Ripe for Resolution: Conflict and Intervention in Africa* (New York: Oxford University Press, 1995); William Zartman, ed., *Governance as Conflict Management: Politics and Violence in West Africa* (Washington, DC: Brookings Institution Press, 1997); I. William Zartman and J. Lewis Rasmussen, eds., *Peacemaking in International Conflict: Methods and Techniques* (Washington, DC: USIP Press, 1997); William Zartman, ed., *Preventive Negotiation: Avoiding Conflict Escalation* (Lanham, MD: Rowman & Littlefield, 2000).

24 United Nations Economic and Social Council, Strengthening the Coordination of Humanitarian and Disaster Relief Assistance of the United Nations, Including Special Economic Assistance," A/50/50/Rev.1.E/1995/100 (June 1995), 17.

25 Roger Cohen, "Europe's Shifting Role Poses Challenge to U.S.," *New York Times*, 11 February, 2001.

26 See Thomas Weiss, ed., *Beyond UN Subcontracting*, 1998.

27 ICISS, *The Responsibility to Protect*, 21–22; John Paul Lederach, *Building Peace: Sustainable Reconciliation in Divided Societies* (Tokyo: United Nations University Press, 1997); Crocker, Hampson and Aall, *Managing Global Chaos*; Rupesinghe and Kuroda, *Early Warning*.

28 David Keen, "The Economic Functions of Violence in Civil Wars," *Adelphi Papers* 320 (1998), 1–96; Oliver Ramsbotham and Tom Woodhouse, *Humanitarian Intervention in Contemporary Conflict: A Reconceptualization* (Cambridge, UK: Polity Press, 1996); Hugo Slim, "Military Humanitarianism and the New Peacekeeping: An Agenda for Peace?" *Journal of Humanitarian Assistance* (1995), http://www.jha.ac/articles/a003.htm (accessed 28 November 2003); Hugo Slim, "International Humanitarianism's Engagement with Civil Wars in the 1990s: A Glance at Evolving Practice and Theory" *Journal of Humanitarian Assistance* (19 December 1997), http://www.jha.ac/articles/a033.htm (accessed 28 November 2003); and Zartman, *Governance as Conflict Management*.

29 See Jean Daudelin in this volume (chapter 1).

30 Romeo Dallaire, "The End of Innocence: Rwanda 1994," in Jonathan Moore, ed., *Hard Choices: Moral Dilemmas in Humanitarian Intervention* (Lanham, MD: Rowman & Littlefield, 1998), 78–80; Kurt Mills, "Sovereignty Eclipsed? The Legitimacy of Humanitarian Access and Intervention," *Journal of Humanitarian Assistance* (1997), http://www.jha.ac/articles/a019.htm (accessed 28 November 2003).

31 Alton Frye, *Humanitarian Intervention: Crafting a Workable Doctrine* (New York: Council on Foreign Relations, 2000).

32 Francis M. Deng, et. al., *Sovereignty as Responsibility: Conflict Management in Africa* (Washington, DC: Brookings Institution, 1996); Ted Robert Gurr, *Minorities at Risk: A Global View of Ethnopolitical Conflicts* (Washington, DC: USIP Press, 1993); Christopher Kilby, "Aid and Sovereignty," *Social Theory and Practice* 25, no. 1 (1999): 79–93; Gene M. Lyons and Michael Mastanduno, eds., *Beyond Westphalia: State Sovereignty and International Intervention* (Baltimore, MD: Johns Hopkins University Press, 1995); Neil S. MacFarlane and Thomas G. Weiss, "Political Interest and Humanitarian Action," *Security Studies* 10, no. 1 (Autumn 2000), 112–42; and Väyrynen, "More Questions than Answers," 1999.

33 Paul F. Deihl, ed. *The Politics of Global Governance: International Organizations in an Interdependent World* (Boulder, CO: Lynne Reinner, 1997).

34 Abiew and Keating in this volume (chapter 5).

35 Kofi Annan, "Peacekeeping, Military Intervention, and National Sovereignty in Internal Armed Conflicts," in Jonathan Moore, ed., *Hard Choices: Moral Dilemmas in Humanitarian Intervention* (Lanham, MD: Rowman & Littlefield, 1998), 55–70.

36 Lyons and Mastanduno, *Beyond Westphalia*; Mathews, "Power Shift," *Foreign Affairs* 76, no. 1 (1997): 50–67.

37 James Rosenau, *The United Nations in a Turbulent World*, 344.

38 Bruce Russett, Harvey W. Starr and David Kinsella, *World Politics: The Menu for Choice*, 6th ed. (Boston: Bedford/St. Martin's Press, 2000), 401.

39 Slim, "Military Humanism"; John Prendergast, *Crisis Response: Humanitarian Band-Aids in Sudan and Somalia* (London: Pluto Press, 1997); Médecins sans Frontières, *World in crisis: the politics of survival at the end of the twentieth century* (London: Routledge, 1997); and Katrina West, *Agents of Altruism: The expansion of humanitarian NGOs in Rwanda and Afghanistan* (Aldershot, UK: Ashgate, 2001).

40 Kathryn Sikkink, "Principled-Issue Networks, Human Rights, and Sovereignty in Latin America," *International Organization* 47, no. 3 (1993): 411–42.

41 In Africa: Angola, Burundi, Congo (Zaire), Ethiopia, Liberia, Mozambique, Sierra Leone, Somalia, Sudan, Rwanda, and Uganda; in the Middle East/Central Asia: Afghanistan, India-Pakistan (Kashmir), Iraq, Turkey, and Yemen; in Southeastern Europe: Croatia, Bosnia-Herzegovina, and Kosovo; in the former Soviet republics: Georgia, Azerbaijan-Armenia (Nagorno-Karabakh), Moldova, Uzbekistan, Tajikistan, and Russia (Chechnya and North Ossetia).

42 Antonio Donini, "Asserting Humanitarianism in Peace-Maintenance," in Jarat Chopra, ed., *The Politics of Peace-Maintenance* (Boulder, CO: Lynne Reinner, 1998), 81–82; Roberta Cohen and Francis M. Deng, *Masses in Flight: The Global Crisis of Internal Displacement* (Washington, DC: Brookings Institution Press, 1998); Patrick Regan, *Civil Wars and Foreign Powers: Outside Intervention in Intrastate Conflict* (Ann Arbor: Michigan University Press, 2000); United Nations High Commissioner for Refugees, "Statistics on Refugees and the Internally Displaced," http://www.unhcr.ch/world/world.htm (accessed 28 October, 2000); see also http://www.unhcr.ch/cgi-bin/texis/vtx/statistics (accessed 28 November, 2003).

43 Anderson, *Do No Harm*; Benjamin Barber, "Feeding Refugees, or War? The Dilemma of Humanitarian Aid," *Foreign Affairs* 76 (July–August 1997): 8–14; Mark Duffield, "The Political Economy of Internal War: Asset Transfer, Complex Emergencies, and International Aid," in Joanna Macrae & Anthony Zwi, eds., *War and Hunger: Rethinking International Responses to Complex Emergencies* (London: Zed Books, 1994), 50–69; Gil Loescher, *Beyond Charity: International Cooperation and the Global Refugee Crisis* (Oxford: Oxford University Press, 1993); Ian Smillie, "NGOs and Development Assistance: A Change in Mind-Set?" in Thomas G. Weiss, ed., *Beyond UN Subcontracting* (London: Macmillan Press, 1998), 184–202; Peter Uvin, *Aiding Violence: The Development Enterprise in Rwanda* (West Hartford, CT: Kumarian Press, 1998).

44 Mark Duffield, "The Political Economy of Internal War," 50–69; Oliver Ramsbotham and Tom Woodhouse, *Humanitarian intervention*; Slim, "International Humanitarianism"; Karin von Hippel, "Democracy by Force: A Renewed Commitment to Nation-Building," *Washington Quarterly* 23, no. 1 (2000): 95–113.

45 Weiss, *Beyond UN Subcontracting*; World Bank, *Annual Report* (Washington,D.C: World Bank, 1998); World Bank *Annual Report* (Washington,D.C: World Bank, 1999).

46 Leon Gordenker and Thomas G. Weiss, "NGO Participation in the International Policy Process," *Third World Quarterly* 16, no. 3 (1995): 543–56.

47 Leon Gordenker, and Thomas G. Weiss, "Pluralizing Global Governance: Analytical Approaches and Dimensions," in Thomas G. Weiss and Leon Gordenker, eds., *NGOs, the UN, and Global Governance* (Boulder, CO: Lynne Reinner, 1996), 42; and Andrew S. Natsios, "Nongovernmental Organizations," in Andrew S. Natsios, *U.S. Foreign Policy and the Four Horsemen of the Apocalypse: Humanitarian Relief in Complex Emergencies* (Westport, Conn: Praeger, 1997), 56–75.

48 Weiss, *Beyond UN Subcontracting*.

49 Stephen Jackson and Peter Walker, "Depolarising the 'Broadened' and 'Back-to-Basics' Relief Models," *Disasters* 23, no. 2 (1999), 93–113; Joanna Macrae and Anthony Zwi, eds., *War and Hunger: Rethinking International Responses to Complex Emergencies* (London: Zed Books, 1994); Terje Tvedt, *Angels of Mercy or Development Diplomats? NGOs and Foreign Aid* (Trenton, NJ: Africa World Press, 1998).

4 Praxis versus Policy

Christopher P. Ankersen

PEACEBUILDING AND THE MILITARY

It is one of the hallmarks of a democratic nation that core societal values should find expression in the tasks given to the military.

JAMES WHITMAN[1]

NATO GROUND FORCES entered Kosovo on 12 June 1999, following a protracted air campaign. These forces were involved across a wide spectrum of conflict and prepared in the first instance to engage in full-scale offensive operations. Later, they were involved in what have come to be known as "peacekeeping" activities–having to use force and the threat of force on a daily basis to maintain order. The international community, in this case manifested by the presence of armed forces and a UN transitional administration, committed itself to the short- to midterm management of Kosovo, and this meant not just "making" or "keeping" the peace, but building, nurturing and developing it. How this was to be executed in practice was (and still is) the subject of much head scratching. One of the issues wrestled with was the role of the military in such circumstances–one of the themes echoed by Bush[2] and Labonte.[3]

The more traditional functions of armed forces were clearly demonstrated during the air campaign, but some of the more subtle and unconventional activities of the soldiers in the province have gone largely unnoticed. It is these functions that are under examination in this chapter: what can the military do in peace support operations? Following from this, one might ask what *should* the military do? In order to address these questions, it is necessary to explore the nature of the tasks performed by soldiers in the province.[4] Only then we can look more closely at whether or not these activities should continue. This discussion closes with a series of recommendations aimed at decision-makers.

Ground forces sent into Kosovo were prepared to face stiff opposition from Yugoslav troops. Contributing nations equipped their units with armored personnel carriers and tanks; artillery and anti-armor assets were deployed; utility and attack helicopters were positioned in and near the theater; and offensive air support was on hand. Robust rules of engagement enabled military commanders on the ground to act and react with vigor, using force where necessary to accomplish the mission. In short, all the tools required to wage modern war were available. As events turned out, the worst-case scenario did not materialize. Yugoslav military and paramilitary forces acted in accordance with the Military-Technical Agreement that prescribed routes, timings, and procedures for their orderly withdrawal. Furthermore, the Kosovo Liberation Army (KLA) complied, for the most part, with the Undertaking it signed providing for its eventual demobilization and disarmament.[5] The military forces found themselves in a situation where fighting a war was not going to occupy their time.

Indeed, from the outset the mission of the military forces was threefold: (1) to provide a safe and secure environment; (2) to perform core civil functions; and (3) to provide humanitarian assistance.[6]

For many forces it was possible—and in some cases, necessary—to begin work on the second and third aspects of their mission immediately upon entry into Kosovo. As an example, a unit that deployed to the town of Glogovac arrived on the heels of the departing Yugoslav forces. They were instantly confronted by "nontraditional" military tasks such as having to arbitrate property disputes between equally needy families arguing over the right to live in a one-room apartment. One commander began to issue birth certificates, with the proviso that the "real" administration system would have to formalize the process at some unknown later date. In an absolute vacuum of civil authority, soldiers assumed functions of the police. Soldiers dealt with emergency life and death matters, as well as issues that police around the world normally handle—and that soldiers generally do. Military personnel, untrained in the nuances of law enforcement, responded to occurrences of domestic violence, sexual abuse, theft, and impaired driving. No judicial system existed, and the only detention facility was also run by the military. Commanders at all levels found themselves to be jurist, judge, and jailer.

Clearly, this was not a peacekeeping mission like those conducted previously. It was not a return to the "Thin Blue Line" of UN Missions where peacekeepers positioned themselves between two warring armed forces. It was not a mature peace enforcement mission, such as the one NATO was conducting in Bosnia, where civil and military authority is well established and well separated.[7] At the same time, though, it was not a warfighting situation, where the military applied force and would not be involved in the administration of the population. In many respects, owing to the lack of indigenous infrastructure or an international administration, it resembled a military governorship, reminiscent of postliberation countries in earlier wars. As the UN Interim Mission in Kosovo (UNMIK) developed over time, many of these functions were transferred from the military to the international civil presence. Still, some remained with the military due to a lack of capability on the part of UNMIK to assume them.

The activities undertaken by military forces in missions such as Kosovo include humanitarian relief, in terms of emergency shelter delivery, critical medical care, and provision of food. However, they go further than this into what has been regarded as the "humanitarian space"—into the realm of peacebuilding.[8] For example, medical personnel in Kosovo helped local doctors establish practices in areas of mixed ethnicity, teaching not only public health principles, but helping people to see the value of coexistence. Even in projects that aimed mainly at providing humanitarian relief, such as the rebuilding of houses or bridges, soldiers strove to build capacity in the community, instructing locals in both the technical and managerial skills required.

In the area of governance, military officers assisted in creating responsible and tolerant structures, paving the way for these structures to become democratic. Joint municipal bodies were convened, with oversight by military and UN administrators, which required the participation of the community. Mixed ethnic schools were established, supported, and guarded by KFOR. All of this activity was the result of work done by the soldiers on the spot, who initially entered the province to fight a war.[9]

Of course, the Kosovo mission was not an isolated incident. Indeed, in many ways it can be seen as the culminating point in a process that began after the end of the Cold War. The 1990s saw the rise of armed humanitarian intervention,[10] beginning with the creation of the "no fly zones" in northern Iraq designed to protect displaced Kurds, continuing through such places as Somalia, Cambodia, Rwanda, Bosnia, and culminating with NATO's 1999 "humanitarian war" over Kosovo and Serbia. While this phenomenon, which connects military and humanitarian motivations and organizations, is not entirely new,[11] the last decade was marked by a significant proliferation of missions in terms of numbers and scope. The "New World Order," proclaimed after the end of the Cold and Gulf Wars seems to rely on a series of military interventions, linked to massive humanitarian aid delivery operations.[12]

The reasons for the development of humanitarian assistance as a method of policing the world order are diverse. Weiss suggests that they are a combination of "the end of East-West tensions, the erosion of sovereignty, the evolution of [international] norms, genuine altruism, domestic politics, media coverage, and the desire to contain refugee flows."[13] Others believe that these missions are indicative of "the people centered approach" popular in development circles being applied in the arena of international politics.[14] Indeed, rhetoric from a number of Western governments, such as Canada and the United Kingdom, highlight the need for a "human security strategy" based on humanitarian values as a substitute for the traditional "state security" paradigm.[15]

There are ideas, though, that situate the rise in humanitarian interventionism as part of a larger scheme. Labeled by Slim as "geopolitical conspiracy theories," they see "humanitarian missions as rehearsals for short notice invasions."[16] Less radical is the notion that military attention on humanitarian activity is grounded in a desire to maintain budgetary funding, in light of defense spending draw-downs. This "substitution theory" posits that militaries look for roles to fill as a way of making themselves indispensable. Therefore, as the threat of the Cold War subsided, humanitarian missions were substituted for more traditional activities.[17]

Whatever the particular reasons behind them, humanitarian missions have become hallmarks of the international community's engagement in world affairs.[18] Despite the fact that these operations are occurring as never before, the so-called "international humanitarian system" behind them "is not a system" at all.[19] The interventions are at best a crude "process of management" at worst a series of *ad hoc* measures.[20] However loosely organized, the occasions of humanitarian assistance of this period do have aspects that set them apart from missions of earlier times. First, they are instances of direct political and military involvement in the internal affairs of a country, with or without explicit consent. What began as "peacekeeping" evolved into something far more intrusive. Traditionally, peacekeeping had generally meant some form of "truce supervision" by a "neutral (usually UN) interpositional force. However, with ideas such as "peace enforcement," "preventive deployment," and even "peacemaking" introduced into the vocabulary of international diplomacy,[21] the lines between the political, the military, and the humanitarian began to blur.

Second (and most interesting for the purposes of the current study), these interventions were responses to "complex emergencies" and consequently they required a mix of political, military, and humanitarian assets and capabilities.[22] As a result, "the certainties of military and civilian roles...have become hazy."[23]

Within this hazy context, the military forces in Kosovo performed "nontraditional" tasks under two circumstances that are worthy of note. First, the military forces felt compelled to conduct them. This was not a case of the militarization of humanitarian intervention, *per se*, as Kenneth Bush has intimated.[24] The soldiers on the ground did not actively seek out these kinds of activities. Often, they were approached by desperate members of the community, or stumbled upon issues that demanded attention. This is significant because it illustrates that any kind of linear modeling of military operations in "postconflict" scenarios is inherently flawed. Conflicts—and by extension the activities that mitigate their consequences—do not proceed in sequential order, from one phase to another. The disputed property issue described above did not wait until after the "entry" or "crisis" phase was over before requiring action. The need for peacebuilding is present at all times, right alongside the need for the application of deadly force or emergency relief, as argued by Labonte.[25]

This highlights the second condition that confronts military forces. Kosovo was very much a "come-as-you-are" affair, with little time between activation of ground forces and their subsequent commitment. Due to the immediacy of the issues confronting military forces, they were forced to conduct peacebuilding with their warfighting hats on. As described above, there was no time to "retool" the units that crossed into Kosovo before the first demands were placed on them. If tanks form the forces in theater, then tank troops will have to be prepared to deal with peacebuilding issues.

The picture painted above only illustrates what *happened*. It does not answer the question of whether or not it *should happen* in the future. There are several schools of thought with opinions on this aspect of military involvement. The soldiers, for instance, "found themselves embroiled in activities—whether intentionally or otherwise—traditionally outside [their] remit."[26] Civilian agencies, on the other hand, were shocked and dismayed to find their domain—the so-called "humanitarian space"—invaded by politicians and soldiers.[27] The relationship was thrust upon the actors and owing to a "mutual lack of familiarity,"[28] many found it challenging. A senior NATO officer admitted frankly, "it is still difficult engaging with the staff of international organizations and NGOs...This is a two way problem."[29] On "both sides" of the debate, practitioners and commentators were asking what role, if any, the "other" should play in complicated and overlapping missions.[30] In spite of this doubt and resistance, civil-military interaction has become a prerequisite for success, which further serves to bring the relationship into the spotlight.[31]

There are two main areas identified as the causes for the difficult nature of civil-military interactions. Many find culture to be the chief culprit.[32] For example, militaries are organized as hierarchies, have established "chains of command," and are accustomed to giving and following orders. NGOs, on the other hand, are portrayed as "horizontally organized," with empowered employees who value their independence. Eisenhour and Marks summarize the dilemma by stating that "the military conditions its personnel to coordinate and be coordinated, while humanitarian organizations [condition their personnel] to be self-reliant in their areas of expertise."[33] However, there are those who believe cultural differences are not so pronounced, while Slim states that the contrast between the groups can be overstated. For example, military officers can be "self-reliant" and international organizations and even some large NGOs have their own bureaucratic processes.[34]

Another area where civilian and military personnel find themselves at odds is that of values, and it seems that matters of principle can be even more divisive than organizational culture. Again, the debate tends to generalize and stereotype and "exceptions to the rule" are rarely acknowledged. Williams, for example, claims that soldiers are inherently conservative in their social outlook, and even form a separate social group. This conservatism clashes most profoundly with NGO culture because "NGOs tend to attract young people, most of whom are social, if not political radicals."[35]

Generalizations aside, "conflicting values"[36] are cited as sources of "reticence and ambivalence on the part of the humanitarian, which extends beyond questions of operational procedure to matters of ethics and identity."[37] Militaries and civilian agencies differ in the ways they value time, efficiency, impartiality and neutrality, and the use of force. Military participation in humanitarian missions is characterized as suffering from "short-sightedness" and a "quick fix" mentality. Military solutions are said to be "cheap, to hand, and temporary."[38] Owing to the fact that—as Abiew and Keating point out[39]—NGOs and other civilians are often *in situ* well before and remain long after the military, they tend to have longer-term interests.[40]

Related to the way in which the organizations view the idea of time, efficiency is understood differently too. Armies see collaboration with their civilian counterparts as a way of getting the mission accomplished.[41] Indeed, some see the provision of humanitarian aid only as a way of captivating the local populations and of winning their hearts and minds. This runs counter to the NGO understanding of humanitarian assistance as leading to longer-term development.[42]

NGOs are protective of their hard-won status as impartial and neutral organizations that provide assistance on the basis of need, and not politics. Therefore, they are wary of tarnishing this reputation through association with the military for fear of losing credibility, or even facing retaliation.[43] The military, conversely, is suspicious of civilian organizations refusing to share information and intelligence, apparently unaware or unswayed by their concerns about taking sides.[44]

If the other three factors can be seen as practical matters, the perspectives on violence are far more fundamental and philosophical. The fact that one party relies on the application of force to do its job while the other abhors it creates a "moral paradox."[45] Most NGOs "have profound reservations about militarism" and "Khaki makes many of them uneasy."[46] This tension is portrayed as far more one-sided than the others because while soldiers can sympathize with and even be motivated by humanitarian principles, the converse is not true for civilian humanitarians.[47]

These cultural and value differences could lead one to believe that civil-military interaction is impossible. However, because "militaries and humanitarians have represented two sides of the same coin—humankind's inability to manage conflict peacefully,"[48] they find themselves thrust together, forced to work side by side. Against this backdrop of pessimism and dissatisfaction, though, are examples (like the Canadian operation in Kosovo) that demonstrate that the military does have a significant role to play in helping to build peace. Collaboration does occur and sometimes it even works.[49] In order to show that military forces should engage in peacebuilding activities we need to look at the complexity of the situations in which they are involved, the competence and capacity of those forces, and the complementary nature of peacebuilding.

The types of conflict situations that the international community is increasingly becoming involved in are by their very nature extremely complex. It has become apparent that simply separating warring parties will not stop the violence, let alone help a country on the road to recovery and resolution. Just as there are several causes to a conflict, be they social, economic, or political, there are several actions that may be taken to help reduce suffering or end war. This being the case, one encounters what Clarke and Smith refer to as the "complexity of joint action," whereby "policies that require something to be done have to use a number of different agencies to achieve a result."[50] It is clear that conflicts that are caused by a number of diverse factors will not be ended by the application of only one policy instrument. A complex problem, such as Kosovo, cannot be solved by a simple unidimensional approach; military force alone will not achieve success. Just as true is the argument that *any* one activity, be it humanitarian relief or diplomacy, suffers from the same inability to address the whole problem. Hayes and Sands assert that "stovepipe strategies for dealing with...crises—that is strategies confined to narrow areas of activity that do not consider how they may effect other areas—are woefully inadequate."[51] Two conclusions can be drawn from this discussion. First, holistic strategies that address as many different aspects of a particular conflict as possible must be developed. Second, each instrument involved in the resolution of the conflict must address as many aspects as it is able and capable of handling.

Professional military forces, such as those deployed under the NATO flag in Kosovo, are made up of talented men and women who, by and large, are well educated and resourceful. The training that they undergo throughout their careers stresses initiative and resourcefulness and, moreover, they are trained how to train; instructing others is a constant part of their job. Soldiers are accustomed to making do in less than ideal situations—improvisation and the ability to get the job done are highly developed skills. These skills make military personnel more than competent to handle new tasks, even nontraditional ones. Weiss believes "the military's 'can-do' mentality, self-supporting character, and rapid response capabilities, as well as its hierarchical discipline, are essential assets within the turmoil of acute tragedies."[52] Recently, with the rise in the number of "operations other than outright war" that professional armies are finding themselves conducting, new training, tailored to preparing soldiers for missions like Kosovo, is being added. Instruction in the subjects of cultural awareness, language, and negotiation forms the backbone of predeployment training. This new training adds a focus to the already present competence found in modern armies. These skills have been developed and demonstrated in any number of situations, including past "peacekeeping" missions as well as domestic and international disaster relief operations. As Whitman claims, the issue of "competence is not on the agenda"; capacity is.[53]

The ground forces deployed into conflicts such as Kosovo are designed with the capacity to use force foremost in mind. Having said that, they bring with them the capacity to do a great deal more than that, too. This capacity is due to the resources they have, the flexibility of the equipment and personnel, and the short reaction time that often sees these forces on the ground ahead of anyone else. Modern military forces are well equipped with logistical vehicles, forklifts and cranes, palletized loading systems, communication systems, food preparation equipment, medical supplies, field shelters, and more. Again, while this equipment exists primarily to provide military muscle, this military capacity can be used to help build peace since military operations can constitute an extremely small percentage of a contingent's time. It makes no sense to have military trucks sitting idle when there are shelters to be built or food to be delivered. The capacity intended to wage war can easily be utilized in the building of peace. This kind of employment of equipment, however, must be done intelligently, and should, where possible, not be committed to projects on a permanent basis—thus avoiding what Kenneth Bush calls "the militarization of peacebuilding,"[54] since "postconflict" situations do not always remain nonviolent.

The military resources may need to be used in the execution of more traditional military tasks at a moment's notice. This potential need, however, does not preclude their use in peacebuilding. It simply means that plans must be developed to allow for their integration, and for their absence. Each request for the use of military resources must therefore be evaluated and judgment must be used in their provision.

When the issue of competence was examined above, it was pointed out that military personnel are generally resourceful people. Equipment, as well, is inherently adaptable. These two qualities mean that military forces are extremely flexible, a trait that allows for a capacity built for one purpose to be redeployed quickly for other purposes. Trucks or medical personnel can be involved in a community health program in the morning and immediately be dispatched to a riot or public disturbance to see to the needs of military personnel in the afternoon. A graphic example existed in Kosovo in the winter of 2000. As the divided town of Kosovo Mitrovica, with its emblematic protests on the bridge separating Serb from Albanian, erupted into violence on television screens around the world, the Canadian soldiers pictured on the evening news (the ones with the long woolly beards) were from an infantry specialist "pioneer" platoon. Only days before, these same soldiers were building bridges and repairing homes with locals, passing on advice and expertise. That platoon had the flexibility to shift from one activity to another—at opposite ends of the spectrum in terms of conflict—with short notice and little difficulty. Furthermore, when they were no longer needed to stand on the bridge between angry mobs, they returned to the business of peacebuilding just as effectively.

Finally, military forces have one more characteristic that makes them ideal candidates as peacebuilders: rapid reaction capability. In some cases, military forces are on the ground more quickly than their IGO counterparts, and sometimes even more quickly than some NGOs. What is more, even when they are not the first to arrive on scene, they are usually the first ones there with any kind of capacity. Military forces arrive ready to operate, with all the personnel and equipment they require. This means that the competence and capacity mentioned above is often all that is available, and often for a considerable time. Looking at Kosovo, KFOR (NATO's Kosovo Force) was established well before UNMIK was able to begin operations. As a result, KFOR personnel ran the international airport, railway, and the coal-fired power station for several months until other agencies were able to assume responsibility for them.

If a military has both the competence and capacity to engage in peacebuilding, it would appear as if there are no impediments to its continued employment in this endeavor. This, however, is often far from the case. Some senior military officials see any activity outside the realm of traditional combat as a dangerous precedent, "claiming that such operations divert the focus of the military from warfighting.... Skeptics believe that peace operations tasks should continue to be narrowly construed, with the focus remaining on achieving a safe and secure environment for target populations, relief workers, and peacekeepers."[55] One author claims that "soldiering and peacekeeping are two quite separate activities...combat-trained soldiers are asked to act as noncombatant soldiers and to perform duties which go against their training, and more importantly, their vocation."[56] For many, though, peacebuilding and even humanitarian assistance during peacekeeping missions will never amount to anything more than an "incidental undertaking."[57]

It is interesting to note that operational level commanders on the ground do not often share this view. The people, who are faced every day with either sitting by or waiting for something bad to happen, or engaging in meaningful activity, have a very different opinion. No less of a warfighter than Major-General Nash, the Commander of the US 1st Armored Division in Bosnia in 1994 said of peacebuilding: "it's not mission creep, it's mission."[58] In a very real and very self-serving sense, the military must do more than keep order and act as a deterrent; winning the hearts and minds of the population has been an objective of military forces for centuries. Hayes and Sands assert that forces must go far beyond merely providing a "safe and secure environment" to ensure that the mission is achieved: "if a military operation fails to transcend immediate humanitarian needs and address future developmental requirements, the best it can hope to achieve is very limited set of objectives."[59] If security is what militaries want, then building peace is one of the best ways to get it.

Luckily, commanders in theaters such as Kosovo do tend to get on with the job and military forces are contributing to peacebuilding in many ways. Despite nay-saying and tough rhetoric which posits warfighting as the only thing militaries do, the real "policy is not what we choose; it is what we are doing."[60] General Doctor Reinhardt, the Commander of KFOR, had this to say of the role his forces were playing in Kosovo: "KFOR and UNMIK are partners in an international effort to restore Kosovo and help the local population to transform the province into a free and democratic society open to all.... The multinational force provides resources, skills, and manpower to various organisations and agencies working under the UNMIK umbrella."[61]

How should partnerships such as these be managed in the future? How do the international community and national governments get the most bang for their buck, and how do the populations of failed states and complex emergencies get the assistance they desperately need? The following portion of this chapter outlines a series of recommendations designed to increase the efficiency of a system of ad hoc cooperation.[62]

Perhaps as a result of the stereotypical views that exist, most cooperation between civil and military organizations is at a very personal or low-rank level, due to traditional distrust and animosity on both sides. This antagonism has led to a lack of any kind of formalized coordination, and this, in turn, has led to inefficiency. As Moore states, "without institutionalising an interagency [mechanism] too much unity of effort will be sacrificed until 'work-arounds' eventually emerge."[63] One such case was observed in Kosovo. Representatives from the Canadian International Development Agency (CIDA), the Canadian military unit, and several NGOs created a successful system of repairing communal buildings, such as schools. The military officer would take information gathered from soldiers in the area and create an assessment of requirements. He then passed the file to the CIDA representative for funding approval. Once funding was available, the military officer would contract work from NGOs and locals, maintaining supervision over the project through the use of liaison officers and a local engineer. Eventually the system worked so well that the CIDA representative left the country and the nearly one million dollars of CIDA funding was devolved to the military officer for use on similar projects. All of this was done without any prior formalized coordination and happened only because of the personalities involved: three of the key players in the above example were from the same hometown and were able to work well together.[64]

As Melissa Labonte argues, no one agency or organization can act alone in complex emergencies or failed states.[65] As the current Secretary-General of NATO has stated, "The Kosovo conflict...emphasised the extent to which the means of responding to an international crisis are inter-linked."[66] Accordingly, interagency coordination has to become a priority. Nationally, this means formalized cooperation prior to deployments, tying the resources, expertise, and money of all affected players together. In the Canadian context, for instance, this means that CIDA, DFAIT, DND and others (such as the Solicitor-General's office when RCMP officers or correction officials are dispatched) need to meet and decide upon a unified plan of action, and put in place the structures and processes to ensure that cooperation is not simply a byproduct of personality.

Not only would formalized policy and implementation rationalization improve efficiency at a national level, it would help ensure that our resources are not squandered. In Kosovo, in addition to the military, over seventy RCMP officers were in the province, as well as officials from Corrections Canada and several forensic pathologists. Moreover, large numbers of Canadian NGOs were present, working in the areas ranging from mine awareness and clearance to shelter provision and rehabilitatory medicine. There was no official contact between the groups and logistical hardships were not resolved nationally. In the United States, Presidential Decision Directive 56, signed in 1999, and titled "Managing Complex Emergencies" demands that this type of lateral planning occur. In Germany, private as well as public agencies are involved in this coordination under the umbrella of an agreement between the German government and its international development arm *Gesellschaft für Technische Zusammenarbeit* (GTZ).[67] Something similar is needed in Canada and elsewhere. As Doug Bland has remarked, "Canada must resist the habit of merely lending troops to others, leaving them to serve some communal interest while assuming it is a common interest."[68] This habit seems to have been extended to other national assets as well.

Progress has taken place on the international front, as UNMIK and KFOR work together and lead agencies, such as UNHCR and the OSCE, have multi-agency relationships and regular coordination sessions. At a national level, it is important to remember that neither the military activity nor the good works of humanitarian agencies and NGOs should be seen to exist in a vacuum. A coordinated approach not only ensures unity of effort and reduces redundancy, it makes sense "in an era of fiscal constraint [where] there is also pressure to synchronize assets for maximum impact."[69]

Any degree of coordination must be reinforced by active measures at the working level. The best way in which this can be achieved is to have, where applicable, joint coordination centers, as well as liaison officers and advisors. Joint coordination centers act, not as a means for any one organization to command or control any other, but rather as information clearinghouses.[70] Issues of mutual concern can be raised and information on such things as the security situation and the effectiveness of programs can be shared between all parties. Backing this up, the employment of liaison officers between military forces and key agencies such as UNHCR or the UN civil administration provides invaluable information and allows all players to focus their efforts in the same direction.

Lastly, the use of political/policy advisors on military staffs is very important from a national perspective. These advisors maintain a link between the military, with its often narrow focus on meeting the immediate requirements of a given situation, and other government agencies, such as DFAIT or CIDA in the Canadian setting. The role of the policy advisor is to ensure unity of effort or "policy coherence" by both advising the commander on the political environment in which the military operates and reporting to the political chain of command the nature and effect of military operations.[71]

Two words of caution are warranted here. First, while the military possesses the competence and capacity to engage in peacebuilding, and should do so in order to both achieve its aim of providing security and aiding in the recovery of conflict-torn societies, it must not be seen as the "silver bullet," the quick fix for all problems. Military forces can help build the peace, but need to do so as a part of a larger peacebuilding team, working together with national governments, international organizations, nongovernmental organizations, and the local populace. As Whitman warns, the international community "cannot let military action replace proper long-term development or specialized civilian peacebuilding."[72] If the situation is grave enough to deserve the attention of the international community and serious enough to prompt the deployment of the military, then it is probably complex enough to need the coordinated and determined effort of several actors and agencies. In this combined effort, the military is essential, but not sufficient.[73]

The second caveat that must be borne in mind is that the primary reason that military forces are deployed is to provide security. This means that their training and force structure will be predicated upon the application of armed force. Their use of "hard power" is what creates the space for other activities to occur. In some cases, humanitarian relief and peacebuilding rely on this "umbrella"; no one can distribute food or construct democratic institutions under a hail of gunfire. The conditions for success must be achieved first. For this task, there is no one else. Military forces alone have the expertise and the hardware to create and maintain order. It so happens that they also have a great deal to offer in the creation of peace as well.

Peacebuilding can and does involve military forces. Furthermore, military involvement in peacebuilding does not have to degrade combat capability, nor taint the peace being built. The Kosovo missions serve to illustrate the opportunities that exist for all actors to cooperate and work together towards the common goal of building a tolerant and secure society. It also demonstrates, beyond what is happening now, what is possible in the future. When organizations come together and overcome their institutional prejudices, powerful results are achievable. As Greenaway notes, "if the moral impetus of humanitarianism were to be harnessed effectively—instead of being dispersed as at present...an increasingly internationalized civil society may have more effective strategies than it suspects."[74] This cannot be seen as a bad thing.

Notes

1 Jim Whitman, "'Those That Have the Power to Hurt but Would Do None': The Military and Humanitarianism," *Journal of Humanitarian Assistance* (3 June 2000), http://www.jha.ac/articles/a012.htm (accessed 15 July 2000)
2 See Kenneth Bush in this volume (chapter 2).
3 See Melissa Labonte in this volume (chapter 3).
4 For the most part, examples will be drawn from the activities of a Canadian infantry battle group based in the First Battalion, Princess Patricia's Canadian Light Infantry. The Battle Group comprised of approximately 600 soldiers and was made up of two mechanized infantry companies, a troop of tanks, a troop of combat engineers, a mortar platoon, an anti-armor platoon, a reconnaissance platoon, an administration company, and a headquarters element. The Battle Group was deployed under command of a British brigade and located in the area surrounding the town of Glogovac, south west of Pristina. A rifle company was deployed with less than 30 days notice, arriving in Kosovo on 8 July 1999. The remainder of the unit arrived by 12 August 1999 and departed 17 December 1999 when another Canadian unit replaced them. The author served as an operations staff officer in the Battle Group headquarters.
5 For a discussion of the decision-making process that lead up to the operations in the Kosovo, see Wesley Clark, *Waging Modern War* (New York: Public Affairs Publishing, 2001).
6 North Atlantic Treaty Organization, (KFOR Objectives)," http://www.nato.int/kfor/kfor/objectives.htm (accessed 28 November 2003).
7 For a discussion of how military and other agencies worked together in one part of Bosnia, see Shane Schreiber, "Creating Compliance: Some Lessons in International Cooperation in a Peace Support Operation," *Canadian Military Journal* 1, no. 1 (2001–2002): 11–22.
8 K. van Brabant, "Understanding, promoting and evaluating coordination: an outline framework," in D.S. Gordon and F.H. Toase, eds., *Aspects of Peacekeeping* (London: Frank Cass, 2001), 141–62.

9 For a list of the kinds of tasks performed by military forces in theater, see Michael Ward et al., "Task Force Kosovo: Adapting Operations to a Changing Security Environment," *Canadian Military Journal* 1, no. 1 (2000): 67–74.

10 See Melissa Labonte in this volume (chapter 3).

11 Hugh Slim," The Stretcher and the Drum: Civil-Military Relations in Peace Support Operations," *International Peacekeeping* 3, no. 2 (1996), 123.

12 Daniel L. Byman, "Uncertain Partners: NGOs and the Military," *Survival* 43, no. 2 (2001), 97.

13 Thomas G. Weiss, *Military-Civilian Interactions: Intervening in Humanitarian Crises* (Oxford: Rowman and Littlefield, 1999), 1.

14 David Chandler, "The People-Centred Approach to Peace Operations: The New UN Agenda," *International Peacekeeping* 8, no. 1 (2001), 1–19.

15 For example see Lloyd Axworthy, "Canada and Human Security: The Need for Leadership," *International Journal* 52, no. 2 (1999), 183–96; Paul Heinbecker, "Human Security: The Hard Edge," *Canadian Military Journal* 1, no. 1 (2000), 11–16; and Tony Blair, "Doctrine of the International Community." Speech by the Prime Minister, Tony Blair, to the Economic Club of Chicago, Hilton Hotel, Chicago, USA, Thursday 22 April 1999, http://www.fco.gov.uk/news/speechtext.asp?2316 (accessed 12 May 2000).

16 Slim, "The Stretcher and the Drum," 137.

17 Michael Pugh, "Civil-Military Relations in the Kosovo Crisis: An Emerging Hegemony? *Security Dialogue* 31, no. 2 (2000): 231–32; See also Jane Barry and Anna Jeffreys, "A bridge too far: aid agencies and the military in humanitarian response," *Humanitarian Practice Network*, Network Paper Number 37 (London: Overseas Development Institute, 2002), esp. 6–9.

18 These have been characterized as "second generation" peacekeeping missions. See Michael C. Williams, "Civil-Military Relations and Peacekeeping," *Adelphi Papers* 321 (August 1998), 1–93.

19 van Brabant, "Understanding, promoting and evaluating coordination," 141.

20 Stuart Gordon, "Understanding the Priorities for Civil-Military Cooperation (CIMIC)," *Journal of Humanitarian Assistance* (2001), http://www.jha.ac/articles/a068.htm (accessed 8 May 2002).

21 Boutros Boutros-Ghali, "An agenda for peace: preventative diplomacy, peacemaking and peace-keeping. Report of the Secretary-General pursuant to the statement adopted by the Summit Meeting of the Security Council on 31 January 1992," A/47/277-S/24111, 17 June 1992.

22 John Howard Eisenhour and Edward Marks, "Herding Cats: Overcoming Obstacles in Civil-Military Operations," *Joint Force Quarterly* (Summer 1999): 86.

23 Pugh, "Civil-Military Relations," 229. See also Francis Abiew and Tom Keating, "NGOs and UN Peacekeeping Operations: Strange Bedfellows," *International Peacekeeping* 6, no. 2 (1999): 90–105.

24 See Kenneth Bush in this volume (chapter 2).

25 See Melissa Labonte in this volume (chapter 3).

26 J.W. Rollins, "Civil-military cooperation (CIMIC) in crisis response operations: the implications for NATO," *International Peacekeeping* 8, no. 1 (2001): 122.

27 Barry and Jeffreys, "A Bridge too Far," 1.

28 Byman, "Uncertain Partners," 106.

29 Rollins, "Civil-Military Cooperation," 128.

30 See, for example, Douglas E. Delaney, "CIMIC Operations During Operation 'Kinetic'," *Canadian Military Journal* (Winter 2000–2001): 29–34; Andrew Rigby, "Humanitarian assistance and conflict management: the view from the NGO sector," International *Affairs* 77, no. 4 (2001): 957–66; Jim Whitman, "Those that have the Power," *Journal of Humanitarian Assistance* (2001), http://www.jha.ac.uk/articles/a012.htm (accessed 8 May, 2002).

31 J. Mackinley, "The role of military forces in a humanitarian crises," in Leon Gordenker and Thomas G. Weiss, eds., *Soldiers, Peacekeepers and Disasters* (London: Macmillan, 1991), 13–32; See also Byman, "Uncertain Partners," 100; and Williams, "Civil Military Relations," 13.

32 K.M. Kennedy, "The relationship between the military and humanitarian organizations in Operation Restore Hope," in W. Clarke and J. Herbst, eds., *Learning from Somalia: The Lessons of Armed Humanitarian Intervention* (Oxford: Westview Press, 1997), 108; See also Byman, "Uncertain Partners," 101; Barry and Jeffreys, "A Bridge too Far," 13–14; Williams, "Civil Military Relations," 15.

33 Eisenhour and Marks, "Herding Cats," 86.

34 Slim, "The Stretcher and the Drum," 124.

35 Williams bases this on Samuel Huntington's idea of "the military mind" first conceived of in the late 1960s. See Williams, "Civil Military Relations," 33–34.

36 F.C. Cuny, "Dilemmas of Military Involvement in Humanitarian Relations," in Gordenker and Weiss, *Soldiers, Peacekeepers and Disasters*, 75.

37 Slim, "The Stretcher and the Drum," 125.

38 Cuny, "Dilemmas," 75.

39 See Abiew and Keating in this volume (chapter 5).

40 Gordenker and Weiss, *Soldiers, Peacekeepers and Disasters*, 10. See also Byman, "Uncertain Partners," 106; Barry and Jeffreys, "A Bridge too Far," 14.

41 Delaney, "CIMIC Operations," 32; Eisenhour and Marks, "Herding Cats," 86.

42 Berry and Jeffreys, "A Bridge too Far," 7.

43 Rigby, "Humanitarian Assistance," 959–60; Byman, "Uncertain Partners," 104.

44 Par Eriksson, "Civil-military coordination in peace support operations—an impossible necessity," *Journal of Humanitarian Assistance* (2000) http://www.jha.ac.uk/articles/a061.htm (accessed 8 May, 2002).

45 Hugo Slim, "Violence and humanitarianism: moral paradox and the protection of civilians," *Security Dialogue* 32, no. 3 (2001): 325–39.

46 Slim, "The Stretcher and The Drum," 125.

47 Barry and Jeffreys, "A Bridge too Far," 7.

48 Slim, "The Stretcher and The Drum," 124.

49 Kennedy, Operation Restore Hope," 104.

50 Michael Clarke and Steve Smith, "Perspectives on the Foreign Policy System: Implementation Approaches," in Michael Clarke and Brian White, eds., *Understanding Foreign Policy: The Foreign Policy Systems Approach* (London: Elgar, 1989), 178.

51 Bradd C. Hayes and Jeffrey I. Sands, "Non-traditional Military Responses to End Wars: Considerations for Policymakers," *Millennium: Journal of International Studies* 26, no. 3 (1997), 820.

52 Weiss, *Military-Civilian Interactions*, 17.

53 Whitman, "Those That Have the Power."

54 See Kenneth Bush in this volume (chapter 2).

55 Hayes and Sands, "Non-traditional Military Responses," 821.

56 Paulo Tripodi, "Peacekeeping: Let the Conscripts do the Job," *Security Dialogue* 32, no. 2 (2001): 155, 160. For a discussion of the difficulties faced by commanders on peacekeeping missions see Canada, *Debrief the Leaders Report: Officers* (Ottawa: Department of National Defence, 2001) and Janet M. Weber, "Demands of OOTW on Ground Forces: Implications for Recruiting and Training," National War College Student Paper 1997, http://www.ndu.edu/ndu/library/n1/97-E-61.pdf (accessed 8 May, 2002).

57 F.T. Liu, "Peacekeeping and humanitarian Assistance," in Gordenker and Weiss, *Soldiers, Peacekeepers and Disasters* (London: Palgrave / MacMillan, 1992), 49.

58 Hayes and Sands, "Non-Traditional Military Responses," 840. Nash, now retired, was appointed as the UN Administrator for Kosovo Mitrovica on March 12, 2000. General Zinni, formerly of the US Marine Corps, echoed this sentiment when he stated, "Even though people will say that supporting [NGOs] of 'mission creep,' the military commander will often become directly involved because there is no one else to do the job" (In Hayes and Sands, "Non-Traditional Military Responses," 839).

59 Hayes and Sands, "Non-Traditional Military Responses," 834.

60 Clarke and Smith, "Perspectives on the Foreign Policy," 168.

61 North Atlantic Treaty Organization, "KFOR Web Page," http://www.kforonline.com (accessed 28 November, 2003).

62 For an introduction to the kinds of mechanisms available to organizations, ranging from partnership to competition, see D. Robinson, T. Hewitt and J. Harriss, eds., *Managing Development: Understanding Inter-organizational Relationships* (London: Sage, 2000).

63 Scott Moore, "Today it's *Gold*, Not *Purple*," *Joint Force Quarterly* (Autumn/Winter 1998–1999): 101.

64 The other point to note in this example is that the military officer in question had no formal training in development or project management. His "primary" responsibility in Kosovo was that of a company commander for over 250 warfighting soldiers, including a troop of tanks and a platoon of anti-tank systems.

65 See Melissa Labonte in this volume (chapter 3).

66 Lord Robertson of Port Ellen, Secretary of State for Defence, "Kosovo: An Account of the Crisis," United Kingdom Ministry of Defence, http://www.kosovo.mod.uk/account/lessons.htm (accessed 28 November, 2003).

67 Byman, "Uncertain Partners," 108.

68 Douglas Bland, "Canada and Military Coalitions: Where, How, and with Whom?" *Policy Matters* 3, no. 3 (2002): 48.

69 Moore, "Today it's Gold," 105.

70 The area of coordination and cooperation is not without its problems. For a detailed discussion of the pros and cons of each of these mechanisms, see Robinson, Hewitt and Harriss, *Managing Development*. Coordination, after all, is easy in theory but difficult once agencies have to be assigned roles—either as coordinator or "coordinatee."

71 For a detailed description of the requirement for political advisors at all levels in peace support operations, see David A. Lange, "The Role of the Political Advisor in Peacekeeping Operations," *Parameters* (Spring 1999): 92–109.

72 Whitman, "Those that have Power."

73 Whitman, "Those that have Power."

74 Sean Greenaway, "Post-Modern Conflict and Humanitarian Action: Questioning the Paradigm," *Journal of Humanitarian Assistance* (2000): 1, http://www.jha.ac.uk/articles/a053.htm, (accessed 8 May, 2002).

5 Defining a Role for Civil Society

Francis Kofi Abiew & Tom Keating

HUMANITARIAN NGOs AND PEACEBUILDING OPERATIONS

THE ACTIVITIES OF NGOs in the areas of economic development, poverty alleviation, and emergency relief have come to play a significant role in multilateral peacebuilding operations. The increased significance of the activities of these NGOs provides them with an important role in all phases of the peacebuilding process—from political advocacy and advisors to governments and IGOs, through to service delivery in the field. The multifaceted nature of peacebuilding,[1] coupled with the sheer number and prominence of NGOs involved in peacebuilding, make it necessary to examine the evolving relationship between NGOs and these multilateral operations.

This current discussion provides a critical reflection on NGO involvement in peacebuilding: it reviews the nature and scope of such involvement and identifies the range of activities that have been pursued by NGOs, as well as the factors that have influenced their participation in peacebuilding operations; it briefly examines the performance of multilateral peacebuilding operations with particular reference to the relationship between NGOs and others involved in these operations, particularly IGOs; and it critically assesses the contribution of NGOs to the peacebuilding process and raises a series of questions about the capacity, effectiveness, legitimacy, and accountability of NGOs involved in peacebuilding operations.

NGOs comprise of a variety of associations involved in a wide spectrum of social, political and economic activities.[2] As Melissa Labonte has noted,[3] while some NGOs seek to maintain a principled position of neutrality, others will not hesitate to identify the perpetrators of violence and abuse. Even within the more limited area of humanitarian relief there is a considerable range of organizations reflecting very different goals, membership, funding sources, size, political, cultural and ethnic affiliation, as well as operational practices. A taxonomy of NGOs might also distinguish these organizations according to their relationship with local, national and international groups, differentiating between local nongovernmental organizations (LNGOs), international nongovernmental organizations (INGOs) and distinguishing state-sponsored nongovernmental organizations from more autonomous ones. This study's reference to NGOs is based primarily on the activities of INGOs providing humanitarian relief in postconflict situations. While we will revert to using the more generic term NGOs, the reader should be aware of these distinctions among various types of NGOs.

The number of NGOs has been growing at a phenomenal rate. Some 400 to 500 INGOs are currently involved in humanitarian activities worldwide. NGOs collectively spend an estimated $9–10 billion annually, reaching some 250 million people living in poverty.[4] The range of NGOs varies from large INGOs whose budgets rival those of governments and multinational corporations to small autonomous local organizations. The size and range of activities of the larger NGOs leave them well placed to be significant institutional players in developing countries and in those experiencing complex emergencies. These NGOs have the potential to circumvent the political, economic, and civil structures of these societies and could alter the balance of domestic forces in situations of political and social conflict.

Among the many NGOs operating in the area of humanitarian relief, eight are responsible for more than 50 percent of relief dollars.

They are: the ICRC, CARE, World Vision International, Oxfam, Médecins Sans Frontières (MSF), Save the Children Federation, Eurostep, CIDSE (Cooperation internationale pour le developpement et la solidarité), and APDOVE (Association of Protestant Development Organizations in Europe). The remainder of relief dollars is distributed among hundreds of others, including many local NGOs. The ICRC has an annual budget of about one billion dollars, about 27 percent of which is devoted to humanitarian relief operations.[5] CARE USA's annual budget is over $364 million, while that of World Vision is over $140 million. The 160 NGOs comprising InterAction, for example, have combined annual revenues of $2.3 billion.[6]

NGOs have on occasion overshadowed major UN agencies in peacebuilding activities. World Vision International, for instance, spent over $180 million in postconflict Mozambique between 1993 and 1994, while the total five-year budget of UNDP for the country was estimated to be about $60 million. On average, INGOs account for about thirteen percent of all development assistance. This amount is larger than that being transferred through the UN system, excluding the Washington-based financial institutions. In 1996, the UNHCR expressed concerns that the increased flow of funds to national NGOs and the proliferation of NGOs in the field to the neglect of international institutions were undermining "systems of cooperation and coordination in large-scale emergencies."

There is a considerable body of evidence to suggest that NGOs are increasingly active as a result of the absence of local authorities, the disinterest and fatigue of donor governments, and the limited capacity of international institutions. INGOs are becoming central agents in the international response to civil conflicts in places like Bosnia, Somalia, Kosovo, and Zaire, and have increasingly been called upon to perform their humanitarian tasks alongside multilateral military contingents operating partly as peace enforcement and partly as peacebuilding units. For some, like Kenneth Bush,[7] this represents "the militarization of the international relief system," as these military contingents signify "the arrival of a major new player in today's humanitarian operations—a large new kid on the block."[8] It can, however, also be read as an expansion in the mandates and activities of humanitarian NGOs.

At the very least, the development of armed humanitarianism is a reflection of the changed character of conflict in global politics and the international community's response to this conflict—the link between peace enforcement and peacebuilding. The increased presence of NGOs in these conflict situations is also a reflection of the relative growth in the resources, fostered by two converging developments. One has been the increased proportion of donor government funding for development assistance that has been channeled through NGOs. Over the past two decades there has been a fivefold increase in the amount of official development assistance (ODA) channeled through NGOs and a marked decline in the amount delivered through recipient governments. NGOs have also increasingly been favored over multilateral IGOs as dispensers of development assistance.[9] A second development has been the increased amount of development assistance funds directed to humanitarian relief operations, many of which are related to peacebuilding operations. In light of these funding developments, there has been a proliferation of NGOs in the area of humanitarian relief and peacebuilding that has sometimes generated a degree of rivalry among NGOs for limited donor support. This rivalry has become even more intense as the proliferation of agencies has coincided with an overall decline in the development assistance budget in most northern states.

INGOs have performed a variety of tasks as part of multilateral peacebuilding operations. In Afghanistan in the early 1990s, where the UNHCR, the governments of Pakistan, and the USA could not handle the 3.5 million Afghan refugees, NGOs filled the void by providing humanitarian assistance.[10] At the height of the Rwandan emergency, an unprecedented number of NGOs responded to the refugee influx with more than 100 groups operating in Goma and North Kivu and another 169 operating inside Rwanda during late 1994. In some instances, NGOs have been on the ground long before outside governments, militaries, or multilateral IGOs become engaged. Amidst the conflicts in such places as Somalia, East Timor, Ethiopia, the former Yugoslavia, Haiti, Cambodia, Afghanistan, and Iraq, NGOs have been in place during the conflict and have often assumed a prominent role in the peacebuilding operations that followed.

Competition among NGOs has encouraged involvement in these high profile conflicts. This was perhaps best demonstrated by the number of organizations that flocked to Eastern Zaire after the Rwanda genocide of 1994.[11] NGOs also respond in the absence of governments and institutions that lack the interest, will, or capacity to get involved. As Baitenmann has noted in examining the Afghan conflict, NGOs can be an effective means through which governments attempt to influence the political direction of a conflict without direct involvement.[12] While this could be read as an explicit policy to offload responsibility from governments onto private agencies, the involvement of NGOs more often bespeaks less a policy option than the lack of policy on the part of governments.

In many instances, NGOs' participation in peacebuilding operations is a natural extension of their engagement in development work. Many humanitarian NGOs have a commitment to long-term projects in support of economic and social development. This includes working in societies affected by conflict. As a result, NGOs are often inside the country or among the first outsiders to enter postconflict environments. Additionally, they are often able to react more quickly and efficiently than the UN or other IGOs. For one, they have shown a greater disregard for sovereignty, a fact that often encumbers international and regional institutions.

In that regard, NGOs have sometimes been able to identify the status of conflicts or provide early warning indicators to governments, the UN, and the international media. To use Eliasson's metaphor, "such activity among NGOs moves the international community from merely extinguishing fires to finding the arsonist before the fire breaks out and to identify the conditions that lead to arson."[13] In acting in this way, NGOs are also able to marshal public support for an international response as they seek to raise funds for their own operations.

In their ongoing development work, NGOs have performed important peacebuilding tasks by engaging in activities relating to economic and social development in a manner intended to contribute to a sustainable peace. They provide services such as building organizational structures for development projects in rural areas and supporting some of the social and economic infrastructure that encourages local individuals and groups to be more active, thus providing a linkage between short-term aid work and medium to longer term political and economic development priorities.[14] Some have challenged the effectiveness of such efforts, but it is this type of work that places NGOs in situations where multilateral peacebuilding operations are, will be, or have recently been active.[15]

It has been suggested that NGOs also possess certain comparative advantages in terms of their capacities. These have included their ability to reach the poorest and to get to remote areas; a capacity to promote local participation and to implement programs in direct collaboration with target beneficiary groups; a capacity to operate on low costs; and a capacity to strengthen local institutions and to facilitate the empowerment of marginal groups. Added to these qualities, NGOs are more flexible and more pragmatic than some governments and IGOs, provide a people to people approach, are less partial, and operate to some extent on rules of neutrality in their delivery of services in conflict situations. As Griffiths, Levine and Weller note,

> The great strengths of NGOs—flexibility, speed of reaction, comparative lack of bureaucracy, operational and implementation capacity, commitment and dedication of the usually young staff—are particular advantages in emergency work. In addition, the political independence of the NGOs, not bound by the rules of the UN Charter, gives them a strong comparative advantage in increasingly complex internal conflicts.[16]

Another factor encouraging NGO involvement in peacebuilding operations is the fact that governments or warring factions are at times more likely to welcome the participation of selected NGOs than other institutional actors. Eliasson makes an important point when he states that "in difficult internal situations, governments are often unwilling to accept intergovernmental involvement, be it by the United Nations, regional organizations, or other states, because of the legitimacy it may seem to bestow on insurgents or opposition groups. NGOs...may instead have unique possibilities to gain access and try to diffuse conflict."[17] It could, however, also be argued that parties to the conflict are able to use NGOs for their own political purposes more effectively than other institutions and foreign governments and thus prefer their involvement because they are easier to manipulate.

Lastly, as the Final Report of the Carnegie Commission on Preventing Deadly Conflict acknowledges, governments and IGOs often lack the mechanisms for acquiring the systematic information that NGOs possess from years of involvement in conflict situations.[18] The UN Secretary-General, Kofi Annan, emphasized encouraging information sharing and exchange between NGOs and other institutional actors in his 1997 report on UN reform.[19] There is considerable evidence, especially from events in the Great Lakes region of Africa during the 1990s, that NGOs were particularly influential in providing information and analysis to the UN and to state actors. De Waal even argues that NGOs were generally a more reliable and credible source of information about developments in Somalia than UN Special Representative Mohamed Sahnoun.[20]

On balance then, NGOs have been seen as very relevant players in complex emergencies. For their part, the NGOs have viewed conflict situations as an opportunity both to respond to a pressing need and to expand their profile and influence in the politics and economics of development and humanitarian relief. Operating in these hostile situations has increased the risks to NGO workers (as well as IGO staff, as the August 2003 bombing in Baghdad so vividly illustrated), in part because of the general level of violence in their surroundings and because of the increased politicization of their work. A fine balance needs to be struck between security and protection and the ongoing reconstruction involved in delivering assistance to the population.

The increased prominence of NGOs in peacebuilding operations has occurred in the wider context of changing security practices in the 1990s, and has been shaped by a number of interrelated developments, *inter alia*, the increased prevalence of civil strife, which has generated many opportunities for postconflict peacebuilding operations, and the growing interest in human security and the increased demand for outside intervention. In the last instance, the international community has confronted the longstanding contradictions between the principle of state sovereignty and its corollary nonintervention amidst demands for humanitarian intervention and pressure to protect civilians. This increased interest in humanitarian interventions has created an historic opportunity to use IGOs such as the UN, NATO and regional organizations to undertake new security initiatives and move into the largely unchartered terrain of peacebuilding.

The change in attitude among UN member governments appeared in the early 1990s as many groups and individuals promoted a more active interventionist role for the UN in conflict management. The euphoria in the aftermath of the Gulf War saw the UN Security Council taking on issues dealing with intra- and interstate wars including nonmilitary sources of instability in the economic, social, humanitarian, and ecological fields. The result was not merely an increase in the number of UN and regional peace operations, but a fundamental change in their character. The UN took on more complex humanitarian tasks ranging from monitoring elections, human rights observation, training of civilian populations in areas of public administration, policing and justice, as well as a variety of socio-economic development activities. In the face of declining levels of bilateral and multilateral aid, the number and complexity of these operations placed significant strains on the already overstretched organization. Many of these newly acquired responsibilities also required skills better suited to civilians than to militaries and encouraged the organization to look for new partners in carrying out these mandates.

Regional organizations faced similar constraints. In this context, NGOs with their capacity to perform peacebuilding tasks became especially useful.[21] They have functioned as implementing agents or subcontractors for the UN and donor governments, carrying out UN mandates, most often informally or by default. As sovereignty-free actors, NGOs are both a window from which governments can observe and monitor developments in the conflict zones and a door through which assistance can be delivered to the victims.

There has also been a stronger linkage between levels of social-economic development and civil conflict. The proliferation of civil conflicts in the impoverished regions of the globe—*e.g.*, Haiti, Somalia, Sudan, Afghanistan—has demonstrated the interconnections between poverty, underdevelopment, and conflict, thus moving development workers to center stage in many conflicts. Even without formal partnerships, peacebuilding has increasingly brought IGOs and intervening governments into direct contact with NGOs active in the arenas of social and economic development and emergency relief. The linkages between economic and social development and civil conflict have also brought humanitarian and development NGOs to the front line of peacebuilding.

Many intervening governments have also shown a limited interest in direct long-term involvement in postconflict peacebuilding. Whereas these states argued for a more assertive multilateralism in the early 1990s, they have subsequently resorted to a more restricted and isolationist view of security and turned away from supporting peacebuilding, particularly in the African region.[23] NGOs have been one way to fill the void. The governments have also withdrawn from direct involvement in many development assistance projects and in the midst of declining budgets have invested in NGOs as the primary service deliverers in this area. This "privatization" of development assistance has, in part, been encouraged by the repeated failures of past IGO efforts in the development field and the more pervasive antistatist ideology, prominent in the West since the days of Reagan and Thatcher.[23] Civil society was viewed as being more effective than governments in delivering assistance to people in need. Thus much of the proliferation of NGO activity has come at the expense of both states and IGOs. The convergence between national governments' interest in downloading responsibility for development to NGOs and the linkages between economic and social development and conflict has enhanced the important prominence of NGOs in peacebuilding operations.

The new role of NGOs in peacebuilding also carries increased responsibilities.[24] While NGOs have their own interests in establishing a presence in a region, they also serve the interests of states and state-based institutions such as the UN. Juan Somavia writes that

> [s]ome would argue that relief development workers have become *de facto* advance-men and women in conflicts where states have no real political intent or practical means to guarantee their safety—let alone, achieve peace. Others allege that the political and humanitarian dimensions of complex emergencies are poorly understood, and that lack of coherent situation assessment, priority-setting, and field operations on the part of the international community not only lengthens the agony of people living in countries in crisis, but also puts at risk those trying to help them.[25]

Reiff has raised the specter of such actions becoming part of the problem rather than the solution:

> The ardour with which governments in the West have embraced the idea of humanitarian aid, even as they have cut almost every other form of development aid, should give one pause.

> For it may be in the attention-grabbing, media-enthralling luster of its real heroism and its apparent success that, paradoxically, contemporary humanitarianism may be providing the great powers with the excuse that they need to turn their backs on a world in which chaos increasingly reigns and in which hundreds of millions of people have become superfluous to the global economy; in effect these people have been excommunicated.[26]

While it would be absurd to suggest that humanitarian NGOs have positioned themselves to be the agents by which the West disentangles itself from the rest of the world, it is perhaps not so absurd to argue that they may unwittingly facilitate such an endgame.

It would seem that the international community has retreated somewhat from the more interventionist practices of the early 1990s. Events in Somalia, Bosnia, and Haiti, among others, have questioned the ability and willingness of the international community to offer an effective and sustained response to civil conflict. Many observers, including members of the NGO community, have criticized the failure of multilateral peacebuilding operations, arguing that "military intervention is no panacea" and that such interventions "too easily become part of the problem" while others view armed peacekeepers as necessary to protect humanitarian relief workers.[27] The problems encountered in these multilateral operations have also raised concerns about the effectiveness and responsibility of the INGOs involved. It is not surprising that both the UN and NGOs have emerged from these conflicts with sizeable scars. The considerable problems experienced by multidimensional peacebuilding operations suggest the need for a reappraisal of the practices of both IGOs and NGOs.

The experiences in which multinational military operations have shared the field with a variety of other interventionists from the NGO community have been the subject of a considerable amount of commentary.[28] Much of it has focused on the differences in personnel, mandates/interests, authority structures and resources, as well as on numerous additional problems of management and service delivery. Indeed, lines of coordination and responsibility in such situations are often blurred and accountability becomes a difficult practice to implement. For example, "[i]n Bosnia, nine agencies and departments of the U.S. Government cooperated with more than a dozen other governments, seven international organizations, and thirteen major NGOs—from the Red Cross to the International Crisis Group to the American Bar Association—to implement the Dayton Peace Accords."[29]

Given the persistence of civil conflicts and the increased demands for peacebuilding, it is readily apparent that intervening military forces will scarcely be able to avoid interacting with NGOs, as both Labonte and Ankersen have pointed out.[30] This has generated increased concerns about the degree of coordination among the different actors involved in peacebuilding. As the Chilean Ambassador to the UN stated:

> [A] stronger link must evolve between the United Nations, the Security Council and organizations like Oxfam—who are on the ground, doing humanitarian work, who are touching those societies, looking into the eyes of the people in danger, learning who they are and what is going on and who the factions are and what relations people have with their leaders—much of which never gets to the table of the Security Council.[31]

The UN's interest in expanding contacts with NGOs also extends to other areas and can be viewed both as a recognition of the growing influence of such groups and the pressing need for greater democratization in its practices. Yet as Somavia has noted,

> The mix of actors involved in these conflicts creates a situation where responsibility for delivering security is at best blurred, but too often delegated to others—by states to IGOs, by IGOs to NGOs, by NGOs to their volunteers, and by the volunteers to the victims à la self-help. The challenge is to develop a series

of interlocking legal and logistical safeguards—shored up by the political will of countries to enforce them, and operationalized through a coherent UN system that functions in tandem with regional, national, and local institutions.[32]

It is evident that NGOs have not been immune to these concerns. Since the mid-1970s, efforts have been made to coordinate the activities of NGOs working in the area of humanitarian relief. One example of such efforts is the SPHERE project that was initiated in 1997 by a coalition of frontline humanitarian agencies including the International Federation of Red Cross and Red Crescent Societies, Caritas Internationalis, the World Council of Churches, Oxfam, Save the Children, MSF, and CARE International. It was designed to coordinate activities in the disaster relief field and to develop a code of conduct for relief agencies in an effort to make them more accountable. Such efforts on the part of NGOs to examine their activities more critically are promising, but they do not overcome the problems generated by competition for declining public and private funds and those that emerge from the complex political environments in which these groups operate.[33]

Some have noted the tendency for NGOs to interfere with local activities as the experience in Kosovo illustrates:

> All the evaluations comment on the large amounts of bilateral aid "thrown" at relief, not—this time—at development. Some see this as having created problems for a population that was already fully employed in reconstruction when the international community intervened. For a decade, Albanians in Kosovo had been forced to create their own parallel civil society, from kindergartens to health clinics, architecture schools and a vibrant independent media. Thus, interventions can be seen as peremptory, non-consultative and over-dependent on "in-and-out" commercial contractors; in a word, these interventions were debilitatingly dispossessing, rather than constructively supportive.[34]

There have also been concerns about the ability of outside NGOs to engage effectively the participation of local NGOs:

> Where there is some evaluation of human resource management, little positive is said; one Kosovar employed by an international NGO reported to me that the organization behaved "just like the communist party, powerful, rich with resources, coming in from afar, and knowing only how to look after their own—in this case foreign—staff." Unprofessional personnel management appears to have been the norm, as in other emergencies, with a familiar pattern of short-term assignments, lack of appropriate training, lack of briefing on arrival and departure—and, as ever, gender issues were reportedly "forgotten again."[35]

NGO operations sometimes cause unintended consequences.[36] Anderson, for instance, asserts that although NGOs "do not generate conflicts, they sometimes contribute to and reinforce violent conflicts preexisting in societies where they work."[37] Commentators have maintained that the negative consequences of relief assistance might include freeing up local relief resources for continuation of war; diversion of aid to warring factions, and thus supporting and financing their activities; escalating violence by attracting raiding; creation of false economies or foreign exchange sources that are fought over in areas such as employment, rents, contracts, transport, and currency exchange; facilitating the isolation or displacement of particular populations; and conferring unrepresentative legitimacy on warlords and leaders of particular factions prosecuting the war.[38]

The provision of relief to Rwandan refugees in Goma drives home the point. In providing assistance to the camps controlled mainly by the Hutu militia, NGOs may have inadvertently impeded peacebuilding by aiding the military objectives of the militia. The intense competition for political power also made it increasingly difficult for these NGOs to retain neutrality as they sought to provide relief to civilian populations. Not only have they been at risk as a result of ongoing fighting, but they have also been more directly implicated as abettors to one side or the other parties to the conflict. Anderson cites the example of a road constructed into a remote area in Ethiopia for purpose of delivering humanitarian assistance that subsequently allowed military vehicles to reach these parts in order to recruit young men into the government army.[39]

As Prendergast writes, "UN military intervention and many NGOs helped refuel and underwrite an extortionist, militarized political economy in many Somali towns. Much of the benefit was captured by General Aidid and his allied militia in Mogadishu South. The intervention greatly exacerbated the conflict, as competing militia positioned themselves for the potential spoils of a resurrected aid-dependent state."[40] Humanitarian assistance has also had an effect on the course of the war in the Sudan. Again, Prendergast maintains, "aid has become directly integrated into the dynamics of conflict through the negotiated access agreements of Operation Lifeline Sudan and the Sudan Emergency Operations Consortium."[41] These examples demonstrate the pressing need for NGOs, the military, and the various interstate agencies to develop a more refined strategy for dealing with emergencies. The effective management of relief resources must be contingent upon an analysis of existing structures and the capacity of the various actors in managing relief in a way that ensures resources are distributed on the basis of need while military actors and activities receive no support.[42]

The local context must be taken into account in decision-making with regard to where, when, and how to engage in peacebuilding operations. Drawing from the experience in emergency relief, Prendergast contends that "any form of aid that ignores local context is potentially destabilizing; that which takes it fully into account can help resolve local conflicts and ease local resource pressures and competition."[43] At a symposium organized by the United States Institute of Peace (USIP) at the request of several concerned NGOs, participants identified eight steps that can be taken to minimize the negative impact of humanitarian aid. These are: improving planning; assessing need more accurately; analyzing the consequences of agreements negotiated to gain access to needy populations and obtaining security for NGO personnel; providing assistance that will have the longest term benefit to particular targeted groups; contracting for independent monitoring and evaluation of aid programs to reduce mismanagement and the diversion of supplies; making the empowerment of local institutions a high priority; coordinating closely with other assistance organizations operating in particular crisis situations; and deploying human rights monitors to help protect local populations from exploitation and repression by the warring factions.[44]

Another issue affecting NGO participation in peacebuilding operations is the claim that NGOs are nonpolitical actors and have the particular advantage of being able to rise above the narrow national interests of states and UN agencies in fulfilling their mandate.[45] Political neutrality is best exemplified and practiced by the ICRC, which endeavors to preserve the humanitarian space needed for dialogue and political settlement in conflict settings. However, the very concept and appropriateness of NGO neutrality has been the subject of intense debate in recent times.[46] Some writers point to the problematic nature of the term "neutrality" in that it inaccurately reflects the activities of many NGOs and instead adopt the term "independence" or "detachment."[47]

The concept is under threat given "the militarisation, the overt politicisation of humanitarian crises and an ever greater reliance on donors to underwrite the costs of humanitarian operations."[48] Some NGOs like the ICRC have argued that implementation of the concept is becoming difficult.[49] For instance, in Rwanda NGOs operated side by side with UNAMIR and became dependent on its support assets, thus compromising their neutrality.[50] Yet the principle remains an important one in clarifying the role of NGOs in the peacebuilding process, for as James Orbinski, past president of MSF, has said:

> It must adhere to basic humanitarian principles of independence, universality, impartiality and neutrality, and in neutrality that is neither silent nor morally neutered. Just as no humanitarian can make war, no humanitarian can make peace. Again, these are political, not humanitarian imperatives. Humanitarian principles and action cannot be subordinated to political or military goals, however legitimate these goals may be. For if they are, this is potentially, and more actually is, to the detriment of both. It is however conditional on political responsibility to ensure that humanitarian space can exist in situations of conflict. The rights that exist under international humanitarian law are not the same rights that exist under human rights conventions, and the responsibilities of the humanitarian organization are not the same responsibilities of the human rights organization. Humanitarian action in war is not development, it is not peacebuilding, it is not enforcement by military means, and nor can it be a substitute for politics by other means.[51]

Examples of difficulty with aid delivery serve to highlight the problem of neutrality. Aid is usually viewed by warring factions as secondary to military and strategic aims and allowed only when it is deemed beneficial to political objectives. In those circumstances, the work of NGO is severely impeded by political interests. Operation Lifeline Sudan, for instance, has suffered prolonged periods of inertia due to a lack of consent by the local government. Similarly, in Mozambique, subsequent to the signing of an accord for the provision of aid to FRELIMO (government) and RENAMO (rebels) controlled areas, the UN committee created to oversee that program was unable to secure the agreement of both sides. Beer[52] notes that the same problem was experienced in Somalia, Bosnia, Ethiopia and Angola, and Haiti.[53]

Given the prevailing state of affairs, commentators have called for NGOs to address more directly the political dimensions of conflicts.[54] Deng notes the importance of recognizing that the work done by NGOs must be linked to the challenge of peace because the ultimate humanitarian objective is that of ending wars. Even though some of the wars may seem senseless, others are waged for a "just cause." Should NGOs therefore merely claim neutrality in situations where a war is fought challenging the oppression of a minority group?[55] For Prendergast, NGO actions often influence the military and political character of conflicts even though this is rarely intended.[56] According to DeMars, in failed states (*e.g.* Somalia and Liberia) where the various factions lack the internal coherence of a state, neutrality can hardly be adapted to fit. A "generic problem for aid operations" in those situations is that "the boundary between the political and humanitarian erodes."[57]

In sum, it seems that whatever the claims of NGOs to neutrality and impartiality, engaging in peacebuilding operations is hardly a nonpolitical activity. In coming to grips with the issues discussed here, Slim makes an important point by stating:

> ...[An] NGO's effectiveness in responding to the suffering of civil wars is heavily dependent on the quality of its people. To operate effectively within the international, regional and local politics of today's civil wars, NGO workers must embody a combination of political sophistication, humanitarian principle and operational imagination. Unless they have adopted a position of solidarity, they must be nonpolitical, but must have a detailed political analysis which informs their work. They must have an understanding of conflict and the role of third parties within it.[58]

As noted earlier, many NGOs have gone well beyond providing relief and are increasingly being asked to perform more politicized roles such as monitoring human rights violations, assisting with conflict resolution, and peacebuilding. Some have even taken over state-type functions in areas like health, education, water and sanitation systems, and agricultural extension services.[59] In many ways, NGO activity can thus be seen as filling a vacuum left by the state. NGO representatives have often made references to their operations "as comprising a continuum of relief efforts, rehabilitation, reconstruction, and sustainable development."[60] Then the question becomes one of whether such expanded roles are appropriate for NGOs.

In light of these developments, there have been calls for a reassessment of the role of NGOs. Should NGOs concentrate on relief work, or engage in both relief and development? Should they respond to complex emergencies wherever they occur, or limit their involvement geographically or sectorally? Are other actors better suited to performing some of these roles? As Natsios suggests, "it may be possible to perform some of these functions well, but it is nearly impossible to coordinate efforts in all...of these very different [spheres] so that they are performed well and do not conflict with one another."[61] Limiting their operations to areas where NGOs have ongoing programs might yield better results. In cases where they have less knowledge of the area, NGOs would need to develop a strong sectoral expertise to make up for lack of experience working in a particular country.[62]

The involvement of NGOs in these different roles has generated greater demands for accountability, transparency, and effectiveness. NGOs must account to the victims, the host governments, and the donors who fund their programs. However, as Harriss points out, those with the "greatest reason to demand accountability—the victims—are those least likely to receive it." Furthermore, failure to consult with victims leads to their marginalization, and results in less efficient programs. Until NGOs "find more systematic ways of genuinely answering to those whom they claim to serve, the problem will remain of accountability to those with power but not to those without."[63] For Slim, NGOs must be held accountable in terms of international humanitarian law, human rights law, and quality of service to those they seek to help and their donors. Their programming standards must be judged on their social and economic impact as well as their technical competence. Ultimately, this process of regulation has to be transparent and public.[64]

The increased prominence of NGOs in peacebuilding operations has coincided with a gradual withdrawal on the part of states and IGOs from long-term sustainable peace projects, and a greater delegation of peacebuilding functions to NGOs. This development has led to increased expectations regarding the capacity, efficiency, effectiveness, and legitimacy of NGOs in addressing the complex set of issues faced by civil societies in postconflict situations. The results to date, however, have been mixed, and while the performance of NGOs has on balance been no worse than that of other players, the results threaten to undermine their long-term credibility in these and other areas.

If the international community continues to lose interest in complex peacebuilding operations, NGOs will likely attempt to fill in the gaps by performing these important tasks. In this context, "the challenges facing international NGOs today," as Anderson suggests, "are to recognize where things go wrong in order that they 'do no harm' and to explore, develop, and implement programs that support local people who seek alternatives to conflict."[65]

NGOs may perhaps be better positioned to work hand in hand with local forces than other institutional actors. It is, however, imperative to recognize that donor governments, the UN, and even NGOs have perhaps reached their political limits in terms of their willingness and their ability to invest in the people, resources and programs needed to address and resolve many of today's conflicts. Increasingly, the burden will shift to the local level and the development of indigenous initiatives and capacities that address the root causes of conflict and support conflict resolution processes. Ultimately, outside NGOs can play only a supporting role in the building of sustainable peace.

Acknowledgment

Research for this paper was supported by a grant from the Social Sciences and Humanities Research Council of Canada, Grant No. 410 971628.

Notes

1 See Keating & Knight in this volume (Introduction).

2 This paper will not address the important matter of defining nongovernmental organizations or civil society organizations. It accepts the diversity of such groups and leans towards Scholte's description of CSOs. As Scholte notes, the membership of civil society organizations is incredibly diverse. He states that CSOs include: "Academic institutes, business associations, community-based organizations, consumer protection bodies, criminal syndicates, development cooperation groups, environmental campaigns, ethnic lobbies, foundations, farmers' groups, human rights advocates, labor unions, relief organizations, peace activists, professional bodies, religious institutions, women's networks, youth campaigns and more" (6).

Scholte also divides their membership into three categories: conformists (those who seek and uphold existing norms), reformists (those who aim to correct the regime's flaws) and radicals (those whose purpose it is to transform the social order). Business or professional associations, think tanks and foundations belong to the conformist category. Social-democratic groups and associations of academics, consumers, human rights, relief or trade unions compose the reformist category. Finally, the radical category consists of anarchists, environmentalists, fascists, feminists, and religious revivalists—those with "respective implacable oppositions to the state, industrialism, liberal values, patriarchy, militarism and secularism" (Jan Aart Scholte, "Global Civil Society: Changing the World?" Centre for the Study of Globalisation and Regionalisation (CSGR), University of Warwick, Working Paper 31, May 1999, 2, http://www.warwick.ac.uk/fac/soc/CSGR/wpapers/wp3199. PDF [accessed 28 November 2003]).

3 See Melissa Labonte in this volume (chapter 3).

4 See Yves Beigbeder, *The Role and Status of International Humanitarian Volunteers and Organizations: The Right and Duty to Humanitarian Assistance* (Dordrecht: Martinus Nijhoff Publishers, 1991), 80–82; J. Bennet and Mark R. Duffield, eds., *Meeting Needs: NGO Coordination in Practice* (London: Earthscan Publications, 1995), xi.

5 Cyrus Vance and Herbert Okun, "Creating Healthy Alliances: Leadership and Coordination among NGOs, Governments, and the United Nations in Times of Emergency and Conflict," in Kevin M. Cahill, ed., *Preventive Diplomacy—Stopping Wars Before They Start* (New York: Basic Books, 1996), 194.

6 Pamela Aall, "Nongovernmental Organizations and Peacemaking," in Chester Crocker, Fen Osler Hampson and Pamela Aall, eds. *Managing Global Chaos: Sources of and Responses to International Conflicts* (Washington, D.C.: United States Institute of Peace, 1996), 435.

7 See Kenneth Bush in this volume (chapter 2).

8 Hugo Slim, "The Continuing Metamorphosis of the Humanitarian Practitioner: Some New Colours for an Endangered Chameleon," *Disasters* 19, no. 2 (June 1995): 110–126.

9 See Mike Powell and David Seddon, "NGOs and the Development Industry," *Review of African Political Economy* 71 (1997), 3–10.

10 For a discussion of the details of NGOs role in Afghanistan see for example, Helga Baitenmann, "NGOs and the Afghan War: The Politicisation of Humanitarian Aid," *Third World Quarterly* 12, no. 1 (1990), 62. For the Rwandan emergency see for example, R. von Bernuth, "The Voluntary Agency Response and the Challenge of Coordination," in "The Rwandan Emergency: Causes, Responses, Solutions," special issue *Journal of Refugee Studies* 9, no. 3 (1996), 283. For Somalia, where about 40 NGOs were working when "Operation Restore Hope" was deployed, see Andrew S. Natsios, "NGOs and the UN System in Complex Emergencies: Conflict or Cooperation?" *Third World Quarterly* 16, no. 3 (1995), 406. Elizabeth G. Ferris notes the tremendous resources that NGOs bring to the field of refugee relief and estimates that hundreds, perhaps thousands, of NGOs are involved in one way or another with refugee work—see Elizabeth G. Ferris, *Beyond Borders: Refugees, Migrants and Human Rights in the Post-Cold War Era* (Geneva: WCC Publications, 1993), 41.

11 Alex deWaal, *Famine Crimes* (New York: St. Martin's Press, 1998), especially 191–203.

12 Helga Baitemann, "NGOs and the Afghan war," 62–85.

13 Quoted in Crocker, Hampson and Aall, *Managing Global Chaos*, 437.

14 See Peter Sollis, "Partners in Development? The State, NGOs, and the UN in Central America," in Thomas G Weiss and Leon Gordenker, eds., *NGOs, the UN, and Global Governance* (Boulder, CO: Lynne Reinner, 1996), 189–206. Sollis describes the role of NGOs in Central America, where they are expected to make a contribution in terms of protecting the environment, reducing poverty, and strengthening the democratization process.

15 Among the skeptics see, for example, Michael Maren, *The Road to Hell* (New York: Free Press, 1997) and Paul Stubbs, "Croatia: NGO development, globalism and conflict, in J. Bennett, ed., *NGOs and Governments: A Review of Current Practice for Southern and Eastern NGOs*, (Oxford; INTRAC, 1997), 77–87.

16 They, however, point out that not all NGO relief operations are professionally competent, and that accounts of operations from Cambodia, Sudan, Ethiopia, and Mozambique reveal that NGOs run programs that are as incompetent as the worst UN programs. See Martin Griffiths, Iain Levine and Mark Weller, "Sovereignty and Suffering" in John Harriss, ed., *The Politics of Humanitarian Intervention* (London: Pinter Publishers, 1995), 72.

17 Jan Eliasson, "Establishing Trust in the Healer," in Cahill, ed., *Preventative Diplomacy*, 332.

18 See Carnegie Commission on Preventing Deadly Conflict, *Preventing Deadly Conflict, Final Report* (Washington, D.C.: Carnegie Commission on Preventing Deadly Conflict, 1997), 45–47.

19 Kofi Annan, *Renewing the United Nations: A Programme for Reform, Report of the Secretary-General* (New York: United Nations, 1997), §207–16.

20 See deWaal, *Famine Crimes*, 179–221.

21 The Lessons Learned Unit of the Department of Peacebuilding Operations has recently undertaken studies of four such multidisciplinary peacebuilding operations and released a report that deals with issues ranging from mandate and means, planning, coordination, intelligence and information analysis, military, security, training of local police and human rights monitoring, logistics, finance and budget, personnel and training, medical and health, de-mining, humanitarian relief in a peacebuilding environment, public information, and relations with local population, to demobilization. See "Multidisciplinary Peacebuilding: Lessons from Recent Experience," Peacekeeping Best Practices, UN Peacekeeping Handbook, http://www.un.org/Depts/dpko/lessons/PBPUHandbook.htm (accessed 28 November, 2003).

22 See Kassu Gebremariam in this volume (chapter 9).

23 See for example the discussion in Antonio Donini, "Surfing on the Crest of the Wave until it Crashes: Intervention and the South," *Journal of Humanitarian Assistance* 3 (October, 1995), http://www.jha.ac/articles/a006.htm (accessed on 28 November, 2003).

24 See for example the discussions concerning emergency relief in Sudan: John Ryle, "Sudan: The Perils of Aid," *New York Review of Books*, 11 June, 1998, 63; John Ryle, "How famine sharpens the hunger for power," *Manchester Guardian Weekly*, 10 May, 1998; and Michael Ignatieff, "Unarmed Warriors," *The New Yorker*, 24 Mar. 1997.

25 Ambassador Juan Somavia, Permanent Representative of Chile to the UN, "The Humanitarian Responsibilities of the United Nations Security Council," 1996 Gilbert Murray Memorial Lecture, Oxford, England, 26 June, 1996.

26 David Rieff, "The Humanitarian Trap," *World Policy Journal* (1995/96): 10–11.

27 Save the Children, *The United Nations and Humanitarian Assistance: A Position Paper*, cited in Hugo Slim, "Military Humanitarianism and the New Peacebuilding: An Agenda for Peace?" *Journal of Humanitarian Assistance* (22 September 1995), http://www.jha.ac/articles/a003.htm.

28 For a sample see contributions in Weiss and Gordenker, eds., *NGOs, the UN, and Global Governance*; and on a more critical note, see Maren, *The Road to Hell*, especially chapters 13–16.

29 Strobe Talbot, "Globalization and Diplomacy: A Practitioner's Perspective," *Foreign Policy* 108 (Fall 1997), 79.

30 See in this volume: Melissa Labonte (chapter 3) and Christopher P. Ankersen (chapter 4).

31 Somavia, "Humanitarian Responsibilities."

32 Somavia, "Humanitarian Responsibilities."

33 See, for example, "International Federation of Red Cross and Red Crescent Societies," http://www.ifrc.org/; http://www.ifrc.org/pubs/sphere/Index.htm (accessed 28 November, 2003).

34 Raymond Apthorpe, "Was international emergency relief aid in Kosovo 'humanitarian'?" Humanitarian Practice Network, Overseas Development Institute, London, http://www.odihpn.org/report.asp?ID=2417 (accessed 28 November 2003).

35 Apthorpe, "Was international...".

36 See for example, Joanna Macrae and Anthony Zwi, eds., *Engaging with Violence: A Reassessment of Relief in Wartime in War and Hunger* (London: Zed Books, 1996).

37 Quoted in David R Smock, "Humanitarian Assistance and Conflict in Africa," *Journal of Humanitarian Assistance* (July 1997), http://www.jha.ac/articles/a014.htm (accessed 28 November, 2003).

38 See Hugo Slim, "International Humanitarianism's Engagement with Civil War in the 1990s: A Glance at Evolving Practice and Theory," *Journal of Humanitarian Assistance* (19 December 1997): 10, http://www.jha.ac/articles/a033.htm (accessed 28 November, 2003); Peter Shiras, "Humanitarian Emergencies and the Roles of NGOs," in Jim Whitman and David Pocock, eds., *After Rwanda: The Coordination of United Nations Humanitarian Assistance* (London: Macmillan Press, 1996), 114; John Prendergast, *Crisis Response: Humanitarian Band-Aids in Sudan and Somalia* (London: Pluto Press, 1997), 140.

39 Similarly, an NGO health training program for Cambodian refugees along the Thai border camps had the effect of conscripting some of the trainees as medical personnel that were returned to Cambodia to care for wounded soldiers on the frontlines. Again, in Tajikistan, NGO assistance focused on rebuilding homes destroyed during the war drew the ire of the "victors" of the conflict, as they saw assistance being channeled to the faction that was defeated in the conflict. See Mary Anderson, "Humanitarian NGOs in Conflict Intervention" in Crocker, Hampson and Aall, *Managing Global Chaos*, 347–48.

40 Prendergast, *Crisis Response*, 140.

41 Prendergast, *Crisis Response*, 140.

42 Joanna Macrae, "Purity or Political Engagement?: Issues in Food and Health Security Interventions in Complex Political Emergencies," *Journal of Humanitarian Assistance* (7 March 1998): 10, http://www.jha.ac/articles/a037.htm (accessed 28 November, 2003). Hugo Slim maintains that since more academic attention is being paid to the negative effects of NGOs involvement in humanitarianism, it is incumbent on NGOs in the years ahead to articulate and assess the positive effects of their operations. He stresses the fact that such an assessment of the positive effects "must move beyond traditional quantitative indications of output (food and blankets given, etc.) to a more subtle analysis of impact and outcome which can stand up to the increasingly rigorous analysis of the dark side of relief in war" ("International Humanitarianism's Engagement").

43 Prendergast, *Crisis Response*, 121. For further discussion on the ten commandments of providing aid without sustaining conflict, see John Prendergast, *Frontline Diplomacy: Humanitarian Aid and Conflict in Africa* (Boulder, CO: Lynne Reinner, 1996), chapter 4.

44 See Smock, "Humanitarian Assistance."

45 In light of the limited impact of NGO operations during the Cold War, NGOs developed the necessary skills and experience in seeking and maintaining the consent of local warring factions. Therefore they were less constrained by the political and strategic conflicts that characterized state actors, or even UN relief programs.

46 Griffiths, Levine and Weller define "impartiality" as the provision of relief solely on the basis of need, and, "neutrality" as the refusal to take sides in a conflict "Sovereignty and Suffering, 78).

47 See Prendergast, *Crisis Response*, 40; Minear and Weiss use the term "nonpartisanship" and define the nonpartisanship principle thus: "[h]umanitarian action responds to human suffering because people are in need, not to advance political,

sectarian, or other extraneous agendas. It should not take sides in conflicts" (Larry Minear and Thomas G. Weiss, *Humanitarian Action in Times of War* [Boulder, CO: Lynne Reinner, 1993], 23).

48 Griffiths, Levine and Weller, "Sovereignty and Suffering," 76.

49 Joanna Macrae notes in this context: "neutrality tends to be identified primarily at the macrolevel, rather than at the meso- and micro-level. In other words, achieving neutrality is associated with not using bilateral—government to government—instruments, but ignores how other institutions—NGOs and UN agencies interact with national and local government authorities, and how decisions regarding distribution strategies function at the community level. Responsibility for neutrality is thus effectively delegated downwards through the system, but not regularly monitored" (Macrae, "Purity or Political engagement," 10).

50 Dallaire writes: "One example occurred during the time when RGF broadcasts were generally attacking both the UNAMIR operation as a whole and some of its senior officials. These broadcasts not only alienated UN personnel from the large Hutu population, thereby hindering the mediation process, but also put numerous NGOs in a difficult situation" (Romeo Dallaire, "The Changing Role of UN Peacebuilding Forces: The Relationship between UN Peacekeepers and NGOs in Rwanda," in Whitman and Pocock, *After Rwanda*, 215.

51 James Orbinski,University of Alberta Visiting Lectureship in Human Rights, University of Alberta, Edmonton, 6 March 2001.

52 See David Beer in this volume (chapter 6).

53 See Griffiths, Levine and Weller, "Sovereignty and Suffering," 77–78.

54 Cited in Smock, "Humanitarian Assistance."

55 Deng, cited in Smock, "Humanitarian Assistance."

56 Cited in Smock, "Humanitarian Assistance."

57 Quoted in Smock, "Humanitarian Assistance."

58 Slim, "International Humanitarianism's Engagement."

59 Donini maintains, "in operational terms, this has led to the emergence of a competitive culture in the international NGO community. In structural and ideological terms, this means that 'development' has ceased to function as a 'mobilizing myth' for the South" (Antonio Donini, "Asserting Humanitarianism in Peace-Maintenance," *Global Governance* 4, no. 1 [1998], 85); See also Andrew Natsios, "An NGO Perspective," in William Zartman and Lewis Rasmussen, eds., *Peacemaking in International Conflict: Methods and Techniques* (Washington D.C.: United States Institute of Peace, 1997), 337; Mark Duffield, "NGO Relief in War Zones: Toward and Analysis of the New Aid Paradigm," in Thomas G. Weiss, ed., *Beyond UN Subcontracting* (London: Macmillan Press, 1998), 139–59.

60 See Aall, "Nongovernmental Organizations," 442–43.

61 Natsios, "An NGO Perspective," 351.

62 For a detailed discussion of these issues, see for example, Shiras, "Humanitarian Emergencies," 106–17.

63 Griffiths , Levine and Weller, "Sovereignty and Suffering," 79.

64 Slim, "International Humanitarianism's Engagement."

65 Anderson, "Humanitarian NGOs in Conflict Intervention," 353.

6 Peacebuilding on the Ground

Reforming the Judicial Sector in Haiti

David Beer

THE POST–COLD WAR ERA has proven to be the world's most violent period since World War II. A central reality of the shift from the bipolar politics was the emergence of intrastate conflict as a threat to international peace and security. Conservative estimates indicate that there were 93 armed conflicts around the world, and that of the 5.5 million people killed (fully 25 percent of all deaths in armed conflict since 1945), 75 percent were civilians.[1] During the same period, the UN launched more peacekeeping missions than it had in the previous 45 years.[2] "Collective intervention" emerged as a viable option for the international community that was now more willing to get involved in intrastate matters.

This change in international behavior also stems from the recognition of the importance of human rights and justice as a foundation for stability, peace and security. In responding to the new challenges posed by intrastate conflict, options beyond the traditional notion of peacekeeping were needed. Boutros Boutros-Ghali introduced "peace building" to the range of strategies of international conflict resolution in his report of 17 June 1992, *An Agenda for Peace* (revised 1995).[3]

Peacebuilding became recognized as a lengthy process of complex transformation of society, culture, politics, and economics.[4] Given its complexity, peacebuilding involves the need for partnerships with recipient states to address the multitude of tasks of rebuilding and sustaining development in conflict torn states.

Haiti represents an interesting case in examining the concept of peacebuilding and the partnerships that emerged in justice development efforts. It is a country with immature institutions that has struggled politically, economically and socially for the 200 years since its independence.[5] The brutality of the military coup that followed Haiti's first truly democratic exercise in December 1991, and the subsequent flight of refugees, garnered international attention. Unlike other situations where peacebuilding efforts have been coordinated with peacekeeping actions, Haiti, in the period following the peacekeeping intervention, offered an environment generally free of civil violence. Still, significant human suffering and human rights violations were evident.[6] To this extent the international intervention in Haiti is an example of shifting norms regarding the sanctity of sovereignty, and the willingness to act against sovereignty in matters of human security and fundamental freedoms.

Haiti's case study is also timely. International development initiatives ended after five years of activity, and one would expect evidence of progress. Multi- and bilateral programs are under scrutiny, and their assessment will certainly impact on decisions regarding future commitment. On 29 February 2004 the legitimately elected President of Haiti was again ousted indicating the failure of peacebuilding in that country.

The rationale for justice development in Haiti as a primary peacebuilding initiative stems from the history of dictatorial rule, the human rights record of the *de facto* military government that ousted Jean-Bertrand Aristide in 1991, and the obvious weakness of all institutions of justice.[7] Independence of the judiciary and procedures for judicial appointment and legal representation were ignored. Detentions were prolonged for indeterminate periods, as

80 percent of the prison population awaited trials. Moreover, trial decisions and detention rulings were often made at the whim of the untrained, corrupt, or politically influenced judiciary. Inasmuch as the penal system has a direct impact on the underprivileged (60 percent of inmates were incarcerated for incidents of theft or assault), these factors contributed to the common belief that the justice system was systemically corrupt.

Beyond arbitrary arrest and illegal detention, health and sanitary conditions in the country's prison system were atrocious. There was no adequate medical treatment of prisoners, children were housed with adults, and women with men, no inmate registration existed, and physical abuse of inmates by guards was common. When available, food was inadequate and often families delivered food for imprisoned family members to ensure they were fed at all.[8]

Policing development represented even bigger challenges. Created in an environment of urgency, a new civilian police force was to fill the security void created when the military was disbanded in 1994 in accordance with the Governor's Island Accord.[9] With no history of policing in a democratic model, this organization was to be created where nothing had existed before.

As peacebuilding continues to evolve as an international response to conflict prevention, understanding the "partnership" arrangements in Haiti arguably is important to future decisions regarding how, how much, and how long to contribute aid. A better understanding of collective efforts will add to our knowledge of strategies leading to success in peacebuilding operations.

While the basic concept of peacebuilding may be easily understood in terms of its broad goals of conflict prevention through development and social transformation, a deeper examination reveals other realities. The influence of external developers and facilitators, and the extent to which they may impose values, beliefs, and standards of behavior, raises questions concerning impingement on sovereignty, the need to respond to humanitarian crises, and the self-interest of intrusive actors.

If international interventions are tainted by self-interest, it stands to reason that there will be further complications when a mix of actors (international, state, and civil society) is involved, all driven by different motivations.[10] The objectives of these actors, their methods of doing business, and the financial and human resource commitments they are able to lend to the intervention can vary greatly. So too can the duration of their missions.[11] Where multiple actors are involved, the unique requirements of the given situation, based on the social and cultural history of the recipient country, may be overshadowed. In fact, as Kumar suggests, the concept of international neutrality at any level is seen as highly misleading, and the very presence of foreign actors (in particular foreign actors with resources) is apt to upset internal power relationships and influence decisions.[12]

Hidden in the concept of peacebuilding is the importance of flexibility, coordination, and cooperation among participating actors.[13] Consensus among donors and ratification by the recipient of the course of action outlined in any plan is an important first step in any peacebuilding operation. Failure to do that can lead to a wide range of undesirable consequences, such as unintended strengthening of corrupt systems, or an unhealthy and counterproductive dependence on donors.

The "environment" within which peacebuilding is undertaken figures prominently in the potential for its success. This environment encompasses local realities (including the economy, culture, and politics), and the extent to which change is required to facilitate sustainable peace. It also includes the notion of "political will," or the extent to which transformation is desired, supported and nurtured by powerful elites and decision-makers in the recipient country.

Sustainability has been defined as a program's ability to produce outputs and benefits that are valued enough to command continued resources and attention to ensure continued outputs.[14] This definition ties sustainability to the "success" measurement. However, success measurement is another fundamental problem in peacebuilding.

Whereas peace, stability and security are long-term goals, the measurement of the success of interim steps remains elusive. To the extent that peacebuilding activities suggest changed behavior over time, it is necessary to judge successes or failures as one goes along.

Measurement and evaluation of activities are important to ensure that plans are on track. This is particularly difficult when considering the intent behind institutional development and capacity building of peacebuilding. At one level, administrative, operational and organizational aspects of institutions are the focus, while changed behavior, attitudes, and norms are ultimately the focus at another. In peacebuilding there may be no better example of this than development within the justice sector. Focusing on short-term objectives of institutional efficiency and effectiveness is not necessarily any indication that the justice sector development is contributing to broader goals of justice, security, and peace. Indeed, it could well be that such development activities could serve only to make a repressive system more effective and efficient, as we see in the Haitian case.

The UN Security Council Resolution 940 of 31 July 1994 authorized the use of all necessary means (including the use of force) to remove the military regime in Haiti and return the legitimate government to power. It also established a mandate for a US-dominated Multinational Force (MNF), called for the establishment of a stable environment conducive to democratic process and economic recovery in the country, and enabled the formation of a UN peacekeeping mission—the United Nations Mission in Haiti (UNMIH)—that would replace the MNF once security was affirmed. Also authorized by the Council was a unit of civilian International Police Monitors (IPM) to assist the MNF during the security transition. A partnership of military personnel and civilian police elements worked in the peacekeeping mode, despite the difficulty of the mission as a result of some continued violence by the Haitian Armed Forces, the Front for Advancement and Progress in Haiti (Fad'h/FRAPH), and mistrust on the part of the civilian population of the Interim

Public Security Force. Other problems to be overcome were the slow deployment of the IPM and a language barrier. The fact that this was the first "armed" UN civilian police mission underlines the difficulty encountered in this mission.

The MNF and IPM transition to UNMIH was considered relatively seamless thanks to the collaborative efforts of the agencies involved, a singular mandate, recognition of a leader (US administrative and technical support), shared planning, and joint communication and reporting.[15] The formation of a civilian ISPF was to facilitate the bridging of the security gap created by the removal of the Haitian military. Meantime, formal plans were moving ahead for the creation of a permanent professional organization, the Haitian National Police (HNP).

The US Department of Justice, International Criminal Investigative Training Assistance Program (ICITAP) directed and provided logistical support to the training of new HNP recruits. It was staffed by contracted US civilians and seconded police officers from Canada and France. In collaboration with ICITAP, the UNCIVPOL provided newly deployed recruits with "field training." By May 1995, eight months following the return to office of President Aristide, the Haitian military was disbanded and the FRAPH declared illegal. Newly trained HNP members had already begun to replace the interim ISPF.[16] With the deployment of some 5,200 HNP throughout 1995, plans emerged for international bilateral programs to join the early US and UN efforts.

The early collaborative efforts between the US and the UN (and later the bilateral programs of Canada, US, and France), focused on the police, but little emphasis was placed on the judiciary and prisons as integrated parts of the justice sector.[17] The first phase of the plan to replace existing Haitian security forces with civilian police focused on separating the police function from that of the Fad'h. The Royal Canadian Mounted Police (RCMP) combined forces with the ICITAP to create a training plan and curriculum. Plans were also established to coordinate the ICITAP "basic training" with "field training" and mentorship provided by the Canadian-led UN civilian police mission, UNMIH.

A 5,000 member civilian police force was to be created between January 1995 and February 1996, timed to coincide with the end of the UN mandate. The result was classes as large as 300, a size totally ineffective for technical learning. The effectiveness of the training was further compromised by the need to move candidates speedily through the process in a fixed period of time. Evaluation and follow-up were not part of the process.[18]

The need to develop such institutions through a "bottom up" approach was overshadowed by the absence of managerial and administrative systems. There was in fact no managerial or supervisory element capable of providing stability, control, direction, and guidance to the inexperienced recruits. To facilitate the large numbers being trained, the program was split between the HNP training facility in Port-au-Prince and an auxiliary center at Fort Leonard Wood, Missouri. Numerous UN mission extensions and renewals were necessary to assure continued stability and to provide security in the country.

The second phase of the plan, beginning in the spring of 1996, called for institutional development of the newly formed police. The peacebuilding partnership exercise was expanded with the arrival of bilateral development programs. Unfortunately, there were no specific ties to the mandates of donors that emphasized the ideas of "common risk" and "common benefit" associated with a partnership. At the diplomatic level, US-Canadian dialogue on the peacebuilding work existed, but the individual country mandates were not closely linked. Yet, the US supported a strong and high-profile Canadian presence to provide evidence that the peacebuilding mission, in spite of the disproportionately large US commitment, was truly international in scope.[19]

If the most powerful states tend to influence international decisions to intervene in conflict situations, their self-interests tend also to have an impact on postconflict activities. US influence over justice development in Haiti had been significant from the outset of the "peacebuilding" activities. Even before the 1994 US-led intervention, an American-designed development plan became the "blueprint" of policing development. This indicated clearly the beginning of US influence on the peacebuilding process. Further indications of that influence in the early stages of postconflict activity included: US funding of the initial police training, the use of US-developed training guides and lesson plans, and the contracting of foreign police (principally Canadian and French) to the US executing agency (ICITAP).[20]

Even as bilateral programs began in 1996 (US, Canada, France, as well as a UNDP mission), US influence persisted, sometimes to the detriment of other development programs. Administratively, while other projects were subjected to an epidemic of rescheduled activities, cancellations, and unexplained delays of all kinds, US problems seemed less acute, and US access to police and government officials unfettered. At an operational level, US influence also tended to have had an impact on other development programs (*e.g.*, the availability of HNP candidates for training).

The pressures of operational deployment soon conflicted with the development opportunities presented by the arrival of bilateral programs. Simply put, the HNP was incapable of meeting the basic challenge—identification of candidates for training. While the "partners" were each preparing for training and expecting candidates to fill their classrooms, there were not enough candidates to go around. Poor coordination and planning resulted in lengthy and expensive delays and inefficient use of resources.[21] Yet, curiously enough, US-sponsored programs for development of "specialty units" like Special Weapons and Tactics (SWAT), Narcotic Investigation, Presidential Guard, and Palace Security, proceeded without delay.

Here, the US concern with issues of narcotics trafficking, and in particular the movement of cocaine by Colombian cartels through Haiti to US destinations, demonstrated the level of American influence. While the emergence of Haiti as a narcotic transhipment point was undeniable, the HNP's ability to counter international drug trafficking activities was clearly well down the list of development priorities. A newborn institution had far greater challenges in legitimizing itself in the eyes of the public at large.

The US also installed its own investigative unit of the Drug Enforcement Administration (DEA). Reported as a group of eight investigators, this group grew to as many as sixteen by the year 2000, in contrast to the one DEA "liaison" position in place in 1996 when bilateral "development" activities began. These American-trained Haitian narcotics investigators rapidly gained a reputation as a corrupt group, and had few operational links with the DEA. Any Haitians involved with US investigators were tightly vetted and often subjected to polygraph examinations.[22]

Also focused on narcotics investigation and intelligence gathering, the US established a Haitian office of the Joint Intelligence Coordination Center (JICC), an American-driven anti-narcotic information network in the Caribbean, Central, and South America, which exists almost entirely to serve US interests. To staff the center, US officials "seconded" criminal intelligence analysts from the ranks of the HNP's *Bureau de Renseignement Judiciare* (BRJ).[23] Despite the fact that the seconded staff had been assigned an important role in the security preparations for national elections (1999 Legislative, 2000 Presidential), they were to be moved to serve US interests. It was clear that the HNP Director-General was under intense pressure to accede to American demands as they related to narcotics issues. "Certification" (a US designation of a country's contribution in matters of international drug trafficking), demanded it and development "aid" generally was tied to such certification.[24] Not only did this action on the part of US authorities have an impact on the Haitian officials' authority, it also affected the Canadian bilateral program.

The focus on US self-interest is not to suggest that Canada and France, as the other major players in justice development in Haiti, are not also concerned with pursuing their own self-interests. In the case of justice development in Haiti, both countries furthered their stature in the UN and "La Francophonie" and Canada within the Organization of American States (OAS). However, in comparison to the US, Canadian or French pursuit of self-interest was much less blatant.

When outside agencies or states are involved in providing the means of change through peacebuilding activities, it is vital for there to be real cooperation and collaboration among all the players to ensure success. With respect to justice development in Haiti, donors were agreed on the importance of collective goals. The language of facilitation (promotion of acceptable standards, strengthening and capacity building, assistance and support, cooperation and collaboration) was ever present in describing the peacebuilding strategies of major contributors.[25] Nevertheless, the distance between the rhetoric and practice was great.

While all donors appeared to emphasize the importance of creating a capable and professional Haitian civilian police force, there was little cooperative effort among them to accomplish this. A joint committee, comprised of the international project directors and headed by the HNP Director-General, was created in 1996 to coordinate initiatives detailed in the HNP Strategic Development Plan.[26] In spite of this positive step, the various development "partners" often worked independently, without consideration of their impact on planned or ongoing programs, on the long-term impact on the HNP, or on the ability of the GOH to sustain the development. For a time there was a virtual competition among international partners to get Haitian police officers off the street and into classrooms so that individual projects might show progress. This not only created tension among the international partners, it also placed great stress on the HNP, which had been struggling to meet its operational commitments. Control and direction on the part of the coordinating committee never materialized. What should have been an international effort quickly deteriorated into a series of poorly integrated independent programs.[27]

The entire process proved difficult and, at best, only achieved a limited degree of success. On the Haitians' part, access to documents such as budgets and financial reports necessary for the mid- and long-term planning of sustainability, was not handed over by government and police officials. Thus, a coordinated business approach was not truly embraced by either the international partners or the recipient state.[28]

Development of the prison system represented yet another example of poor collaboration on the part of the international partners. Among the major development partners, only the UNDP and USAID were actively involved in prison reform.[29] Most of the other actors paid little attention to prison reform, and it could be argued that even less attention might have been paid had it not been for publicity surrounding the court martial of US Army Captain Lawrence Rockwood. Concerned about prison conditions, he paid a late-night visit to the National Penitentiary, and was disciplined as a result.

In the wake of that publicity, problems within the prison system were unearthed and some immediate attention was given to them. US Army engineers assisted with some urgent repairs on prisons, US Special Forces began training guards, a facility for women and children was established in Port-au-Prince, and coordination was attempted with MICIVIH [United Nations Civilian Mission in Haiti (Human Rights)] and certain NGOs. CIVPOL (outside of its mandate), assumed responsibility for prison administration at the local level and coordinated with a Haitian NGO to deliver meals to inmates.[30] Much of this new focus on the prison system, however, was on the initiative of local commanders and managers; it was certainly not part of any multilateral plan. By the time major bilateral programs began in 1996, international interest in assisting with prison development had waned. From there on, prison development was severely stunted by the minimal resources available to address the complete range of development needs. While the conditions within the Haitian prison systems were recognized as a fundamental weakness of the judicial sector, policing commanded the main focus of the vast majority of development efforts in the country.

The absence of a collaborative and cooperative relationship amongst international partners was exacerbated by the extent to which they brought different experiences, resources, and interests to the development table. Here, a detailed analysis of the "baggage" of each of the international partners is not as important as an understanding of why these differences were not overcome and how ideals of cohesive working relationships simply fell by the wayside.

The primary bilateral actors in justice development, the United States and Canada, were clearly important multilateral participants in the UN peacebuilding mission in Haiti. At the same time, France dominated the UN civilian police missions after 1996 by virtue of having the largest representative contingent and exercising control over the missions' executive positions. As it turned out, the switch in control of the UN police mission from Canada to France signaled the breakdown of multilateral cohesion in policing development.[31] Prior to the change in CIVPOL leadership, international civilian police deployed in the field were well coordinated, with bilateral initiatives focused on basic training of police recruits. Generally considered as a highly successful initiative, this program ceased abruptly when the French contingent took command of CIVPOL.[32]

Steeped in traditions of reactive and garrisoned paramilitary policing, the new commander was totally unfamiliar with the principles and philosophies of community policing, considered fundamental to the training program itself and important for the public to accept the new police. Under French command, CIVPOL retracted from a close working relationship with the young HNP members and returned to a strict monitoring and formal training regimen. Joint patrols by HNP and CIVPOL were no longer the norm, and routine and purposeful interaction with the public was discontinued.[33] This represented a clear example of colliding principles and philosophies.

The utility of multiple actors in the service delivery of peacebuilding activities is generally restricted by the complexity and inflexibility of their bureaucracies, and by the limited financial resources available for seed money. The notion of inflexibility focuses on the fact that "off the shelf" training or development plans, successful in a donor country, may not necessarily be effective or sustainable in the context of the recipient state. This was a recognized problem in Haiti. Attention was often paid only to the immediate results—emphasizing the number of candidates trained, rather than the quality or utility of the training. In the absence of local input, the notion of sustainable processes was easily lost.[34]

The total irrelevance of some of these programs to the Haitian realities was comic. The US major crime investigation course, where forensic evidence in the context of the O.J. Simpson murder investigation was discussed, is a prime example. Not only did Haitian law not recognize forensic evidence; their police had never been exposed to it, nor were they capable of collecting and preserving it. The course instructor was oblivious to the fact that the puzzled looks on trainees' faces was due in large part to the fact that they had never heard of Simpson. Other examples were equally bizarre. Among them was the US-led drug investigators course, with its emphasis on shooting skills, running in troop formation, and chanting Marine Corps spirit songs. The playing of the Michigan State University fight song by the Haitian police band was another oddity.

The UNCIVPOL had no generic format for development. The capacity to provide training and development was left to the discretion of the Commander. When Canada was in charge, Canadian entreés were presented; when France assumed command, the menu changed.

In the case of the UN, the "training and development" contribution to the peacebuilding exercise was very much a function of the mission itself. A large number of countries contributed, representing a wide variety of experience and expertise. When the peacekeeping role gradually transformed into a peacebuilding role, the UN simply could not adjust to the changed mandate. For instance, it was not uncommon for less developed countries' partners to send in peacekeepers who were slightly more capable in policing than the Haitians to coach and mentor the Haitian police.[35] This did nothing to improve HNP/UN relations on the ground.

At another level, UN missions were subject to regular renewal on the basis of the extent of the willingness of major countries to contribute to the missions. The difficulties involved in planning a long-term and sustainable contribution in such circumstances is obvious. To make matters worse, the UN mission had no financing to kick start programs.

The absence of real coordination and collaboration by peace-building partners also affected the attitude of the recipient. When one international partner or another was slow to react to a particular local need or request, there was a not so subtle tendency by the Haitian authorities to shop around among the international partners, looking for a quicker or more lucrative deal. It was also the case that training or development programs were often started, but not followed through. If neither the donor nor the recipient were able to expend the resources needed to see a project through to completion, it simply died. When development contributors had limited cash, they were less likely to grab and hold the attention of the recipient. Overlapping activities and wasted time and resources became a source of real frustration among partners, and most assuredly the governments or agencies they represented.

Over time, a greater degree of coordination became evident. However, it was not in the form of a collective arrangement involving all partners. Limited cooperative efforts between individual donor/partners were, more often than not, motivated by a desire to economize through the sharing of financial and human resources, rather than a rooted desire to work together for the greater good of the HNP.

Generally, the need of the Haitian justice system to deal with even the most rudimentary elements of forensic evidence was recognized, among other priorities, as being important to development in this sector. This need called for training and development within the police and the judiciary at all levels, from the collection of evidence to the judicial recognition of its value in criminal inquiry. The magnitude of development challenges in this area made it an undesirable project for any individual donor. While the US had significant resources to contribute, it was incapable of providing training in French. The Canadian International Development Agency (CIDA), on the other hand, without the same financial resources, could provide program administration through the RCMP, which had training and development systems in place, human resources available, and the capacity to deliver the service in French.

A development partnership was struck between the Canadians and the Haitian Director of the "Police Scientifique" in planning and executing development activity. A general split in activities saw the Canadians generally responsible for the development of Police Identification Technicians and administrative/managerial mentoring to the Director, with ICITAP responsible for Laboratory development. Despite some early and significant progress, this joint project fell victim to a number of unforeseen realities. First was the absence of parallel development in other areas of the Judicial Police. Such parallel development was important because the capacity in forensic sciences exists to support investigative branches. When the investigative branches showed little development progress, and simply ignored the forensic technicians, rapid early progress came to a standstill. Likewise, within the Judiciary: while some introductory training in matters of criminal justice science was available, it was *ad hoc* at best and the new "experts" were not accepted. By the time a technical forensic capability emerged within the police, development in the Judiciary had been all but abandoned by donor countries as well as by the Haitian government.

The typical problems of peacebuilding (whether identified with the mission, the actors, or the environment) were in evidence in the Haitian example of justice development undertaken by multilateral and bilateral actors. Kumar identified the abstract nature and multiplicity of the peacebuilding goals in Haiti as the primary weakness of justice development. He suggested that rather than having evolved out of a strategy of risk management, international peacebuilding initiatives emerged as a "laundry list" of individual projects that were poorly coordinated, lacking in continuity, without logical conclusion, and most critically, without a singularity of purpose. Initiatives addressed symptoms of the dysfunctional justice system, rather than focusing on the cause.[36] When there was no concrete planning among development partners, including the participation of the recipient government, initiatives were disjointed, stalled, and unsuccessful.[37]

Planning across all levels of development should have started with a broad vision of the recipient's needs (as defined by the recipient in collaboration with the international community), and its capacity to sustain development. This should have been linked with the capacity of international partners, and recognition of the need for a "fit" between the realities of local history, politics, culture and the economy. While the international partners bore responsibility here for the failures, so too must the Haitian Government, which did not show a concerted effort or willingness to take responsibility for its own development.

The Haitian Government's failures in justice sector development did little to instill confidence that fundamental change in justice was on the horizon.[38] More disturbing, was the fact that Haitian officials showed little desire for change. Such perceptions must affect public opinion regarding the effectiveness of government processes, surely an important factor in terms of state stability. Further, such perceptions have an impact on political decisions among the international partners, as questions are asked about continued funding of expensive development programs that seem to make little or no progress.

The collective security partnership that emerged from the peacekeeping phase of the international intervention in Haiti in 1994–95, anchored by the clarity of its mandate, for the most part proved successful. The Haitian military was removed with practically no violence, and a secure environment was created for peacebuilding activities. Save for the contentious issue of the negotiated departure of the Cédras military regime, the first phase of the international partnership represented collaboration, cooperation, and a singularity of purpose.

Yet, for the international partners, the shift to the peacebuilding phase represented a vague and more complex mission of professionalization, institutional development, and capacity building. In 1996, bilateral programs in justice development were added alongside the UN mission, which was transformed from one of peacekeeping to peacebuilding. After five years of international partnership efforts in development, justice issues continued to be most pressing. Indeed, the success of the development partnership to bridge the gap between "inputs" and "outcomes," must be questioned.

From the perspective of "impact," a glaring failure is evident. The human rights situation in Haiti, a principal reasons for the international intervention, did not improve significantly. A deep division continued between the police and the public and widened as human rights violations persisted. Specialty units of the police were identified as particularly abusive. Prisons remained overcrowded, and general conditions were still abysmal. The justice system remained inefficient and developmentally stagnant.[39] Added to this was mounting evidence of widespread police corruption and politicization.[40] Data collected by MICIVIH on allegations of human rights abuse by security officials offer no indication of changing trends.[41] This remained the case despite joint UN/OAS human rights initiatives since 1993, a multilateral presence in police development since 1994–95, and bilateral development in the justice sector since 1996. Not even mentioned among routinely gathered statistics was the number of people arrested for being "threats to the security of the state," a convenient catchall that was used frequently. These facts alone call into question the success of justice sector peacebuilding partnership in the Haitian case.

In light of the evidence, developing capacity in the Haitian justice sector was at best unsuccessful and, at worst, may have only served to strengthen institutions carrying out human rights abuse. In failing to recognize the history of the state as perhaps the most important challenge to overcome, the peacebuilding partnership may have failed by moving to correct symptoms without considering more basic and underlying causal factors. Indeed, the international partnership at no point laid out collective goals beyond those of elementary benchmarks—the numbers of people trained, the amount of equipment purchased, the numbers of facilities refurbished, or the policies and procedures created.

Most disturbing in unraveling this failure is the fact that the international partnership seems to have recognized its own weaknesses. The need for clear, attainable goals, real evaluation of progress, coordination of programs and projects, and an overall commitment to working cooperatively were regularly discussed. The time and resources wasted as a result of overlapping projects and irrelevant training were reported repeatedly.[42] Further, the international community also recognized that the Haitian government was failing to support the partnership, was reluctant to take responsibility for the development of its own institutions, and showed no leadership as champions of change. Yet there was seemingly no effort to rectify the problem. Instead, the following excuses were offered as rational explanations for slow progress at the beginning of development activities: the institutions were young, systems needed to mature, and patience was required.

As the years went by, these excuses became timeworn. Justice sector programs that reached their prescribed level of development because of the international partners, often withered on the vine as the Government of Haiti failed to assume its responsibility as a development partner. Where the government did take a more active position, it conspicuously favored those aspects of the new police that were rapidly becoming ugly reflections of the old. The desperate needs of the Administrative Police, the rank and file with front line responsibly to citizens of the country, were over-shadowed in favor of specialty units like the "*maintien d'ordre*" (tactical riot units) teams, SWAT (Special Weapons and Tactics), the Presidential Guard, and Palace Security—units mandated to keep order and protect government officials. The international community (MICIVIH) was reporting that these units were the most glaring examples of human rights violators, and the US' own investigations identified these units as being responsible for politically motivated assaults and murders. At the same time, international partners had focused attention on development without meaningful follow-up or scrutiny of the impact of their work.

The differences among international partners, be they philosophical, resource-based or based on self-interest, while real, need not be barriers to unity of action. What is needed is forward-thinking leadership capable of overcoming the inherent difficulties of a multinational model. Specifically, greater attention needs to be directed at developing collective goals, and a "success" framework that takes into consideration the collective impact of operations. It is also important that the recipient-partner has the political will to facilitate change. In the absence of such a formula, the goals of multinational peacebuilding will remain elusive and unattained.

Many lessons emerged from the experience of working in an environment of relative calm (political chaos notwithstanding) with bilateral and multilateral partners sharing the same development turf, and all addressing the challenges of rebuilding a totally dysfunctional set of institutions. The most important lesson may be that the development of the justice sector in Haiti will not be successful until it is recognized that peacebuilding demands a "common vision of the future and a living social pact."[43] This suggests that the complexity of the peacebuilding exercise needs to be acknowledged, and that attacking the challenges successfully requires a singularity of focus and unity of action among international partners. Simply continuing to attend to the "laundry list" of activities, in the absence of a coordinated long-term strategy, will lead to failure.[44]

The next order of business in justice development in Haiti must be the political task of encouraging the international community to return. The first priority of any new partnership that evolves (a partnership that must include a committed Haitian Government), must be to reorganize justice development on the basis of the lessons learned, real collaboration and cooperation, singularity of purpose, and a focus on the outcomes, particularly with respect to issues of human rights.

Acknowledgment

This chapter is extracted from a larger work. All references to "interviews," "notes," or "reports" are made in the context of events and writings concerning "development business," not in the context of academic research.

Notes

1 Jarat Chopra, "Introducing Peace Maintenance," *Global Governance* 4, no. 1 (1998): 1.
2 Trevor Findlay, *Challenge of the New Peacekeeper* (New York: Oxford UP, 1996).
3 See Keating and Knight in this volume (Introduction).
4 Jonathon Goodhand and David Hume, "From wars to complex political emergencies: understanding conflict and peace-building in the new world disorder," *Third World Quarterly*, 20, no. 1 (1999): 13–27.
5 Irwin P. Stotzky, *Transition to Democracy in Latin America and The Role of the Judiciary* (Boulder, CO: Westview Press, 1993): 14.
6 Francis Kofi Abiew, *The Evolution of the Doctrine and Practise of Humanitarian Intervention* (The Hague: Kluwer, 1999): 212.
7 *Human Rights Watch 1992*, "Thirst for Justice: A Decade of Impunity in Haiti," http://www.hrw.org/reports/1996/haiti.htm (accessed 20 December, 2003). Despite the "1992" of the title, the report concerns events in 1991. The report notes that despite his tolerance of vigilantism, including the killing of suspected criminals and political opposition, Aristide as a human rights violator, paled by comparison with the military government that threw him from office.
8 Notes, interviews and observations (1998–1999). Discussions in Port-au-Prince with Jean-Paul Lupien, Program Manager, Prison Reform Development, UNDP.
9 Robert B. Oakley, Michael Dziedzic, Eliot M. Goldberg, eds., *Policing the New World Disorder* (Washington DC: National Defense University Press, 1998).
10 Jared Wright, "Conclusions: Problems and Prospects in Peace building," in Ann L. Griffiths, ed., *Building Peace and Democracy in Post Conflict Societies* (Dalhousie Univ: Centre for Foreign Policy Studies, 1998): 163.
11 Derick W. Brinkerhoff and Jean-Claude Garcia-Zamor, Politics, *Projects and People—Institutional Development in Haiti* (New York: Praeger, 1986): 271.
12 Chetan Kumar, *Building Peace in Haiti* (Boulder, CO: Lynne Reinner, 1998): 88.

13 David J. Whittaker, *United Nations in the Contemporary World* (New York: Routledge, 1997): 55.

14 Derick W. Brinkerhoff, *Improving Development Program Performance* (Boulder, CO: Lynne Reinner, 1991): 194.

15 Discussions with J. O'Neil G. Pouliot (1996). See also: Michael Bailey, Robert Maguire, and J. O'Neil G. Pouliot, "Haiti: Military-Police Partnership for Public Security," in Oakley, Dziedzic and Goldberg, *Policing the New*, 215–34.

16 Bailey, Maguire and Pouliot, "Haiti: Military-Police Partnership."

17 Bailey, Maguire and Pouliot, "Haiti: Military-Police Partnership."

18 Instructors trained in "systems delivery" found the process of training in "bulk" both frustrating and ineffective. Efforts to economize on time, at the expense of quality training, were common. For instance, if a particular piece of kit or equipment was to be issued to candidates, training might be suspended while the entire school of candidates was assembled (Interviews with instructors attached to the ICITAP program). Follow-up training "in the field" was conducted, but only during the brief period when Canada led the UN civilian police mission. Field training ended when France took charge of the CIVPOL mission.

19 Prior to deployment of the bilateral missions, Canadian-American dialogue was routine, even daily. In contrast, discussions with the UN and France, the other partners in the peacebuilding effort, were far less frequent.

20 ICITAP (International Criminal Investigation Training Assistance Program) is a coordinating agency of the US Department of Justice. The agency led US justice development activities in Central America and has, since beginning in Haiti, expanded to other development programs in South Africa, Lebanon, and Bosnia and elsewhere.

21 Such delays were particularly costly to Canadian programs, which at this particular time were focused on management training. At considerable expense, a management training program had been created that was unique to the Haitian experience. Instructors trained specifically to deliver the material, and to identify Haitian candidates as future instructors, were often left to "make work" projects on lesser priorities.

22 The use of polygraph examinations was a fairly standard practice of the American agencies where there was a considered security risk in dealing with Haitian police officers. This was particularly evident in the area of narcotic investigations and related activities.

23 The BRJ, the analytical branch of the HNP Judicial Police, was developed and trained by the CIDA-RCMP bilateral program. The branch had gained a reputation as a highly competent and honest group, to the degree that they had been called upon by the Director-General of the HNP to conduct sensitive investigations in lieu of other mandated units. Interestingly, this unit had no formal investigative training and no mandate to conduct investigations. Many were civilian police employees.

24 The writer had developed a relationship with the HNP Director-General that permitted frank discussion of this nature. There was no denying that the movement of competent HNP personnel was an important loss. Fortunately, negotiation between the HNP and US and Canadian officials resulted in a reduction

of the proposed secondment, but with alternative training for some JICC employees to facilitate US needs.

25 See: Edmundo Jarquin and Fernando Carrillo, *Justice Delayed* (Washington DC: Johns Hopkins Univ Press, 1998).

26 The writer, in his capacity as director of the Canadian policing development effort (bilateral), was the Canadian representative to this group.

27 Author's observation based on experience and notes, 1996–1999.

28 The international partners on the United Nations Development Programme (UNDP) (policing development program), embraced the process. In the absence of real support and willingness to be guided by the process on the part of the largest donor partners (US in terms of dollars, UNCIVPOL in terms of human resources), the real potential was never attained. Canada, and to a lesser degree, the UNDP, used the documents and the business planning process as guidelines for their development contribution.

29 USAID efforts in reform of justice administration have failed miserably. A December 1999 report by CBS Television, "60 minutes" (Walt Bogdanovich, Producer) revealed that very little progress had been made. The report also uncovered the questionable qualifications of individuals working for the company contracted to do the development work. This included an executive within the contracted company (hired at the suggestion of USAID), who it was later discovered was a disbarred California lawyer, convicted of fraud against the US Govt.

30 Michael Bailey, Robert Maguire, and J. O'Neil G. Pouliot, "Haiti: Military-Police Partnership," 234–37. In another judicial program sponsored by the US Department of Justice and managed by the Office of Professional Development, $1.9 million was available.

31 Robert B. Oakley and Michael Dziedzic, "Conclusions," 525.

32 This change in command of the international police representation reflected a political reality within the UN. Canada had taken over command of the UN military forces and could not simultaneously hold control of the police mission as well.

33 There were situations of successful police-community interaction, the small city of Jacmel being one such example that was widely reported. Here the initiative on a local HNP commander was recognized and supported by the local CIVPOL commander. This relationship, on both levels, was not usual.

34 Brinkerhoff and Garcia-Zamor, Politics, *Projects and People*, 267.

35 The minimum UN standards for peacekeepers include a minimum level of service, the ability to drive a four-wheel drive vehicle, and the ability to speak the language of the mission. Participating countries interpret even these minimum standards liberally. In one example, an entire contingent was sent home when it was discovered that few in the group could drive and none were capable of speaking either French or English, or Haitian Creole.

36 Kumar, *Building Peace in Haiti.*

37 E.T. Jackson and Associates, Ltd. *Learning for Results: Issues, Trends and Lessons Learned in Basic Human Needs* (Ottowa: CIDA, June 1996), para 5.4.2, http://www.acdi-cida.gac.ca/cida_ind.nsf (accessed 5 October, 1999). Recurring costs and sustainability are rarely addressed before projects begin. Recipient governments are then unable to deal with the impact of development.

38 Haiti's growing reputation as a transshipment point for the traffic of cocaine between Columbia and North America has been widely reported. Politicization of officials in the Justice Sector has been a fear of the development partners since the outset of international assistance activities (Notes, reports and experience 1996–1999).

39 Human Rights Watch, *World Report 1999: Haiti Human Rights Developments*, http://www.hrw.org/hrw/worldreport99/americas/haiti.html, 1–6 (accessed 16 December 2003).

40 Information drawn from notes, interview, and discussion.

41 A complete review of the human rights situation in Haiti is available in the quarterly reports of the UN Mission (MICIVIH), Human Rights Review, (October–December 1998, April–June 1999); See also: Human Rights Watch World Report http://www.hrw.org/wr2k1/americas/haiti.html (accessed 16 December 2003); and Human Rights Watch, Haiti Human Rights Developments, http://hrw.org/wr2k/americas-06.htm (accessed 16 December 2003).

42 The writer's own reports on the project management regularly reported on the partnership failings.

43 Kumar, *Building Peace in Haiti*, 29–31.

44 Kumar, *Building Peace in Haiti*, 77.

7 Women and Gender Equality in Peacebuilding

SOMALIA AND MOZAMBIQUE

Sumie Nakaya

THE ROLE OF WOMEN in conflict resolution and peacebuilding is increasingly emphasized in multilateral policy discourse. Following the 1995 Beijing Platform for Action, which called for an increased participation of women in conflict resolution at decision-making levels,[1] the UN Security Council adopted its first resolution focusing on the role of women in the maintenance of international peace and security in October 2000.[2] In November 2000, the European Parliament adopted a similar resolution encouraging women's participation in conflict resolution.[3]

In essence, Security Council Resolution 1325 calls for (1) an increased in the representation of women in decision-making related to peace and security, including UN peace operations, (2) the better protection of women and girls under international humanitarian and human rights law, and (3) special attention to women in the pursuit of postwar justice, disarmament and demobilization, and repatriation and reintegration of refugees. In the follow up, two major studies are being prepared to enhance the understanding of critical issues facing women in conflict and postconflict situations. The UN Division for the Advancement of Women is leading the Secretary-General's study on women, peace, and security, while the UN Development Fund for Women (UNIFEM) has commissioned independent experts to assess the impact of armed conflict on women and the role of women in peacebuilding.[4]

These policy developments have provided political visibility and recognition to women's movements for peace, disarmament, and reconciliation at local, regional, and global levels. They also suggest institutional frameworks in which intergovernmental organizations could enhance women's participation in peace processes. To ensure that women and their "common agenda" are represented at the peace table, the UN, regional organizations, donors, and civil society alike are increasingly supporting conflict resolution training and informal dialogues for women, and brokering their participation in official negotiations. Women were made party to official negotiations in Burundi (2000), Afghanistan (2001–02), and the Inter-Congolese Dialogues (2001–02).

Through these forums, women's groups have proposed the issues they wish incorporated in peace agreements. Their proposals often include: (1) statutory guarantee of women's rights and equal treatment; (2) a minimum 30 percent quota for women in decision-making processes; (3) special measures ensuring the safe return and re-integration of displaced women; (4) women's rights to property ownership and inheritance; and (5) the end of impunity.[5] In Burundi, Northern Ireland, and Guatemala, women have managed to incorporate some of these proposals into peace agreements, making each more progressive and inclusive of political commitments towards women.

The role of women in conflict resolution and peacebuilding is multidimensional. First, women's participation is an issue of equitable representation, for legitimate conflict resolution and peacebuilding requires an inclusive and participatory process.[6] Second, it is frequently argued that women bring gender perspectives to the substance of negotiations. According to Swanee Hunt, "Common sense dictates that women should be central to peacemaking, where they can bring their experience in conflict resolution to bear."[7]

As such, women are expected to articulate and negotiate favorable terms for women and gender equality based on their experiences as single heads of households, community leaders, humanitarian and social workers, and peace activists. Some claim an even more substantial role for women. Noeleen Heyzer, Executive Director of UNIFEM, states, "Women's commitment to peace also remains critical to ensuring the sustainability of peace agreements signed by political and military factions."[8] It is thus no accident that Resolution 1325 places a strong emphasis on the increased representation of women in peace-related functions.

In spite of the increased participation of women in peace negotiations, however, the short- to medium-term results of many peace processes point to the contrary: women continue to be discriminated against and marginalized in postwar society. In Kosovo, despite the introduction of 30 percent electoral quotas for women, only 8.2 percent of those elected to the Municipal Assemblies in the October 2000 elections were women.[9] In Burundi, despite the historic convention of the All-Party Women's Conference in July 2000 in which two women from each of nineteen political parties participating in peace negotiations formulated recommendations and managed to incorporate 23 of them into the final peace agreement, conference-goers could not agree on which one delegate would represent them at the accord signing. To date, the role of women in the implementation of the accord has been minimal.[10] In Guatemala, Cambodia, and Bosnia-Herzegovina, women's representation in parliament has decreased from prewar levels. With international financial institutions advocating the downsizing of the civil service, women are often the last and the least favored in obtaining public sector employment.

These shortcomings seem to derive from the continued asymmetry of power relations in postconflict society, namely in patriarchal traditions, state structures, and state-society relations. The pronounced international policy discourse focusing on the representation of women in conflict resolution and peacebuilding[11] has had a limited impact on changing gender relations in postconflict societies. By definition, gender refers to a socially constructed designation of women and men, their roles in a culture-specific context, and the relationship between the two sexes.[12] In wartime, gender relations become even more complex when "women's and men's gender identities and behavior fluctuate and change in response to external forces, including armed conflict."[13] Not only does the "standpoint" approach emphasizing the commonality of women and their "experiences" fail to take into account the diverse identities, needs, and responses of war-affected women and men, but the inclusion of women and their proposals does not necessarily lead to the integration of gender perspectives in peacebuilding.

Promoting gender equality in peacebuilding is an open-ended process and part of a broader commitment to equality. For instance, the recruitment of Tutsi women for high-level government positions in post-genocide Rwanda may make it look as though women are making progress. However, this may not amount to gender equality for Hutu women.[14] In the Balkans, women's groups and their external supporters were vocally critical of the absence of women in the Dayton process,[15] but they have not explored with the same rigor the gender impact of the ethnic partitions model employed for Bosnia-Herzegovina and in Kosovo. Women of minority or those who have entered into interracial marriages often experience double discrimination in partitioned societies—as outsiders to the community and as women.[16] Where there is inequality in political, social, and/or economic conditions among groups, there is likely to be gender inequality, both intragroup (men–women) and intergroup (*e.g.* Hutu women–Tutsi women).

Such underlying power relations in war-torn societies are key to understanding not only postconflict gender equality but also the sustainability of peace. The main task of peacebuilding from a gender perspective is to carry out structural reforms that promote intra- and intergroup equality both institutionally and within structural power relations. To build sustainable peace after prolonged and protracted conflict, "the task is not only to broker a formula for postwar power-sharing and to return the economy of peacetime conditions, but to establish the basic structures within which these processes are to take place."[17] Mainstreaming a gender perspective in this process requires "the process of assessing the implications for women and men of any planned action, including legislation, policies or programs, in any area and at all levels."[18]

One can posit, therefore, that gender equality in postconflict peacebuilding is contingent upon (1) the institutional framework of postconflict governance, including power-sharing arrangements; (2) the structural base of power relations in society, such as class, clan, and other forms of group membership, from which the gender interface cannot be constructed independently; and (3) international support to gender mainstreaming in peacebuilding. The incorporation of 30 percent quota for women in peace agreements is part of the institutional framework, while the structural base of power continues to dictate gender relations in households, communities, and decision-making processes in many of the postwar societies. International support to peacebuilding often encompasses a transition to a market economy and liberal democracy.

Postconflict institutional reforms encompass power-sharing arrangements and, in some cases, the formation of a new government. In particular, postwar elections can serve the "demilitarization" of politics by transforming intergroup security dilemmas into cooperative norms and institutions[19] and, if devised properly, the political accommodation of minority and opposition groups. Accordingly, postwar elections are now included in the mandates of many multilateral peacekeeping/peacebuilding operations that oversee or administer the transitional period.

Affirmative action in the institutional reforms would promote *de jure* gender equality in decision-making. As one of the major safeguards for their electoral representation, women have called for the introduction of quotas.[20] In addition, proportional representation (PR) or multimember district systems are empirically recognized as more advantageous to women than majoritarian or single-member district systems.[21]

Yet, quotas do not necessarily guarantee *de facto* gender equality in policymaking. Qualitative equality enabling women (and men) to effectively represent themselves and gender issues in the legislature is dependent upon other institutional innovations. Such variables include the equal provision of adequate authority, resources, and policy and technical assistance to policymakers, gender awareness and expertise of representatives, and their outreach and communication with a wider constituency. Equally important is the efficacy and integrity of the legislature.

In postconflict institutional reforms, the establishment of the rule of law is also recognized as a priority for both peacebuilding and peace maintenance.[22] In postwar societies, the restoration of law and order, as well as security sector reform, addresses political violence and common crimes.[23] Otherwise, "public insecurity presents a political opportunity for any group that has sufficient organization and weaponry to present itself as a protector of a given community."[24] The establishment of law and order is a necessary condition for gender equality, too, given that women continue to face gender-based violence, exploitation, and the predatory economy of war in many postconflict situations.

In addition, the principal of equality enshrined in constitutional, electoral, legislative, and judicial reforms is the first step toward combating gender inequality and discrimination. Women's movements are increasingly mobilized to engender such legal reforms. During constitutional drafting in South Africa, East Timor, and Cambodia, women's groups organized consultations, studied various constitutional models, and developed a "women's charter,"[25] which included (1) the principle of gender equality and equal citizenship for women; (2) affirmative action or quotas for women in decision-making bodies; (3) social and economic rights, including women's rights to land and property ownership and inheritance; and (4) the establishment of a gender focal point in government structures.[26]

Nonetheless, the reform of other basic laws that would criminalize domestic violence, improve the status of women in civil matters, and implement employment laws to protect domestic workers and ensure equal opportunities for women has encountered considerable delays in many postconflict countries. Civil and family laws are among the most difficult to reform, as they are seen to challenge customary practices, thereby clashing with traditional power relations. The delay is also in part due to donor interests in property law and criminal law that would promote internal order and foreign investment. Even when laws are updated, their implementation and women's access to law and justice remains problematic due to the lack of legal infrastructure, outreach, advocacy, and human resources.

One of the most urgent tasks of postconflict reconstruction is the restoration of core state functions, including the provision of public goods and maintenance of basic infrastructure. The public provision of basic services, including health care, water, sanitation, and education constitute the "dividends of peace" that visibly and immediately affect the lives and minds of war-affected people. From a gender perspective, it is important that the distribution of the dividends of peace be equitable, for "if equal access to land, education, health, etc. is not addressed initially, the macroeconomic policies and growth patterns may easily institutionalize such inequalities and make them more difficult to change at a later stage."[27] Yet, the macroeconomic policies prescribed by international donors, in particular the privatization of land, education, and even water, have exacerbated such inequalities in many instances. The privatization of property rights tends to deny women's pre-existing access to common land and customary and joint land holding when productive resources are crucial for their survival, because land tenure is tied to other substantive resources such as irrigation systems and forest products.[28]

Gender equality may also be promoted within the government apparatus through national women's machineries (NWMs) set up for the empowerment of women and gender equality in the form of a Ministry of Gender or Women's Affairs, a Women's Bureau, or other agency within government.[29] More often than not, NWMs are placed under a functionary dealing with social and economic issues without receiving adequate authority and resources to influence major legislation or the design and implementation of postconflict reconstruction. In Afghanistan and the Palestinian Territories, the gender offices are entirely funded by bilateral donor contributions. In East Timor, the 2002 national budget allocates to the Office of Equality six permanent staff, out of 14,819 civil servants, and a budget of $38,000 (0.049 percent).[30] In Kosovo, the UNMIK Consolidated Budget for 2000 does not mention women or gender;[31] the 2001 budget mentions only one gender-specific project, gender training, with a budget of $40,000 (0.003 percent). As such, the danger is that NWMs may be treated as tokens of good intention, expected to be a program delivery agency for 50 percent of the population despite meager human and financial resources, or required to raise external funds to operate. As a result of such shortfalls, the entire responsibility for change may be placed on women themselves. This could lead to significant disparities between women and men in such sectors as politics, law, finance, education, trade, industry, and others.[32]

Against this background, this study reviews two cases: Somalia and Mozambique. It examines both aspects of the issue discussed above: (1) whether the representation of women at the peace table resulted in the expressed commitment toward women and gender equality, and (2) whether the explicit commitments achieved gender equality. It is argued that the structural base of power is the decisive factor in promoting postconflict gender equality, and that the current international interventions assisting women in peace processes have exercised little influence in the reform of such power structure.

For instance, in Somalia, institutional devices were established to bring nearly 100 women to the latest round of peace negotiations, and women managed to secure 25 seats in the 245-member Transitional National Assembly established in August 2000. Yet, women in Somalia continue to be marginalized, gender equality is un-institutionalized, and the implementation of peace agreements has stalled. In contrast, in Mozambique, women did not play a visible role during peace negotiations, nor were they granted statutory quotas. Yet, today Mozambique is one of the few countries in the world where women occupy more than 30 percent of the parliament, due in part to the history of women's emancipation within the country's national liberation movement and the current ruling party.

Peacebuilding in Mozambique and Somalia would have required completely different sets of priorities, challenges, and processes. Although devastated by nearly two decades of civil war, Mozambique maintained a central authority with a government structure in the capital of Maputo. There were only two main actors involved—the government of FRELIMO (Frenet de Libertacao de Mocambique) and the opposition, RENAMO (Resistencia National Mocambicana). In contrast, Somalia was divided into a number of factions, warlords, and clans. Nonetheless, the international response to the two countries was fundamentally similar. Peacekeeping missions in Somalia (UNOSOM I, II) and Mozambique (ONUMOZ) involved multidimensional mandates ranging from disarmament and demobilization to humanitarian assistance to civilians and security sector reform. While the intervention in Somalia subsequently assumed and then abandoned a controversial "peace enforcement" mandate, the main approach to peacebuilding in both Somalia and Mozambique was "nation building" with the deployment of multinational forces for a relatively short timeframe.

Although the success rate of the two interventions varied considerably (ONUMOZ as a success and UNOSOM as a failure), the operations imprinted legacies on the postwar structures of both countries. Their impact on the political outcomes of the peace process and gender implications is reviewed below in both cases.

A total of thirteen conferences were convened after the collapse of the Somali state in 1991. All failed to make significant progress, leaving Somalia without a central government for nearly a decade. Women's participation in the Somali peace process was first formalized at the Conference on National Reconciliation in March 1998, convened in Addis Ababa with the facilitation of the Ethiopian president and the Swedish Life and Peace Institute.[33] This meeting resulted in the establishment of a Transitional National Council (TNC) that required that one woman be included in each of the three-member delegations from the eighteen regions. The agreement soon disintegrated as fighting resumed. The Addis Ababa framework was a failure because of its power-sharing scheme among the fifteen faction leaders did not engage clans that are part of the traditional decision-making bodies.[34]

The Somali women's movements emerged out of humanitarian necessity during the prolonged civil war, during which women provided shelter and medical care to the combatants, supplied clean water in war-affected communities, and restored destroyed schools. The women's groups also initiated an inter-clan dialogue for peace, mobilizing their access to political elite through humanitarian and community work, and cross-clan connections; in Somali society, women not only belong to their father's clans, but also form close ties with their husband's clans, since their children belong to the clan of their husbands.[35] To strengthen the cross-clan dialogues, seventeen NGOs, mostly led by Somali women, formed an umbrella organization to coordinate peacemaking and peacebuilding activities. By linking gender-specific roles in clan systems, women were able to influence the structural base of power relations and link it to institutional peacebuilding initiatives.

Recognizing that clan engagement was critical to sustained peace in Somalia, President Ismail Omar Guelleh of Djibouti, in his capacity as chair of the Intergovernmental Authority on Development (IGADD), argued that any Somali peace process should be moved away from the faction leaders and warlords. Against this background, the March 2000 Symposium, convened by President Guelleh, recommended a clan-based formula for the next National Reconciliation Conference.[36] On 2 May 2000, the Somali National Conference was formally opened in the town of Arta, Djibouti, and attended by a total of 810 delegates, consisting of four clan delegations of 180, each including twenty women, and ninety minority alliance representatives (including ten women).

As a result, the power-sharing arrangement conceived in the Arta conference resembled a consociational model whereby major clans were ensured participation in national decision-making while maintaining their territorial, political, and economic autonomy. The Transitional National Charter (TNC) was adopted, and a 245-member Transitional National Assembly (TNA) was established in August 2000. The TNA seats were allocated according to clan membership: 44 seats were allocated to four major clans and 24 seats to the Clan Alliance comprised of smaller clans, and an additional twenty seats for the independent, non-clan affiliates. Women had vigorously pursued a twelve percent quota in the TNA, calling themselves the "sixth clan," and took the proposal to the host country, Djibouti, when faced with opposition from religious leaders and male delegates. Subsequently, women were granted 25 seats in the TNA, to be equally divided among the four major clans and the Alliance.

Another critical feature of the TNC was the decentralization of state functions, both in decision-making and defense/policing authorities.[37] In principle, the TNC recognized and legitimized *de facto* autonomy of eighteen regions and, in particular, partition of the north, which is home to a relatively homogenous clan composition. In some parts of Somalia, however, decentralization equaled the disintegration of state authority. Both Somaliland and Puntland have refused to endorse the Transitional National Government (TNG), and a number of the faction leaders from Mogadishu did not participate in the Arta process.

In the decentralized state model, most decision-making authority remains at the local level, within each clan. Clans use a mix of traditional and Islamic dispute resolution discourses, which exclude women from decision-making mechanisms. In judicial cases, elders and religious specialists are called upon to mediate negotiations between parties in conflict. Negotiations often involve references to customary law and legal precedent, and various kinds of compensation for the offended party. A woman's value in terms of blood money is half that of a man's and women rarely receive compensation, since payments are made strictly between male relatives. In some instances, a woman may be offered as spouse to the offended party if intercommunal ties are at stake.[38]

International interventions, including UNOSOM II, practically endorsed decentralization, focusing on the strengthening of local authorities instead of the transitional government apparatus. UNOSOM II made the establishment of national police forces one of its top priorities, but as the establishment of the TNG stalled, it allowed the police forces to remain under the command of district and regional councils, and hastily withdrew from Somalia.[39] UNDP assistance, for example, focused on capacity building in local authorities such as local police and traditional clan leaders, instead of supporting the transitional government apparatus.[40] The two separate processes launched by the UN—

> Factional reconciliation at the national level and grassroots political development at the district and regional level—both had their own problems. In the short term, this type of support would have facilitated the development of effective governance at the intraclan level, albeit at the cost of strengthening the existing territorial divisions among the various Somali clans.[41]

While economic conditions have continued to deteriorate in the past decade, the arrival of large-scale, externally supplied foreign troops certainly had a destabilizing effect on the local economy, exacerbating the "economy of war." Service-sector oriented commercial activities, with no state regulation or intervention, preyed upon the weak and the poor and flourished. Public commodities, from security to water, were privatized, giving the least access to women. Faced with the dire humanitarian situation in Somalia (in which 45 women die every day in labor and one in four children do not reach the age of five[42]), ongoing humanitarian assistance is coordinated by the Somali Aid Coordination Body.[43] According to one account put together by women's groups, however, "The Somali Aid Coordination Body does nothing for Somali women. The United Nations and the European Union are not interested in women's issues either. How can we organize ourselves politically and be expected to participate in decision-making if we have no support?"[44]

Due to the deteriorating security situation in Somalia, little has been achieved in the way of gender equality. Furthermore, the prolonged period of civil conflict has led to the spread of religious fundamentalism. More militant, conservative, and politicized than traditional Somali Muslim beliefs, new versions of Islam are increasingly introduced into local Islamic courts, together with harsh punishments and strict standards that govern the behavior of women. Interestingly, however, many Somali women seem to be supportive of the introduction of Islamic *Sharia* law for curtailing the widespread looting and robbery, which is a sign of nonconfidence in state-sponsored law enforcement.[45]

In conclusion, women's representation at the peace table in Somalia resulted in the expression of political commitment to women's empowerment in the Transitional National Charter and the institutional framework of TNA, which provided 12 percent quota for women. There was also ample international support for this endeavor. Asha Hagi Elmi, a leader of the Sixth Clan and Vice-Chair of the Chairmanship Committee testified:

> Women made their own identity on non-ethnic base as the Sixth Clan to differ with the other five ethnic based groups. From there, the Sixth Clan, united by gender equality, national aspiration and vision for peaceful and modern Somalia, became an acquainted national stakeholder with an independent quota/identity in participation.... As a result, the National Charter of Somalia is very reconciliatory to modernity, with affirmative action quota for women participation in the Transitional Assembly, refined clauses for preservation of human rights of women, child, minority etc, together with other sound democratic principles included. It ranks among the top in the region and best in the Muslim world.[46]

Yet, these breakthroughs failed at the level of implementation. The real decision-making authority continues to rest within clans. Without conceiving measures that improve the status of women and gender equality within the clan system, the representation of women at the national legislature remains a nominal and minimal change. Although women's groups continue inspiring work amidst deteriorating security situations, their impact on the national policy-making process has been limited in scale. The disconnect between these women's groups and female members of the TNA can be striking, some of whom mistook CEDAW for the Conference on Racism taking place in South Africa.[47]

The Mozambican peace process features a faith-based conflict resolution model and the role of the Catholic Church as the largest *supra* civil society organization. Over a period of fourteen years, the Vatican-based Community of St. Egidio established solid relationships with both parties to the Mozambican conflict—the government of FRELIMO and the opposition, RENAMO—through its development and humanitarian assistance projects. While St. Egidio went on to host all twelve rounds of the Rome talks, the Mozambican Peace Movement (MPP) was launched in 1992 to mobilize public support for peacemaking. Church groups were heavily involved in the MPP as well.

Furthermore, the UN and outside donors made a concerted effort to accommodate RENAMO from the early stage of the peace process. The UN Peacekeeping Operation in Mozambique (ONUMOZ) was deployed in early 1993, and by mid-April 1994, 55 percent of the government's and 81 percent of RENAMO's soldiers were cantoned. Italy contributed approximately $35 million to help finance RENAMO's commitment to the peace process and its transformation from a guerrilla force into a political party. Similarly, a UK-based multinational corporation, Lonrho, which had established oil business relations with RENAMO, contributed millions of dollars to buy RENAMO's compliance with the terms of the general peace accord. Consequently, the peace agreement was crafted with great flexibility for political accommodation to RENAMO. Parliament agreed to give RENAMO one-third representation on the Electoral Commission. The country's first multiparty elections were held in October 1994 and the government's party, FRELIMO, won the parliamentary (51 percent) and presidential (53 percent) elections.

Although women constituted the majority of church membership in Mozambique and were active in community-based development and reconciliation, women and gender issues were largely absent during the peace negotiations. The 1994 creation of a women's section within MPP reflected women's frustration that the major political parties were not addressing their needs. Likewise, the general peace agreement did not contain any gender-specific provisions.[48]

However, today Mozambique is one of only eight countries worldwide to have achieved a 30 percent representation of women in the legislature. The high representation derives from Mozambique's longstanding policy of women's emancipation, which extends to formal employment and liberal family laws. When FRELIMO won independence from Portugal in 1974, most of the colonists left the country, taking with them nearly all of the skilled labor force and sabotaging the industrial and commercial infrastructure.[49] To compensate for the shortage of skilled labor and infrastructure, FRELIMO adopted a policy of nationalization and state-sponsored social services, and encouraged women to participate in full-time employment. In 1971, the Women's Detachment was established within the nationalist movement, and in 1973, OMM (Organizacao da Mulher Mocambicana) was founded within FRELIMO to mobilize women for national development.[50]

The creation of the Women's Detachment was in recognition of the role of women in national liberation movements. The OMM played an instrumental role in enhancing the status of women, providing women with immunization, literacy training, and candidacy to local assemblies. The first Constitution of the People's Republic of Mozambique in 1975 enshrined gender equality, which was reiterated in the postwar Constitution, enacted in 1990. In 1976, the OMM and FRELIMO developed a new family law that provides for monogamous marriage, joint ownership of property, joint decisions regarding place of residence, and men's child support responsibilities.

FRELIMO continued women's emancipation through education, political mobilization, and formal sector employment. For the first democratic election in 1994, FRELIMO formulated gender-inclusive electoral policies, including the allocation of one-third of the candidacy to women. Women were also distributed among favorable positions within the party's master lists, and a large number of women candidates were drawn from OMM. In the end, FRELIMO presented 37 percent female candidates, as opposed to RENAMO's 9 percent female candidates.

Yet, challenges to gender equality remain. Two of the gender-specific indicators used in UNDP's Human Development Index, Gender-related Development Index (gender disparity of life expectancy, literacy, gross enrollment, and income) and Gender Empowerment Measure (economic and political participation) ranks Mozambique among the lowest in the world,[51] which is a testament to the remaining gap between women's political representation and gender equality.

The Constitution and the new 1997 land law guarantee women equal rights to own and inherit land. The progressive language of the 1997 land law has yet to be supported by institutional development. The 1997 law offers land rights for all, but on a "the-user-pays" basis, and coupled with the shift to a market economy, access to land is being consolidated in the new power alliance between local government and traditional authorities.[52] Rachel Waterhouse notes that

> Given peasant women's generally low social status and weaker access than men to labor and capital resources, they tend to be weaker players in the market, which reinforces their dependence on men.... It suggests that strategies aimed to protect women's independent land rights, without associating men in the process, may not be successful.[53]

In addition, legal pluralism poses a grave challenge to gender equality in many postconflict societies. During the civil war in Mozambique, community courts supplanted the role of traditional authorities, which, for women, have been the most accessible venue to legal redress. Portuguese colonial laws and customary practices continue to be used widely as the basis of Mozambican rule of law. The pre-existing Civil Code, defining men as heads of households, discriminates against women in matters of marriage, maintenance, custody and succession, and other aspects of family law.[54] The Penal Code includes gender-differentiated definition of adultery: when adultery is committed by women, the penalty involves a prison term of between two and eight years; when conducted by men, the crime is punishable by a fine.[55] The gaps among constitution, colonial law, and customary law are recurrent phenomena in peacebuilding, and constitute a problem of codification that prevents the systematic development of gender equality.

In terms of institutional framework, some ministries have set up gender units (*e.g.* education, agriculture, and environment) and some of the public policies have properly integrated a gender perspective.[56] The Ministry for Coordination of Social Action (MICAS) has responsibility for women's affairs. As such, MICAS's comparative advantage lies with its experience of working with "vulnerable" groups. In general, social policy favors community-based services rather than institutional provision.[57] After the Beijing conference, an interagency task force (*Grupo Operativo*) was set up in 1997, with the representatives of twelve different ministries, NGOs, and an academic institution. It produced a government Plan of Action that sets out responsibilities and targets in each sector,[58] but since then the group has been plagued by a lack of resources and the absence of a clear definition of its mandate and authority.[59]

While the Somali peace process is often labeled as "good practice" in terms of the participation of women, women and gender issues remain marginalized in clan decision-making. This poses one of the challenges to the current international assistance to women. International advocacy and donor funding may be shortcuts to bring women to the negotiating table in the short term, but the categorization of women's participation as an "international priority" may not guarantee the sense of ownership for social transformation at the local level. It is ultimately the responsibility of the local society to promote and institutionalize gender equality, which requires long-term commitment, resources, empowerment, and partnerships with various groups in society.

In some instances, women explored unconventional ways to engage political leadership through advocacy, kinship, personal connections, and other methods available to foster an environment for ceasefire, disarmament, and the restoration of law and order. Somali women's cross-clan initiatives to promote dialogues for peace, and the cultivation of non-ethnic, non-clan based identity in the "sixth clan" movements are examples. These movements, however, did not influence in a major way the existing structural power base, the clan system. As a result, the status of gender relations in the Somali state structures is influenced by (1) power-sharing schemes based on existing social categories, (2) the decline of women's political mobilization and power after the agreements were signed, and (3) inadequate international support for the implementation of peace agreements. The case of Somalia underlines that the state-building models based on existing social categories could undermine the opportunity for women and men to gain new identities and political powers that are independent of traditional systems, and thus fail to remedy existing patterns of gender relations.

In contrast, women and gender equality was not incorporated in the institutional framework established by the peace process in Mozambique. The 30 percent representation of women in Mozambican politics derived from socialist structures and policies during the national liberation movement. The emancipation of women and gender equality, however, could be reversed by privatization and macroeconomic policies that do not take gender analysis into account. Thus, the case of Mozambique supports the essence of the critique presented by Roland Paris against the dominant "single paradigm" favoring the transition to a market economy and liberal democracy. The forces of the market economy, particularly the privatization of public goods, could be a major obstacle for gender equality in the future, as it reaffirms the old patterns of power relations and inequality by concentrating resources in the hands of the minority. Prior to embarking upon a transition to a market economy, the redistribution of resources, the elimination of inequality, and the installation of protection mechanisms that tackle the existing power asymmetry in political and economic arenas (which are often intrinsically linked) needs to take place.

The contrasting outcome of Mozambique and Somalia confirms the obvious: security, the rule of law, and a government apparatus must be in place to consolidate peacebuilding. Thus, as both Labonte and Ankersen suggest,[60] the deployment of multidimensional peacekeeping forces contributes to the stabilization of environments enabling the building of peace. Similarly, the cases highlight that gender equality should be an integral part of international political, operational, and technical assistance to postconflict societies, including electoral assistance, peacekeeping missions, and transitional aid for the reconstruction of governance.

Women's groups continue their pioneering work in difficult situations. They form support groups, generate environments conducive for reconciliation, and lead community development. Conflict resolution and peacebuilding provide a window of opportunity for social transformation, and the integration of gender equality into the design of emerging state and social structures. To this end, international assistance to women and gender mainstreaming needs to take place at the two levels: postconflict institutional framework and the structural base of power, so that (1) structural change takes place, particularly in power relations at all decision-making levels, and (2) the qualitative and quantitative equality of gender relations is promoted in the emerging governance frameworks. This requires long-term commitment to technical and operational assistance, cross-sectoral partnerships, outreach and advocacy. In addition, international approaches to peacebuilding, including macroeconomic policies and the financing of transitional and reconstruction aid, need to involve gender analysis as part of structural reforms toward equality.

Notes

1 United Nations Division for the Advancement of Women, "Beijing Declaration and Platform for Action," Strategic Objective E.1, http://www.un.org/womenwatch/daw/beijing/platform (accessed 28 November, 2003).

2 United Nations Security Council, Resolution SC/RES/1325/2000, http://www.un.org/events/res_1325e.pdf (accessed 28 November, 2003).

3 European Parliament, Resolution on the participation of women in peaceful conflict, Resolution 2000/2025 (INI), http://www3.europarl.eu.int (accessed 28 November 2003).

4 The author has been closely involved in the process leading up to and resulting from Resolution #1325, preparing background documents for the Security Council debates and the adoption of the resolution and as a member of the team assisting the UNIFEM-commissioned independent assessors. This article is largely informed

by the research, interviews, and field visits undertaken by the author during this time. This paper, however, is submitted in the author's personal capacity as a doctoral candidate and is not meant to reflect the views of UNIFEM or its experts' assessments.

5 The draft of the Secretary-General's study on women, peace and security (internal document, p. 58).

6 I. William Zartman, "Putting Things Back Together," in Zartman ed., *Collapsed States: The Disintegration and Restoration of Legitimate Authority* (Boulder, CO: Lynne Reinner, 1995), 267–73.

7 Swanee Hunt and Cristina Posa, "Women Waging Peace," *Foreign Policy* (May/June 2001), 46.

8 *Women at the Peace Table: Making a Difference* (New York: UNIFEM, March 2000), Preface.

9 *Getting it Right? A Gender Approach to UNMIK* (Sweden: The Kvinna till Kvinna Foundation, 11 May 2002).

10 Interview with International Crisis Group representatives covering Burundi, 16 January 2002.

11 Craig Calhoun, *Critical Social Theory: Culture, History and the Challenge of Difference* (Massachusetts: Blackwell Publishers, 1995), 171.

12 See Council of Europe, *Gender Mainstreaming: Conceptual Framework, Methodology and Presentation of Good Practices*, Final Report of Activities of the Group of Specialists on Mainstreaming, EG-S-MS (98) 2, Strasbourg (May 1998), 3.

13 Judith Large, "Disintegration Conflicts and the Restructuring of Masculinity," *Gender and Development* 5, no. 2 (June 1997), 25.

14 For instance, Rwanda's Minister for Women and Social Services, Aloysia Inyumba, is one of the eminent members of the Rwandan Patriotic Front. In February 1998, Inyumba was put in charge of building up a national RPF network of women's groups using funds for women's empowerment allocated to her ministry. *"Consensual Democracy" in Post-Genocide Rwanda: Evaluating the March 2001 District Elections*, ICG Africa Report No. 34 (October 2001), 7.

15 See *Getting it Right?* and also another report from the Kvinna till Kvinna Foundation, *Engendering the Peace Process. A Gender Approach to Dayton—and Beyond* (Sweden: The Kvinna till Kvinna Foundation, June 2000).

16 Testimonies of Roma women and women who are married to ethnic Serbians in Kosovo in interviews conducted in September 2000.

17 Astri Suhrke, Arve Ofstad and Are Knudsen, *A Decade of Peacebuilding: Lessons Learned for Afghanistan* (Oslo: Chr. Michelsen Institute, April 2002), 5.

18 The definition adopted by the UN Economic and Social Council, E.1997.L.10, 17 July 1997), §4.

19 Terrence Lyons, "The Role of Postsettlement Elections," in Stephen John Stedman, Donald Rothschild and Elizabeth M. Cousens, eds., *Ending Civil Wars: The Success and Failure of Negotiated Settlements in Civil War* (New York: International Peace Academy, September, 2002), 215–36.

20 Joni Lovenduski and Azza Karam, "The Effect of Electoral Systems on Women's Representation," *International IDEA Women in Politics: Women in Parliament* www.idea.int/women/parl/ch3c.htm (accessed 28 November, 2003).

21 First, proportional representation systems have a higher number of seats per district (higher district magnitude), which allows winning parties to go further down the party lists, where women are usually listed. Second, high electoral thresholds of proportional representation systems discourage the creation of "mini-parties" which can nominate only one or two representatives, usually male.

22 United Nations, *Report of the Panel on United Nations Peace Operations*, A/55/305-S/2000/809 (New York: The United Nations), 19; See also Mark Plunkett, "Reestablishing Law and Order in Peace-Maintenance," *Global Governance* 4, no. 1 (January–March 1998): 66.

23 Charles T. Call and William Stanley, "Civilian Security," in Stephen John Stedman, Donald Rothchild and Elizabeth Cousens, eds., *Ending Civil Wars: The Implementation of Peace Agreements* (Boulder, CO: Lynne Reinner, 2002), 303–26.

24 Call and Stanley, "Civilian Security," 306–7.

25 Federation of South African Women, "Women's Struggle in the African National Congress," Women's Charter, http://www.anc.org.za/ancdocs/history/women/wcharter.html (accessed 28 November 2003); "Women and the Reconstruction of East Timor," *The La'o Hamutuk Bulletin* 2, no. 5 (August, 2001), The East Timor Institute for Reconstruction Monitoring and Analysis, http://www.etan.org/lh/bulletins/bulletinv2n5.html (accessed on 28 November, 2003).

26 Reports of the United Nations Development Fund for Women (UNIFEM), including: *A New Gender Sensitive Constitution for Rwanda* (Kigali: UNIFEM, June 2001); *Draft proposal: Strengthening Gender Justice in Post-Conflict Peace Building* (New York: UNIFEM, July 2001); *A Climate of Fear: Gender in the 1993 Cambodian General Elections* (Bangkok: UNIFEM, October 2000).

27 Susan Woodward cited in Astri Suhrke, Arve Ofstad and Are Knudsen, *A Decade of Peacebuilding*, 48.

28 Susana Lastarria-Cornhiel, "Privatization of Land Rights and Access to Factor Markets: a Path to Gender Equity?" (Paper presented at the Agrarian Reform and Rural Development: Taking Stock Conference, sponsored by the Social Research Center, American University, Cairo, October 2001).

29 The Commonwealth Secretariat, *Gender Management System Handbook* (June 1999), http://www.thecommonwealth.org/gender (accessed 28 November 2003).

30 The East Timor Combined Sources Budget 2002–2003, Budget Paper No. 1, Draft (pending final clearance of text by council of ministers, 7 May 2002).

31 UNMIK Kosovo Consolidated Budget for 2000, www.seerecon.org/Kosovo/UNMIK/Budget2001/index.html (accessed 28 November, 2003).

32 UNMIK Kosovo Consolidated Budget for 2000.

33 Brigitte Sorensen, *Women and Post-Conflict Reconstruction: Issues and Sources*, War-torn Society Project Report (Geneva: UN Research Institute for Social Development, 1 June 1998), http://www.unrisd.org/wsp/op3/op3-03.htm (accessed 15 June, 2000).

34 The Secretary-General's report to the Security Council on 17 August 1994 noted that conflicts within the dominant Hawiye clan (to which General Farah Aidid belonged) constituted the major obstacle to national reconciliation.

35 "Somalia: Supporting Local Capacities for Peace," in *People Building Peace: 35 Inspiring Stories from around the World* (The Netherlands: The European Centre for Conflict Prevention, 1999), 201.

36 Sixty Somalis from various parts of the country as well as from the diaspora, all invited in their individual capacities, attended the symposium. Somalia: *IRIN Guide to the Somali National Peace Conference* (UN Office for the Coordination of Humanitarian Affairs: Integrated Regional Information Networks, 2000), http://www.reliefweb.int/IRIN/cea/coutnrystories/somalia/20000630a.phtml (accessed 3 April, 2001).

37 Article 31 states: "Structure of the State: The Structure of the State shall be decentralized and shall consist of a) Central Authority, b) Regional and District Authorities, c) Authority of Independent Agencies"; Article 38 sates: "Formation of Security and Defense Forces; Every region of the country shall form its own police force with adequate capacity to maintain law and order" (Transitional National Charter, adopted at Arta, Djibouti, July 2000).

38 United Nations Development fund for Women, *Somalia Between Peace and War* (Nairobi: UNIFEM, 1998), 51.

39 Ameen Jan, "Somalia: Building Sovereignty or Restoring Peace?" in Elizabeth M. Cousens and Chetan Kumar ed., *Peacebuilding as Politics: Cultivating Peace in Fragile Societies* (New York: International Peace Academy, 2001), 68–69.

40 UNDP, *Governance Foundations for Post-Conflict Situations: UNDP's Experience* (New York: UNDP, January 2000), 75.

41 Ameen Jan, "Building Sovereignty," 78.

42 *Consolidated Inter-Agency Appeal for Somalia 2002* (UN Office for the Coordination of Humanitarian Affairs, 26 November 2001), www.reliefweb.int (accessed 30 November, 2003).

43 There are over 100 international and local aid agencies currently working in Somalia. In the year 2000, more than US $115 million from donors was given to aid projects in Somalia. The Somali Aid Coordination Body (SACB) is the umbrella group for assistance to Somalia, and is comprised of UN agencies, nongovernmental organizations, and donors.

44 Interview, Somalia, September 2001.

45 Bridget Byrne, Rachel Marcus and Tanya Powers-Stevens, *Gender, Conflict and Development: Volume II: Case Studies: Cambodia, Rwanda, Kosovo, Algeria, Somalia, Guatemala and Eritrea* (Brighton: Institute of Development Studies, July 1996), 97.

46 Asha Hagi Elmi, email message to author, 12 August 2002.

47 Notes from the field visit to Somalia, September 2001.

48 Ruth Jacobson, *Gender and Democratization: the Mozambican Election of 1994* (Bradford, UK: University of Bradford, Department of Peace Studies, 1996), www.brad.ac.uk/research/ijas/rjijasel.htm (accessed 17 April, 2001).

49 Natalina Teixeira Monteiro, "The War of Liberation/Frelimo. Mozambique: Women in the Informal Sector" (Unpublished Research Paper presented at Northern Arizona University, 2001), http://dana.ucc.nau.edu/~nm5/Independence.html (accessed 4 June, 2001).

50 Sally Baden, *Post-Conflict Mozambique: Women's Special Situations, Issue and Gender Perspectives to be Integrated into Skills Training and Employment Promotion* (Geneva:

International Labor Organization, 1997). The text is electronically available at www.ilo.org/public/english/employment/skills/training/publ/pub7.htm (accessed 30 November 2003).

51 Mozambique ranks 144th among 146 countries for Gender-related Development Index (GDI), which adjusts the average achievement of each country in life expectancy, literacy and gross enrolment, and income in accordance with the disparity in achievement between men and women, and 170th among 173 in the Gender Empowerment Measure. It is made up of two dimensions: (1) Economic participation and decision-making is measured by the percentage of female administrators and managers, and professional and technical workers; and (2) Political participation and decision-making are measured by the percentage of seats in parliament held by women. Power over economic resources is measured by women's estimated earned income (PPP US$).

52 Rachel Waterhouse, "Women's Land Rights in Post-war Mozambique," paper presented at the Inter-Regional Consultation in Kigali, Rwanda, February 1998, 3.

53 Rachel Waterhouse, "Women's Land Rights," 4.

54 Sally Baden, *Post-Conflict Mozambique*, 64.

55 *Gender, Women and Human Development: An Agenda for the Future* (United Nations Development Program: National Human Development Report on Mozambique, 2002), 56.

56 Sally Baden, *Post-Conflict Mozambique*, 78.

57 Sally Baden, *Post-Conflict Mozambique*, 78.

58 For the summary of the action plan, see the UN Division for the Advancement of Women site at http://www.un.org/womenwatch/confer/beijing/national/africsum.htm (accessed 30 November 2003).

59 *Gender, women and human development*, 53.

60 See Melissa Labonte in this volume (chapter 3); see also Christopher P. Ankersen (chapter 4).

8 West Africa's Tragic Twins

Adekeye Adebajo

BUILDING PEACE IN LIBERIA AND SIERRA LEONE

THIS ESSAY EXAMINES the peacebuilding role of the Economic Community of West African States (ECOWAS)[1] and other international actors in building peace in Liberia and Sierra Leone between 1990 and 2001. It begins by providing the background to the civil wars in the two countries and discusses the interrelationship that exists between them, before going on to describe some of the political and economic motives for waging war and assessing the role of subregional actors within ECOWAS, as well as that of two important external actors: the US and Britain. The efficacy of various peacebuilding tasks and tools employed in Liberia and Sierra Leone is evaluated, including disarmament, social, economic and humanitarian assistance and transitional elections. The essay then examines the nature of peacebuilding in post-1997 Liberia, the prospects for peacebuilding in postwar Sierra Leone, and Charles Taylor's attempts at destabilizing the West African subregion. The conclusion analyzes some of the lessons learned and mistakes made in the two West African cases, and offer policy recommendations to remedy these errors in future peacebuilding efforts.

Liberia and Sierra Leone are West Africa's tragic twins. Both have endured almost a decade of civil wars that resulted in nearly 250,000 deaths and the spilling across borders of over one million refugees.

The ECOWAS Ceasefire Monitoring Group's (ECOMOG) involvement in Sierra Leone's civil war was inextricably linked to its eight-year peacekeeping efforts in neighboring Liberia's civil war. The Revolutionary United Front (RUF) invaded Sierra Leone from Liberia in March 1991 with the assistance of Charles Taylor's National Patriotic Front of Liberia (NPFL). ECOMOG's role in Sierra Leone increased exponentially after the late Nigerian autocrat, General Sani Abacha, diverted peacekeepers from their mission in Liberia (which was drawing to a close) to Sierra Leone in an attempt to crush a military coup by the Sierra Leone Army (SLA) in Freetown in May 1997. ECOMOG reversed the coup in February 1998 and restored the elected president, Ahmed Tejan Kabbah, to power. However, the unsuccessful but devastating rebel invasion of Freetown in January 1999 showed that ECOMOG was unable to eliminate the rebels as a military threat. ECOMOG's ill-equipped and poorly-funded peacekeeping mission[2] was unable to defeat rebels in guerrilla warfare. As a result, the military stalemate forced political accommodation and the appeasement of local warlords.

Liberia's civil war lasted from December 1989 to early 1997 and was fought mainly by eight factions.[3] The largest, the NPFL, was led by Charles Taylor and consisted largely of ethnic Gios and Manos. Two factions broke off from the NPFL: the Independent National Patriotic Front of Liberia (INPFL) and the NPFL-Central Revolutionary Council (CRC). The Armed Forces of Liberia was the remnant of murdered Liberian autocrat Samuel Doe's Krahn-dominated army. The United Liberation Movement of Liberia for Democracy (ULIMO) split into two factions, with Roosevelt Johnson, a Krahn, heading ULIMO-J, while Alhaji Kromah, a Mandingo, headed ULIMO-K. George Boley headed the Krahn-dominated Liberia Peace Council (LPC). Francois Massaquoi, an indigene from Lofa County, headed the Lofa Defence Force (LDF).

Sierra Leone's civil war lasted from March 1991 until a ceasefire in July 1999, when the UN mission in Sierra Leone (UNAMSIL) took over ECOMOG's peacekeeping duties.[4] The RUF attacked UN peacekeepers in May 2000, leading to the arrest of its leader, Corporal Foday Sankoh. Between May 1997 and February 1998, the rebels formed an alliance with the putschist Sierra Leone army under Major Johnny Paul Koromah to form the ruling Armed Forces Revolutionary Council (AFRC). The relationship between Sankoh and Charles Taylor was cemented by the exchange of Sierra Leonean diamonds for the NPFL's arms and men.

In both Liberia and Sierra Leone, the largest factions (the NPFL and RUF) aimed to win military victory and inherit the state by controlling its political institutions. In both countries, battles were fought for control of areas rich in economic resources such as diamonds, timber, rubber and iron ore. Taylor derived an estimated $75 million annually from these exports, including $10 million a month from a consortium of North American, Japanese and European miners,[5] as well as $300,000 a month from foreign timber firms.[6] ULIMO-K was keen to restore the Mandingo's diamond trading links with Sierra Leone, from which it had been excluded in March 1991. ULIMO-J was involved in diamond mining in Bomi County, while the LPC exported rubber from Buchanan port.[7] In Sierra Leone, RUF rebels and rogue military officers and units controlled an estimated $250 million annual diamond trade.[8]

In Liberia, the legitimacy of the warlords was based on building ethnic support. Some populations supported the factions only to secure protection from attacks launched by other ethnic groups. However, territory did not always conform neatly to ethnic coalitions. While the brutality of Liberia's factions was directed at rival factions or ethnic groups, the horrific violence of the RUF, including the severing of limbs, decapitation and the mutilation of bodies, was often indiscriminate. Both wars witnessed widespread human rights abuses and atrocities.[9] Underfed and underpaid soldiers, many of whom were drug-induced children, were often only nominally controlled by their leaders.[10]

An intricate network of personal relationships and shifting alliances often determined the policies of individual states towards the conflicts in Liberia and Sierra Leone. The NPFL was backed initially by Côte d'Ivoire, Burkina Faso and Libya. In Liberia, Sierra Leone and Guinea backed ULIMO, while Nigeria provided military assistance to the AFL and LPC. Nigeria, Ghana, and Guinea supported successive beleaguered governments in Freetown against the RUF, while Nigeria provided military assistance to the *Kamajors*.

Nigeria provided at least 80 percent of ECOMOG's troops and 90 percent of its funding during both military interventions in Liberia and Sierra Leone, thus effectively determining ECOMOG's policies. Historically, Nigeria's military leaders have been keen to portray their country as the indispensable power in West Africa in pursuit of a *Pax Nigeriana*.[11] They were concerned about the impact of the civil war on the stability of the subregion and on ECOWAS, an economic integration scheme launched with strong Nigerian leadership in 1975. Nigeria remained involved in Liberia and Sierra Leone in part because its generals personally benefited from revenues written off as ECOMOG expenses, and because the ECOMOG mission helped the Nigerian leader, General Sani Abacha, to ward off the threat of severe international sanctions against his regime. By restoring democracy in Liberia and Sierra Leone, Nigeria's late autocrat sought to portray himself as a good international citizen, without seeming to realize the irony of denying democracy to his own people.

Following Abacha's death in June 1998, a democratic transition in Nigeria led to the withdrawal of about 8,500 of its 12,000 peacekeepers from Sierra Leone. The remaining Nigerian troops were subsumed under a new UN peacekeeping mission. Faced with enormous socio-economic problems and buckling under constraints from an increasingly isolationist public and cantankerous parliament, the civilian regime of Olusegun Obasanjo was no longer prepared to pay $1 million a day and suffer hundreds of fatalities.

Though both ECOMOG interventions are often erroneously portrayed as a bid for hegemonic domination by Nigeria,[12] several ECOWAS states also had their own interests in supporting ECOMOG. Gambian dissidents fought with the NPFL in Liberia, and the unsuccessful

1981 coup in Gambia was widely believed to have been sponsored by NPFL ally, Libya. Guinea, Côte d'Ivoire, and Sierra Leone were eventually flooded with about 750,000 Liberian refugees. Fighting from Liberia and Sierra Leone spilled over into Guinea, while Liberian factions made border incursions into Côte d'Ivoire. The NPFL had Sierra Leonean dissidents within its ranks who launched a decade-long civil war from Liberia. Guinean and Sierra Leonean soldiers fought alongside ULIMO against the NPFL in Liberia, while Guinean troops fought with ECOMOG in Sierra Leone mainly in areas near the common border between both countries. Approximately 500,000 Sierra Leonean refugees spilled into Guinea and Liberia, and after being elected president of Liberia in July 1997, Charles Taylor continued to support the RUF against the elected government and subregional peacekeepers. Between 1999 and 2001, Guinea backed former ULIMO rebels (Liberians United for Reconciliation and Democracy—LURD), who launched incursions into Liberia. Charles Taylor also supported armed dissidents in Guinea.

The United States, who in the 1980s was the major external Cold War ally of Liberia's autocrat, Samuel Doe, abandoned the Liberian leader to his fate when the civil war erupted in December 1989. With the end of the Cold War, Washington perceived little strategic interest in the country and was, furthermore, distracted by the annexation of Kuwait by Iraq. The US contributed $500 million in humanitarian assistance to Liberia during the civil war, but did not support ECOMOG substantially until the end of the mission. Britain, the former colonial power, has been the most influential external actor in Sierra Leone, mobilizing international support for peace-building efforts. Britain, like the US, lent mostly diplomatic and humanitarian assistance to ECOMOG's peacekeeping efforts, and desisted from playing a direct military role in Sierra Leone. Both interventions in Liberia and Sierra Leone illustrated the growing indifference of external actors to African conflicts in the post-Cold War era, and the rising influence of regional actors. What follows is an examination of three areas of peacebuilding in Liberia and Sierra

Leone in which the international community was involved: (1) disarmament, demobilization and reintegration; (2) humanitarian assistance; and (3) electoral support.

ECOMOG's commitment to disarming Liberia's factions was aided tremendously by international assistance. During the fierce factional fighting in Monrovia in April 1996 that resulted in 3,000 deaths,[13] the US helped to create the International Contact Group on Liberia to identify how international actors could assist Liberia and ECOMOG. Between August and December 1996, Washington released $40 million for helicopters, communication equipment, uniforms and medical equipment. This, along with the arrival of EU assistance, gave the peacekeepers the logistical support to deploy confidently to the countryside for the first time since the start of their mission. The Minister for Development Cooperation of the Netherlands, Jan Pronk, launched a fundraising drive in October 1996 that culminated in three donor conferences that eventually provided the vital funds to support Liberia's disarmament, demobilization, and electoral process.[14] The British-led International Contact Group on Sierra Leone has also been useful in helping to raise funds for Sierra Leone's postwar reconstruction.

The disarmament process in Liberia started on schedule on 22 November 1996. Fighters were given food rations and provided with transportation to chosen destinations in exchange for the surrender of a serviceable weapon or a hundred rounds of ammunition. The second Abuja accord of 1996 did not provide even small assistance packages for former combatants. Despite these difficulties, Liberia's factions largely cooperated with disarmament drives. By 9 February 1997, an estimated 74 percent of the fighters had been disarmed and demobilized. Over 9,570 weapons and 1.2 million pieces of ammunition were also surrendered, while ECOMOG's cordon-and-search operations around the country yielded another 122,162 pieces of ammunition and 917 weapons.[15] There were, however, reports of arms caches hidden away in parts of the Liberian countryside.[16]

The UN Observer Mission in Liberia (UNOMIL) sent 368 unarmed military observers to Liberia in 1994 and about 100 of them assisted ECOMOG's disarmament efforts, investigating ceasefire violations and verifying arms and ammunition collections by ECOMOG. Tensions between ECOMOG and UNOMIL had hampered earlier disarmament efforts. ECOMOG soldiers often complained that UNOMIL withheld its vehicles and helicopters from their use. UN personnel were paid much higher stipends than ECOMOG's, a fact that fuelled further envy.[17] Four other disagreements emerged between the peacekeepers: first, ECOMOG wanted UNOMIL to have a passive rather than a leading role in disarmament; second, ECOMOG officials were angered by what they regarded as UN Special Representative Trevor Gordon-Somers' unilateral disarmament negotiations with the parties; third, in contrast to UNOMIL's Chief Military Observer, Kenyan General Daniel Opande, ECOMOG's Field Commander, Nigerian General John Inienger, distrusted the NPFL's commitment to disarmament; and finally, ECOMOG criticized UNOMIL for its failure to consult with it before deploying its troops.[18] Similar problems were reported in Sierra Leone.

Following the signing of the Lomé agreement with Sierra Leone's parties in July 1999, there were major difficulties in the implementation of the agreement. Fighting occurred between the RUF and its former Armed Forces Ruling Council (AFRC) allies and between the RUF and CDF; the rebels held ECOMOG and UN peacekeepers hostage, some of the peacekeepers were killed, and their freedom of movement was restricted.[19] Between 18 May 2001 and the end of disarmament on 17 January 2002, the 47,706 fighters were finally disarmed after UN peacekeepers took a firmer military stance against RUF intransigence. Despite the apparent success of disarmament in Sierra Leone, both the government and rebels in Liberia began recruiting some of Sierra Leone's disarmed fighters.[20]

As civil administration and social services collapsed and the economy declined during their respective civil wars, Liberia and Sierra Leone depended on the UN and various NGOs to provide humanitarian assistance. In Liberia, the WFP, EU and UNDP established a Civil Reconstruction Team bridging program to support demobilization. The UN spent $3.3 million on bridging activities: the UNDP's 110 public works projects created 10,000 jobs for civilians and ex-fighters, while the UN Humanitarian Coordination Office funded 44 projects involving 8,352 temporary jobs. The EU's 128 microprojects also provided short-term employment for nearly 8,000 civilians and ex-combatants. Some 30,000 former fighters and civilians had benefited from the short-term employment and training opportunities by June 1997. But such efforts proved short-lived and the emergence of a second armed rebellion reversed many of these gains.

In Sierra Leone, the office of the UN High Commissioner for Refugees helped in the repatriation of 68,698 refugees to Sierra Leone from Liberia and Guinea. UNICEF reunited 3,000 children with their families. UNDP has been involved in establishing a Small Arms Trust Fund to help Sierra Leone's police curb the scourge of illegal arms flows. The WFP and an assortment of NGOs were also involved in providing emergency relief particularly to Sierra Leone's rural population. Much more humanitarian assistance will still be needed, however, if the country is to return to a functioning state.

On 7 April 1997, Liberia's Independent Elections Commission and the Supreme Court were installed in Monrovia. Three weeks later, an ECOWAS Foreign Ministers' delegation met with the Elections Commission and Liberia's political parties to discuss the draft electoral law, the electoral timetable and the Elections Commission's budget. A budget of $5.4 million was approved and ECOWAS decided to assume greater responsibility for the physical and logistical aspects of the electoral process.

ECOWAS' assertiveness in organizing Liberia's elections reflected the tension that pervaded the electoral preparations. Following tense bilateral relations between Washington and the military junta in Abuja, Nigeria was keen not to allow external actors to steal the glory for ending the Liberian war. A minimum $100,000 levy was imposed on ECOWAS members to help pay for the elections and to raise $1.5 million on top of the $5.4 million approved earlier for the electoral process. ECOWAS and the UN established a Joint Electoral Coordination Mechanism that met regularly with Liberia's Elections Commission to discuss operational and other issues related to electoral preparations. In June 1997, the United States contributed $7.4 million for Liberia's elections, and the EU funded civic education programs and paid election workers.

Liberia's elections were held on 19 July 1997, with ECOMOG providing security at the 1,864 voting stations and 500 international observers observing the poll.[21] Charles Taylor scored a landslide victory with 75.3 percent of the presidential vote. Taylor's National Patriotic Party also won 21 of the 26 Senate seats and 49 of the 64 seats in the House of Representatives. An impressive 85 percent of the 750,000 registered voters turned out to cast their ballots on polling day. ECOWAS and the UN issued a joint statement declaring the elections "free and fair." There were some logistical and technical deficiencies: voter education had been inadequate; no census was conducted; and ballot secrecy was sometimes compromised by assistance given to illiterate voters. But these difficulties were expected after seven years of civil war in the first election in twelve years.

Sierra Leone held parliamentary and presidential elections on 14 May 2002.[22] Nine candidates contested the presidency, which the incumbent Ahmed Tejan Kabbah comfortably won with a landslide 70 percent majority in the first round. His SLPP party also won a parliamentary majority. The RUFP, the political party of the former rebels, performed abysmally at the polls. The US-based National Democratic Institute and the UK-based Westminster Foundation for Democracy provided support to strengthen political parties, while the UN, ECOWAS and the OAU electoral observers declared the elections "free and fair."

Taylor's government inherited a national treasury that contained only $17,000, a domestic debt of $200 million, and an external debt of $3 billion.[23] His first years in office were difficult financially and marred by controversy over human rights violations.[24] The UN established its first peacebuilding support office in Liberia after the 1997 elections to coordinate postconflict programs and to promote international support for Liberia's reconstruction efforts, but foreign assistance trickled rather than flooded in.

Felix Downes-Thomas, the UN Special Representative in Liberia, became deeply unpopular with Liberian civil society groups who accused him of being too close to Taylor's regime. Downes-Thomas argued that his mandate was to mobilize support for the regime to recover from its civil war rather than to criticize it. As an internal UN report of July 2001 admitted, the UN peacebuilding office was poorly resourced and its mandate was weak and not politically intrusive due to the initial reluctance of the UN Security Council to establish the office. The Liberian government accepted the office in the full knowledge that the UN would not interfere with its running of the country.[25]

Liberia's National Reconstruction Program (NRP) sought $433 million over the first two post-election years and aimed to revive government institutions, provide essential social services, rehabilitate public infrastructure, protect civil liberties as well as national and personal security, repatriate refugees and internally displaced persons, reintegrate demobilized fighters back into society and provide them with increased employment opportunities.[26] Many of these plans remain unfulfilled. This response was similar to the failure of donors to deliver on pledges of $232 million in Sierra Leone after the signing of the Abidjan Agreement in 1996.[27]

Taylor cracked down on Liberia's opposition groups and attempted to institutionalize his domination of the Liberian state. Former Taylor ally and later opponent, Sam Dokie, as well as members of his family were brutally murdered in November 1997. Journalists have been harassed and jailed for criticizing the government. Two radio stations and four newspapers were closed down. Most opposition politicians went into exile.

Until Charles Taylor agreed to leave office in 2003, Liberia's security situation remained precarious and contained many lessons for postwar Sierra Leone. Rebellion, armed robbery, and banditry thrived in rural Liberia. Crime and insecurity plagued Monrovia. The mobilization of armed ethnicity in support of the agendas of rival warlords during the civil war continued to strain the country. A shooting incident involving ULIMO-J's former Krahn leader, Roosevelt Johnson, led to 52 deaths and the flight of over 4,000 Krahn to Côte d'Ivoire.[28] Mandingos have been violently attacked by Lorma in Lofa County and by Gios and Manos in Nimba County in clashes over land and resources as refugees return to areas abandoned during the civil war. Some of the land reform or redistribution measures and the extension of agricultural credit that UN peacebuilders implemented in El Salvador between 1991 and 1995 may have to be considered in both Liberia and Sierra Leone.

A linked tale of insecurity can be told about Liberia's neighbors. Fighting in Sierra Leone in September 1997 forced 200,000 refugees to flood into Liberia. In an outbreak of violence that signified the start of Liberia's second protracted civil war, Liberian dissidents invaded the towns of Voinjama and Kolahun in Lofa County in 1999. A group calling itself Liberians United for Reconciliation and Democracy (LURD) launched these attacks from Guinea. It is thought that the group consisted mostly of Mandingo and Krahn fighters of the former ULIMO-K and ULIMO-J militias. Since May 1999, Taylor-backed RUF rebels have launched attacks into Guinea, destroying property and lives.[29] The relationship between Liberia and Guinea worsened following renewed attacks into Lofa country by LURD rebels between July and November 2000, forcing thousands of refugees to flee the area. Taylor's continued military support for RUF rebels led to friction with the peacekeepers. ECOMOG, frequently criticized by Taylor for being an external army of occupation, finally withdrew its peacekeepers from Liberia by the end of 1998. Taylor included many of his former NPFL fighters in the new Liberian army and created the notorious Anti-Terrorist Unit (ATU) as a private army directly under his command. By filling the army with ethnic loyalists and using it as a tool against political opponents, Taylor created conditions for the mobilization of ethnic groups to protect their own people against a partisan army. The institutionalization of violence as a way of life that had been a hallmark of the Doe era was further entrenched during Liberia's savage civil war.[30]

Most of Taylor's opponents viewed the state apparatus as an extension of his own personal power. This created potential conditions for the breakdown of law and order. Events in postwar Liberia paralleled those in prewar Liberia: widespread insecurity, a weak economy, patronage-fuelled corruption, harassment of the press and civic groups, interethnic clashes, and trumped-up coup plots. The lack of security and of the rule of law made donors cautious and kept away foreign investors. Liberian diamonds continued to be smuggled out of the country,[31] and there were accusations of lucrative contracts being awarded to Taylor's close political associates.

A donor conference for Liberia's reconstruction that was held in Paris in April 1998 led to pledges of $200 million, but these funds were made conditional on progress in the areas of security and human rights, and were not disbursed because of the government's poor human rights record. Little of Liberia's infrastructure was restored and the promised provision of social services did not occur. Taylor maintained close political relations with Burkina Faso and Libya and sought to court Taiwanese and French investors, but traditional trading partners like the US, Japan and Germany continue to stay away.

Amidst these domestic difficulties, Taylor faced unprecedented external pressure. In March 2001, the UN Security Council demanded that Liberia halt the importation of Sierra Leonean diamonds, end Liberian support for the RUF and pressure the rebels to allow the UN mission in Sierra Leone access to rebel-controlled territory. On 7 May 2001, the UN Security Council imposed a ban on the export of diamonds from Liberia and placed travel sanctions on senior government officials and their spouses. The Council also tightened an existing arms embargo by prohibiting the sale or supply of arms and related material to Liberia and banning the provision of military training to the government. These sanctions were renewed in May 2002.

In order for the UN sanctions to be effective, it was important for the Security Council to secure ECOWAS' cooperation for this approach. The diamond sanctions were not watertight, since Liberian gems were easily smuggled through third countries. Furthermore, no effective enforcement mechanism existed on the ground. France and China, who together import about 45 percent of Liberia's timber, blocked more devastating economic sanctions on Liberia's $13 million annual timber trade in the UN Security Council.[32] However, the sanctions clearly rattled Taylor, forcing him to reduce support for the RUF, and weakening his ability to fight the LURD. Eventually, the pressure from the international community— particularly from the US—forced Taylor to resign and go into exile.

Even as Liberia's security situation worsened, Sierra Leone's internal problems were ameliorated by the introduction of a large UN peacekeeping presence in the country. On 19 August 1999, Nigeria's President Obasanjo wrote to UN Secretary-General, Kofi Annan, informing him of Nigeria's intention to withdraw the bulk of its peacekeepers from Sierra Leone. Annan, strongly supported by Britain, suggested to the Security Council that a United Nations peacekeeping Mission in Sierra Leone (UNAMSIL) should take over from ECOMOG under the leadership of the Indian Force Commander, General Vijay Jetley.[33] The UN mission in Sierra Leone was established and its costs totalled $692 million annually.

The peacekeepers soon faced problems as Foday Sankoh employed "spoiler" tactics to frustrate the UN. Sankoh complained that RUF members were not being appointed to government positions as agreed at Lomé.[34] The RUF prevented the deployment of UN peacekeepers to the diamond-rich eastern provinces and attacked UN peacekeepers, holding them hostage, killing some of them, and seizing their heavy weapons and vehicles.[35] UNAMSIL also experienced its own internal problems. A UN assessment mission sent to Sierra Leone in June 2000 found serious managerial problems in UNAMSIL and a lack of common understanding of the mandate and rules of engagement. The mission also noted that some of UNAMSIL's military units lacked proper training and equipment.[36]

A confidential report written by General Jetley was published in the international press in September 2000, accusing senior Nigerian military and political officials of attempting to sabotage the UN mission in Sierra Leone by colluding with the RUF rebels to prolong the conflict. No evidence was provided for the allegations. Nigeria refused to put its peacekeepers under Jetley's command and India subsequently announced the withdrawal of its entire 3,000-strong contingent from Sierra Leone.

Following its humiliation, UNAMSIL responded more forcefully against the RUF in July 2000 by freeing some of its hostages in Kailahun, recapturing the strategic town of Masiaka, and clearing illegal checkpoints from Occra hills.[37] A brief British military intervention helped stabilize the situation in Freetown and its environs. Following the difficulties with the RUF, Nigeria, Ghana and Senegal sent a 3,000-strong American-trained rapid reaction force to Sierra Leone.

Recognizing the importance of a long-term strategy for the survival of Sierra Leone's civilian government and keen to devise an "exit strategy," two external peacekeepers have promoted security sector reform in Sierra Leone.[38] Nigeria helped to train officers for a new 8,500-strong Sierra Leonean army, and Britain played the lead role in training the army and police in Sierra Leone.

There are parallels between the Lomé peace settlement in Sierra Leone and that of Abuja in Liberia. Both were basically efforts to appease local warlords by giving them political power in exchange for military peace. Both agreements were an open invitation for warlords to enjoy the spoils of office in a giant jumble sale of the national wares. In both cases, few alternatives existed once ECOMOG, and particularly Nigeria, had made it clear that it was no longer willing to continue to sacrifice men and money. Under these circumstances, Liberian and Sierra Leonean politicians were forced to seek a political solution that inevitably left them at the mercy of wealthy armed warlords. Though civil society groups played important roles in mediation efforts, they were unable to break the military grip of warlords on their countries.[39]

It is important that some of the lessons learned from these peacebuilding cases be applied to future peacebuilding efforts, particularly in the African context. We offer five key lessons from these two cases:

First, regional peacekeepers in West Africa and other parts of Africa must be provided, in a timely manner, with the logistical and financial resources they need if such missions are to achieve their goals. The Liberian case revealed that if external actors provide these resources and funds, and if there is a will on the part of the parties to disarm their factions, even a poorly resourced regional body can achieve some success. The presence of unarmed UN peacekeepers in Liberia was insufficient, and the UN decided to subsume some of the regional peacekeepers under its own command in Sierra Leone. Former UN Secretary-General Boutros Boutros-Ghali had proposed the same solution for Liberia in 1995. The UN Security Council rejected the proposal, since after debacles in Somalia (1993) and Rwanda (1994), the Council was reluctant to approve new UN missions in Africa.

Second, the cases of Liberia and Sierra Leone show that the role of Nigeria and other aspiring regional hegemons in peacekeeping missions must be carefully considered if resolutions to local conflicts are not to be unduly delayed. While regional powers like Nigeria are often indispensable, their actions can also arouse fear and suspicion among local and subregional actors. ECOWAS leaders have recognized the need to establish decision-making institutions and to ensure broader participation in subregional peacekeeping by signing a Protocol on Conflict Prevention at its summit in Lomé in December 1999.[40] The introduction of UN and OAU peacekeepers from outside West Africa into Liberia was a conscious attempt to dilute the Nigerian dominance of ECOMOG and to reassure local actors of the peacekeepers' impartiality.

The UN peacekeeping mission in Sierra Leone, with its sizeable Bangladeshi and Kenyan contingents, signified a new, innovative approach to UN peacekeeping in Africa based on regional pillars supported by local hegemons. By placing largely regional forces under the UN flag, the hope is that the peacekeepers will enjoy the legitimacy and impartiality that the UN's universal membership offers, while some of the financial and logistical problems of regional peacekeepers can be resolved through greater burden-sharing. These new missions should also be more accountable.[41]

Third, any successful postconflict strategy must be subregional and take into account the interconnectedness of the conflicts in West Africa. Liberia's civil war spilled into Sierra Leone, Côte d'Ivoire and Guinea, subregional governments backed various warring factions, and most significantly, warlords in Liberia and Sierra Leone assisted each other through supplying fighters, trafficking arms and smuggling diamonds. Ways must be found to support ECOWAS in its efforts to channel resources to joint commercial and infrastructural projects that link countries in the region together to promote peaceful cooperation. To this effect, the establishment of a new UN office in West Africa to support ECOWAS and civil society groups in their security, development and democratization efforts is a welcome development.

Fourth, the UN and its agencies, along with international NGOs, must continue to provide the humanitarian assistance to beleaguered civilians during civil wars such as those in Liberia and Sierra Leone. Despite ECOWAS' ambitions to play such a role, the resources are simply not available in a subregion that contains some of the poorest countries in the world. ECOMOG should restrict itself mainly to supporting peacekeeping and providing security to relief convoys traveling to volatile parts of the countryside, as it did in Liberia and Sierra Leone.

Finally, the donor conferences that provided crucial electoral and postconflict assistance in Liberia and Sierra Leone must continue to mobilize resources in support of peacebuilding in both countries. In Sierra Leone, funding must be provided for transforming the RUF into a genuine opposition political party, as was done with RENAMO in Mozambique. Though programs were developed in Liberia to provide jobs for demobilized fighters and to reintegrate them into their local communities, these were mostly short-term programs. This error must be avoided in Sierra Leone. The political problems of the Taylor regime in Monrovia (including his indictment by an international criminal tribunal for war crimes committed in Sierra Leone) caused the international community to withhold the financial assistance needed in Liberia. The result was increased crime and continued instability within Liberia that spilled over into neighboring territories. Local civil society groups must also be supported in efforts to entrench peace.

We offer four policy recommendations for international efforts to bring peace to West Africa: First, the UN Security Council must provide timely support and resources to UNAMSIL troops in Sierra Leone, and avoid a precipitous withdrawal of the 17,500 peacekeepers that could create a destabilizing security vacuum.

Second, the international community must provide the resources necessary to restructure Sierra Leone's new army and other security forces and to fund the Special Court and the Truth and Reconciliation Commission. It is crucial for future stability that a truly national army and police force be created that includes equitable regional and factional representation and that enjoys the confidence of the population. The government in Sierra Leone needs security forces that are capable of defending democratic institutions from internally and externally inspired threats. A Truth and Reconciliation Commission was called for in the Lomé agreement of July 1999, along with a controversial amnesty for war crimes. Many Sierra Leoneans consider the confession of crimes by perpetrators and the offering of testimonies by victims, as well as the documentation of evidence of war crimes committed since 1991 as vital components of an attempt at national reconciliation. A war-weary Sierra Leonean population has, however, mainly backed the forgiveness of rebels as a necessary sacrifice for peace. Aside from the Truth Commission, a Special Court will try former RUF leader Foday Sankoh and other alleged violators of human rights. This court must be established with the utmost transparency. Many Sierra Leoneans have questioned the wisdom of putting scarce resources into a court to try war criminals rather than into a fund to rehabilitate war victims and develop the country.

It will be crucial to establish fair and transparent criteria for determining potential war criminals if the Special Court is to avoid accusations of undertaking a witch-hunt against the RUF. Members of other factions who committed human rights abuses must also be tried if the Court is to have any legitimacy. The court has now received enough funds for the first year of its work, while the Truth Commission is yet to receive adequate funding. The fact that these funds are voluntary contributions rather than compulsory UN assessments leaves these two bodies vulnerable to the changing priorities of capricious external donors.

Third, international efforts to cut off the illicit flow of diamonds to world markets—a trade that forms the sinews of war in Sierra Leone—must be vigorously pursued. Many Sierra Leonean diamonds find their way to the main Belgian market through Côte d'Ivoire and Liberia. To deprive warlords of the benefits of resources that fuel their violence, international pressure must be applied to the international buyers, companies and regional states involved in this sordid trade. The government of Sierra Leone must be assisted in establishing security in this area through the deployment of sufficient numbers of UN peacekeepers, and the Kabbah administration will also need help in regulating the diamond trade in ways that are transparent and that ensure that revenues from diamond sales reach government coffers. The government's dependence on diamond exports can also be reduced through financial assistance aimed at reviving the country's potentially lucrative rutile exports.

Finally, the international community will have to dig deeper into its pockets to increase the derisory amounts dedicated to postconflict peacebuilding tasks in Sierra Leone and Liberia. Disproportionate attention has been focused on the tragedies in Kosovo and East Timor, while Africa's civil wars have often been left to fester. Donors often demand stability before committing resources, but as in Liberia, if factions show signs of wanting to settle conflicts, it is better for the international community to invest the resources to implement agreements. The security climate may then become more propitious for achieving other peacebuilding goals.

Donors must show more understanding for the plight of cash-strapped governments in countries like Liberia and Sierra Leone that have been devastated by civil wars. Debts will have to be forgiven or substantially reduced, while borrowing restrictions and stringent aid conditions must be eased on these countries until they have recovered sufficiently from the ravages of war. Donors will have to go beyond empty promises, get over their fatigue, and start delivering on their pledges if they intend to prevent a return to full-scale war. It is crucial that this golden opportunity to secure peace in Sierra Leone and end the current war in Liberia is not squandered by the frugality of an indifferent international community.

Notes

1 The fifteen current members of ECOWAS are Benin, Burkina Faso, Cape Verde, Côte d'Ivoire, Gambia, Ghana, Guinea, Guinea-Bissau, Liberia, Mali, Niger, Nigeria, Senegal, Sierra Leone and Togo. Mauritania withdrew from the organization in December 2000.

2 For further details on ECOMOG's military shortcomings, see Herbert Howe, "Lessons of Liberia: ECOMOG and Regional Peacekeeping," *International Security* 21, no. 3 (Winter 1996/1997): 145–76; and Robert Mortimer, "From ECOMOG to ECOMOG II: Intervention in Sierra Leone," in John W. Harbeson and Donald Rothchild, eds.,

Africa in World Politics: The African State System in Flux, 3rd ed. (Colorado and Oxford: Westview Press, 2000), 188–204.

3 For accounts of the Liberian civil war, see Colonel Festus Aboagye, *ECOMOG: A Subregional Experience in Conflict Resolution, Management and Peacekeeping in Liberia* (Accra: Sedco Enterprise, 1999); Adekeye Adebajo, *Liberia's Civil War: Nigeria, ECOMOG and Regional Security in West Africa* (Boulder, CO and London: Lynne Reinner, 2002); Abiodun Alao, John Mackinlay and Funmi Olonisakin, *Peacekeepers, Politicians, and Warlords: The Liberian Peace Process* (Tokyo, New York and Paris: United Nations University Press, 1999); Stephen Ellis, *The Mask of Anarchy* (London: Hurst and Company, 1999); Karl Magyar and Earl Conteh-Morgan, eds., *Peacekeeping in Africa: ECOMOG in Liberia* (London: Macmillan / New York: St. Martin's Press, 1998); Klaas Van Walraven, *The Pretence of Peace-keeping: ECOMOG, West Africa and Liberia (1990–1998)* (The Hague: Netherlands Institute of International Relations 1999); and Margaret Vogt, ed., *The Liberian Crisis and ECOMOG: A Bold attempt at regional peacekeeping* (Lagos: Gabumo Press, 1992).

4 For accounts of the Sierra Leone conflict, see Ibrahim Abdullah and Patrick Muana, "The Revolutionary United Front of Sierra Leone: A Revolt of the Lumpenproletariat," in Christopher Clapham, ed., *African Guerrillas* (Oxford: James Currey / Kampala: Fountain Publishers / Bloomington: Indiana University Press, 1998), 172–95; Adekeye Adebajo, *Building Peace in West Africa: Liberia, Sierra Leone and Guinea-Bissau* (Boulder, CO and London: Lynne Reinner, 2002); "Youth Culture and Political Violence: The Sierra Leone Civil War," special issue of *African Development* 22, nos. 2 and 3 (1997); John Hirsch, *Sierra Leone: Diamonds and the Struggle for Democracy* (Boulder, CO: Lynne Reinner, 2001); Mark Malan, Phenyo Rakate, and Angela McIntyre, *Peacekeeping in Sierra Leone: UNAMSIL Hits the Home Straight* (Pretoria: Institute for Security Studies, 2002); William Reno, *Warlord Politics and African States* (Boulder, CO and London: Lynne Reinner, 1998); Paul Richards, *Fighting for the Rainforest: War, Youth and Resources in Sierra Leone* (Oxford: James Currey / New Hampshire: Heinemann, 1996); and A.B. Zack-Williams and Steve Riley, "Sierra Leone: the coup and its consequences," *Review of African Political Economy* 20, no. 56 (1993): 91–98.

5 William Reno, "The Business of War in Liberia," *Current History* 96, no. 601 (May 1996): 215.

6 *Africa Confidential*, 17 May 1992, 3.

7 Reno, *Warlord Politics*, 104–5.

8 Reno, *Warlord Politics*, 126–127.

9 See Amnesty International, "Sierra Leone: Human Rights Abuses in a War against Civilians," *AIIndex* (13 September 1995); Human Rights Watch/Africa, "Waging War to Keep the Peace: The ECOMOG Intervention and Human Rights," *Human Rights Watch Publications* 5, no. 6 (June 1993), http://www.hrw.org/reports/1993/liberia/ (accessed 22 December 2003); Human Rights Watch/Africa, "Liberia: Emerging from Destruction," *Human Rights Watch Publications* 9, no. 7 (November 1997), http://www.hrw.org/press97/nov/libngvt.htm (accessed 23 December 2003); and the United Nations Secretary-General's Reports to the Security Council on Liberia and Sierra Leone.

10 See Paul Richards, "Rebellion in Liberia and Sierra Leone: A crisis of youth?" in Oliver Furley, ed., *Conflict in Africa* (New York and London: Tauris Academic Studies, 1995), 134–70.

11 See, for example, Joseph Garba, *Diplomatic Soldiering: Nigerian Foreign Policy, 1975–1979* (Ibadan: Spectrum Books, 1987); Yakubu Gowon, "The Economic Community of West African States: A Study of Political and Economic Integration" (PhD diss., Warwick University, 1984); Olusegun Obasanjo, *Not My Will* (Ibadan: Ibadan University Press, 1990).

12 See, for example, Neil Macfarlane and Thomas Weiss, "Regional Organizations and Regional Security," *Security Studies* 2, no. 1 (Autumn 1992): 6–37; and Robert Mortimer, "ECOMOG, Liberia and Regional Security in West Africa," in Edmond Keller and Donald Rothchild, eds., *Africa in the New International Order: Rethinking State Sovereignty* (Boulder, CO and London: Lynne Reinner, 1996), 149–83.

13 For a detailed account, see: United Nations, *Seventeenth Progress Report of the Secretary-General on the United Nations Observer Mission in Liberia*, S/1996/362, 21 May 1996.

14 For an assessment of the Dutch role in Liberia, see Klaas Van Walraven, *The Netherlands and Liberia: Dutch Policies and Interventions with Respect to the Liberian Civil War* (The Hague: Netherlands Institute of International Relations, 1999).

15 United Nations Security Council, *Twenty-second Progress Report of the Secretary-General on the United Nations Observer Mission in Liberia*, S/1997/237, 19 March 1997, 3–4.

16 For further details, see Victor Tanner, "Liberia: Railroading Peace," *Review of African Political Economy* 25, no. 75 (March 1998): 133–47.

17 Personal Interview with Trevor Gordon-Somers. UNDP, New York, May 1997.

18 See "Liberia: problematic peacekeeping," special issue of *Africa Confidential*, 4 March 1994, 2–3; Clement E. Adibe, "The Liberian conflict and the ECOWAS-UN partnership," *Third World Quarterly* 18, no. 3 (1997): 471–88; Binaifir Nowrojee, "Joining Forces: UN and Regional Peacekeeping, lessons from Liberia," Harvard Human Rights Journal 18 (Spring 1995): 129–52; and Funmi Olonisakin, "UN co-operation with regional organizations in peacekeeping: the experience of ECOMOG and UNOMIL in Liberia," *International Peacekeeping* 3, no. 3 (Autumn 1996): 33–51.

19 United Nations, *Third Report of the Secretary-General on the United Nations Mission in Sierra Leone*, S/2000/186, 7 March 2000, 6.

20 United Nations, *Thirteenth Report of the Secretary-General on the United Nations Mission in Sierra Leone*, S/2002/267, 14 March 2002, 1–2.

21 See Terrence Lyons, *Voting For Peace: Post Conflict Elections in Liberia* (Washington D.C.: The Brookings Institution, 1998).

22 For a pre-election assessment, see "After the horror, a new beginning," *The Economist*, 18 May 2002, 45–46.

23 "Liberia," *The Economist Intelligence Unit*, Fourth Quarter 1997, 1–10.

24 See Jon Lee Anderson, "The Devil they Know," *New Yorker*, 27 July 1998, http://www.newyorker.com/archive/content/?30728fr_archive01; and Baffour Ankomah, "Knives out for Taylor," *New African Magazine*, September, 1998, http://www.africasia-com/newafrican/na-php?ID17&back_month=06.

25 Baffour, "Knives."

26 See Norwood Langley, "The National Reconstruction Program in Liberia," in *State Rebuilding after State Collapse: Security, Democracy and Development in Post-War Liberia*, Report of the Strategic Planning Workshop on Liberia (London: Centre for Democracy and Development, 1998), http://www.cdd.org.uk/.

27 United Nations, *Report of the Secretary-General on Sierra Leone*, S/1997/80, 26 January 1997, 6.

28 "Liberia," *The Economist Intelligence Unit*, First Quarter 1999, 8.

29 ECOWAS, *Meeting of ECOWAS Ministers of Foreign Affairs, Final Communique*, Lomé, 24–25 May, 1999, 5.

30 Amos Sawyer, "Foundations for reconstruction in Liberia: Challenges and Responses," in *State Rebuilding*, 69.

31 "Liberia," *The Economist Intelligence Unit*, Third Quarter 1998, 11.

32 "Liberia," *The Economist Intelligence Unit*, March 2001, 49.

33 United Nations Security Council, *First Report on the United Nations Mission in Sierra Leone (UNAMSIL)*, S/1999/1223, 6 December 1999, 1–6.

34 United Nations Security Council, *Fourth Report on the United Nations Mission in Sierra Leone*, S/2000/455, 19 May 2000, 4.

35 United Nations Security Council, *Third Report on the United Nations Mission in Sierra Leone*, S/2000/186, 7 March, 2000, 3–4; and United Nations Security Council, *Fifth Report on the United Nations Mission in Sierra Leone*, S/2000/751, 31 July 2000, 4.

36 See: United Nations Security Council, *Fifth Report*, 9.

37 See: United Nations Security council, *Fifth Report*, 4–5.

38 See Comfort Ero, *Sierra Leone's Security Complex*, Working Paper no. 3, (London: Centre For Defence Studies, June 2000).

39 See D. Elwood Dunn, "Liberia's Internal Responses to ECOMOG's Intervention Efforts," in Karl Magyar and Earl Conteh-Morgan, eds., *Peacekeeping in Africa: ECMOMOG in Liberia* (London: MacMillan / New York: St. Martin's Press, 1998); Yasmin Jusu-Sheriff, "Sierra Leonean Women and the Peace Process," *Accord* 1 (2003), http://www.c-r.org/accord/s-leone/accord9/women.shtml (accessed 20 December 2003); Augustine Toure, *The Role of Civil Society in National Reconciliation and Peacebuilding in Liberia* (New York: International Peace Academy, 2002); Thomas Mark Turay, "Civil Society and Peacebuilding: The Role of the Inter-Religious Council of Sierra Leone," Special issue of Accord, *Accord* 9, http://www.c-r.org/accord/s-leon/accord9/society.shtml (accessed 20 December 2003); and Samuel Kofi Woods, "Civic Initiatives in the Peace Process," *Accord* 1 (2003), http://www.c-r.org/accord/lib/accord1/woods.shtml (accessed 20 December 2003);.

40 See: ECOWAS, *Protocol Relating to the Mechanism For Conflict Prevention, Management, Resolution, Peacekeeping and Security* (Abuja: ECOWAS Secretariat, 1999). See also Adebajo, *Building Peace in West Africa*; and Eric G. Berman and Katie E. Sams, *Peacekeeping in Africa: Capabilities and Culpabilities* (Geneva: UN Institute for Disarmament Research / Pretoria: Institute for Security Studies, 2000).

41 See Adekeye Adebajo and Chris Landsberg, "Back to the Future: UN Peacekeeping in Africa," in Adekeye Adebajo and Chandra Lekha Sriram, eds., *Managing Armed Conflicts in the 21st Century* (London and Portland: Frank Cass, 2001), 161–88.

9 Peacebuilding in the Horn of Africa

THE ROLE OF AFRICA'S REGIONAL ORGANIZATION

Kassu Gebremariam

PEACE AND HOPE are rare commodities in the Horn of Africa. The negative lessons of the Somali experience, the decline in the strategic importance of the Horn, and the preeminence of personalist rules have slackened the efforts of international organizations and major powers to rescue Ethiopia, Eritrea, Somalia and Sudan. The intensification of social and physical crises has led those countries to sink deeper into hopelessness and despair. Yet reforms undertaken by the Organization of African Unity (OAU), now the African Union,[1] such as the establishment of a Mechanism for Conflict Prevention, Management, and Resolution and the creation of the Intergovernmental Authority for Drought and Development (IGADD), aimed at enhancing the goals of peacebuilding undertakings, are inherently flawed. The principal problem with OAU reforms is that they still fail to address systematically how diversity within unity (or a community of communities) can be instituted. This study challenges this failure.

The analytical framework used here is the model of layered loyalties (otherwise referred to as a community of communities) employed at the local, state and subregional and regional levels. The use of this model to investigate the question of peacebuilding in the context of the Horn of Africa is advantageous for several reasons. First, the place that the approach assigns to local conditions guards one against the fatal flaws of universal prescriptions. Second, the importance attached to the state enables one to determine the state's ability to ensure political legitimacy. Third, the place assigned to a region allows one to identify truly regional problems that require cooperative undertakings by countries in the Horn of Africa. On the contrary, the OAU's Mechanism for Conflict Management and Resolution inhibits us from determining what kinds of proactive peacebuilding responses need to be initiated based on a commitment to common principles.

The plausibility of the framework of layered loyalties is well supported by the reality of countries in the Horn of Africa. In most instances during the precolonial days, people saw themselves primarily as members of a tribe or clan. This changed after independence. Many started to see themselves as members of a country as well as of a particular tribe or clan. However, the consolidation of the loyalty of citizens to their respective states was eroded due to the inability of the political elites to respond to popular demands. Today, the challenge is to foster policies that maintain proper equilibrium between loyalties at the levels of the local, the state and the region in a complementary and reinforcing manner. Failure to nurture such an approach would perpetuate divisiveness, demonic stereotyping, xenophobia, and lack of resolution on overdue issues. In short, it would be a major impediment to building sustainable peace. Without instituting such layered loyalties, one cannot strengthen the abilities of the OAU and IGADD to settle conflicts in a legitimate manner and deepen cooperation around regional problems.

The first section of the current discussion deals with the OAU's potential in managing conflict and how it failed to provide strong leadership to resolve border conflicts between Somalia and its neighbors. The second section explains how the Cold War international order basically undercut the OAU's role in conflict resoltion and the extent to which regional countries depended on either the United States or the former Soviet Union for their survival. The third section shows that despite reforms at the level of the OAU, very little is expected from the regional organization in the near future with respect to peacebuilding initiatives. The final section analyzes the current situation in the Horn of Africa (which embraces Ethiopia, Eritrea, Somalia and Sudan) and demonstrates ways in which the formulation of policies set in line with the principle of layered loyalties can indeed strengthen OAU and IGADD peacebuilding roles.

The formation of the OAU is generally considered to be one of the most important milestones in Africa's search for peace, security and economic development. The political genesis of the OAU can be traced to the development of pan-Africanism. The priority pan-Africanist forces assigned to the question of termination of colonial rule culminated in the independence of most African countries in the late 1950s and early 1960s.[2] Subsequently, serious cleavages developed over such issues as the nature and extent of pan-African cooperation and the character of social and economic policies in African countries. The most outstanding difference was between those who upheld and legitimized the principle of national sovereignty and those who saw the political federation of Africa as the most urgent issue.[3] However, antagonism between competing visions for the future of the continent was muted when Emperor Haile Selassie of Ethiopia initiated the events that led directly to the creation of the OAU.

The OAU was formed on 25 May 1963. Thirty independent African states participated at the Addis Ababa Conference that brought this regional organization into being. The inviolable integrity of each state and its right to choose whether it would be bound by organizational decisions were recognized as the key features of the relationship between member states and the OAU. This principle is expressed most clearly in Article III of its Charter. The Article echoes the UN Charter in stipulating several conditions: first, the sovereign equality of all members states; second, noninterference in the internal affairs of states; and third, peaceful settlement of disputes by negotiation, mediation, conciliation or arbitration. Ever since then, conflict management by the OAU has been bounded by its adherence to "the support of member states for the territorial boundaries inherited from the colonial era, and their opposition to secessionist movements and to external assistance to such movements."[4] In consequence, the Commission on Conciliation, Mediation, and Arbitration, created in July 1965, had its jurisdiction limited to interstate conflicts. The Commission could only act when requested by one of the parties involved, the Assembly, or the Council, and only when both disputants accepted its intervention.

Although the OAU's voting rule (a two-thirds majority) allowed it to intervene in a conflict, it seldom did so. Decisions premised on a two-thirds majority vote were of a nonobligatory nature. Nor was the Assembly of Heads of State and Government as the "Supreme Organ" of the OAU given the authority to impose its will on members. The Conciliation Commission remained largely inactive for the last three decades, as the OAU used *ad hoc* committees in its stead. There was no enforcement structure in place. Reasons revolving essentially around the narrow interpretation of sovereignty created difficulties for the OAU in formulating procedures for the resolution of conflicts among its member states.[5] The assumption was that conflicts within African states fell within the exclusive competence of the states concerned. In consequence, the organization stood by in apparent "helplessness" as many of these conflicts caused enormous challenges.

Despite these difficulties, the OAU in the main depended on less formal means of "mediation" for conflict resolution—a legacy of the founding fathers whereby political means for settling conflicts were favored.[6] *Ad hoc* means such as the Assembly of Heads of State and Government, or eminent persons, served as the dominant means of settling conflicts. Individual heads of state had the tradition of intervening in conflict situations on behalf of the Assembly of Heads of State and Government.

The conflicts of the Horn of Africa in the 1960s and 1970s were essentially marked by Somalia's claim on the territories inhabited by its kinsmen in Ethiopia, Kenya and Djibouti, coupled with nationalism that espoused creation of a nation-state under the banner of "Greater Somalia." This presented a major challenge to regional peace. Another challenge from Somalia, particularly with regard to the OAU's authority, lay in the principle of self-determination.[7] Somalis are tied by a common ancestry, language, and culture. This is declared in Article VI of its Constitution and symbolized by the five stars of its flag. The five stars of Somalia's flag represent the aim of unification of the Somali inhabited regions of the Ogaden of Ethiopia, the Northern Frontier District (NFD) of Kenya, Djibouti, and former British and Italian Somalilands. Mogadishu's adherence to the ideals of "Greater Somalia" and the principle of self-determination challenged the OAU's adherence to the principle of respect for colonial boundaries.

The recalcitrant behavior of Mogadishu, combined with the impotence of the OAU as peacemaker among the Horn of Africa countries, became all too apparent during the 1964 and 1977–78 Ethio-Somali wars. In the latter part of 1963 and early 1964, the Somali-Ethiopian war erupted when Somalia supported armed groups conducting intermittent raids into the Ogaden province of Ethiopia.[8] This was followed by Somalia's attack against Ethiopia on 7 February 1964. Somalia requested intervention by the UN Security Council. This tack met with failure when both the former USSR and the UN Secretary-General requested Ethiopia and Somalia to settle their disputes within an inter-African context. On 9 February 1964, Ethiopia and Kenya appealed to the OAU Council of Ministers to call for a ceasefire and pass a resolution reiterating the inviolability of the existing borders of the states in the Horn. The Council at a meeting in Lagos on 24 February asked the warring parties to settle their conflict in conformity with Article III (3) of the OAU Charter. The belligerents appeared to end their hostilities when the Sudanese

President Ibrahim Aboud intervened as a mediator between Ethiopia and Somalia.

As subsequent developments disclosed, peace was not achieved because Somalia failed to renounce its territorial claim. Between 1965 and 1967, it organized guerrilla forces that harassed Ethiopian and Kenyan government officials.[9] This prompted both Ethiopia and Kenya to adopt a deterrent policy. They closed their borders to the Somali nomadic clans' intrusions into their respective territories for grazing lands and water. In particular, Ethiopia's aerial counter-offensive against Somalia was most successful. The combination of these measures compelled Mogadishu to initiate a policy of detente. At the Kinshasa OAU Summit Conference in September 1967, Mogadishu normalized relations with its neighbors through President Kenneth Kaunda's personal diplomacy.

Somalia's elite persistent search to implement the goals of "Greater Somalia" posed a major obstacle to that country's ability to adhere to the OAU's rules of the game and settle its border conflicts with Ethiopia. Mogadishu's defiance of the OAU peacemaking role was clearly demonstrated in its invasion of Ethiopia during the 1977–78 Ethio-Somali war. At the time, Ethiopia was preoccupied with internal reforms and gripped by turmoil. Addis Ababa found itself under attack first from the Western Somali Liberation Front (WSLF), the Somali Abo Liberation Front (SALF), and eventually from Somali troops.[10] By June 1977, the SALF and WSLF controlled 85 percent of the Ogaden region of Ethiopia. The OAU's role did not develop beyond passing implicit criticism of Somalia's claims. The Ethiopian government's search to secure a two-thirds majority vote to convene an emergency session of the OAU failed. The eight-nation mediation committee created in 1973 to arbitrate the border dispute between Ethiopia and Somalia merely issued a statement confirming the inviolability of frontiers inherited from the colonial era.

What ensured the territorial integrity of Ethiopia at the time was the coincidence of a radical ideology between Moscow and Addis Ababa and the former Soviet Union's desire to displace the US in the region. Both Ethiopia's and Somalia's capabilities of ensuring their territorial unification and independence were tied to the transfer of arms from either Washington or the former Soviet Union in exchange for the strategic services each country rendered to them. The ideology of pan-Africanism and the principles of the OAU did not deter the superpowers from relentlessly pursuing their interests. Moscow and Washington designed their policies on the Horn's strategic and political importance not on the conflicting claims of Ethiopia and Somalia. Somalia deployed over 1,000 tanks, 600 pieces of artillery and canons, anti-aircraft guns, surface-to-surface missiles and rockets, 48 artillery pieces, and eight fighter aircraft. Ethiopia, on the other hand, deployed about 70 tanks, 48 artillery pieces, and eight fighter aircraft.[11] The Ethiopian government's army, numbering less than 40,000 men, was spread all over the country in an effort to contain insurgent groups.

Ethiopia's ability to dislodge the invading army of Somalia and resort to an offensive strategy was facilitated by the Soviet Union's shipment of arms and equipment worth nearly one billion dollars.[12] Ethiopia's survival was further reinforced when the Soviet Union urged client states, such as Cuba and South Yemen, to provide fighting personnel. Twelve thousand Cuban troops fought on the side of the Ethiopian army. The consequence was the expulsion of Somalia's regular troops from the southeastern provinces of Ethiopia and the restoration of the *status quo ante*.

In the same manner, Somalia's capability to weather the consequences of the war and ensure its unity rested on its alignment with Washington. The US sought to buttress Somalia's survival with its desire to displace the Soviet Union from that country and obtain base rights and access to Berbera, a former Soviet military base in Somalia.[13] In return, Mogadishu received $40 million in military aid for 1981 and 1982. The US sent 250 troops to Berbera to assist with the "Bright Star" exercises in November 1981.[14] It then spent $66 million to expand naval facilities at the port of Kisimayo.[15] Its military assistance program from 1983 to 1986 averaged $36–40 million per year.[16] Most important, in November 1983, the US helped arrange a $1.5 billion loan for the ailing Somali economy.[17]

The reliance on the bipolar structure of the international system rather than on OAU principles for securing national borders and unity is further illuminated by the alignment pattern Ethiopia and Somalia maintained with Washington and Moscow respectively. In the case of Somalia (being suspicious of British interest in Kenya, French interests in Djibouti, and the US ties with Ethiopia), an alliance was built with the former Soviet Union. Mogadishu broke off diplomatic relations with Britain in 1963. In October 1963, it accepted a Soviet military credit of $30 million that was used to expand its army from 4,000 to 20,000.[18] The Soviet Union's help to bolster Somalia's defense took a very decisive turn after the 1969 *coup d'état*. For instance, when the Soviet defense minister, Marshall Andrei A. Grechko, visited Somalia in 1972, there were about 3,600 Russians, of whom 1,200 to 1,400 were military personnel.[19]

Ethiopia's capability to preserve its unity rested primarily on the patron-client relationship with the US. Addis Ababa and Washington signed a defense pact in 1953. As a rental cost, Ethiopia received military training and equipment worth about $147 million between 1953 and 1970.[20] The US interest in Ethiopia declined when the Kagnew station was no longer considered part of its strategic interest. The US replaced Kagnew with a military base at Diego Garcia, situated in the middle of the Indian Ocean. Revolutionary developments within Ethiopia exacerbated the deterioration of Ethio-US relations. In consequence, when Somalia invaded Ethiopia, the map of the Horn might have been redrawn had the Soviet Union not come to the rescue of Ethiopia.

With the end of the Cold War, the OAU had to review its approach to conflict management in order to cope with the challenges of the collapse of African states and escalation of domestic conflicts. To this end, the Heads of State and Government at the 26th ordinary session in July 1990 adopted a "Declaration on the Political and Socio-economic Situation in Africa and the Fundamental Changes

Taking Place in the World." In that declaration, many African leaders expressed their determination to work together towards the peaceful and speedy resolution of all the conflicts on the continent.[21] This was a major shift in attitude in the sense that African leaders accepted the limitations imposed on the OAU simply on account of arguable technicalities of sovereignty. Member states recognized that where national means of conflict resolution proved unsuitable or inadequate, they needed to be supplemented by "international" action, especially within the purview of the OAU.

The 29th ordinary session of the Heads of State and Government adopted the "Report of the Secretary-General on the Establishment of the Mechanism for Conflict Prevention, Management and Resolution." This guaranteed that the OAU would play a pivotal role in trying to prevent conflicts from breaking out among African states.[22] The Division for Conflict Management is guided by the OAU Charter principles of sovereign equality, noninterference in domestic affairs, territorial integrity, and commitment to the peaceful settlement of disputes. Its main pillar is the central organ consisting of elected members of the Bureau of the Assembly of Heads of State, which functions at the level of heads of state as well as of ministers and ambassadors. This central organ can be summoned by the Chairman, the Secretariat, the Secretary-General, or at the request of a member state.

All this marked a major departure from the assumption that domestic conflicts fell within the exclusive competence of member states. Member states' attitude moved away from a position of total opposition to the involvement of the OAU in internal conflicts to accepting the organization's role in assisting in their resolution. The Secretary-General of the OAU is now able to take the initiative to intervene personally or, through special envoys, to promote pacific settlement of conflicts.[23] The enhancement in the stature of the OAU and the shift in the position of states is evident in the number of member states that have asked the organization to observe elections. Between 1991 and 1998, the OAU has been able to observe

39 elections in 25 member states. Member states responded favorably to the OAU's requests for troops to engage in peacekeeping operations under UN auspices in the cases of Rwanda and Burundi. During the 1998 summit in Addis Ababa, the African heads of states decided that member states of the OAU should earmark and train contingents from their national armies so that they can be called upon to perform tasks relating to peacekeeping and conflict prevention.[24]

However, the Mechanism for Conflict Prevention, Management and Resolution is confronted with major limitations despite its attempt to address conflict situations on the continent. There is a shortage of human-resource capacity to serve the mechanism. There is also a structural problem related to the position and composition of the Conflict Management Division.[25] In addition to these constraints, there is little financial and political commitment by member states for the Division's organizational capacity. For instance, in 1994 only seven Member states and the Group of African Ambassadors' wives in Addis Ababa made a contribution to the OAU's Peace Fund. In this regard, the Division depends heavily on the International Community. The organization appears to depend mainly on financial donations from European countries, the EU, Canada and the US. Belgium made valuable contributions to the OAU's efforts in Burundi.[26]

Beyond human-resource and financial limitations, the OAU has assigned a greater priority to Conflict Prevention and Management than to peacekeeping to make the Division adequate for the tasks of dealing with the rise in regional domestic conflicts. Interestingly, peacekeeping tasks are now generally carried out by subregional organizations. The role of ECOWAS (the Economic Community of West African States) and ECOMOG (the West African Community's Monitoring Group) are cases in point. In the context of the Horn of Africa, cooperation with the Intergovernmental Authority for Drought and Development (IGADD) is perceived as a means to further the goals of peacebuilding in the region.

Although it was created in 1986 to control drought in the subregion, the IGADD has been the major forum for conducting negotiations to deal with conflict in the Horn of Africa. Djibouti, Ethiopia, Eritrea, Somalia, Kenya, the Sudan and Uganda are member states of this subregional organization. This institution was the consequence of discussions among the ministries of foreign affairs and the IGADD countries' representatives in the UN General Assembly. The severe drought of 1984–86 brought these actors together and they agreed to pool their resources since, individually, they could not face the problem of drought.[29] The authority provided a ready-made forum in which heads of state could meet to mobilize and coordinate resources needed for drought control projects to achieve some results. At the time, food security, environmental protection, water resources and desertification control defined IGADD's activities. The authority's food security strategy for the region was endorsed and accepted by all member states in Kampala in October 1990.[30] The objective of this project was to develop a data bank that covers the entire food security spectrum.

However, the role assigned to IGADD as a subregional organization in peacebuilding enterprises stemmed from the recognition that neighboring countries have an important role to play in conflict resolution and peacemaking, and that their cooperation should be sought whenever possible.[31] This became evident in light of the intensification of domestic and interstate conflict in the region. Conflict reduction is a precondition for carrying out the authority's plan of action with respect to peacebuilding. Utilizing IGADD, the "Standing Committee on Peace in Sudan" was formed in 1994. The National Islamic Front's (NIF) Government in Khartoum welcomed the initiative. The Committee was chaired by President Daniel Arap Moi of Kenya and included the presidents of Ethiopia, Eritrea, and Uganda. The Committee sought reconciliation between John Garang and the southern secessionists without registering the support of Khartoum. The NIF denounced the Committee's measure as a hostile act. The Committee further startled the NIF when it presented its views regarding the terms of the Sudanese conflict known as the Declaration of Principles (DOP). The document was a dramatic condemnation of the ideology and policies of the NIF. Khartoum rejected the DOP on the grounds of the centrality assigned to a secular and democratic state and to self-determination.

IGADD's meaningful role in promoting peace in Sudan was practically over when relations between Sudan and most member states of the "Standing Committee on Peace in Sudan" soured. Relations between Asmara and Khartoum deteriorated sharply when Asmara broke off diplomatic relations with Sudan, accusing the NIF of arming Islamic groups active in Eritrea.[32] In April 1995, Kampala broke off diplomatic relations with Khartoum after a series of clashes along their common border.[33] Relations between Addis Ababa and Khartoum declined sharply following the attempted assassination in Ethiopia of Egyptian President Hosni Mubarak, because it was believed that Sudan had encouraged the failed assassins.[34]

Other peace initiatives through IGADD can also be cited. In the case of Somalia, IGADD has been very active in trying to resolve that country's crisis. President Ismael Omar Gulleh of Djibouti has been at the forefront in putting forward plans that envisage a transitional government of national unity to run Somalia for two years, similar to what has been done recently in Afghanistan.[35] The Djibouti peace conference, which was backed by IGADD and the UN, is the latest of thirteen attempts to reunite Somalia under a central government. The failure of twelve previous conferences has been blamed on the machinations of either Ethiopia or Egypt.[36]

Beyond the task of helping in the management of active conflicts in the subregion, IGADD member states have sought to address a number of peacebuilding issues. The Heads of State and Government of the IGADD met on 26 November 1999 under the chairmanship of Djibouti's president[37] and underlined the importance of developing a regional infrastructure, such as road and railway links among member countries. However, it appears that the scarcity of funds and the reluctance of international financial donors pose a major constraint in this connection. A group of states calling itself the "Friends of IGADD," which was formed as a pressure group to help advance the peace process in the subregion, is now more poised to resolve conflicts in the region than the initiative Washington adopted, otherwise known as ACRI (the African Crisis Response Initiative) which so far has failed to bring about any peaceful and negotiated solutions to the conflicts in the Horn of Africa.[38]

The US, prompted by a desire to reduce costly intervention in Africa, launched the ACRI to prevent another Somalia-type situation. The primary objective of ACRI is to enable Africans to manage their own conflicts without outside help. Even if Washington's alignment with the Horn of Africa countries in the aftermath of the Cold War is no longer tied to its strategic and ideological competition with the former Soviet Union, it has a number of incentives to promote means for resolving conflicts in the region.[39] In the first place, Washington finds it imperative to promote the goals of peacebuilding in order to offset the influence of powers hostile to its interests in the region. Second, it seeks to accelerate Africa's integration into the global economy. Finally, it hopes to counter transnational threats—terrorism (particularly since 9-11), organized crime, environmental degradation, drug trade, weapon proliferation, refugee crises, and the spread of disease (particularly HIV/AIDS)—emanating from Africa.

To achieve these goals, Washington provides training for African forces through the International Military Education and Training Program (IMETP). The IMETP aims at improving the capabilities of African forces in peacekeeping missions so that the OAU and subregional organizations can take on a more active and constructive role. The idea of creating an African peacekeeping force is supported by the OAU's Division of Conflict Management. The IMETP constituted the background that prompted the OAU to set up a Continental Peacekeeping and Intervention Force during the Yaounde Summit in July 1996. The ACRI also aims at making African forces more professional, more efficient, and more in tune with participatory political systems.[40] The US European Command is entrusted to manage security programs in Africa, including those of the ARCI.

In the Horn, acceptance of ACRI by Ethiopia, Eritrea and Uganda appears to have played a role in stabilizing the region. These countries were among the target states whose policies tended to converge with Washington's strategic interests in isolating the fundamental Islamic government in Khartoum. They received military aid worth US$20 million in 1996.[41] However, the stabilizing role of the ACRI in the Horn has been eroded by the outbreak of Ethio-Eritrean conflicts and Ethiopia's defiance of the US-initiated peace agreement in the ongoing war between Ethiopia and Eritrea. The reaction of other African countries to the ACRI was mixed and mostly lukewarm. While Senegal backed the proposal, southern African countries like South Africa and Zimbabwe were noncommittal. So what is the future of peacebuilding in the Horn?

In focusing on the transformational role of the OAU in implementing the goals of peacebuilding, it is necessary to examine whether attainment of the objectives would be feasible independent of adopting the model of layered loyalties. The unsuitability to peacebuilding of remedial measures suggested by donor countries and analysts stems from the inherent shortcomings of their frameworks. Large parts of their prescriptions are based on individualistic assumptions. The paradigms of classical liberals, contemporary classical liberals, and *laissez-faire* conservatism all make individuals their starting points. Individuals cannot be treated in isolation from their respective communities. Community provides them with history, traditions, culture, and a sense of commitment to shared values—a point Masciulli makes.[42]

What is evident in the Horn of Africa is that people see themselves as belonging to one "tribe/clan" or another, and that their loyalty to the encompassing community of communities (states) has diminished. In the context of Ethiopia, Eritrea and Sudan, their capacity to avoid disintegration and institute a state that enjoys the loyalty of its citizens is hindered by the consolidation of patrimonial dictatorships. Personalist leaders speak in the name of their societies, leaving little leeway for communities to negotiate in intergroup peace-making or peacebuilding. This characteristic is reinforced by the absence of loyal opposition groups that promote peace negotiation and of political debate with estranged or hostile groups.[43]

Sudan's Islamic fundamentalist government's resort to genocide to solve the conflict with the animist Christian south and the Eritrean and Ethiopian governments' unwillingness to negotiate a mutually acceptable compromise with the opposition, have hardened the resolve of groups to choose armed rebellion. The preoccupation of forces in outflanking one another with the development of networks of alliances, and the use of blackmail and disinformation obstruct the development of the psychological conditions for forming peaceful coalitions at national and regional levels.

The deeply inbred authoritarian political cultures and the persistence of the fragmentation of the loyalty of citizens exacerbate differences and downplay commonalities. The division of Somalia into clan and sub-clan based units, the separation of Eritrea from Ethiopia, and the Sudanese government's policy of Islamization have intensified the antagonism of groups towards one another. The inhabitants of Eritrea, Ethiopia and Sudan are divided into a multiplicity of ethnic groups that are also separated by religion, regional and tribal loyalties. The three countries are troubled by regional imbalance and armed conflicts that search either for secession or representation at government levels. Whether the further balkanization of the states can be curtailed and whether Ethiopia, Eritrea and Sudan can hold out against the forces of separatism and remain in their present form is uncertain despite the current state of fragile unity in these states.

The Somali state is essentially dead. The fragmentation of power under autonomous warlords in the southern part of the country and the prominence of bandits and militiamen who profit from an economy of plunder and other unlawful dealings perpetuate Somalia's statelessness—at least in the short term. The lack of common curricula and common schools of learning between the Somaliland, the Puntland, and the southern parts of the country undermine the emergence of a nationally integrated elite. The flight of the majority of Somalia's trained state personnel—administrators, accountants, lawyers, medical doctors, and other classes of professionals—further weakens prospects for the restoration of the state.

Another factor that undermines institutionalization of a sense of regional community premised on cross-cultural communication and understanding is the Ethio-Egyptian rivalry. Their rivalry is intimately linked to the "hydropolitics" of the Nile River.[44] Egypt prefers a weakened Ethiopia and provides support to Ethiopia's enemies so that Ethiopia becomes bogged down in a costly security problem on its borders. Ethiopia's capacity to counter Egypt's ambition is undermined by a host of other factors. One is the absence of a mutually acceptable compromise between major political groupings. Another is the rise of ethnic parochialism as a result of implementation of the policy of "ethnic federalism."

Promotion of the goals of peacebuilding through the instrumentality of the OAU and IGADD is unlikely. In the first place, the principles of the OAU that have binding effect on member states, such as the principle of noninterference in domestic affairs and respect for the colonial boundaries, are violated in this part of Africa. Proxy warfare has become most blatant and disruptive in Ethiopia, Eritrea and Sudan. Ethiopia, Egypt, Libya, and Eritrea are pursuing sub-regional hegemonic aspirations by providing military training and equipment to competing Somali factions. Second, the OAU's maxim of respect for existing boundaries is discarded.

Violation of respect for inherited colonial boundaries came with the independence of Eritrea and the death of Somalia. OAU members and the rest of the international community accepted the change they had opposed because of the agreement between the Eritrean People's Liberation Front (EPLF) and the Ethiopian People's Revolutionary

Democratic Front (EPRDF) that replaced the military government of Colonel Mengistu Hailemariam in Ethiopia.

IGADD's role in peacebuilding is also very precarious. Its efforts to foster peacebuilding are inherently limited because of the involvement of member countries such as Ethiopia and Eritrea in interstate conflict and the disintegration of Somalia, and these same factors deligitimize IGADD's role in peacekeeping undertakings. What further undercuts IGADD's effectiveness is that its roles are not clearly formulated. It can be effective only if neighbors sharing borders are excluded from certain conflict management exercises. Some analysts, for instance, oppose the use of troops in either peacekeeping or peacemaking efforts in countries that share borders and where the perception of bias towards one or the other of the parties is likely to hinder the process. The experience of multilateral forces that have intervened in Somalia demonstrates that military intervention can put an end to fighting, but that political and diplomatic initiatives as well as active participation of civil society are crucial to peacebuilding.

The principal theme of this analysis has been that reforms confined to the levels of the OAU (now the African Union—AU) and IGADD remain inadequate for the realization of the objectives of peacebuilding that call for multifaceted adoption of the framework of the community of communities. This model enables one to implement a host of peacebuilding measures at the levels of the local, state and regional organization. The modest success story of peacebuilding in Somaliland (ex-British Somaliland) highlights the effectiveness of the multilayered approach to peacebuilding in the Horn of Africa. In the wake of the overthrow of General Siyaad Barre's regime in the north, and in the absence of any effective centralized government, northern Somalis attained peace through the "bottom up" approach. The government formed by the Somali National Movement (SNM) withered away because of its failure to achieve popular support.

It was left to the local clan elders to weave a web of peace at the local, district, and national levels. The highest level of Council of

Elders (known as Guurti) represents the various clans in national peace conferences and other matters of common interest.[45] The goals of peace, security, and economic development are best served when members of any one community view themselves as citizens of a country as well of the Great Horn. It is within this context that I suggest a number of possible solutions to improving the peacebuilding process in the Horn of Africa. Topping the list would be the strengthening of the institutional capacity of the AU and IGADD and the initiation of collaborative undertakings between the subregional/regional institutions and the UN. This will allow for an exchange of views, strategies and relevant experiences. Such an undertaking involves a host of other measures.

First, the role of the AU and IGADD in conflict management calls for a commitment to the promotion of political and economic reforms in the region. These institutions need to foster national reconciliation and unofficial dialogue that would bring together a wide array of interests—including opposition groups, academics, respected senior leaders, religious leaders, trade unions, and women's groups. Indigenous conflict resolution methods should be explored.

Second, access is needed to a profile of country-based conflicts and the stakes of the warring factions. An example of this is the initiation of the Social Movement Learning Project based on a collaborative study among three sets of actors: social movements, universities and educational research institutions, and the OAU and IGADD as well as global policy networks. Each set of actors is committed to doing reflective studies and assessing the implications of their own activities upon civil society.

Third, there ought to be the creation of a documentation center with proficient personnel.

Fourth, a standing working or mediation team within the IGADD should be constituted.

Fifth, there should be closer coordination and cooperation between the Division of Conflict Management in the AU and IGADD's mediation team.

Enhancing the authority of states in the Horn of Africa to a level that will allow them to transcend political and social fragmentation and to bring about the emergence of a value consensus on the legitimacy of IGADD and the AU requires three major reforms at the local and national levels. These are: (1) the promotion of policies of integration through administrative and other types of reforms; (2) the change of electoral laws; and (3) the construction of insulated bureaucracies.

Special attention should be given to strengthening judicial and legal structures and institutions and instruments aimed at protecting minorities. It is important as well to establish various arrangements that would maintain the unity of the regional states but grant substantial rights of autonomy and self-determination to states in the region. There should be no support for claims of substate self-determination that would shatter an existing state unless a "people" was being victimized either by genocidal behavior or through repeated crimes against humanity. Finally, reactivation of indigenous knowledge that resides in people, their oral histories, stories, sets of beliefs, poems, dances and music, and legends and folk tales should be a priority of any sustainable peace project in this region of the world.

If one wants the AU to implement objectives of peacebuilding in the Horn of Africa, one needs to adopt the model of community of communities. The implementation of measures that curb conflicts at the local, state and regional levels is necessary for the promotion of peace, security and development in the long term. In this broad sense, the AU and IGADD have the potential to create conditions for political, economic and social progress as well as to equip the Horn of Africa countries with the necessary instruments and skills to manage their social and physical crises. Current approaches in peacebuilding offer limited theoretical and practical guidance for determining the contents of policies of such regional and subregional bodies.

Much of the peacebuilding literature is overly deterministic. We cannot have uniform policies for all countries in that region. In the last two decades, the countries there have become a much more diverse group. Somalia has deteriorated into statelessness. The inhabitants of Eritrea, Ethiopia, and Sudan are divided into a multiplicity of ethnic groups that are separated by religious as well as regional and ethnic loyalties. People in those countries speak more than 150 languages. Competitive elections and parliamentary forms of government are not institutionalized in Ethiopia, Eritrea and Sudan. Civil societies in all instances are not strong enough to enforce the accountability and transparency of officials. Therein lies the benefit of situating peacebuilding in the context of local conditions, the state, and the region. This omission has been a costly error.

The OAU has been faced with Ethio-Somalia conflicts and the Somalia crisis of 1992, but on the whole it has failed to play a decisive role in their management. The pan-Somali ideal undermined the consensus of territorial integrity. Although one of the main reasons why the OAU was created arose from the desire of Africans to exclude international rivalry from the continent, it is clear from the evidence that the great powers undercut the OAU's role in conflict management during the days of the Cold War. The post–Cold War neoliberal world order has done nothing to enhance the OAU's role in conflict management or peacebuilding. The major effect of the neoliberal world order is a diminution of the state as well as the strengthening of political and security ties with the great powers, particularly the US. Taking the UN's debacle in Somalia as a point of departure, what we have witnessed so far has been the reluctance of major powers to contribute positively to peacebuilding in the region. Washington's ACRI is really nothing more than a token gesture. The US appears poised to let events in the Horn run their course. This is best evidenced by its reluctance to become involved in Ethio-Eritrean war, particularly after the debacle in Somalia.

Another lesson drawn out of this study is that the failure to attain the goals of peacebuilding stems from erroneous assumptions of international aid donors and moneylenders. The cultural and ethnocentric arrogance of international financial institutions and their inherent biases against indigenous knowledge prevent them from accepting the local people, as well as their culture, on their own terms. Strategies of peacebuilding require cooperation between international regimes and in-country peacebuilding measures. If the AU and IGADD are to serve the regional countries, acceptance of the people on their own terms and formulation of programs based on the experiences of the various localities and countries is crucial. As Chopra and Hohe confirm,[46] the weakness of past peacebuilding undertakings consisted in their failure to heed the historical specificity of a society and in their treatment of peacebuilding as something with very little connection to local conditions, the state and the region. For sustainable peace to come to the Horn of Africa, more attention must be paid to local wisdom and to strengthening the regional and subregional institutions of governance.

Author's Note

Note that in July 2002, the OAU was reformulated and renamed the African Union—modeled after the European Union.

Notes

1 The acronym "OAU" will be used throughout this chapter, as most of the analysis was done when the organization still went by that name.
2 Colin Legum, *Pan-Africunism: A Short Political Guide* (New York: Praeger, 1962): 32.
3 Vincent Bakeptu Thompson, *Africa and Unity: The Evolution of Pan-Africanism* (New York: Humanities Press, 1969): 181–94.
4 Robert Good, "Changing Patterns of African International Relations," *American Political Science Review* 58, no. 3 (1964), 637; and N.J. Padelford, "The Organization of African Unity," *African Quarterly* 33, no. 1 (1993): 82.
5 Salim Ahmed Salim, "Searching Solutions to Internal Conflicts: The Role of the OAU," (Address to the Consultation of the International Peace Academy on Internal Conflicts in Africa: In Search of Response, Arusha, 23 March, 1992), 6.
6 Organization of African Unity, *Resolving Conflicts in Africa: Implementation Options* (Addis Ababa: OAU Information Publication, 1993), 60.

7 Somali Government, *The Somali Peninsula: A New Light on Imperial Motives* (St. Albans: The Information Services of the Somali Government, 1962), 25–30, 31–33; Somali Government, *Northern Frontier District (NFD): Problem Planted By Britain Between Kenya and the Somali Republic* (Mogadishu: Ministry of Information, 1963), 86–91.

8 "Somalia/Ethiopia Hostilities," *Africa Currents* 5 (1979): 137.

9 I.M. Lewis, "The Nation, State, and Politics in Somalia," in David R. Smock and Kevumena Betsi, eds., *The Search for National Integration in East Africa* (New York: Collier MacMillan Publishers, 1975), 291.

10 John Markakis, *National and Class Conflict in the Horn of Africa* (New York: Cambridge University Press, 1987), 181.

11 President Mengistu Haile Mariam, Secretary-General of the Workers Party of Ethiopia, Address to the National Shengo, *FBIS*, 26 April 1991.

12 Robert G. Patman, *The Soviet Union in the Horn of Africa: The Diplomacy of Intervention and Disengagement* (Cambridge: Cambridge University Press, 1990), 223.

13 United States Department of State, "Access Agreement with Somalia," *State Bulletin* 80, no. 2043 (1980), 19.

14 Paul B. Henze, "How Stable Is Siyaad Barre's Regime?" *Africa Report* 27, no. 2 (March–April 1992): 57.

15 Henze, "How Stable Is Siyaad Barre's Regime?" 57.

16 David D. Laitin and Said S. Samatar, *Somalia: Nation in Search of a State* (Boulder, CO: Westview Press, 1987), 44.

17 Patman, *The Soviet Union*, 287.

18 J. Bowyer Bell, "Strategic Implications of the Soviet Presence in Somalia," *Orbis* 19, no. 2 (1975): 403.

19 Brian Crozier, "The Soviet Presence in Somalia," Occasional Paper (London: Institute for the Study of Conflict, 1975): 4.

20 United States Government. The Mutual Security Act of 1951 (65 Stat. 377), October 10, 1951; Text of the Agreement Between Ethiopia and the United States Concerning the American Military Base in Eritrea; and United States Senate, *US Security Agreements and Commitments Abroad, Senate Foreign Relations Committee, Subcommittee on US Security Agreements and Commitments Abroad.* Vol.2, Part 8, 1935–37, 1971. Also United States Senate. *US Policy and Request for Sale of Arms to Ethiopia.* Hearings Before the Subcommittee on International Political and Military Affairs, 94th Congress, 1st Session, Washington, 1975.

21 Salim Ahmed Salim, "The Architecture for Peace and Security in Africa," http://www.uneca.org/eca_resources/speeches/2002_speeches/030603salim.htm (accessed 13 January 2004).

22 Organization of African Unity, *Declaration of the Assembly of Heads of State and Government on the Establishment Within the OAU of a Mechanism for Conflict Prevention, Management and Resolution*, AHG/DECL.3 (29), 1993.

23 Salim Ahmed Salim, "An Introduction to IGADD," in Lionel Cliffe, et. al., eds., *Beyond Conflict in the Horn: Prospects for Peace, Recovery and Development in Ethiopia, Somalia and Sudan* (New Jersey: The Red Sea Press, 1992), 5.

24 Salim Ahmed Salim, "The OAU Role in Conflict Management," in Olara Otunu and Michael W. Doyle, eds. *Peacemaking and Peacekeeping for the New Century* (New York: Rowman and Littlefield Publishers, 1998), 47–49.

25 Organization of African Unity, *Introductory Note to the Report of the secretary-general*, CM/1851 (LX1), 23–27 January 1995, 5–6.

26 Organization of African Unity, *Introductory Note*, 7.

27 Arie M. Kacowitz, "Negative International Peace and Domestic Conflict, West Africa, 1957–96," *Journal of Modern African Studies* 35, no. 3 (1997): 367–85.

28 Salim Ahmed Salim, "The OAU and the Future," in Tajudeen Abdul-Raheem, ed. *Pan-Africanism: Politics, Economy and Social Change* (London: Pluto Press, 1996), 232.

29 Ahmed Salim, "Searching Solutions," 114.

30 Ahmed Salim, "Searching Solutions," 115

31 International Peace Academy, *Chairmen's Report of Joint OAU/IPA on the OAU and Conflict Management in Africa* (New York: International Peace Academy, 1993), 7.

32 *Africa Confidential* 35, no. 25 (December 16, 1994), 6.

33 *Africa Research Bulletin* 32, no. 2 (February 28th, 1995): 1174–75.

34 *Africa Confidential* 37, no. 1 (January 5th, 1996): 1–2.

35 Ian Fisher, "With Warlords at Home, Somalis Talk Peace," *New York Times*, August 6, 2000.

36 Ian Fisher, "An Oasis of Peace in Somalia Sees Freedom," *New York Times*, November 26, 1999.

37 The Proceedings of the Summit of Heads of State and Government of IGADD Member States for the Launching of Revitalized IGADD, Djibouti, 25–26 November 1996, http://www.iss.co.za/AF/RegOrg/unity_to_union/pdfs/igad/5thIGADSUMMIT.pdf (accessed 13 January 2004); and Walta Information Center, "Declaration of the 7th IGADD Summit of Heads of State and Governments," Djibouti, 26 November 1999, www.waltainfo.com/conflict/basicfacts/1999/december/fact1.htm (accessed 13 January 2004).

38 "Interview with Prime Minister Meles Zenawi," *AlL-Shafi Al-Dawli*, November 1, 1999, 1–16.

39 Paul Omach, "The African Crisis Response Initiative: Domestic Politics and Convergence of National Interests," *African Affairs* 99, no. 394 (2000): 82–83.

40 Paul Omach, "The African Crisis Response Initiative," 90.

41 Paul Omach, "The African Crisis Response Initiative," 90.

42 See Joseph Masciulli in this volume (chapter 15).

43 William Zartman, "Inter-African Negotiation and State Renewal," in John W. Harbeson and Donald Rothchild, eds., *Africa in World Politics: Post–Cold War Challenges*, 2nd ed. (Boulder, CO: Westview Press, 1995), 142.

44 Wondimneh Tilahun, *Egypt's Imperial Aspirations Over Lake Tana and the Blue Nile*. (Addis Ababa: United Printers Ltd, 1979).

45 Samuel S. Makinda, *Seeking Peace From Chaos: Humanitarian Intervention in Somalia*, International Peace Academy Occasional Paper Series (Boulder, CO: Lynne Reinner, 1993), 16.

46 Chopra and Hohe in this volume (chapter 11).

10 Peacebuilding in Southeast Asia

AN ASSESSMENT OF ASEAN

Shaun Narine

ASEAN (The Association of Southeast Asian Nations) was created in 1967. In the intervening years, the organization has undergone many changes. The question of what ASEAN has evolved into, however, remains the subject of considerable scholarly debate. Is it the embodiment of regional norms and values, a weak instrument of state power, or something in-between? The object of this study is to assess ASEAN's ability to contribute to "peacebuilding" within Southeast Asia. I conclude that, insofar as "peacebuilding" requires physical intervention within postconflict societies, ASEAN is more of an impediment to regional peacebuilding than a help. Its fundamental norms are at odds with the idea of external intervention in the affairs of regional states. However, insofar as peacebuilding is concentrated on preventing the outbreak and escalation of conflict, ASEAN has a meaningful, but limited, role to play in laying the foundations for a "culture of conflict prevention" in Southeast Asia. Even so, ASEAN's role in peacebuilding must not be exaggerated.

ASEAN's potential as an instrument of peacebuilding in Southeast Asia has implications for the larger Asia-Pacific region. ASEAN's methods and philosophy of interaction have been widely adopted by the Asian states of the Pacific.[1] These practices have been extrapolated to other regional institutions, such as the Asia Pacific

Economic Cooperation (APEC) forum and the ASEAN Regional Forum (ARF). The ARF is the only Pacific-wide forum that addresses regional security issues. Canada is a full and active participant in the ARF and APEC. Understanding the motivations and implications of ASEAN's regional approach is, therefore, of basic concern to Canadian efforts at promoting human security and peacebuilding in the Asia Pacific.

To many observers, ASEAN has helped promote strongly held norms of international interaction in Southeast Asia.[2] Like the African Union (formerly the OAU), ASEAN is committed to respecting the sovereignty of its members. An extension of this principle is the norm prohibiting the use of force to settle regional disputes between states. ASEAN merits examination as an instrument that could already be making a significant contribution to peacebuilding within Southeast Asia. Other observers take a much more skeptical approach to the question of ASEAN's organizational efficacy. From this other perspective, ASEAN is a relatively weak organization that has never been seriously tested. The force of the regional norms that it claims to embody is highly suspect. To these more "realist" critics of ASEAN, the organization has been far more effective in creating the illusion of regional unity than actually producing this reality.[3]

This study argues that ASEAN's more optimistic supporters have exaggerated and misinterpreted the extent of the organization's normative influence upon its member states. On the surface, it appears that the ASEAN member states have firmly upheld the organization's basic norms. However, on closer examination, it is clear that the reasons for upholding these norms are more complex and instrumental than ASEAN's advocates recognize. While ASEAN is the foundation of a collective identity shared by its members, the ASEAN identity is only one of many others, and is held strongly by only an elite few within the foreign ministries of its member states. Overall, ASEAN has not created a "culture of conflict prevention" in Southeast Asia. However, the chapter does not dismiss ASEAN's potential as the basis of such a culture. ASEAN's survival and development in the post–Cold War era reflects, in part, the reality that states exist within an international society that is shaped and governed by norms and rules. ASEAN is a symbol of these normative structures. However, this is an international society of states; the norms that ASEAN currently embodies are, primarily, designed to further and protect the sovereign capabilities of the ASEAN members. As a result, they may be at odds with some of the basic requirements of "peacebuilding."

This study uses the definition of "peacebuilding" offered by Kenneth Bush as its starting point. According to Bush, "peacebuilding" is an attempt

> (t)o foster and support sustainable structures and processes which strengthen the prospects for peaceful coexistence and decrease the likelihood of outbreak, recurrence, or continuation of violent conflict.[4]

We must assess ASEAN as a possible instrument of intervention in the conflicts—and the aftermath of conflict—in Southeast Asia. Peacebuilding does not need to focus only on the intricacies of intervention, however. As Keating and Knight suggest,[5] it can include consideration of the avoidance of conflict by creating a "culture of conflict prevention." This analysis of ASEAN considers the organization from both of these perspectives: what is the likelihood of ASEAN functioning as an effective interventionary force and what are its prospects for contributing to the creation of a culture of prevention in Southeast Asia?

Andy Knight and Annika Bjorkdahl describe a "culture of conflict prevention" in the following terms:

> The notion of "a culture of prevention" is based on the values of the moral rightness to prevent deadly conflict. Having more modest goals than the complete elimination of violence, "a culture of prevention" attempts to reduce the use of war as a policy tool for solving disputes within and between states

through constructing norms of prevention.... "[A] culture of prevention" socializes states and non-state actors by prescribing norms of "appropriate" behavior.... [W]e are not claiming that norms of prevention are part of a fully developed robust intersubjective normative structure. These norms are contested norms-in-process, competing with other set of norms.[6]

Developing a culture of conflict prevention requires creating the willingness—*i.e.*, the political will—on the part of the international community to undertake preventive action to stop areas of tension from becoming full-blown regional or international conflicts. Assessing the development of a "culture of prevention" requires answering the following set of questions about the evolution of international norms of state conduct:

Are norms of prevention emerging within the existing international system? Do these norms matter, and under what circumstances do they matter, and how can we identify their importance? Is "a culture of prevention" developing within the international system? How can "a culture of prevention" contribute to increase political will?[7]

The theoretical foundation of this concept of "peacebuilding" is *constructivist theory*.[8] *Constructivism* is a theoretical approach that focuses on the role of identity in explaining state actions. Alexander Wendt defines "constructivism" in the following terms:

Constructivism is a structural theory of the international system that makes the following core claims: (1) states are the principal units of analysis for international political theory; (2) the key structures in the states system are intersubjective, rather than material; and (3) state identities and interests are in important part constructed by these social structures, rather than given exogenously to the system by human nature or domestic politics.[9]

The constructivist approach claims that states' identities and interests are socially constructed. Understanding state behavior means understanding the international social context in which it evolves.

States possess *social identities, i.e.*, how they see themselves in relation to other states in international society. On the basis of these identities, states construct their interests. States may have many different social identities. States define their interests in the process of defining the social situations in which they participate.[10] The Cold War is an example of a social structure that ceased to exist once its participants redefined their relationships and identities. International structure consists of social relationships, which give meaning to material capabilities.

Wendt defines an "institution" as "a relatively stable set or "structure" of identities and interests.... Institutions are fundamentally cognitive entities that do not exist apart from actors' ideas about how the world works."[11]

Institutions and states are *mutually constituting entities*. Institutions embody the constitutive and regulative norms and rules of international interaction; they shape, constrain and give meaning to state action and define what it is to be a state. However, institutions exist because states produce and reproduce them through practice. The social relationships that define state identity and, therefore, state interests, develop within the context of institutions. States usually assign meanings to social situations on the basis of institutionally defined roles. Because states and institutions are constantly in process, there is always the possibility that one can bring about change in the other. Constructivism suggests that state identities and interests—and how states relate to each other—can be altered at the systemic level through institutionally-mediated interactions.[12] Constructivists focus most of their attention on institutions that exist at a fundamental level of international society, such as international law, diplomacy, and sovereignty. Organizations such as ASEAN are superficial manifestations of these deeper institutional structures.

Constructivist analysis of international relations focuses on understanding the social structures governing state relationships. Constructivists ask: what are the social structures and relationships presently characterizing a region? How do states perceive their identities, and those of their neighbors? What interests follow from these perceptions? It is important to recognize that constructivist theory does not privilege any particular answer to these questions. Unlike traditional realist or liberal theories, both of which make assumptions about the basic interests of states, constructivism can predict and explain violent conflict between states as easily as peaceful interaction. How states interrelate depends upon the social environment they have created and reinforced through their interactions.

How international norms are transformed is not clear. Wendt suggests that processes of interaction could contribute to changes in normative standards and, as a result, actor identity. For current purposes, we do not need to explore these processes. Assessing ASEAN's contribution to creating a culture of conflict prevention requires examining the norms that underpin the regime and the extent to which they affect the actions of the ASEAN member states.

ASEAN is underpinned by a number of fundamental norms and practices. The practices have evolved over the course of the organization's history; ASEAN's basic norms have been present from the organization's inception, though they were only fully articulated in 1976. Most of ASEAN's social structures contribute to the organization's potential as an instrument of peacebuilding. Importantly, however, some of ASEAN's basic norms conflict with the requirements of peacebuilding.

The Treaty of Amity and Cooperation in Southeast Asia, ASEAN's blueprint for intraregional interaction, specifies the following fundamental norms as guiding ASEAN's members:[13]

(1) Respect for the sovereignty and territorial integrity of all nations;
(2) Noninterference in the internal affairs of member states;
(3) Settlement of disputes by peaceful means;
(4) Renunciation of the threat or use of force.[14]

ASEAN represents a nonaggression pact between its members, and the norms of the organization underline this fact. It is focused on preserving the sovereignty of its members from encroachment by each other as well as by outsiders.

The "ASEAN way" is the method of intra-ASEAN interaction that has enabled the organization to maintain itself. Supposedly based upon the Malay cultural practices of *musjawarah* and *mufukat*, the ASEAN way requires that the organization make decisions on the basis of consensus. If the members cannot agree upon a common stand on a particular issue, they agree to disagree, and adopt positions that reflect their particular national interests. ASEAN itself then takes no position on that issue. As a result, ASEAN's decision-making process moves no faster and goes no further than the slowest member. ASEAN deliberately avoids discussing or attempting to resolve conflicts between its members. As part of its structure, ASEAN has a formal disputes-resolution mechanism. This mechanism has never been utilized. The ASEAN states have learned, instead, to cooperate around contentious issues. Conflicts are not allowed to block the development of cooperation in other, noncontentious areas. Over time, the issues of conflict will either fade into obscurity or be tempered by the cooperative linkages fostered in other areas. The ASEAN way, therefore, has more to do with creating a particular kind of social environment than resolving, or even addressing, conflict.[15]

When ASEAN was created in 1967, its founding members were Indonesia, Malaysia, the Philippines, Singapore and Thailand. The states of the region had just gone through a three-year period of "Konfrontasi" (Confrontation), wherein Indonesia had politically (and, on occasion, militarily) challenged the legitimacy of the Malaysian state and, by extension, Singapore. The Philippines, locked in a territorial dispute with Malaysia, also questioned its legitimacy. *Konfrontasi* ended with a change of government in Indonesia, but it left lingering tensions and uncertainties within the region.[16]

ASEAN was created with three interrelated objectives. These were to alleviate intra-ASEAN tensions, to reduce the regional influence of external actors, and to promote the socio-economic development of its member states as a further hedge against communist insurgency. During its first eight years, ASEAN implemented very few concrete organizational initiatives, though this period may have been necessary to build the interpersonal contacts that would later prove essential for institutional growth. However, in 1975 the reunification of Vietnam under communist rule galvanized ASEAN's members into trying to strengthen the organization. The Bali Conference of 1976 was the first meeting of the ASEAN heads of government. At that meeting, the ASEAN states signed the Treaty of Amity and Cooperation (TAC). The TAC was open to accession by non-ASEAN states.

Initially, the relations between the new Socialist Republic of Vietnam (SRV) and individual ASEAN states were not particularly good, though they warmed with time. However, on 25 December 1978, Vietnam launched an invasion of Cambodia. This action deposed the brutal Khmer Rouge and ended a series of border battles between Vietnam and Cambodia. However, the action also violated the principles of ASEAN, primarily its prohibitions against the use of force and its call to respect state sovereignty and territorial integrity. The Vietnamese invasion also allowed the Soviet Union, which had recently become Vietnam's primary benefactor, unprecedented access to Southeast Asia. The ASEAN states became the political vanguard of a coalition (principally backed by China and the United States) opposed to Vietnam's occupation of Cambodia. From 1978–1990, this single issue was the primary focus of ASEAN's activities. ASEAN organized the international community against Vietnam and attempted to broker a diplomatic resolution to the conflict. Intra-ASEAN cooperation and coordination improved dramatically.[17] The Vietnam experience demonstrated to ASEAN that, as an organization, it could exercise considerable international political influence. However, ASEAN's ability to affect events in Indochina was heavily circumscribed by what China and the US would allow. Moreover, different perceptions of threat and national interests within ASEAN divided the organization over how to approach Vietnam. In the end, dealing with the Cambodian invasion defined ASEAN, but highlighted its real limitations.[18]

The international dimension of the Cambodian situation ended in 1991 with the Paris Peace Agreement. At that time, ASEAN was faced with a crisis of purpose. It appeared that ASEAN would need to find a new focus for its energies or risk dissolution. ASEAN soon rallied, however. Since 1991, ASEAN has increased its organizational scope considerably and has added four new members.[19] The entire self-defined region of Southeast Asia now falls under the ASEAN umbrella. Nonetheless, its decision to rapidly expand its membership threatens to undermine whatever normative and political unity may have existed between the established ASEAN states. ASEAN's inability to play a meaningful role during the recent Asian Economic Crisis has encouraged further doubts about the organization's continued viability.[20] These doubts were exacerbated by ASEAN's reluctance to deal with Indonesia's conduct in East Timor.

Given its normative structure, methods of interaction and history, can ASEAN intervene to build peace within member states recovering from conflict? Recent developments in Southeast Asia have made some political actors argue that regional political and economic interdependence require ASEAN to address the domestic affairs of member states when those affairs have regional effects. Attempts to reform ASEAN's principle and practice of nonintervention, however, have been unsuccessful. An examination of ASEAN's handling of the struggle over East Timor, and the debate over "flexible engagement" shall demonstrate why reform has, so far, failed.

The events surrounding the independence of East Timor represent the best test of ASEAN's potential to be an interventionary peacebuilding body. East Timor encapsulates many of the political factors that have made the preservation of state sovereignty fundamental to ASEAN's normative structure. East Timor was incorporated by Indonesia in 1975 and, since that time, has been the victim of a brutal military campaign and massive human rights violations. Almost one-third of East Timor's population died under Indonesian occupation before the territory gained its independence in 1999.[21] During this period, the ASEAN countries generally supported Indonesia's claims to East Timor, treating the issue—in accordance with ASEAN norms—as an internal Indonesian matter.[22] ASEAN's silence also reflected its members' unwillingness to antagonize Indonesia.

In 1997, the East Asian Economic Crisis led to the overthrow of Indonesian President Suharto. His was replacement was President Habibie, who announced that Indonesia was willing to allow East Timorese to vote on whether they wished to remain in Indonesia or establish an independent state. A UN-supervised referendum on this issue was held on 30 August 1999. Despite massive intimidation from Indonesian-backed militias and the military, East Timorese voted overwhelmingly in favor of independence.[23] This result sparked an orgy of killing by the militias, who also forced refugees into West Timor. The situation attracted international condemnation and eventually led the Indonesian government to accept the intervention of a UN peacekeeping force.

The events of 1999 created a dilemma for ASEAN.[24] The organization was faced with the need to address an important regional security issue and to demonstrate its ability to manage regional affairs. However, its basic norms and general inclinations argued against any ASEAN involvement in East Timor. A number of factors, normative, practical and political, explain this reluctance to become involved.

ASEAN was afraid independence for East Timor could cause the disintegration of Indonesia by encouraging other dissatisfied groups to push for independence. A weakened Indonesia would hobble

ASEAN. Upheaval in Indonesia could cause refugee outflows to neighboring states and spark regional instability. Moreover, a successful insurgency in East Timor might encourage separatist movements in other ASEAN states.

Beyond these immediate concerns, ASEAN countries also suspected that Western states were using human rights issues as a pretext for unilateral armed intervention in the affairs of developing countries. The NATO action against Yugoslavia had set the precedent that some regimes could be held responsible for gross human rights violations. ASEAN was bothered by the question of who would determine when the use of force against a sovereign state was justified. Malaysian Prime Minister Mahathir was most vocal in expressing these concerns, and in castigating the West for its "hypocritical" application of its principles, but his views were widely accepted in the region (and in much of the developing world):

> Southeast Asians generally believe that humanitarian intervention could subvert the region's dominant non-intervention norm, weakening political and social cohesion and allowing the West to call into question the legitimacy of governments and regimes not of their liking.[25]

In addition, ASEAN states were unhappy that UN intervention was authorized under Chapter VII of the UN Charter, which allowed the International Force for East Timor (INTERFET) and, later, the UN Transitional Authority in East Timor (UNTAET) to use force to fulfill their mandates. ASEAN regarded this as an insult to Indonesia, which had not yet formally ceded its claim to sovereignty over East Timor when INTERFET was deployed.

The ASEAN states were also concerned with the practical difficulties of undertaking a peacekeeping mission in East Timor. With the exception of Malaysia, the ASEAN countries had little experience in UN peacekeeping. Singapore and Thailand worried about a domestic political backlash if their troops were killed. The ASEAN states were apprehensive about the consequences for ASEAN if their troops exchanged fire with Indonesian-backed militias or Indonesian troops. Finally, they worried about the expense of participating in an armed intervention when the effects of the economic crisis were still being felt. Some Southeast Asian states made their participation in INTERFET conditional on financial support from Australia and Japan.[26]

The Indonesian government encouraged substantial ASEAN participation in INTERFET because it wanted to minimize Australian influence. This formal request from Indonesia removed some of the political barriers to ASEAN's involvement in the peacekeeping force. In the end, ASEAN did make a substantial contribution to the INTERFET force. Of the 9,900 troops deployed, around 2,500 were from ASEAN, and the deputy commander was from Thailand. Malaysia pushed hard to have a Malaysian appointed as UNTAET force commander, but the East Timorese regarded Malaysia as too sympathetic to Indonesia and made their opposition to such a move very clear.[27]

The consequences to ASEAN of the East Timor situation are uncertain. In the short term, ASEAN's perceived inability to act on East Timor confirmed the view of many Western states that "ASEAN is chronically incapable of taking meaningful action even when its own interests are directly engaged."[28] East Timor was widely perceived as ASEAN's opportunity to demonstrate that it could manage regional security problems without external actors playing security roles in the region. Yet, ASEAN was divided over East Timor. Burma, unsurprisingly, opposed any external intervention in East Timor, and Vietnam was unenthusiastic about the UN's regional role. Debate within ASEAN centered on the interpretation of "noninterference" in the East Timor context. Thailand and the Philippines, the ASEAN states most willing to modify the principle of nonintervention, also made the largest contributions to the UN operations in East Timor. Thailand contributed 1,580 personnel, including 1,230 troops. The Philippines committed 600 personnel, though no ground troops. However, the Philippines also voted against a UN Human Rights Commission resolution to launch an international inquiry into the East Timor situation (the resolution still passed), justifying its vote by claiming to follow the ASEAN policy of noninterference.[29] In Thailand, the Deputy Foreign Minister, Sukhumband Paribatra, defended Thailand's active role, arguing that "(i)t is not necessary to be under the ASEAN banner to help restore peace in East Timor. We are a good UN member and a good neighbor of Indonesia." However, many Thais criticized the government for acting too quickly, and expressed the fear that Thailand would bear the brunt of worsened relations with Indonesia if the situation in East Timor deteriorated.

ASEAN's reaction to East Timor underlines the inability of the organization to play any interventionary role in peacebuilding. For ASEAN to initiate an armed intervention into the affairs of a member state contradicts the fundamental norms and established practices of the institution. None of the ASEAN states are inclined towards active intervention, especially not under ASEAN auspices. Allowing intervention into one ASEAN state invites intervention into all. ASEAN may become involved in an internal conflict if it is invited to by a member state, but this entails obvious risks, particularly if a conflict could not be resolved quickly. Moreover, ASEAN's ability to broker peace between a member state's government and insurgent factions is compromised by ASEAN's inherent tendency to favor the state position. In short, it is almost inconceivable that ASEAN would forcefully intervene to build peace within a member state.

ASEAN's ability to launch a diplomatic intervention is also questionable. Even before the East Timor crisis erupted, the East Asian Economic Crisis and the problem of Indonesian forest fires had led various ASEAN leaders and academics to challenge ASEAN's practice of nonintervention. In the weeks preceding the July 1998 ASEAN Ministerial Meeting (AMM), Thailand's Foreign Minister, Dr. Surin Pitsuwan, advanced the concept of "flexible engagement."[31] "Flexible engagement involves publicly commenting on and collectively discussing fellow members' domestic policies when these have either regional implications or adversely affect the disposition of other ASEAN members."[32] When Surin Pitsuwan raised the concept at the

July 1998 AMM, however, all of the other ASEAN governments, with the exception of the Philippines, strongly opposed the idea. Arguments against the concept focused on its lack of clarity, and uncertainty over which domestic issues would remain off limits to public criticism. ASEAN states feared that making intra-ASEAN criticism acceptable would promote mistrust and resentment and renew the tensions that had divided the region before ASEAN was formed. Criticism could foster internal instability, and provide outsiders with the means to divide ASEAN. To most of ASEAN's members, flexible engagement—and any true relaxation of the nonintervention principle—would more likely lead to ASEAN's disintegration than its renewal. To placate Thailand, the ASEAN foreign ministers decided to allow "enhanced interaction." This permitted individual ASEAN states to comment on their neighbor's domestic activities if those activities affected regional concerns. However, ASEAN, the organization, would not intervene in members' domestic affairs.[33]

Enhanced interaction was tested almost immediately. In September 1998, the arrest and imprisonment of former Deputy Prime Minister Anwar Ibrahim in Malaysia evoked powerful reactions across the region. Presidents Estrada of the Philippines and B.J. Habibie of Indonesia, both personal friends of Anwar, criticized Malaysia's actions. The Malaysian government indicated that it would tolerate quiet, private expressions of concern from its ASEAN allies over Anwar's plight, but not public condemnation. Malaysia struck back. It questioned the legitimacy of the Habibie government. It raised the possibility of blocking Filipino and Indonesian workers from employment in Malaysia. It cancelled security exercises with the Philippines' military, and even suggested it might support Muslim insurgency in the Philippines. The fears of the statesmen opposed to relaxing the nonintervention principle were realized.

In November 1998, US Vice-President Al Gore delivered a speech to the pre-APEC Business Summit in Kuala Lumpur, condemning Malaysia's actions against Anwar. Gore's speech ultimately reinforced the "ASEAN way." ASEAN states perceived Gore's speech as displaying a lack of respect for the region and as an attempt by the US to intimidate Southeast Asia into following political and economic systems acceptable to the United States. The American intervention forced the ASEAN states to rally around the "ASEAN way" and helped set back the tentative efforts at reform. It appeared to the ASEAN states that enhanced interaction actually reduced ASEAN's international political relevance by revealing internal tensions which then undermined the unity that is essential to ASEAN's international standing. Under these circumstances, the future of "enhanced interaction" remains unclear.[34]

If ASEAN's norms and practices argue against its playing an interventionary role in its members' affairs, a far stronger case can be made that ASEAN can foster a "culture of prevention" in Southeast Asia, thereby avoiding interstate conflict altogether. ASEAN has articulated norms of peaceful interaction within Southeast Asia that have significantly affected the conduct of regional relations. What is more difficult to gauge are the reasons why these norms have been influential.

Some theorists make a constructivist argument that the ASEAN states have gradually adopted a "Southeast Asian/ASEAN identity" which defines their regional relations. ASEAN's norms underpin that identity and have been internalized by the regional states.[35] This transformation in identity is required to create a culture of conflict prevention. An alternative reading of the ASEAN states' conduct, however, is that they follow ASEAN norms largely out of self-interest; indeed, ASEAN's norms are not meant to impede the exercise of self-interest.[36]

The potential for the ASEAN identity to shape its members' behavior does exist. However, the preponderance of evidence favors the latter interpretation: ASEAN's states adhere to its norms for a combination of reasons, the most important being long-term self-interest. The ASEAN states recognize their mutual interest in cooperating; but this does not mean that they are defined by a strong regional identity. Busse makes a strong constructivist argument that ASEAN constitutes such an identity. He focuses on ASEAN's handling of Vietnam's invasion of Cambodia and its ongoing attempts to deal with an increasingly-assertive China as examples of ASEAN's strong commitment to the organization's norms. These analyses, however, fail to account for the many other factors motivating ASEAN's actions in both of these situations.

ASEAN opposed Vietnam's invasion of Cambodia mostly through diplomatic initiatives. It rallied opposition to Vietnam in the United Nations and created the Coalition Government of Democratic Kampuchea (CGDK) as an alternative to the Vietnamese-appointed regime in Cambodia. In the late 1980s, ASEAN sponsored the Jakarta Informal Meetings (JIMs) that helped forge the diplomatic basis for the eventual settlement of the Cambodian conflict. Ultimately, however, the conflict was ended by the decline of the Cold War and through the intervention of the great powers.[37]

Busse argues that ASEAN's norms were fundamental in causing it to follow its course of action against Vietnam. ASEAN could have followed three different options: (1) ignoring the invasion altogether, since Vietnam was not a direct military threat to any of the ASEAN states; (2) forging a military alliance against Vietnam; (3) launching a diplomatic and political campaign against Vietnam. ASEAN pursued the third option. Vietnam's challenge to ASEAN's basic norms meant that the invasion could not be ignored. ASEAN rejected the second option, forging a military alliance, because it saw such a confrontational strategy as counterproductive, too provocative, and in conflict with a "deep-seated cultural dislike for confrontational social behaviour."[38] ASEAN followed the third option because it was most in line with ASEAN's norms: "Opposing Vietnam on the grounds of principle underlined the validity of ASEAN's model but at the same time avoided the confrontational atmosphere surrounding alliance formation."[39]

Defending ASEAN's regional normative vision was an important factor behind ASEAN's decision to oppose Vietnam. However, this analysis underestimates the complexity of the other forces at work and the pragmatic calculations supporting the ASEAN states' actions. ASEAN's opposition to Vietnam's invasion was, in fact, not limited to nonconfrontational initiatives. By organizing the CGDK, ASEAN directly supported armed opposition to the Vietnamese-backed Cambodian regime.[40] ASEAN's decision to not form a military alliance against Vietnam did not only reflect a normative dislike of such an option. Other important factors included the calculation that Vietnam was not a real military threat to most of the ASEAN states, the fact that the ASEAN states lacked the military power to balance against Vietnam anyway, and the reality—highly relevant in the context of this discussion—that intra-ASEAN tensions precluded the trust necessary to form a military pact. Another fundamental consideration is the role of China. Without China's military might arrayed against Vietnam, Thailand would not have pushed the other ASEAN states towards opposing Vietnam. Instead, it would have accepted the Vietnamese invasion of Cambodia as a *fait accompli*, however unpleasant, and learned to live with it.[41] These considerations undermine the credibility of the argument that ASEAN's response to the Vietnam action in Cambodia primarily reflected normative commitments.

Throughout the conflict, the ASEAN states were at odds over perceptions of threats to regional security. Indonesia and Malaysia were far more concerned with China as a regional threat than with Vietnam; Thailand and Singapore saw Vietnam as the immediate threat. It is to ASEAN's credit that the organization maintained a common front for as long as it did, but significant actions indicating cracks in ASEAN solidarity did occur on occasion. ASEAN took measures to relieve these fissures. Thus, Indonesia became ASEAN's "interlocutor" to Vietnam. However, it is unlikely that ASEAN could have maintained its solidarity on Cambodia indefinitely.

Thailand was little influenced by considerations of ASEAN solidarity when formulating its own policies. This point is illustrated by Thailand's about-face in 1988 concerning its policy towards Vietnam. In Thailand, emerging business interests and new intellectual elites wanted unfettered access to Indochina. The newly-elected Prime Minister, Chatichai Choonhaven, represented these constituencies. Without consulting ASEAN, Chatichai declared his intention of converting Indochina from a battlefield to a marketplace by strengthening economic ties with Vietnam. This policy directly undermined the actions and initiatives of ASEAN to that point in time.[42] Indonesia was pursuing its own agenda in relation to Vietnam while trying to maintain ASEAN unity by endorsing punitive actions against Vietnam. Thailand's actions collapsed the ASEAN united front and undermined Indonesia's efforts and status in the region. Thailand's policies were dictated by economic interests as well as traditional security concerns, and altered as its perceptions of these issues changed. ASEAN's solidarity and coherence were not significant concerns.

Thailand's abrupt policy change occurred after almost a decade of being at the forefront of ASEAN, shaping the institution's policies, and participating in community-building exercises. The fact that it could act on such a fundamental issue without considering the consequences of its actions for ASEAN is an important indication that ASEAN's ability to function as a unit is limited by individual state interests and the perspectives of the government in power. For reasons particular to its political and historical circumstances, Indonesia maintained a high degree of ASEAN solidarity. Thailand did not. ASEAN's handling of the Vietnam/Cambodia affair reflected a wide range of considerations. Upholding ASEAN norms was only one part of a complex picture.

ASEAN's failure to establish a military balance against China reflects a host of considerations. The primary reasons for ASEAN's uncertain and contradictory relationship with China are mostly strategic. The refusal to balance against China reflects a hard-headed interpretation of the real limits of ASEAN's abilities and its lack of faith in the American commitment to Asian security. To some extent, the military modernization that swept Southeast Asia before the economic crisis was a response to a possible Chinese threat.[43] However, trying to match China's military power was not something that the ASEAN states ever intended to do. At best, they hoped to construct militaries capable of dissuading China from engaging in aggressive activities in the region.

The failure of the ASEAN states to seek external balancers is largely due to the fact that there are no reliable external balancers to be found. In the region, Japan is the only country with the military and technological potential to hold China in check. However, the countries of Asia find the prospect of a remilitarized Japan to be even more disturbing than a regionally belligerent China.[44] The preferred balancing power in the region is the United States. ASEAN states perceive the United States as an external actor with no significant historical baggage in the region. However, they do not regard the United States as a reliable ally. Asian states are unconvinced that the US would risk military conflict with China to support its regional allies.[45] This perception is likely to become stronger as China increases its military and technical abilities.

Thus, ASEAN's response to China is less a reflection of a particular ASEAN approach to international relations than a frank calculation of ASEAN's abilities to keep China in check. The ASEAN states cannot physically restrain China, nor can they rely on others to restrain China for them. Their only option is to engage China on the diplomatic and political fronts. ASEAN hopes to "socialize" China into the Asia Pacific regional community by impressing upon China the need for it to conform to standards of conduct that are acceptable to the other states of the Asia Pacific.[46] These acceptable standards reflect ASEAN's norms.

In the post–Cold War period, ASEAN countries have often pursued their individual regional interests without consulting ASEAN. Examples include individual ASEAN states arriving at separate arrangements with the US and Australia regarding regional security issues, inconsistent approaches to China over the Spratly Islands, and tensions between the original ASEAN states over how to incorporate the newest members.[47] These cases of inconsistency and disunity should not be exaggerated, but they do indicate that tension between ASEAN and individual state interests remain a common part of regional relations.

ASEAN cannot contribute to peacebuilding as an interventionary force. ASEAN's most basic norms require respect for its members' sovereignty and the practice of noninterference in members' domestic affairs. New pressures in the regional environment have encouraged some ASEAN states to challenge the conventional interpretation of nonintervention, but the great majority of ASEAN's members are vehemently opposed to any substantial redefinition of these established practices. The reasons for this are clear: most ASEAN members are weak states that are in the process of state-building. They joined the organization to enhance their sovereignty and, in the case of the newer members, enjoy greater international standing. As the experience with "enhanced interaction" demonstrated, opening themselves to criticism from their fellow members evokes tensions that the organization cannot resolve and creates disunity that undermines ASEAN's influence.

This being said, ASEAN can, conceivably, help smooth relations between East Timor and Indonesia. East Timor is deeply suspicious of ASEAN because of the organization's support for Indonesia's occupation. However, the Timorese recognize that their membership in ASEAN symbolizes a regional recognition of their state's legitimacy and accords them a level of protection. Playing an intermediary role between Indonesia and East Timor may help ASEAN gain experience in managing future conflicts within and between member states. However, any such intervention could only occur with the permission of the affected state(s). ASEAN will always need to be aware of the sensitivities of the governments of its member states—a requirement that compromises its ability to be an honest broker between governmental and nongovernmental factions in internal disputes.

In contrast, ASEAN contributes significantly to the creation of a culture of conflict prevention in Southeast Asia. However, this influence is not simply attributable to the construction of a regional identity that eschews violent confrontation. ASEAN *has* helped to create a regional identity, but this remains rather weak. The logic of self-interest is the major reason that the ASEAN states adhere to the organization's norms. The ASEAN states reject violence in their dealings with each other largely because it is not in their interests to engage in violent conflict. The corollary to this is that if an issue ever arose between ASEAN states that one or more saw as important enough to resolve through violence, then military force would become a viable option. However, it is difficult to imagine any circumstances under which this would happen. The importance of regional stability to the political and economic security of the ASEAN countries cannot be overestimated. Still, the ASEAN states have not rejected violence as a matter of cultural development, but as a matter of pragmatic political and economic calculation.

This argument does not reject the importance of norms and social structures in shaping the actions of the ASEAN states. Indeed, traditional realist interpretations of state action have little application in the case of ASEAN.[48] ASEAN's ability to promote norms that may influence the conduct of state action in Southeast Asia is probably the single greatest reason for its members' commitment to the organization. The ASEAN states are, indeed, part of a regional society. However, it is a *pluralist* international society, one that is based around the norm of sovereignty, which supports the practice of nonintervention.[49] This norm promotes the right of states to act as they deem necessary in their domestic affairs, even as it supports the norm prohibiting the violent resolution of disputes between states. The evidence that ASEAN countries still pursue narrow self-interests—sometimes to the detriment of ASEAN itself—is consistent with this analysis. ASEAN has not crumbled under this pressure because its structures are designed to demand little of its members. In addition, its members have recognized the diplomatic and economic advantages of speaking with one voice on the international stage, though these advantages have been compromised by ASEAN's recent indecision and ineffectiveness.

Eventually, ASEAN's collective identity may be enough to define its members' actions. At that point, the ASEAN states would identify strongly with each other, and their self-identity would be strongly tied to ASEAN. For now, however, the depth of the ASEAN identity—and, by extension, the norms that promote and reinforce (and are reinforced by) that identity—is mitigated by other factors. There are really only a few hundred foreign ministry officials and academics across the ASEAN states who genuinely feel part of an "ASEAN identity." For most other government officials—including those involved in economics and defense—the ASEAN identity is superficial, if it is felt at all.[50] At the least, it is overshadowed by much more important and parochial identities. These other identities have a critical effect on state policy, depending on the issues and circumstances. It is necessary to account for the numerous identities of each state, and their relative strengths and compatibilities, before it is possible to understand state actions.

One of the criteria for creating an active culture of conflict prevention is that regional organizations directly address and attempt to resolve, or at least defuse, issues of contention. ASEAN explicitly avoids doing this. However, it is advisable to modify the understanding of what is necessary to create a culture of conflict prevention: the ASEAN approach to conflict may be subtle, nonconfrontational and indirect, but it may also be very effective, to a point. The ASEAN countries have avoided violent conflict between themselves for over thirty years. Nonetheless, this assessment must be tempered with the recognition that the reality of external threat was fundamentally important to causing the ASEAN states to put aside their own conflicts and work together.[51] This implies that ASEAN's internal methods and effectiveness may be highly vulnerable to changes in the external environment.

Constructivist analysts of ASEAN emphasize the nonconfrontational dynamics of the "ASEAN way" as an important cultural artifact that supports a particular kind of international relations within Southeast Asia. The argument that Asians are nonconfrontational in their cultures and that this translates into meaningful differences in the conduct of regional politics is debatable. It is true that the manner in which political interaction is conducted can make a significant difference to outcomes, so an "Asian approach" to politics may affect regional relations. It may also be true that Asian cultures, in general, are nonconfrontational, particularly in the conduct of personal relations. However, the mode of conduct does not change the interests that are at stake in interstate relations. The ASEAN states have consistently demonstrated that they define their interests fairly narrowly and on the basis of domestic political considerations. The ASEAN way encourages this narrow definition of interests by ensuring states do not need to make difficult choices between regional and more parochial interests. The idea that "Asian culture" is nonconfrontational is also contentious. During the Cold War, Asia was the most violent continent on Earth. Many Asian countries are not averse to using violence to maintain political order and control. Indeed, the military and ideological threat from communist insurgencies was a major motivating force behind ASEAN.

Sovereignty remains the primary guiding principle of ASEAN, and is the norm from which its other basic norms derive. The collective identity embodied by the organization is a factor, but only a secondary consideration, in understanding the behaviour of its member states. This does not mean that ASEAN cannot and has not already made a significant contribution towards peacebuilding in Southeast Asia. However, ASEAN's members still do not accept that the organization has a legitimate role to play in addressing their domestic affairs. This tension will only be resolved if ASEAN's members agree to redefine the practice of sovereignty and accept that their long-term sovereign goals may actually be enhanced by strengthening ASEAN. Until this happens, ASEAN can continue to promote the norms of non-violence and the peaceful settlement of disputes between states in Southeast Asia.

ASEAN's norms of peaceful interaction do influence the ASEAN member states, but they do not define the social context within which these states operate. Instead, these norms have operated through a complex interaction of gradual social change and states' recognition of their self-interest. If these factors change, then the norms of ASEAN, and ASEAN itself, face the prospect of being seriously undermined. ASEAN contributes to the creation of a culture of conflict prevention in Southeast Asia. It is a good starting point. However, it still does not constitute a strong collective identity. The ASEAN states have largely supported ASEAN for the political advantages that it affords them. If the ASEAN states come to believe that ASEAN is no longer a political advantage, they will probably abandon the organization. Until the ASEAN states accept ASEAN's norms as correct in themselves, the culture of conflict prevention in Southeast Asia will be contingent on how well its values correspond to the narrower political and economic self-interests of the regional states.

For Canada, this analysis has important implications. Canada has invested considerable resources in the ASEAN Regional Forum (ARF) and in building a diplomatic profile in Southeast Asia. Nothing in this analysis should dissuade Canada from continuing these efforts. ASEAN represents its members' commitment to rule-based, peaceful interaction in Southeast Asia. As such, it complements Canada's commitment to state action based on international law and institutions. However, Canada's expectations of what ASEAN and its associated organizations can achieve must be realistic. ASEAN cannot intervene in its members' affairs; trying to do so would precipitate its self-destruction. ASEAN's contribution to peacebuilding cannot extend far beyond what it already is, at least for the foreseeable future.

Notes

1 Amitav Acharya, "Ideas, Identity and Institution-building: From the 'ASEAN way' to the 'Asia-Pacific way'?" *The Pacific Review* 10, no. 3 (1997): 319–46.

2 See, for example: Michael Antolik, *ASEAN and the Diplomacy of Accommodation*, (Armonk: M.E. Sharpe, 1990); Linda Martin, ed., *The ASEAN Success Story* (Honolulu: University of Hawaii Press: 1997); Nikolas Busse, "Constructivism and Southeast Asian Security," *The Pacific Review* 12, no. 1 (1999): 39–60; Chin Kin Wah, "The Long Road to 'One Southeast Asia'," *Asian Journal of Political Science* 5, no. 1 (June 1997): 1–19.

3 See: Michael Leifer, *ASEAN and the Security of Southeast Asia* (London: Routledge, 1989); Shaun Narine, "ASEAN and the Management of Regional Security," *Pacific Affairs* 71, no. 2 (Summer 1998): 195–214; Jurgen Ruland, "ASEAN and the Asian crisis: theoretical implications and practical consequences for Southeast Asian regionalism," *The Pacific Review* 13, no. 3 (2000): 421–51.

4 See Kenneth Bush in this volume (chapter 2).

5 See Keating and Knight in this volume (Introduction).

6 W. Andy Knight and Annika Björkdahl, "Towards a Culture of Prevention: the Evolution and Influence of Norms," Paper presented at the 1999 ISA Annual Convention, Washington D.C., February 1999.

7 Knight and Bjorkdahl, "Towards a Culture of Prevention," 2.

8 Much of the following discussion of constructivism is taken from an earlier article by the author. See: Shaun Narine, "Institutional Theory and Southeast Asia: the Case of ASEAN," *World Affairs* 161, no. 1 (Summer 1998): 39–40.

9 Alexander Wendt, "Collective Identity Formation and the International State," *American Political Science Review* 88 (June 1994): 385. For the purposes of this paper, I rely on Wendt's version of constructivism. See: Alexander Wendt, *Social Theory of International Politics* (Cambridge: Cambridge University Press, 1999). Amitav Acharya's excellent study of constructivism and ASEAN is also essential to the following discussion. See: Amitav Acharya, *Constructing a Security Community in Southeast Asia* (London: Routledge, 2001).

10 Wendt, "Collective Identity," 385–86; Alexander Wendt, "Anarchy is what states make of it: the social construction of power politics," *International Organization* 46, no. 2 (Spring 1992): 397–98; Alexander Wendt, "Constructing International Politics," *International Security* 20, no. 1 (Summer 1995): 74.

11 Wendt, "Anarchy," 399.

12 Wendt, "Constructing," 72–74; Wendt, "Anarchy," 398–99.

13 The Treaty of Amity and Cooperation (TAC) was signed in 1976, after being developed over the course of several years.

14 Busse, "Constructivism," 46.

15 For discussions of the "ASEAN way" see: Shaun Narine, "ASEAN and the ARF: The Limits of the 'ASEAN Way'," *Asian Survey* 37, no. 10 (October 1997): 964–65; Antolik, *ASEAN and the Diplomacy*, 94–96; Arnfinn Jorgenson-Dahl, *Regional Organisation and Order in Southeast Asia* (London: Macmillan, 1982), 165–69.

16 For a comprehensive history of ASEAN to the 1980s, see: Jorgenson-Dahl, *Regional Organisation*, 1–67; Robert O. Tilman, *Southeast Asia and the Enemy Beyond* (Boulder, CO: Westview Press, 1987). Amitav Acharya offers an excellent historical overview of Southeast Asian international relations. See: Amitav Acharya, *The Quest for Identity: International Relations of Southeast Asia* (Singapore: Oxford University Press, 2000).

17 Michael Leifer, *ASEAN and the Security of Southeast Asia*, 74–75; Carlyle Thayer, "ASEAN and Indochina: the Dialogue," in Alison Broinowski, ed. *ASEAN into the 1990s* (London: Macmillan 1990), 138–61.

18 Narine, "ASEAN and the Management of Regional Security," 195–214.

19 Vietnam joined ASEAN in 1995, Laos and Burma in 1997, and Cambodia in 1999.

20 For a deeper analysis of these points, see: Shaun Narine, "ASEAN into the Twenty-first Century: Problems and Prospects," *The Pacific Review* 12, no. 3 (Summer 1999): 357–80;

Michael Wesley, "The Asian Crisis and the Adequacy of Regional Institutions," *Contemporary Southeast Asia* 21 (April 1999): 54–73; Shaun Narine, "ASEAN in the Aftermath: The Consequences of the East Asian Economic Crisis, *Global Governance* 8, no. 2 (2002): 179–94.

21 This comes to approximately 200,000 people ("ASEAN's commitment to new nation tested," East Timor Action Network, http://www.etan.org/et2000a/january/22-31/31ASEAN.htm [accessed November 27, 2003]).

22 Note that, initially, Singapore was uneasy about Indonesia's invasion of East Timor in 1974. It did not support Indonesia in the first UN vote on the invasion, in order to register its discomfort. Singapore feared the image of a large state invading a smaller neighbor was too close to its own situation. Subsequently, however, it fell into line with the other ASEAN states.

23 98.5 percent of eligible voters cast ballots in the referendum; 78 percent voted for independence. John Taylor, *East Timor: The Price of Freedom* (New York: Zed Books, 1999), xiv.

24 Alan Dupont, "ASEAN's Response to the East Timor Crisis," *Australian Journal of International Affairs* 54, no. 2 (2000): 163–70.

25 Dupont, "ASEAN'S Response," 165.

26 Japan provided US $100 million of a $107 million INTERFET fund established to help developing countries cover expenses. Dupont, "ASEAN's Response," 166.

27 "ASEAN' commitment," 3; Dupont, "ASEAN's Response," 168.

28 Dupont, "ASEAN's Response," 167. For further commentary, see Lee Kim Chew, "Politics behind ASEAN's inaction," *Strait Times*, October 17, 1999, http://www.iidnet.org/apcet/views-aseaninaction.htm (accessed October 21, 1999).

29 Sangwoh Suh, "Unease over East Timor," *Asiaweek* 25, no. 41 (1999), http://www.asiaweek.com/asiaweek/magazine/99/1015/easttimor.html (accessed November 28, 2003).

30 "ASEAN's commitment," 2.

31 Robin Ramcharan, "ASEAN and Non-interference: A Principle Maintained," *Contemporary Southeast Asia* 22, no. 1 (April 2000): 74–76.

32 Jurgen Haacke, "The concept of flexible engagement and the practice of enhanced interaction: intramural challenges to the 'ASEAN way'," *The Pacific Review* 12, no. 4 (1999): 583.

33 Haacke, "Flexible Engagement," 592–98.

34 Haacke, "Flexible Engagement," 592–98.

35 See, for example: Nikolas Busse, "Constructivism,"; Amitav Acharya, "Imagined Proximities: The Making and Unmaking of Southeast Asia as a Region," *Southeast Asian Journal of Social Science* 27, no. 1 (1999): 55–77.

36 Tobias Ingo Nischalke, "Insights from ASEAN's Foreign Policy Cooperation: The 'ASEAN Way', a Real Spirit or a Phantom?" *Contemporary Southeast Asia* 22, no. 1 (April 2000): 89–112.

37 Shaun Narine, "ASEAN and the Management of Regional Security."

38 Busse, "Constructivism," 50.

39 Busse, "Constructivism," 50.

40 The CGDK was a coalition of anti-Vietnamese Cambodian parties, including the despised Khmer Rouge. Though all of the CGDK parties fielded militaries, of a

sort, only the Khmer Rouge was moderately successful as a military force against Vietnam. For a comprehensive overview of the political machinations from this period, see: Grant Evans and Kevin Rowley, *Red Brotherhood at War: Vietnam, Cambodia and Laos since 1975* (London: Verso, 1990).

41 Leifer, *ASEAN and the Security of Southeast Asia*, 96–97.

42 It is important to note that the Thai Foreign Ministry, under Foreign Minister Siddhi, actively opposed the government's change in policy and actually sabotaged Chatichai's earlier initiatives by quietly refusing to pursue them. Siddhi was forced to resign in 1990 for domestic political reasons. The new Foreign Minister, Subin Pinkayan, agreed with Chatichai that the war in Cambodia was over as far as Thailand was concerned, and emphasized economic considerations. See: Michael Haas, *Genocide by Proxy: Cambodian Pawn on a Superpower Chessboard* (New York: Praeger, 1991), 216–17, 264; Evans and Rowley, *Red Brotherhood*, 265, 288–89.

43 The question of whether or not there was a Southeast Asian arms race is a complex one. In general, the answer is "no." There were many factors contributing to the ASEAN states military buildups. However, these buildups never became "economically irrational." See: Amitav Acharya, *An Arms Race in Post-Cold War Southeast Asia? Prospects for Control, Pacific Strategic Paper No. 8* (Singapore: Institute of Southeast Asian Studies, 1994); Amitav Acharya, *Constructing a Security Community*, 136–141; Dewi Fortuna Anwar, "The Rise in Arms Purchases: Its Significance and Impacts on South East Asian Political Stability" (Unpublished paper, University of Toronto, April 1993).

44 Michael J. Green and Benjamin L. Self, "Japan's Changing China Policy: From Commercial Liberalism to Reluctant Realism," *Survival* 38, no. 2 (Summer 1996): 42–43; Chin Kin Wah, "Regional Perceptions of China and Japan," in Chandran Jeshurun, ed., *China, India, Japan and the Security of Southeast Asia* (Singapore: Institute of Southeast Asian Studies, 1993), 11.

45 "Innocents Abroad: Bill Clinton's commitment to Asia," *Far Eastern Economic Review*, May 2, 1996, 2; "America's Chinese Puzzle," *The Economist*, May 25, 1996, 35–36.

46 Author interview with Rear Admiral R.M. Sunardi, Assistant to the Minister of Defense and Security, Jakarta, Indonesia, February 20, 1995.

47 Nischalke, "Insights from ASEAN's Foreign Policy Cooperation," 95–103.

48 For a complete analysis of the inapplicability of realism to ASEAN, see Narine, "Institutional Theory and Southeast Asia," 33–47.

49 This analysis of international society is based on the "English School" of international relations, and the work of Hedley Bull. For further information, see Hedley Bull, *The Anarchical Society* (London: Macmillan, 1977); Tim Dunne, *Inventing International Society: A History of the English School* (New York: St. Martin's Press, 1998).

50 There is widespread recognition that the "ASEAN identity" is mostly felt within ASEAN foreign ministries, though less understanding of the limitations this implies. See the earlier discussion of the Thai foreign ministry's resistance to Prime Minister Chatichai's initiatives. See also: Busse, "Constructivism," 55; Alistair Iain Johnston, "The Myth of the ASEAN Way? Explaining the Evolution of the ASEAN Regional Forum," in Helga Haftendorn, Robert Keohane, Celeste Wallander, eds., *Imperfect Unions* (New York: Oxford University Press, 1999), 287–324.

51 Narine, "ASEAN and the ARF."

11 Participatory Peacebuilding

Jarat Chopra &
Tanja Hohe

THE FRONTLINE for international interventions that exercise any degree of political authority in transition has proved to be at the level of local administration. Here, the Western-style paradigm of state-building, which is preoccupied with forming a national executive, legislature and judiciary, confronts resilient traditional structures, socially legitimate powerholders, abusive warlords out to win, or community coping-mechanisms relied on under conflict conditions. The options for establishing or reconstructing governing institutions seem stark: either reinforce the *status quo* and build on it, further empowering the already strong; or replace altogether what exists with a new administrative order. But there may be a middle road.

In the past, in Somalia and Cambodia, or later in Kosovo and East Timor, interveners invariably followed the line of least resistance, rendering themselves irrelevant in terms of the impact they had where the overwhelming majority of the population lives. The result was a social and political reality that developed by itself, regardless of the size of the international presence or the scope of its mandate. By contrast, the dimensions of the social engineering project to invent and introduce an entirely new governance system are vast. Planners have never assessed the number of elements and the breadth of such an assignment, nor have implementers ever adequately prepared for the task, let alone effectively accomplished it. Appreciating the scale of the venture might have led to the conclusion that it was impossible, certainly in the relatively short timeframe of most interventions.

Instead, what may be feasible is a longer-term transition, in which space is provided for local voices to be expressed and communities to get directly involved in the evolution of their own cultural or political institutions, as part of a gradual integration into the national state apparatus. This means giving time for an indigenous paradigm to coexist with and gradually transform during the establishment of modern institutions. Integral to the process is the design of mechanisms for genuine popular participation in administrative bodies at the local level, which can also guarantee representation upwards throughout the government-building enterprise from the very beginning to ensure its social viability.

The exercise of political authority by the international community in postwar states has taken four distinct forms: (1) *assistance* to an interim government (Afghanistan); (2) *partnership* with the existing occupier (Namibia); (3) *control* of divided factions (Cambodia); and (4) *governorship* of territory and population (East Timor). Two particular factors led interveners to temporarily assume these increasing degrees of political power: First, in the midst of complex emergencies, a wide range of intergovernmental agencies and nongovernmental organizations independently addressed security, humanitarian, developmental, human rights, judicial, policing, and economic concerns. To achieve unity of effort for greater effectiveness, civilian unity of command was institutionalized in multifunctional operations with multiple components or pillars. The aim was to improve harmonization across the various sectors, both horizontally and vertically within missions. Second, it became clear (as Kenneth Bush has so eloquently stated)[1] that military forces alone, or massive humanitarian assistance could only stem some of the worst symptoms of violence, but could not resolve the sources of conflict.[2] Doing so required direct involvement in the local political process, and as the national government was fragile, fragmenting or had altogether collapsed, international interventions began to assume increasing degrees of political authority over the territory and population. Transitional administrations finally exercised total executive, legislative and judicial powers as interim governments.

Excluded from the equation, extraordinarily, were the people of the country.[3] The subculture of UN missions, their leadership and much of their staff, was rooted in a diplomatic habit, relating institution-to-institution or at most talking to a minority elite. Civilian bureaucrats were not as accustomed to interacting with the local population in their operations as some militaries are. That asocial form of alienation was tenable in limited types of intervention, but it was disastrous when assisting or acting as a governing authority attempting to build capacity for a self-sustaining state.[4]

The institutional mindset had also plagued early adventures, as in Somalia, when UN officials wasted months under famine conditions seeking consent to international deployments from a sovereign government that no longer existed. The question of consent was subsequently overwhelmed by the formula of declaring particular crisis zones a "threat to international peace and security" and then intervening under the broad terms of Chapter VII of the UN Charter. In the wake of radically intrusive transitional administrations, perhaps the issue of consent should be revisited in a considerably broader sense—socially through the direct participation of local communities in international operations of whatever variety, thus fostering a degree of downward accountability and legitimacy that has so far been absent.

Indeed, following the doctrinal evolution of interventions throughout the last decade—spanning "second generation" uses of force in peace operations during the early years to the comprehensive exercise of political authority until now—the next step is to identify the means for better popular participation in international efforts to establish governing structures in postconflict settings.[5] UN Secretary-General Kofi Annan has acknowledged the necessity of "participatory governance" if a domestic peace is ever to be sustainable.[6]

However, other than reflecting the familiar ingredients of the Western state, the idea of participation amongst the democratization and peacebuilding cognoscenti is still at the stage of labels or headlines, and the notion lacks clear definition, any kind of effective strategy or as much appreciation of the local mindset as of the model to be imported.[7] Similarly, the bulk of General Assembly debates about popular participation have focused on specific disadvantaged groups, such as women and minorities, and addressed how they can be better empowered and included in government. This narrow, albeit important, perspective cannot accommodate the much broader task of holistically integrating a population during as well as after the formation of public administration.

In order to actually address the sources of civil conflict, focusing on armed factions competing for control of a capital or filling the appearance of a central vacuum when an occupier has withdrawn could never be enough. There has to be an intimate understanding of why the population is engaged in strife and what fuels it. What drives the villager to take part in war? What can make him or her stop? Appreciating such perceptions at the grassroots level is a key piece of information around which to design a meaningful approach to conflict resolution and peacebuilding. The answer may be rooted in nothing less than an entire worldview through which the conflict is filtered. Historical facts surrounding why war broke out may pale in comparison to a religious belief system or set of values that functions as the motor for continued violence.

The blunt approach of international interventions has been to rely on "free and fair" electoral exercises as a single event, that function according to global standards of human rights and North Atlantic concepts of democracy but which do not resonate with local communities and are not translated into their paradigm. Individuals may turn out to vote *en masse*, but their understanding of the ballot may be defined according to a parallel cosmos. A democratically elected powerholder may be recognized internationally though not locally, since the voting process was unrelated to beliefs regarding sources of political legitimacy.[8] The problem is more acute when voting for distant national representatives than for more familiar local leaders. The result can be a recycled conflict between what the people and the rest of the world understand as the rightful powerholder.

Similarly, an international mission may appoint or empower a young university graduate as a new administrative official on the basis of modern skills and merit. But that person may not have local acknowledgment, since the community continues to adhere to an aged chief approved by ancestral spirits, a warlord that has protected the village or another type of leader with whom people identify. Building a state in this manner results in a superficial layer on top of the reality of social life, and can lead, again, to conflict between the two perspectives.[9]

Despite the long-term presence of some kind of state apparatus, either in the form of colonial rule or an independent, though authoritarian, regime, local communities in the developing world have often functioned according to their own, fundamentally stateless structures, regardless of the paramountcy of the machine controlled by the capital city. Considerably older than the national identity, such social structures have proved profoundly resilient and defied quick interventions to build new "democratic" institutions to replace the ones that have previously collapsed. Relying, therefore, on an election as the sum total of popular participation in building a state simply replicates the utter disconnect between the people and the government, laying the foundation for institutions to fail again.

To avoid this scenario, and bridge the local-national gap, communities have to be integrated in the process of institution-building, where they live as well as at higher levels, in order to foster a sense of identification with the greater whole and a feeling of ownership of the alternative structure.[11] In this manner, through improved trust in their, now more responsive, administrative bodies, the idea of "citizenship" can begin to have a logical meaning. This kind of realignment is assuredly an arduous and lengthy prospect, and yet it must start at the very beginning of an intervention. A transitional period generally, and its earliest phases particularly, provides a unique opportunity to minimize factional politicization of public administration before a new government can replace civil service officials with the party faithful. In fact, the broadest approach to popular participation may be most feasible before a transfer of power has occurred and an electoral victor begins reshaping the instruments of control.

One of the overall dangers of such an effort, though, is a breakdown of indigenous social structures and a population thereafter having to rely on the successful functioning of state mechanisms. Should the government or its administration become fragile or collapse for whatever reason in the future, a worse set of anarchical conditions may result, in which people have lost any checks and balances that may have been inherent in their social order. Conflict under such circumstances can become "cannibalistic," as Somalis described the early 1990s.

There has been varied practice in bottom-up approaches by development agencies, including the World Bank, UN Development Programme (UNDP) and US Agency for International Development, in the whole range of assistance activities.[12] There have been comparable attempts to specifically strengthen civil society and to improve capacity-building for "governance" according to multiple definitions. The word has been used narrowly to mean efficient and effective public management, or more broadly to encompass the mechanisms, processes and institutions through which citizens and groups articulate their interests.[13] However, there have been relatively few occasions when the international community has aimed to increase popular participation in the actual establishment of local administration.

Furthermore, development agencies have treated "participation" in a universal sense. There are different kinds of participation that have to be matched to the kind of society existing in any particular area. For instance, the approach to a stratified, hierarchical society—like a Timorese kingdom—should vary from one designed for a segmentary group without centralized leadership, as amongst historically nomadic clans in Somalia. These approaches will also vary according to the degree of social change intended and the scale of time required to alter existing structures. Deciding on the amount of social engineering to be conducted will directly affect the balance of power of local stakeholders, given the inevitable empowering or disenfranchising effect of any such project.

In Afghanistan, the traditional *shura* (council) was often employed as an interface for delivering humanitarian assistance and implementing aid projects. Rather than being an internationally-sponsored body, the *shura* was an indigenous, ad hoc means of local decision-making that could provide ownership of outside assistance. It could be composed of elders, religious authorities or other influential personalities, who are well-respected community members, have good negotiations skills and are knowledgeable. Sometimes existing traditional village or tribal *shuras* were used, while in other cases ad hoc *shuras* were instituted. All individuals relevant to the task to be accomplished had to participate in meetings in order to reach nominal consensus, though not all voices were equal. The process met with varying degrees of success and was open to claims that *shuras* were manipulated to the benefit of local leaders and/or that it amounted to social engineering at the hands of foreigners. The speed with which *shuras* learned "aidspeak" was a good indicator of whether the *shura* was homegrown or functioning as part of an external agenda.

Modeled after the *shura*, UN-HABITAT and UNDP established Community Forums that elect Consultative Boards to guide and provide advice on community affairs. While a form of self-government in the absence of formal governing structures, these neighborhood bodies have yet to form the basis of a state administration.[14]

The *shura* concept has also been adapted at the national level in the form of the *Loya Jirga* (Grand National Council) since the eighteenth century. The 2002 *Loya Jirga* convened by the UN Assistance Mission in Afghanistan and the Afghan Interim Authority was "a hybrid-model of traditional selection, popular representation, and central government prerogative."[15] In order to guarantee broad, balanced representation, a free-and-fair universal suffrage election was neither feasible nor desirable. However, many Afghan groups felt the *Loya Jirga* had been pre-orchestrated and was not an endogenous political process.[16]

As part of a "regionalization" strategy attempted by the two UN Operations in Somalia, regional and district councils of elders were formed to outmaneuver factional fighting in Mogadishu. However, in the clan system, elders played more of an advisory than leadership role, and so Somalis never regarded the councils as anything more, contradicting international intentions to create alternative political centers of gravity. Eventually, the competition for control of the capital consumed any efforts outside the city and below the "national" level.[17]

In Rwanda, the World Bank initiated a Community Reintegration and Development Project (CRDP) in 1997 that tested a decentralized and participatory approach to community development. The premise of "decentralization" was to transfer decision-making and expenditure authority to lower levels of government. The project established Community Development Committees (CDC) at the *commune* (later "district") level, based on elections from the *cellules* and the *secteurs*. "Participation" meant a partnership between the *commune* administrations and the local population around sectoral planning and project implementation. The CDC concept and structure laid the groundwork for the first ever elections of district administrators (formerly the *commune burgomasters* appointed by the President since independence). Furthermore, the CDCs have now become a formal part of local government.[18]

Still, the project did lead to some resentment amongst other local leaders. The Rwandan government subsequently created politico-administrative committees (CPAs). The CPAs complemented the work of the CDCs, and members were elected at the same time. But the separation of CPA members from the CRDP project cycle led to several misgivings and delays in implementation, until the relationship between the two was improved.[19]

Perhaps the most extensive experiment of its kind, and indeed a valuable one from which to learn lessons, was the "Community Empowerment and Local Governance Project" (CEP) established by the World Bank and Asian Development Bank in East Timor. Although it had a more development-focused precursor in Indonesia, in the context of the UN's transitional administration of East Timor the CEP aimed to establish the actual local administration of the country.[20] The dramatic scope of the project illustrates well the dilemmas associated with creating local governance structures and the need for deep knowledge of social dynamics.

The UN structure extended formally to the level of the thirteen districts, with a minimal presence in the subdistricts, where 80 percent of the population lives. The CEP concept envisioned elections at the lowest strata of society, in the hamlets, for equal numbers of men and women to form village councils. The village councils would elect equal numbers of men and women to form subdistrict councils. Grants would be provided directly to the subdistrict councils, which would then spend the funds based on proposals it received from the villages. This, it was hoped, would result in a degree of self-determination in reconstruction, as well as reverse centuries of reporting upwards to authority and introduce accountability downwards to a constituency. Ideally, in time, these structures, with the funding that they would have, would be consolidated and officially constitute a nascent form of self-administration.

An interesting question arises whether or not this model could be extended further upwards, with subdistrict councils electing district councils, which in turn would elect a national council. Although politically impossible under the circumstances in East Timor, the speed with which CEP elections were held indicated a rapid means of involving the population directly in some manner at the beginning of an intervention, thus avoiding reliance on appointed bodies that are less representative.

When negotiations began between the two banks, the UN and the Timorese resistance regarding the establishment of the CEP, the first joint project of its kind, it became apparent that one part of the resistance had already started conducting elections independently for chiefs of villages and subdistricts, as wells councils of elders for both, composed of representatives of youth, women and other civil society groups. By this time, the process had been completed at the village level in half the country, and so the issue was raised about the relationship between the CEP councils and these other structures. The two were reconciled in a rudimentary kind of separation of powers. Logically, therefore, to respect this division, neither the village chief as an executive nor any member of the council of elders corresponding to a quasi-judicial entity, could stand for election in the CEP process. For lack of anthropological knowledge, the implication of this particular issue was not anticipated.

In traditional Timorese society, only certain leaders, in most cases the village chief, can acceptably function as a political authority. His source of legitimacy is heredity as part of a family ordained by ancestral approval. If the wrong person exercises political power, upsetting the cosmic order and the continuation of fertility, then villagers will fear ancestral sanctions that endanger the survival of the community, such as harvests failing or children falling ill. Furthermore, the separation of political powers does not make sense, since the village chief exercises his authority in a distinct hierarchy that functions in strict opposition to ritual power as part of the overall sociocosmic order.[21]

Therefore, by excluding the village chief, the CEP councils were not perceived by the community to have any political authority, which in turn meant that they could not form the basis of local administration. Instead, people elected to the councils precisely those individuals who were not older and senior or able to exercise political authority, but who were young, literate and capable of interacting with foreigners. The village chief continued to rule as the acknowledged political head.[22]

Also, a principle carried over to East Timor from the World Bank's Indonesian experience, was to focus on the subdistrict level because it was seen as a weaker layer of society in comparison to the power of the districts and villages. By financing that level, there had been an attempt to subvert the influence of the other two, above and below it, thus creating the opportunity for a new center of gravity, with space for alternative voices, to develop and facilitate genuine community empowerment. With comparable logic, it was also felt that by funding the CEP councils, despite the separation of powers agreed on, the other structures would atrophy without comparable resources. Precisely the opposite happened, both vertically and horizontally, because the CEP councils could not compete with the social power of the village chief whom they had excluded.[23]

This experience poses a typical dilemma. It could be argued, for instance, that in order for the CEP councils to have better fulfilled the intentions behind them, the village chief should have been included—as one amongst many other issues affecting the project. Through him they would have commanded authority in accordance with local perceptions. Doing so, however, would simply reinforce existing power structures, which internationally would be regarded as inequitable and gender-biased and conflicting with individualistic values of human rights and democracy. Alternatively, a decision could be made to challenge the existence of the village chief and dismantle traditional structures, replacing them altogether with administrative institutions of the central state. That would be a radical social engineering campaign that could be conducted brutally or if done humanely, might simply fail. A more sophisticated approach is necessary.

In East Timor, however, the decentralizing logic of the CEP confronted the hierarchical institutional culture of the UN transitional administration. More anthropological knowledge would not have avoided an acrimonious negotiation regarding the establishment of the project, which had been opposed by officials preoccupied with power at the center. Resenting their loss of control as part of the logic of a program aimed at community empowerment, UN negotiators turned down twice the only project that had been funded at the time. The ensuing conflict overwhelmed matters of substance regarding the CEP's design and would later squander the opportunity for popular participation provided by the transitional period. Only coordinated visits by the Secretary-General and World Bank President James D. Wolfensohn forced a signature on the first ever collaborative effort. In the absence of international consensus prior to the project's implementation, the territorial struggle amongst interveners themselves undermined the CEP more than any other single factor, including interests of Timorese stakeholders.[24] Still, the experience with this model is worth considering in future government-building interventions.

There is never a vacuum of power on the ground. Even when there is the complete absence of an identifiable state government or any semblance of governing institutions—as was the case when Indonesian forces withdrew from East Timor or when Somalia disintegrated—traditional structures evolve, social organization is redefined, people continue to survive, filling the space, if it was ever there in the first place.

Learning from past experiments for future participatory projects, the first step is to assess and appreciate the dynamics of perception. Popular perspectives will equally affect any form of intervention, however minimal or extensive, in conflict, postconflict and nonconflict environments, at any level, local or national. What is the system of ideas and values that constitute the local worldview, that influence how people are acting, how they interpret the conflict, and how they will perceive an outside intervention? For instance, is the power of a warlord based on the possession of arms, or is he legitimated by a social structure? Attempted disarmament is a military response in the first case; but the second requires the complicated undertaking of a social transformation. What kind of incentive can there be for people to question existing power structures, seek alternatives and assume ownership of the forces of change?

Answering such questions will require a role for anthropologists and regional experts in international interventions. Though, to be accepted, they will need to adapt and adjust their methodologies to keep pace with an operational context. So far anthropologists have identified the problem of national and institutional cultural differences amongst peacekeepers and between them and the local population.[25] However, work has not yet focused specifically on how to approach the complex policy puzzle of increased participation in state-building. In practical terms, area expertise needs to be incorporated into training for local-level interveners, development of the plan and the concept of participation to be attempted, and the determination of a strategy for implementation and adaptation on the ground. Predeployment anthropological assessments need to be combined with ongoing deep intelligence analysis of internal domestic politics as part of the initial negotiated acceptance of mission intentions and throughout all activities to be undertaken.

In this sense, specialized knowledge is one tool to help tackle the dilemma surrounding the scope of social engineering by identifying objectives according to what is possible or what degree of international commitment will be feasible. For instance, one national faction may be consolidating its power through local structures and to challenge local leaders may not be possible without an intervention that decides to comprehensively confront that faction and create the political environment for other parties to have a place in a peace process. Avoiding the issue may amount to an implicit acceptance of the will of the strong and the reality of a balance of power, or it may lead to the explicit conclusion that an intervention need be something only minimal given the dimensions of the circumstances. Consequently, the right knowledge can dictate planning by adjusting approaches to avoid predictable failures and defining the best means both for establishing local administration and conducting the overall national state-building enterprise, including the structuring of government, the formation of judicial institutions for the rule of law, and the reform of the security sector.

The second step is to actually turn collated information into a detailed concept for genuine participation and to design the mechanisms necessary to support social transformations that are both effective and legitimate. The contours of what is to be done can only be determined according to the specifics of the case. Nevertheless, four options for participatory intervention can be identified that vary in the degree of social engineering to be undertaken. Listed in descending order of intrusiveness at the local level, they are not neat categories; there may be overlap between them or one may become another in the course of an intervention or subsequently. Still, these rough distinctions each lead to substantially different operational plans and decisions that flow from the amount of change interveners intend to result on the ground. In every case, the process must begin at the start of an intervention, in the greatest window of opportunity for change—before new individuals are empowered who either exclude altogether the local level or are rejected by the population.

Local structures may be fully intact but fundamentally abusive, either because they are historically oppressive by nature or because they have been brutalized by conditions of conflict. They may have become factionalized and serve as the core engine for continued conflict. Fighting warlords may be legitimized by social structures in their respective home communities. Competing sets of local structures in the same place may constitute a source of violence. Alternatively, despite persisting social identities, indigenous political structures may have broken down either from the effects of war or mass displacement, or because they were reconstituted by a state-formation enterprise that has now collapsed.

With the objectives of protecting human rights or underwriting a peace process, interveners may attempt to introduce across the country an entirely new and standardized administration at the local level. Existing structures would have to be challenged, outmaneuvered or co-opted as new institutions are established. The effort would require a significant degree of socialization for each community to identify with the proposed outcome. Significant preplanning, international political consensus and human and financial resources will be needed to have any impact, as will a high degree of harmonization with all other aspects of a mission if the effort is not to unravel. As difficult as something of this magnitude sounds, not much less could fulfill the prevailing rhetoric about "democratization."

Indigenous social and political structures may have proved resilient and continue as the operating paradigm for much, if not the majority, of the population at the local level. They will have survived colonial occupations and perhaps decades under a newly independent state, but they may have never been integrated as part of the central governing apparatus. While competing factions, occupying powers or a previously functioning government may have manipulated the existing structures and selectively replaced local leaders, the logic and concept of political legitimacy has remained intact.

As part of a new state-building enterprise, planners may decide that the short timeframe of an intervention is insufficient to conduct a total social engineering project, or that the specifics of a transitional peace process require the support and legitimization of acknowledged leaders to ensure short term results on the ground. However, the disconnection between the indigenous paradigm and the idea of the modern state may be too great to be sustainable. An ungovernable local level may lead to central authoritarianism in response, undermining objectives of democratization and possibly abusing human rights, in turn triggering potentially violent opposition and threatening eventual fragmentation. Alternatively, the local structures themselves may have been somewhat perverted from too much manipulation and it might not be feasible to restore the integrity of the previous system. There may also be power struggles in individual villages as old rivalries emerge in the wake of a withdrawing occupier and competing claims for legitimate leadership.

Therefore, to avoid building state-failure and repeating another cycle of conflict, the long-term objective would be to establish a modern state at all levels through a process of gradual transformation of existing structures into a formal, local administration. This strategy must form an inherent part of the transitional plan, which will need to provide for selective correction of any seemingly abusive practices or violations of human rights in the short term. Key to this model will be creating space for the continuation of local ideas in some form while the community is gradually integrated into the state-building effort from bottom to top.

Indigenous structures may be fully functioning and constitute the reality of social and political life of the population. They may already have transformed to some degree over time, in response to conflict, under colonial occupation or due to a previous national state-formation experience, and resulted in a hybrid form of self-governing institutions. They may actually be stronger than a nominal and weak central government and more capable of delivering basic services to communities. They may even be the only functioning structures in the event of a total collapse in the capital city or before a new authority has been established after the withdrawal of an occupier. Also, the local structures themselves may be wholly appropriate as part of a future administration.

Therefore, it may not make sense to conduct a social engineering project in the short term, displacing what is effectively functioning while also attempting to construct a national executive, legislature and judiciary, with all that that entails. Equally, it may not make sense to transform the existing structures in the long term, because of their acceptability or usefulness as the foundation for state-building efforts. Alternatively, interveners may lack the political will, sufficient time or resources to make many changes at the local level, or they may be characteristically preoccupied with institutions in the capital, either by habit or as an exit strategy, withdrawing as soon as some semblance of a new authority can be recognized. There may also be an operational imperative to use what exists to produce some quick results, or empowerment of existing local leaders may be the consequence of their support to a military intervention.

In all of these instances, the local level as it exists, acting entirely independently as it has, may be integrated as a whole in the state-building effort, and it is not expected to change much over time. The model is one in which the central government and the local paradigm are connected, but the one will not eventually replace the other. Instead, their relationship may be articulated in a constitution, perhaps with a separation of powers at different levels of administration. Additionally, there may be local representation at the national level and an official government presence at the local level. Serious offences would be the responsibility of the judiciary but communities may resolve other forms of conflict according to their own rules. While there may be selective correction at the local level because of human rights standards, government policies or legislative acts, the structures themselves nevertheless continue largely intact.

If operational convenience is the rationale for wholesale integration, then local structures cannot be unacceptably abusive or a factional source of conflict, otherwise this approach will fail after international withdrawal. Integration has to be a carefully harmonized process, made possible in the design of a mission's campaign plan and implemented accordingly. If the gap between local institutions and national government-building efforts is not reconciled during a transitional period, then a new pattern of disconnection will prevent integration from occurring. Instead, widescale disenfranchisement, opposition, authoritarianism, fragmentation and conflict may be the sequential outcome.

Local social and political structures may be far too resilient to contemplate their alteration and they may already have been integrated in some previously decentralized governmental arrangement. Their role in national life may have been officially recognized and overwhelmingly accepted. While they have not constituted a source of conflict, they may nevertheless have been weakened somewhat by a violent environment, politically misused by central authorities or debilitated by a lack of basic resources. Some local leaders may have been killed or fled as refugees, but the concept of local governance understood by the community has not been perverted in any way. The structures mostly in place are largely acceptable according to international standards of human rights and democratization. Alternatively, the international intervention is a minimal one with little capability beyond assistance.

The basic objective in this situation is to restore to their full capacities the existing bodies and repatriate, restore or help identify and support local leaders. Improving the relationship between these structures and a fragile central government being rebuilt, an authoritarian regime democratizing or a new authority to which an occupier is transferring power may be the kind of limited activity performed during a transitional period. Any selective correction of the local institutions would be largely as the result of an overall strengthening of a national rule of law.

The profound danger of this option is that superficially it may be attractive to international donors who lack the political will or resources to do more, or to military forces that have been supported in their isolation of a faction or regime and therefore are unwilling to open up political space for alternative voices during the reconstruction phase. Due to imperatives of political convenience during a peace process, a mission following the line of least resistance will merely accommodate existing realities. In such a context, if local structures are factionalized and abusive, or serve as an integral element in the dynamics of conflict, then to reinforce them will lead to the irrelevance of the intervention, if not an exacerbation and deepening of socially-driven violence.

At the international level, there has to be agreement on the selection of one of these options and organized unity of effort in the field. Political competition amongst international agencies, no less than amongst local leaders or national elites, will profoundly affect the rearrangement of power that increased popular participation will imply. The level of education, the breadth and depth of the skills base in the country, the amount of poverty and imbalance of wealth distribution, the relative sizes of urban versus rural populations, and the degree of identification of local groups with the elite all affect the choice of category. Unless a much more sophisticated approach to participation along these lines can be developed, exclusion of people from any aspect of state-building will continue to cause costly interventions to founder. This means, in the midst of a world of national governments, having to forge a much more direct relationship between international and local communities, paradoxically, to underwrite the state.

Acknowledgment

A version of this chapter appears as an article in *Global Governance* 10, no. 3 (2004) forthcoming. The authors are grateful to the following individuals for their comments on earlier drafts of this chapter: Scott Guggenheim, Leni Dharmawan and Markus Kostner of the World Bank; Antonio Donini of the UN Office for the Coordination of Humanitarian Affairs; Guglielmo Colombo of the European Union; Nicolas Garrigue of the UN Development Programme; Mark Singleton of the Netherlands Ministry of Foreign Affairs; and James McCallum of the US Army Peacekeeping Institute.

Notes

1 See Kenneth Bush in this volume (chapter 2).

2 See for instance Anna Simons and P.H. Liotta, "Thicker than Water? Kin, Religion and Conflict in the Balkans," *Parameters* 28, no. 4 (Winter 1998–99): 11–28.

3 Clement E. Adibe, "Accepting External Authority in Peace-Maintenance," in Jarat Chopra, ed., *The Politics of Peace-Maintenance* (Boulder, CO: Lynne Reinner, 1998), 107–22.

4 Sally Morphet, "Current International Civil Administration: The Need for Political Legitimacy," *International Peacekeeping* 9, no. 2 (Summer 2002): 140–63.

5 John Mackinlay and Jarat Chopra, "Second Generation Multinational Operations," *The Washington Quarterly* 15, no. 3 (Summer 1992): 113–31; and Jarat Chopra, Peace-Maintenance: The Evolution of International Political *Authority* (London: Routledge, 1999), 3–18.

6 Report of the Secretary-General, "No exit without strategy: Security Council decision-making and the closure or transition of United Nations peacekeeping operations," UN Doc. S/2001/394 of 20 April 2001, 2.

7 Charles T. Call and Susan E. Cook, "On Democratization and Peacebuilding," *Global Governance* 9, no. 2 (2003): 233–47.

8 Tanja Hohe, "Totem Polls: Indigenous Concepts and 'Free and Fair' Elections in East Timor," *International Peacekeeping* 9, no. 4 (Winter 2002): 69–89.

9 Tanja Hohe, "Clash of Paradigms: International Administration and Local Political Legitimacy in East Timor," *Contemporary Southeast Asia* 24, no. 3 (December 2002): 569–590.

10 Anna Simons, *Networks of Dissolution: Somalia Undone* (Boulder, CO: Westview Press, 1995), 195-201.

11 Sukanya Mohan Das, "Process Issues: An Argument for Inclusion of Grass-Roots Communities in the Formulation of National and International Initiatives in Rebuilding Afghanistan," *Journal of Humanitarian Assistance* (2 February 2002), www.jha.ac/articles/a076.htm.

12 See for example UNDP, "Decentralized Governance Programme: Strengthening Capacity for People-Centred Development," Management Development and Governance Division, September 1997 (accessed 13 January 2004), www.magnet.undp.org/Docs/dec/DECEN923/Decenpro.htm.

13 Robert Orr, "Governing When Chaos Rules: Enhancing Governance and Participation," *The Washington Quarterly* 25, no. 4 (Autumn 2002): 140.

14 Rasna Warah, "Afghanistan's Silent Revolution," *HABITAT Debate* 8, no. 1 (March 2002): 19–20.

15 International Crisis Group, *The Loya Jirga: One Small Step Forward?*, ICG Asia Briefing Paper, Kabul/Brussels, 16 May 2002, 7, www.crisisweb.org.

16 International Crisis Group, *The Afghan Transitional Administration: Prospects and Perils*, ICG Asia Briefing Paper, Kabul/Brussels, 30 July 2002, 3, www.crisisweb.org.

17 Ken Menkhaus, "International Peacebuilding and the Dynamics of Local and National Reconciliation in Somalia," in Walter Clarke and Jeffrey Herbst, eds., *Learning From Somalia: The Lessons of Armed Humanitarian Intervention* (Boulder, CO: Westview Press, 1997), 54–55; and Jarat Chopra, Åge Eknes and Toralv Nordbø, "Fighting for Hope in Somalia," *Journal of Humanitarian Affairs* (1995), www.jha.ac/articles/a007.htm.

18 World Bank, Rwanda: Community Reintegration and Development Project, Report No. PID6101, 23 November 1998, www.worldbank.org.

19 Gillian Brown et al., "A Tale of Two Projects: Community-Based Reconstruction in East Timor and Rwanda," *Social Funds Innovation Update* 2, no. 4 (July 2002), www.worldbank.org/sp.

20 World Bank, East Timor: Community Empowerment and Local Governance Project, Project Information Document, 27 December 1999, www.worldbank.org.

21 Elizabeth G. Traube, *Cosmology and Social Life: Ritual Exchange among the Mambai of East Timor* (Chicago: University of Chicago Press, 1986), 98–124.

22 Sofi Ospina and Tanja Hohe, *Traditional Power Structures and the Community Empowerment Project—Final Report* (Dili: World Bank/UNTAET, 2001), 130.

23 Ospina and Hohe, *Traditional Power*, 130.

24 Jarat Chopra, "Building State Failure in East Timor," *Development and Change* 33, no. 5 (November 2002): 992–94; La'o Hamutuk, "The World Bank in East Timor," *The La'o Hamutuk Bulletin* 1, no. 4 (31 December 2000), www.etan.org/lh/bulletin04.html; and Joel C. Beauvais, "Benevolent Despotism: A Critique of U.N. State-Building in East Timor," *New York University Journal of International Law and Politics* 33, no. 4 (Summer 2001): 1126.

25 Robert A. Rubinstein, "Cross-Cultural Considerations in Complex Peace Operations," *Negotiation Journal* 19, no. 1 (January 2003): 29–49; Tamara Duffey, "Cultural Issues in Contemporary Peacekeeping," *International Peacekeeping* 7, no. 1 (Spring 2000): 142–69; and Marianne Heiberg, "Peacekeepers and Local Populations: Some Comments on UNIFIL," in Indar Jit Rikhye and Kjell Skjelsbaek, eds., *The United Nations and Peacekeeping: Results, Limitations and Prospects: The Lessons of 40 Years of Experience* (London: Macmillan, 1990), 147–69.

12

Sustainable Peace

Satya Brata Das

WHO PAYS THE PRICE?

WHEN XANANA GUSMAO was sworn in as the first elected President of the new country of East Timor in May 2002, it was one of those rare moments when hope bears fruit. As so many present noted, it was thanks to the intervention of the United Nations and the international community that East Timor was at last able to assert its independence—and to have a reasonable hope of crafting a civil society and a sustainable future.

Some of the success was undoubtedly due to luck. The Asian economic crisis of 1997, which led in part to the downfall of the Suharto dictatorship in Indonesia, was a momentous step in East Timor's transition from Indonesian occupation to independence. Yet this mixture of luck and design does not diminish the fact that East Timor is the least ambiguous success story in UN-led efforts to build civil society in the aftermath of conflict. Indeed, the notion of building civil society rather than merely keeping a peace reflects a move away from conventional UN roles towards new models better suited to an age when the emerging agenda of human security demands that peace not only be kept, but also sustained. However, as this analysis will make clear, the UN needs more stable political and financial support to properly take on the new roles of peacebuilding.

The UN needs a permanent commitment of armed forces if it is to rapidly respond to violent conflict. It also needs an enhanced supply of material and human resources that make up the infrastructure of a stable civil society if it is to facilitate a lasting peace. To fund the complex system that is required for true peacebuilding, the UN needs to have a more reliable source of funding that could be gained through taxing the international arms trade and managed through the development of a High Commissioner for Peace. Tragedies in places like Rwanda and successes in countries like East Timor demonstrate the need for commitment and the potential that a strong UN can bring. The central thrust of this study is to explore the concept of "sustainable peace" and to offer some observations on how it might pass from theory to practice. This study aims to make a case for Canadian leadership in crafting and implementing the notion of sustainable peace as part of a broader agenda of "human security."

To trace the evolution of the idea of sustainable peace, let us recall what UN Secretary-General Kofi Annan said in his address at University of California, Berkeley on 20 April 1988:

> The evolution of United Nations peacekeeping from the traditional kind of patrolling buffer zones and cease-fire lines to the modern, more complex manifestations in the former Yugoslavia has been neither smooth nor natural. It has created conceptual confusions and inflated expectations, betrayed hopes and blemished reputations. It has made us review our responsibilities and question our most basic assumptions about the very nature of war and the very high price of peace in the post-cold war era.
>
> Peacekeepers were asked the impossible, and sometimes, therefore, even failed to achieve the possible....
>
> We were asked to step in when all others had failed, and when no power or alliance equipped to act on behalf of the world

had the political will to do so. When global opinion calls for the world to "do something" about a crisis, we become the "doers," whether we have been given the tools or not."

Two years and after Kofi Annan's landmark speech at Berkeley, a smaller-than-planned deployment of UN peacekeepers-cum-peacemakers, lacking the tools they had been promised, found themselves face to face with a potential catastrophe. Indian General Vijay Jetley commanded a largely pan-African UN force in Sierra Leone that was armed with a standard ceasefire mandate offered by the Security Council on 22 October 1999. A more robust mandate sanctioned on 7 February 2000 enabled Jetley's soldiers to actually begin building a peace rather than merely monitoring a ceasefire. They were on the front lines of a conflict within a nation, the model of warfare that has become more common than the conflict between nations that marked the first UN peacekeeping mandates.

Until the first days of May, it appeared that success was in sight. Yet the peace was nearly undone by the madness of Foday Sankoh, leader of the Revolutionary United Front, whose army of mostly child soldiers had been singularly successful in spreading terror and chaos. Sent to guarantee a peace in the aftermath of Sierra Leone's civil war, and charged with creating a climate wherein civil society and civil institutions could be rebuilt, Gen. Jetley's peacekeepers faced a virulent recurrence of the conflict.

There was no logical reason why this should be so—Sankoh had not given up control of the illicit diamond trade that fuelled his rebellion, and he had a role in government. The hard-won peace covered by the UN mandate seemed as durable as any in the immediate aftermath of a conflict. Civil wars are inherently illogical, yet when they end with a peace accord that shares power and gives each party some of the responsibility for governance, one might believe that there is some basis for building a peace. This had certainly been the thinking amongst the members of the Security

Council, which had authorized a force of 11,000 soldiers, and many civilians and volunteers to establish peace in Sierra Leone.

Stung by the lessons of Rwanda and Sierra Leone's neighbor, Liberia, the UN determined that it could not afford to stand by yet again in an African conflict. In the internal politics of the United Nations, there was a stark contrast drawn between the resources diverted to address the European conflict in the Balkans, and the lack of both political will and resources in quelling African conflicts. Indeed, in the aftermath of the Central African debacle in April 1994, there was clear evidence that the UN had repeatedly ignored the warnings of Canadian General Romeo Dallaire that a slaughter was imminent in Rwanda. Faced with genocide, the small UN contingent took the bodies of dead peacekeepers with them and fled Rwanda. The United Nations Under-Secretary-General of the time, who gave insufficient weight to Dallaire's warnings, also took the lesson to heart—Kofi Annan would not make the same mistake again.

Sierra Leone, then, was to be the fruit of Lessons Learned—the UN would provide proper resources, and a large enough force, and lay the postwar foundations to rebuild a country that ranked dead last on the UN Human Development Index. The UN thought it had time—although most of the peacekeepers on the ground in May 2000 were Nigerian, Kenyan and Zambian, a larger international contingent was on the way.

The inclusion of both parties to the civil war in government brought the hope that armed forces might be disarmed and displaced populations returned to their homes. Despite all the preparation and all the hopes, 500 UN peacekeepers, hampered by a mandate to return fire only in self-defense, found themselves the captives of drug-fed boys and teenagers in early May. Of the many eventualities the UN had anticipated, it had perhaps taken too lightly the probability that Foday Sankoh suffered from a serious mental illness. He heard voices. These voices told him to resume the war. And the children and teens he led looked to him as a messianic force. This armed force, animated by a leader who hears voices, threatened to unravel the entire UN mission in Sierra Leone despite Annan's assurances that lessons had indeed been learned.

Yet the mission did not collapse, thanks to sheer luck. Rather than fleeing after the mass abduction of 500 of its members, the UN forces regrouped around the capital city, Freetown. They were aided by British paratroops originally brought in to evacuate British nationals and foreigners from its former colony. Foday Sankoh's rebels ignored the peace accord their leader had signed and resumed the battle.

Sankoh's murderous brigade of mostly child and teenaged soldiers had spent several years rampaging through the countryside, hacking off limbs, shooting whom they wished. Even though they were repelled from the capital, victory for the government was by no means assured, until on 17 May 2000 government forces captured Sankoh. More of the UN hostages were released. More international troops began to arrive; the contingent was to be 17,000—the largest international peace force ever assembled.

Yet the Sierra Leone crisis is not necessarily a story with a happy outcome. The UN was fortunate, but it should not have been in a position to depend on luck and happenstance to assure the success of its missions. It pointed out the crying need for a UN standing army. An effective military intervention in the cause of restoring order and laying the foundations for peace building needs a sense of purpose and cohesion. That most frequently comes from training together, living together, building the fraternal bonds between individual soldiers that enable mutual trust and confidence under fire.

Moreover, it enables a common standard of training for UN peacekeepers, and allows for the integration of command structures. A war zone is not the ideal place to mesh different commands or to forge unity amongst soldiers from different countries and cultures. Peacekeepers and peacebuilders need to train together and work together before they are sent to contain a crisis.

The UN needs the proper resources and the proper mandate to keep and build peace. However, in a world accustomed to warfare, the imperatives of peacebuilding represent new ground, with a paucity of resources and an absence of clear direction. Had Sierra Leone indeed ended in catastrophe, the isolationists in the United States surely would have seen this as yet another sign of UN failure. Wealth and technology created a new hubris in the US and the NATO. It was the belief that policing and peacekeeping ought to come without risk.

This attitude deeply influenced the US conduct of its membership in the Security Council and contributed to the general impasse amongst the five veto-bearing permanent members. The serious answer to Annan's recurring analysis—the provision of adequate funding, troops and indeed a proper mandate—was nowhere to be seen. The UN crisis in Sierra Leone in May 2000 shows that the imperatives of building a peace, of trying to establish order and civil society in the chaotic aftermath of civil war, have yet to be learned.

Building a peace takes the international community into new areas: into violating the sovereignty of other nations, ignoring territorial integrity, and demanding the right to act aggressively against governments that violate the Universal Declaration of Human Rights. It is an implicit facet of human security—at least as advocated by Canada and several other middle powers—that the primacy of individual security must prevail in situations where civilians are caught up in internal conflicts. The human security agenda in theory at least promises a future wherein human rights are paramount.

With more and more intrastate rather than interstate wars protecting civilians in armed conflict becomes a priority. NATO's bombing of the former Yugoslavia as it intervened in the civil war in the rebellious Serbian province of Kosovo was a turning point. It marked the first large-scale decision by western democracies to violate a country's borders and its national sovereignty in the name of rescuing people from the persecution directed against them by their own government. This "illegal" and unilateral measure—the bombing was conducted without the authorization of the Security Council—did not sit well with many countries, because one of the founding tenets of the United Nations is that national borders are inviolate. Yet the argument in the post-Cold War era, fully embraced by Annan and advanced by Canada, is that the protection of innocents comes first; thus human rights supersede all other concerns. The Canadian view holds that ultimately, peacebuilding aims at building human security, including democratic governance, human rights, the rule of law, sustainable development, and equitable access to resources.

Peacebuilding must start from a narrower mission: the requirement to end a conflict so that the foundations of justice can be established. Both tasks are necessary and Annan has consistently stressed that the UN cannot do it alone. The world body cannot impose a miraculous settlement, nor can it reasonably be expected to build a peace if there is no organic desire to end a conflict. "Political motivation and political persuasion are critical elements in a peace process," Annan told a peacekeeping seminar in November 1997. "When the parties are genuinely interested in a settlement, mountains can be moved in the interest of peace. However, in chaotic conditions in which power has devolved to splinter factions that have no real interest in peace, there are palpable limits to what the international community can accomplish. A sense of community—the will to reconcile—cannot be imposed."

The principal question of Sierra Leone and Kosovo, and indeed of every jurisdiction trying to rebuild after civil war, remains: Can peace be built if the combatants do not show a real willingness to work together? While the UN mission is meeting limited success, is it really in a position to build a viable society? In Kosovo, where the drug traffickers of the officially defunct Kosovo Liberation Army (KLA) were back in business in the autumn of 1999—the limits of the UN's ability to build peace are clearly demonstrated. As vengeful attacks by Albanians against Serbs continued, the UN found it difficult to establish the credibility and trust necessary to create a society in which all the ethnic groups could coexist.

There remains a lack of political will to build a lasting peace. British Prime Minister Tony Blair hailed Kosovo as the first military intervention by the outside world to stop human rights violations against civilians. He saw it as a new frontier. But against the reality of entrenched Balkan hatred, just how far can the UN succeed? The counterpoint to that is to do nothing—and in today's world of borderless communications, there is little scope to do nothing, as horrifying images of faraway conflicts are rendered all too intimate and familiar by modern communications media.

Taking some sort of effective action may seem like common sense, but it is much easier said than done. While the UN Charter foresees intervention and, by extension, peacekeeping, there is no explicit provision for peacebuilding. As the need for peacebuilding evolves, the UN must develop the mechanisms and instruments necessary to engage Annan's broad notion of human security, and to make it a reality. The notions of creating civilian police, beginning reconstruction of a ravaged society, and creating civil authority are all new areas of joint international endeavor in the aftermath of conflict. For a UN that has become accustomed to using soldiers to keep peace, the assembly of the military-civilian cohesion necessary to build peace is a monumental challenge.

Whilst many countries have surplus soldiers, only a handful of these have paramilitary police. And few if any jurisdictions have a surplus of police whose main duty is to maintain peace and order within a given community. Even fewer nations or communities have a surplus of police officers, doctors, nurses, teachers, engineers, lawyers, waterworks builders, judges and other skilled personnel necessary to rebuild a normal life in a postconflict society.

Annan's broader preoccupation with human security is also a cornerstone of Canadian foreign policy. It comes from a recognition that it is not enough just to establish a truce—building a lasting peace is the only way to bring about true security. In the foreign policy that has evolved over the past two decades, Canada brings to the table a new definition of what security means—one based on the primacy of human rights and individual well being. This means saving people caught in war, rescuing people from terror, fighting poverty, empowering people and nations, being partners in development, giving people tools to build lives of meaning and purpose. This is bound with the belief shared by Annan: all this should be done with little regard for traditional notions of national boundaries, because individuals come first. Just as Canada was a pioneer in introducing the notion of peacekeeping, so it must continue to be a leader in developing and implementing the concept of peacebuilding, in partnership with other likeminded nations.

The central dilemma—in a world where $1.5 trillion Cdn flows annually into "defense" spending, preparations for war fighting, and the legal portion of the global arms trade—is determining who pays for peace. The United Nations is chronically hampered by a lack of funds. The annual budget for all UN operations, all agencies and programs, is about that of a medium-sized Canadian province.

The question of who pays, therefore, sits front and center: not just in properly funding the campaign in Sierra Leone, but in any theater where the UN has been given a peacebuilding mandate. The United Nations was *de jure* and *de facto* the government of two territories emerging from conflict, Kosovo and East Timor. In the case of Kosovo especially, lack of money has made the lofty goal of establishing a lasting peace rooted in a civil society difficult to attain. As former Czech foreign minister Jiri Dienstbier famously put it after a visit to Kosovo in the fall of 1999, the spring ethnic cleansing of Albanians has been replaced by the fall ethnic cleansing of Serbs. The UN's difficulties in restoring civil society in Kosovo aptly illustrate the challenges of peacebuilding.

Who will pay for extra police, nurses and the like that are essential components of any peacebuilding operation? That is a key question as countries buy into the notion of peacebuilding.

Would Canada and likeminded nations, for instance, allocate part of an enhanced peacebuilding budget to municipalities and provinces?

Without the resources for a long-term presence, the UN cannot work effectively at rebuilding governance structures, civil society and individual lives in postconflict situations. Already, the world's wealthy countries are asking questions about the reconstruction of East Timor. "In the Security Council, they're asking if it's really worth spending $3 billion or $4 billion to build a civil society for only 850,000 people," Robert Fowler, Canada's Permanent Representative to the UN, remarked in a conversation with the author in November 1999. The irony is that the world spends that $4 billion Cdn daily on weapons and defense. In that context, peace building in Timor is surely a low cost.

By contrast, the costs of failing to build peace could be enormous. The UN has kept combatants apart in Cyprus for decades. It appears as though the island will be divided between Greeks and Turks in perpetuity. How long does the UN have to keep peace there? At what cost? How much better off might Cyprus be if peacebuilding had ended the divisions?

The funding for East Timor is seen as the essential investment needed to put the 850,000 Timorese on a level playing field so that they can enjoy equality of opportunity after winning their independence from Portugal and Indonesia. This investment is already showing returns as East Timor begins to work with its newly elected government. Like an insurance policy, investing in peacebuilding helps to prevent future conflict, and in the particular case of East Timor, it would provide the tools to enable the potentially oil-rich country to develop health care, education and the other building blocks of long-term peace and stability.

Yet this brings us back to the central question: Who will pay for peace? Even if the world assumes a collective responsibility, where will the money come from? How will it be distributed? And how much will be enough?

Equally important is the question of control. Should the UN distribute peacebuilding funds, or should it be done in some other way? Would the people who balk at paying US $3 billion to build East Timor anew continue to resist, even if the money was at hand, unless they had absolute say about how it was used? Because this is uncharted territory for the United Nations, flexibility and accommodation become essential in collecting and delivering funds for peacebuilding. It is surely an irony of our age that the very powers reluctant to fund the UN on grounds that it is inefficient or incompetent should be the ones who render it so. The streaks of exceptionalism and isolationism in the conduct of the foreign policy of the United States lead it to restrict or diminish funding for the United Nations. Yet it is the exercise of the Security Council veto by the US and the four other permanent members that prevents the UN from swift, decisive, cohesive action with a broad and open-ended mandate. Inevitably, there will be conflict and controversy regarding the collection and disbursement of peacebuilding funds.

A magnificent philanthropic gift like the US $1 billion donated by media magnate Ted Turner to the United Nations is a rare and happy event. Yet one magnanimous act is not enough, and it would be foolhardy to rely entirely on voluntary donations to build peace, and fund the necessities of postconflict reconstruction. Civic-minded individuals and donor governments would have to give many billions more into a global fund, so that the investment revenue from that fund could fund peacebuilding.

Voluntary donations alone cannot work. The notion of a global facilities fund, as proposed in 1999 by scholars at the University of New York, relies too much on philanthropy and voluntarism. A more formal mechanism is vital to ensure long-term, stable funding. The most reliable instrument, if it can be implemented, might be a global tax on militarism. A legal framework would be challenging to develop. One way to proceed might to build on the jurisdictional liberty offered to the new International Criminal Court (ICC). If criminal laws are applied internationally, can the same not be done with certain civil laws, particularly relating to international trade and taxation?

Yet the absence of an international legal framework to permit global taxation of the legal portion of the arms trade need not be an insurmountable barrier. Countries like Canada, and the other vigorous champions of peace, might begin by "taxing" their own defense and military spending—by designating ten percent of their military budgets specifically for a global peacebuilding fund. In Canada's case, this would come to an annual "tax" that would yield roughly four times as much money as Canada now pays in United Nations dues. National budgets taxed at that level would yield about $75 billion Cdn a year. This would be entirely voluntary, but it would set an example. It would fit in well with the evolving "soft power" regime in international relations, because it would stand as a classical instance of using moral suasion to achieve a greater good. If Canada and other military powers began to set aside parts of their own defense spending, and levied a special export tax on their arms manufactures, it would set a compelling example for others. More practically, it would enable the beginning of what would end up as a permanent fund to enable peacebuilding and post-conflict reconstruction. Since there is little chance that it would yield the dividends of a fully-fledged international tax on the arms trade, an initial target should be to raise enough to make the very idea of the tax credible—perhaps an amount as large as the annual budget for all other UN operations.

If one carries the castles-in-Spain thinking a step further, one can see that a viable international tax on the world's $1.5 trillion war spending could yield the revenues to fund peacebuilding. A relatively modest tax would bring substantial funds—taxing the arms trade and defense expenditure at five percent, for instance, would also bring $75 billion Cdn a year. That is a huge amount of money, considering that the UN budget for all its operations—from peacekeeping to development to health and children's services—

is about one fifth that size. Taxing the arms trade and defense spending would be relatively straightforward, if a consensus were built to do so—the rationale being that the developed countries of the world, including the leading democracies, are the principal suppliers of arms that fuel conflict the world over. They are also the principal suppliers of peacekeepers, and of the meager funds that are eventually used to build peace in the wake of these conflicts.

There is surely a sense of proportion and natural justice in the thought that those who provide the tools of war should pay to provide the tools of peace. Moreover, not all of this money would be poured into a conflict zone. A sizeable fund would enable the development of the civil capacity needed to build a peace. Funding would enable the creation of surplus civilian police, doctors, nurses, teachers, judges, engineers and so forth. Canada, for instance, might use a good portion of its contribution to global peacebuilding to increase municipal budgets, so that municipalities would be able to develop surplus capacity that could then be channeled to postconflict situations as the need arose. This capacity development in turn would enable rapid deployment of peacebuilders that could be assembled just as troops are for peacekeeping.

Nonetheless, there remains the practical issue not just of tax collection, but also of tax administration and disbursement. Who would control the fund? It is highly unlikely that the members of the United Nations would be content to see the funds administered by a third party beyond their control, even one as benign as the foundation set up to disburse Turner's largesse.

It is possible to foresee an entity either led or mandated by the United Nations and modeled on Britain's QUANGOs (quasi autonomous governmental organizations) to gather and distribute a tax on the arms trade and defense spending. This agency or entity would effectively extend taxation influence, if not power, away from national governance to global governance. This would be a momentous step, which may be extremely difficult to attain—unless the post-September 11th climate can create a receptive consideration of such a scheme. The Security Council, particularly the P-5, might entertain such a concept, particularly if the money initially came from voluntary taxation on the part of Canada and others.

One viable idea might be to extend a United Nations concept that has proven its worth, and its level of acceptability amongst both the General Assembly and the Security Council—a High Commission. It could work whether the global peacebuilding fund came from self-imposed taxes on defense spending by Canada and others or from globally imposed taxes on the arms trade under a jurisdictional framework that has yet to be developed. A United Nations High Commissioner for Peace Building and Postconflict Reconstruction would provide the focal point that is so far lacking in global peacebuilding efforts. It would be a logical evolution of the UN system and the evolving UN role in implementing Annan's sweeping vision of human security and the protection of civilians in armed conflict.

A High Commissioner for Peace might be a necessary bridge between the military and civilian facets of peacebuilding and postconflict reconstruction. The role might be particularly important in areas where there is a UN-sanctioned deployment rather than a UN-led deployment—as in the case of NATO's mandate in Bosnia and Herzegovina, or the initial Australian mandate in East Timor. A High Commissioner for Peace would use the surplus civil capacity generated by the fund to assemble peacebuilders—Canadian nurses, Indian computer technicians, French paramilitary police, and the like. Because this would occur under the aegis of a UN High Commission, there would in effect be a permanent General Assembly and Security Council authority, executed under the aegis of the Secretary-General. This may not be ideal, in that countries in the past have refused to put troops under UN command and would not be particularly persuaded that a High Commissioner for Peace, who carries even less authority than the Secretary-General, ought to have troops at his or her disposal.

Yet a High Commissioner is not the only model, nor necessarily the most viable one. It might be simpler to begin, for instance, with a Special Representative of the United Nations Secretary General, appointed on a case-by-case basis. The Military Staff Committee of the UN already has the authority to handle troops, and that constitutional grounding in the UN Charter may in some cases make a Special Representative more palatable than a High Commissioner for Peace. Nonetheless, we need to think of ways to entrench a peace-sustenance consciousness. A vigorous debate about an expanded role for a peace-maintenance agency would be a valuable contribution.

The United Nations' August 2000 peacekeeping review stopped short of recommending an independent force for the UN, and instead recommended that national governments and regional alliances prepare units of troops that might be readily deployed under UN auspices. Could such troops be at the disposal of a High Commissioner for Peace? If they were, their deployment might be more readily seen as part of a complex and ongoing process of shaping a peace, rather than as a military intervention that is not necessarily connected to other civil-society efforts. Certainly, the idea of putting UN troops directly under the aegis of a Peace Commissioner would send an important signal that the UN's longer-term goal is to craft a durable peace, rather than merely supervising a ceasefire or the end of overt conflict.

Ironically, the development of a European standing army in October 2000, the most robust manifestation of the Franco-German entente that shaped postwar Europe, may provide the substance of a peacebuilding movement. The 60,000 strong force, nominally independent of NATO, could indeed be the basis of a rapid-deployment UN force. Canada has worked to give the UN a rapid reaction capability—its 1995 report, *Towards a Rapid Reaction Capability for the United Nations*, was essentially means of projecting Canadian values into the realm of peace enforcement. Along with the Dutch and the Norwegians, Canada has long sought the development of an effective rapid deployment capability for the UN—one that could be seen as a necessary corollary to soft power measures. If the European Union were to develop a corollary civil capacity, a peacebuilding and postconflict reconstruction component, one could foresee a joint military-civil Canadian and European intervention force at the service of both NATO and the UN.

This is precisely the sort of resource that would give a UN High Commissioner for Peace Building and Postconflict Reconstruction a strong foundation and bring legitimacy and credibility to international interventions. Additionally, the High Commissioner for Peace could work closely with the High Commissioner for Refugees and the High Commissioner for Human Rights in providing a comprehensive and coherent matrix for peace building and postconflict reconstruction. The very creation of the office would send a strong signal about the international community's commitment to building peace. It would go a long way towards creating a more capable institutional framework to implement Annan's vision of human security. Moreover, since the purpose would be to encourage the development of the peacebuilding capacity within nations—as in Kosovo and Timor, bringing in outsiders only until the local population and indigenous resources are able to sustain a civil society based on peace and just governance—there is no question of these interventions being seen as a new tentative attempt at colonialism, nor as a neo-imperialist agenda entering by the back door.

Under the aegis of a UN High Commissioner for Peace, the international presence should be diverse and multilateral enough to banish any taint of imperialist intent. Yet the High Commissioner's role is vital if outside aid and indigenous resources are to mesh effectively. One of the gaps in the present climate is the absence of widespread integration between the hard power and soft power options. Military intervention and humanitarian assistance often exist in a postconflict intervention, and indeed both are necessary to achieve stability and lay a foundation for postconflict reconstruction.

The Canadian military has been among the first to recognize that finding the ideal blend of hard power and soft power will become the principal challenge of future peacebuilding interventions: soldiers and civilians working in a coordinated manner to achieve the same objectives. By establishing a High Commissioner for Peace, the UN might create the institutional framework to blend hard power and soft power, bringing together expert practitioners of each option.

Hard power alone cannot create or build a sustainable peace. That is the task of soft power: creating and nourishing civil society. Yet we must recognize, as Labonte and Ankersen have done,[1] that civil society cannot be created in a climate of violence, imminent war, a tenuous ceasefire and incipient chaos. The elements of civil society must be established before anyone can talk of true stability. The rule of law, representative government, the assurance of fundamental human rights, broad access to education and health care, are the foundations of any lasting peace. Representative government should by its definition include an element of democracy, but in many war-ravaged regions, the guarantee of human rights may be a more important factor in building peace. Given these conditions, a working democracy can evolve from the other elements of civil society. The other attraction of soft power solutions to conflict is that they carry a much cheaper price tag than war. Education and health care are relatively low cost investments, but they pay enormous dividends in enabling the growth and development of a society. Establishing the rule of law, too, can be relatively painless if it is done while an international peacekeeping force is at hand.

The evolution of peacebuilding and the necessity for postconflict reconstruction require new ideas and new approaches. A stable and permanent global fund built by a tax on defense spending and the arms trade, and a UN High Commissioner to make use of that fund, would be logical extensions of Annan's bold strides towards making human security the very *raison d'être* of the United Nations. They could indeed provide the building blocks for ensuring that sustainable peace becomes a reality in the many parts of the globe where the culture of violence has, in the past, prevailed.

Notes

1 See Melissa Labonte (chapter 3) and Christopher P. Ankerson (chapter 4) in this volume.

13

Prospects for the Emergence of a Global Small Arms Regime

Carolyn Elizabeth Lloyd

IN JULY 2001, the United Nations Conference on the Illicit Trade in Small Arms and Light Weapons In All Its Aspects was held in New York. This event represented a milestone in the movement to regulate small arms and light weapons (SALW) at the global level[1] and helped draw attention to the fact that the sheer number of small arms in circulation is inescapably related to the incidence of hostilities and levels of crime in the world. The human death toll caused by such instruments of war since the end of the Cold War is over four million, far exceeding the toll caused by weapons of mass destruction. A significant proportion (between 35 and 40 percent)[2] of the slain and injured are civilians. Sustainable peace, at the local or global level, cannot be built unless small arms are brought under control.

What are the prospects for the emergence of an international regime in this issue-area? This study addresses that question by exploring the conditions under which states decide to abide by emerging international norms and rules. It offers an avenue for the examination of the larger question of how and when we can expect global actors to cooperate in sustainable peace projects. The central hypothesis is that three variables (knowledge, power, and interest) are indispensable for such regime formation. These variables could be seen during the creation of other arms control regimes, such as those governing nuclear, chemical and biological weapons. They were *not*, until recently, in place for small arms and light weapons. SALW have been the "forgotten" weapons in international arms control. This situation is changing, however. With increased knowledge of the problems small arms pose, we are witnessing significant movement towards a set of global controls.

How has the study of small arms cooperation been treated in the past? First, few systematic attempts have been made to apply theory to the concrete phenomenon of small arms availability and proliferation. With the exceptions of Keith Krause's work,[3] Edward Laurance's report to the Carnegie Commission on Preventing Deadly Conflict[4] and Suzette Grillot's study on small arms,[5] there is a dearth of theoretical exploration of this issue. What literature does exist on small arms supply and cooperation is an uneven medley of government[6] and international organization publications,[7] nongovernmental organization (NGO) recommendations[8] and occasional declarations by academics that "something ought to be done." For example, Michael Renner's conceptualization of small arms as "orphans" of arms control opens the way for discussion on why cooperation *did* take place for other categories of weapons but *did not* for small arms.[9] Unfortunately, Renner's idea remains underdeveloped. The conditions required for light weapons to be "adopted" or "remembered" as an issue-area of cooperation are left unexplored.

Some academic, government, NGO and IGO publications focus on specific recommendations: expanding the UN Conventional Arms Register to encompass SALW, developing regional and international codes of conducts on the arms trade, providing assistance to states for the destruction of surplus weapon stocks, tightening import and export regulations, and formulating stricter enforcement of laws on illicit trafficking. These documents tend to dwell on the *form* of cooperation envisioned while giving short thrift to how the international community is expected to get from point A to point B. To date, few academics have offered more nuanced theoretical and reflective vantage points. Lamentably, the most respected catalogue of the literature to date—an annotated bibliography published by the Canadian government, considered a "must-have" for researchers worldwide, lumps together papers by NGOs like Saferworld and BASIC and reports released by foreign ministries with scientific outputs from research institutes and universities. All are listed as "scholarly studies."

One might argue that the general lack of attention to explaining how this area has evolved and the failure to apply theories of international cooperation to explain this is due to the fact that small arms control is not properly a transboundary concern. In fact, it is becoming more and more difficult for the case to be made that small arms control is purely within the domestic purview of states.[10] Too many "weak states" exist that have lost control over their security functions to make that claim. Borders, across which "excessive and destabilizing" quantities of weapons flow, are too permeable for the opposite to be said. The complex trajectories of light weapons criss-crossing the globe are creating a need for states to cooperate with one another to address the issue:

> Guns left behind by the United States in Vietnam in the 1970s [have] showed up in the Middle East and Central America; US and Soviet armaments pumped into Central America in the 1980s are now part of a black market feeding violence in Colombia and Mexico; weapons from Lebanon's civil war of the 1970s and 1980s were used in Bosnia; leftover weapons from conflicts in Mozambique and Angola are now being smuggled into South Africa, Namibia, Zimbabwe, and Zambia; and in a recent exposé in the *New York Times*, Raymond Bonner traced arms flows from the former Yugoslavia, Cambodia, Afghanistan, and Mozambique to the Tamil Tigers, the guerillas waging a bloody struggle for Tamil independence in Sri Lanka.[11]

Clearly, it is time to move beyond the stage of establishing the issue and begin theorizing about solutions to the SALW problem at a systemic level.

In our case, the assignment is undertaken by isolating the determinants of regime formation in the global sphere and then applying them to small arms. The concept of a regime, or "a set of principles, norms, rules and decision-making procedures around which actors' expectations converge in a given issue-area"[12] has come to occupy a central place in the field of International Organization.[13] In order to make sense of the different theories that have arisen around the concept of regimes, it is useful to typify them. To begin, many of the theories have been designed to account for the creation, the extent of influence on other actors, and the maintenance of regimes. Andreas Hasenclever, Peter Mayer and Volker Rittberger have divided the studies on regime creation into three schools of thought (elaborating upon earlier distinctions made by Ernst Haas).[14]

The first school of thought is cognitivist in accent. Forwarding the position that "ideas matter," writers like Ernst Haas, Peter Haas and Christer Jonsson have highlighted the intersubjective nature of regimes. A centerpiece of cognitive theory is the role of "epistemic communities," or a group of experts that operate as a "thought collective" to spur movement towards the formation of regimes in a given issue-area. Most recently, a group of "strong cognitivists" have advanced a rather radical research method under the banner of constructivism.[15] The second group counts realists among its members. The proponents' most important contribution to regime creation is the notion of "hegemonic stability," inspired by the economic regimes established under the preponderant powers of Great Britain and the United States respectively.[16]

Building on economist Charles Kindleberger's ideas, International Relations scholars such as Duncan Snidal, Barry Eichengreen and Robert Gilpin have adapted those economic insights to their discipline. These neoliberal[17] analysts have engaged in thinking on what is required for common interests to be forged in order for a regime to be created through analysis of actors' evaluations of what they stand to lose or gain. Keohane, Stein, Frohlich and Oppenheimer are interested in dilemmas of collective action expressed in the form of prisoner's dilemmas, the tragedy of the commons or Rousseau's parable of the stag hunt. For each school of thought, a corresponding dependent variable is emphasized.

The knowledge-based variable: The first determinant of regime formation (underlined by cognitivists) is knowledge, or "the sum of technical information and of theories about that information which commands sufficient consensus at a given time among interested actors to serve as a guide to public policy designed to achieve some social goal."[18] New knowledge leads to the eventual redefinition of state interests (states "learn"). Learning does not automatically translate into policy change, however. The "how" and "when" of this process is presently at the source of much spirited discussion among cognitivists. One of the group's most promising leads concerns the role of epistemic communities—a group of experts and/or NGOs sharing a common set of ideas about a given problem, and employing effective means to spread information about it. The persuasiveness of ideas alone, however, is not necessarily enough to sway policy makers. As Peter Haas explains,

> ...it often takes a crisis or shock to overcome institutional inertia and habit and spur [policy-makers] to seek help from an epistemic community. In some cases, information generated by an epistemic community may in fact create a shock, as often occurs with scientific advances or reports that make their way into the news, simultaneously capturing the attention of the public and policymakers and pressuring them into action.[19]

The discovery of the "ozone hole" over Antarctica in 1985, which became a driving force in negotiations to ban substances that deplete the ozone layer, is a perfect example.[20]

Depending on the nature of the issue-area, certain types of newly introduced information simply do not hold shock value. Additionally, not every epistemic community finds itself in a position of unanimity.[21] Nevertheless, various members of an epistemic community may infiltrate the channels of political power and generate change. Additionally, principled ideas (not to be confused with causal ideas) may have a "profound impact on political action."[22] Principled ideas, like "slavery is unjust," are larger and more comprehensive than strategies for tackling a problem based on an understanding of causal relationships. This means that even though issue-related experts may be divided on their plan of action, there is room for the knowledge variable to have effect. "[P]rincipled ideas enable people to behave decisively *despite* causal uncertainty. [They] can shift the focus of attention to moral issues and away from purely instrumental ones...."[23] We will look for change at both the causal and principled level.

The power-based variable: The second variable (usually stressed by Realists) is power. Cooperation in a regime requires the existence of a major country with the desire to induce other states to act, or a middle-sized country/coalition of countries with the will to assume the responsibility of institution-creation. Inertia will govern the issue-area without a leader.

We state, in contrast, that world powers are not the only actors capable of serving as leaders in regime formation. Taken to the extreme, the stricter version translates into the failure of any global cooperative endeavor not supported by the United States.[24] More IR scholars are admitting that the vast number of issues precludes the world hegemon from extending its influence over every one.[25] In addition, there are instances in which the influence of the United States in the process of regime creation is largely immaterial. The regime to control pollution in the Mediterranean Basin and the Treaty of Tlatelolco, which established a nuclear weapon free zone in Latin America, are cases in point. France's regional dominance at the time of treaty negotiations allowed it to pressure states to join the Mediterranean Action Plan.[26] Similarly, Mexico played a central role in bringing the Treaty of Tlatelolco to life.[27]

These examples and others illustrate that it is (sometimes) of greater value to turn to issue-specific hegemons (as opposed to a world hegemon) in order to predict state behavior. In the words of Keohane and Nye, "the strong make the rules; but it is strength within the issue area that counts."[28]

At the same time, because the United States is directly implicated in the light weapons trade by being a major supplier, and because "nations that are most influential in many circumstances in fact do possess, most of the time, the attributes normally associated with power,"[29] a commitment by the United States to leadership in the given issue will *strongly* sway the chances of regime formation. Yet, an absence of commitment by the hegemon does not rule out success. Rather, there is room for lesser powers, often working together and possessing a "home-field advantage"[30] (such as experience in humanitarian or environmental fields), to exert enough influence for the condition of power to be met.

The interest-based variable: The final determinant is self-interest as often advanced by neoliberals. Here cooperation is said to occur when a solution to a given problem is as compelling as possible—enough to reassure states that a shift in their interests would be worthwhile. Actors offset the costs of establishing a regime with the advantages expected from it.[31] States wavering in their decision to forego their interests must be convinced that the potential agreement will prevent others from cheating, that close to universal participation is secured, and that the regime is intuitively appealing. If the regime meets these criteria in a satisfactory manner, its future is brighter. We argue that all three variables are essential ingredients in creating a light weapons regime.

Our framework follows the wisdom of Frederic Pearson who asserts that the world presently relies on four main regimes to restrain the spread of military weapons and their delivery systems. They are: (1) the ensemble of mass destructive weapons accords; (2)

the Missile Technology Control regime (MTCR)—an agreement among a number of powers to consult and limit the export of ballistic missile technology; (3) the Coordinating Committee on Multilateral Export Controls (now modified from the Cold War to seek restrictions on sensitive military transfers to LDCs but formerly an agreement among Western countries to restrict high-tech technology flows to the East); and (4) and an evolving set of conventional arms transfer controls.[32] General regime theory permits us to compare the norms, rules, principles and decision-making procedures in these security areas and to ask why it has taken so long for a SALW regime to be created.

In the past five to ten years, the international community has learned a lot about the extent of the problem posed by the rampant proliferation and use of small arms and light weapons, as the war zones realities are being brought to awareness (over 108 armed conflicts in 73 countries took place between 1989 and 2000, most of which were fought and/or continue to be fought with light armaments).[33] Also acknowledged are the experiences of those living in places where low-level violence and other after-effects continue despite the signing of a peace accord. On a different level, one finds increasingly addressed the experiences of individuals living in cities and towns across the globe who must contend with weapon-related crime in their daily lives.

A significant portion of what we know is owed to case study work on Africa, Guy Martin[34] writes "between 1955 and 1995, some seven to eight million people died as a result of violent conflict in Africa, including about 850,000 in the 1994 Rwanda genocide alone. Of forty-eight recorded 'genocides' in the world, twenty have occurred in Africa. At the end of 1992 there were 23 million refugees—almost half of the total world refugee population—and about as many internally displaced persons in Africa."[35] Atrocities like Rwanda are likely to recur, since a veritable culture of violence has taken or is beginning to take hold in numerous parts of the continent.[36] A surplus of SALW has meant that many communities are replacing peaceful practices of conflict resolution with resorting to violence. Individuals have begun to arm themselves, provoking group fear[37] and impeding both democracy and development.

In Central America, too, the "constant recirculation and re-distribution of weapons that have been in the region for decades"[38] is an ongoing concern. The abundance of weapons has made "both petty crime and massacres like the one that occurred in Chiapas [in 1997] easy and inexpensive to carry out."[39] Narco-activity, which invariably goes hand in hand with small arms, is high. Light weapons are often used as payment for narcotics by traffickers, for protection of marijuana plantations or drug caches, and for carrying out kidnappings, extortion and bank assaults.[40] In South Asia, Tara Kartha observes some worrisome trends such as the ongoing rapid diffusion of weapons eastward of some six to eight billion dollars worth of weapons supplied to Afghanistan by the US and China in the 1980's with Pakistan becoming a particular trouble spot.[41] In the former Yugoslavia, "the statistics of war deaths are a measure of infinite numbers of individual experiences of suffering and grief."[42] Many Kosovars suffer from posttraumatic stress disorder, as a result of their encounters with small arms.[43] Nor is North America immune to the problem of SALW. While the overall homicide figures in North American have declined in recent years, firearm murders and knifings are on the rise in US cities like New York, Phoenix, San Antonio, Los Angeles and San Francisco[44] and in the Canadian provinces of Ontario, Manitoba, Saskatchewan and Alberta.[45] Violence depicted in the media and by the entertainment industry has not relented in frequency or explicitness, leading some, such as writer Dave Grossman, to call for a "resensitization of America."[46]

Area specialists play an important role in highlighting the gravity of the issue. However, the information contained in these case studies is frequently "not comparable across countries and regions."[47] There is now a need for systemic and systematic thinking when it comes to theories of cooperation and small arms and light weapons. For a global regime to emerge, a global understanding of these dynamics is vital. Keith Krause stresses this point in the following quote:

> Although the trade in small arms and light weapons is estimated at between *two and three billion dollars a year,* we have no overall picture of which weapons are flowing between which states. Similarly, although the total number of military-style firearms in circulation worldwide is estimated at anywhere between *100 and 500 million* (not including the weapons held by police and security forces), we have no clear idea of where these weapons are concentrated, and in whose hands. Finally, although we know that more than *200,000* people are killed each year by these weapons, we know little about where the greatest concentrations of casualties are, how and why they are killed, and what might be done to reduce this toll.[48]

Fortunately, an epistemic community is emerging with the potential to supplement the knowledge of area specialists and fill these "knowledge gaps." Researchers with the Small Arms Survey at the Institute Universitaire de Hautes Études Internationales (IUHEI) in Switzerland, the Norwegian Initiative on Small Arms Transfers (NISAT) and the Peace Research Institute OSLO (PRIO) in Norway, the Institute for Security Studies (ISS) in South Africa, and the Bonn International Center for Conversion (BICC) are making some headway on this front. Key to knowledge contribution is the *Small Arms Survey,* which aims to be "the principal source of public information on all aspects of small arms, and as a resource center for governments, policy makers, researchers and activists."[49]

Complementing the work of experts is a budding global campaign in the issue-area of SALW (the International Action Network on Small Arms [IANSA]). Officially launched at the Hague Appeal for Peace in 1999, the group's aim is to "promote effective global action to curb the proliferation and misuse of small arms."[50] Composed of over 340 religious, humanitarian, arms control and other NGOs, IANSA, concerned that "governments will take a piecemeal approach,"[51] has stressed coordination of issues and transnationalism.

Let us recall that a shock is often required for policymakers to be moved to act. The fact that we live in a world of "mini-holocausts"[52] has not been enough to create the needed shock. Arguably, a shock, in today's age of the "sound byte" is best generated by advocacy groups like those under the umbrella of IANSA. The latter are skilled at promoting certain facts for the consumption of both the public and decision-makers in a way that evokes high drama. According to Canadian foreign minister Lloyd Axworthy, "Civil society activism is the major factor in ensuring that governments actually take up the responsibilities that they have now acknowledged are theirs."[53] That said, NGOs dealing with small arms and light weapons will continue to need a solid, independent base of knowledge from which to draw, a resource that can be provided by the academic epistemic community.

Change at the principled level has already been deep. Learning has occurred in the following overarching areas: a change in thinking away from a strict definition of national security to include elements of human security, a greater acceptance of linkages between development aims and peace building (exemplified in the OECD's Development Assistance Committee's Guidelines on Conflict, Peace and Development[54]), the introduction of "microdisarmament," and an accent on the fact that humanitarian law should be taken seriously. These global principled beliefs have "seeped into the consciousness of policy makers and other influential groups and individuals"—the point at which "knowledge becomes salient to regime construction."[55] This is the point at which we find ourselves now with respect to the small arms and light weapons issue.

Few would dare posit that knowledge of the problem as a variable is enough to herald a regime or that power dynamics are irrelevant. So, what kind of leadership exists to shape a regime on

SALW? As specified earlier, the US is directly implicated in the issue by being the largest supplier of conventional weapons in the world. The historical list of foreign military sales involving SALW is long.

To provide a few examples, between 1980 and 1991, the US government sold 33,274 M16 assault rifles, 3,120 40-mm grenade launchers and 267,000 hand grenades to El Salvador, 38,000 M16 assault rifles, 60,000 hand grenades, 120,000 81-mm high explosive mortar rounds, 2,944 antipersonnel mines and 4,000 antitank mines to Lebanon, 4,800 M16 assault rifles to Somalia, 347,588 hand grenades to Thailand and 1,000 M16 assault rifles to Zaire. More recent data reveals that sales have not significantly slackened with buyers such as Egypt, Bosnia and Bolivia topping the list.[56] Critics of US foreign policy point out instances where sales have been made to repressive regimes. They also single out the dangers in the US practice of giving away unneeded weapons rather than destroying them. This trend has risen since 9-11 with the US "more willing than ever to sell or give away weapons to countries that have pledged assistance in the global war on terror."[57]

Overall, it would appear that the Bush administration is not as cooperative-minded on the matter as was the Clinton administration. During the Clinton presidency, former Secretary of State Madeline Albright chose to speak out on tackling the obstacles presented by the excessive flow and indiscriminate use of small arms and light weapons in a series of major speeches. In contrast, the US under Bush has shown signs of hostility towards the issue as exhibited, for example, in a much-talked about speech given by John Bolton, the US Under Secretary of State for Arms Control and International Security at the UN conference—noteworthy for his brusqueness in tone and its attacks on the global small arms process.[58]

Studies that strive to show that we are living in an era in which "soft power" carries the day tend to ignore that appearances can be deceiving. As Lisa Martin point outs, "Governments that give in to U.S. pressure, for example, may need to conceal this behind a veil of 'multilateral agreement,' for domestic purposes."[59] Conversely, when the US is not interested in cooperating, other countries may abstain, too, having been released from perceived or real obligation—as occurred when the US refused to ratify the nuclear test ban treaty and interest by other states subsequently crumbled. Weak American interest in a potential SALW regime equals weak prospects for its emergence.

All promise is not lost for an outcome favorable to regime supporters, however. Presently, a major stumbling block to stronger US commitment to leadership is anxiety over interference in legal global sales and the fear that movement towards a global regime will rouse the ire of the domestic gun lobby. Such worries are reflected in the US's careful crafting of its current strategy. "The strategy," according to Daniel Nelson, "is to appear 'activist' and show concern about the 'cheap and deadly arms' in which the world is awash, while pushing the arms trade discourse decisively away from the legitimate trade in arms or the sale of individual weapons to sportsmen, collectors, businesspeople, and homeowners."[60] But this could change if activists in support of a regime exert stronger pressure. The US government could furthermore arrive at the conclusion that global controls need not unduly interfere with domestic legislation that permits ownership of nonmilitary-style weapons.

Another source of promise emanates from signs of fledgling leadership in other quarters of the world. Increasingly, middle powers *can* make a difference, lending support to those who place faith in the pull of "soft power." Here one must consider the support of European countries. The flexible Human Security Network is also proving to be a viable avenue for small arms dialogue and alliance building.[61] Furthermore, Canada has expressed interest in taking up the reigns of power. What we see presently is leadership "by small arms niche"—France and Switzerland taking charge with respect to initiatives on tracing small arms, Canada on war-affected children, and so on.

While the world waits for leadership, economic and military interests will need to be overcome in the meantime. These interests, though very real to policymakers and military heads, are to a certain degree malleable: "States may not always know what they want and are receptive to teaching about what are appropriate and useful actions to take."[62] In time, with heightened knowledge and through learning, states *may* become convinced that a global small arms regime is in their interest. Why? Because multilateral controls are intuitively appealing in that they are generally in the *global interest* of humanity.

Following the logic of interest-based theories, it is fair to say that most states will not consider changing course and working towards a common goal unless certain stringent criteria are met (specifically, enforcement, participation and solution-salience) that will optimize the expected value of a regime. Any sign of a defect in a proposed small arms institutional arrangement will predictably be used by nations as an excuse not to participate.

Without a concrete regime proposal on the table, it is difficult to speculate how these issues will be treated in the future. Current agreements and proposals are regional in scope. Among the most important agreements on SALW in place to date are: the Organization of American States Inter-American Convention Against the Illicit Manufacturing of and Trafficking in Firearms, Ammunition, Explosives and Other Related material and their Component Parts, the Moratorium on the Manufacture, Export and Import of Light Weapons in West Africa, the European Union Code of Conduct on Arms Exports, and the European Union Joint Action on Small Arms and Light Weapons. Unfortunately, these initiatives are not sufficient and coordinated action at the multilateral level is a must. While some global proposals exist, mobilization is still in the process of being gathered.

A key place where preliminary talks on a comprehensive approach[63] to the problem are occurring is at the United Nations.[64] A "Programme of Action to Prevent, Combat and Eradicate the Illicit Trade in Small Arms and Light Weapons in all its aspects" was agreed upon by UN member governments. However, US intransigence has caused some to label this effort as a potential failure.[65]

But apart from this fly in the ointment, the Programme of Action itself has major flaws that will not adequately address the problem of SALW proliferation. As Krause notes, the language of the document is "nonconstraining," and many important issues that needed to be addressed were not in the document. For instance, there is no mention of the creation of an international body to trace illicit SALW. No attempt was made to set up a regulatory mechanism for civilian possession of these weapons. There was no expressed commitment to increase the transparency in the way these weapons are produced, stockpiled or traded. There was also no indication of the need to address the issue of developing a code of conduct among the countries exporting these weapons legally. Finally, no mention is made of developing a process of regulating arms brokers.[66]

Despite this negative evaluation of the UN Conference on SALW, there is a sense that information brought to light at this event has helped to raise the level of consciousness within the international community. As Jacques Fomerand understands the matter, "genuine diplomacy"[67] is normally not what goes on at such conferences. These events are "not meant to be arenas for making authoritative decisions." Instead, "UN global conferences encourage a process of action-oriented reflection and research that feeds and sustains international discussions. In doing so, they are an important factor in the sharing of information at the planetary level...." Beyond knowledge creation, "their key function is to act, in the name of the international community, as a source of legitimization—that is to say, to give a seal of approval or disapproval to the competing claims, policies, and action of the participants involved in the international political process." Their usefulness "hinges on the intensity of the energies" mobilized and unleashed at these global conferences.[68] The United Nations Conference on small arms should be seen as an opportunity for a send-off—a true beginning to the diplomatic process. The success of the Programme of Action "will ultimately be measured by its ability to catalyze a wide range of multilateral and national measures."[69]

However, the Programme of Action *does* contain some important ideas upon which states can build their commitments: enhancing national legislation on the production and transfer of light weapons, improving marking, transparency, improving the system of end-user certificates to help prevent diversion and illicit trafficking of SLAW, and protecting stockpiles of SALW. Special attention is paid to peacebuilding in the document. This means commitments to effective disarmament, demobilization and reintegration programs, including the collection, control and destruction of SALW.

The UN Secretary-General and his Under-Secretary-General for Disarmament Affairs wish to contain the SALW regime creation process within the confines of the organization postconference. As a locale for attention raising and norm building, the United Nations is ideal. As a negotiating platform, the UN is less so. This is because a forum where consensus is required waters down the content of a regime to the lowest common denominator so that the regime's components can be acceptable to all. A consensus would be unlikely to obtain even in the slightly more intimate setting of the Conference on Disarmament. Those living in societies afflicted by overflowing supplies of SALW cannot afford to wait a long time. Nor do they wish for an agreement so diluted in content that its implications would be essentially meaningless. A freestanding arrangement outside UN channels, similar to the Ottawa Convention on Landmines, might better meet the challenges of enforcement and solution-salience.

The eventuality of a regime unfolding in this manner is quite plausible for two reasons. Firstly, the process that governed the creation of the landmines treaty is increasingly viewed as a model for future weapons restriction regimes (solution-salience). Secondly, such a way of proceeding is historically grounded. Ken Rutherford argues that "the Ottawa diplomacy process is not as new as some have thought."[70] He cites the Hague Conventions of 1899 that called for a ban on certain weapons like dum-dum bullets and chemical gases as a valid earlier precedent. He furthermore suggests that "consensus-based voting at international conferences is a relatively recent phenomenon." The similarities between the Hague and Ottawa Conventions are remarkable: "[E]ach lacked the support of many major state powers, each was negotiated by majority voting, and each was achieved in a very short time." Both agreements were moreover initiated at the behest of a political leader and not an international organization. Of course, regulating small arms presents challenges that

> Hague and Ottawa supporters did not [have to] face: first, civilian ownership of light weapons is legal in many states, and second, light weapons have legitimate uses in certain circumstances. Such obstacles will inevitably attract state opposition and increase the costs of educating the public and governments....[71]

Nevertheless—history, while an imperfect guide to predicting state behavior—is as reasonable as any other guide at this premature stage. Nay-sayers cannot refute the fact that agreements have been reached before despite strong countervailing interests. There are occasions when rational self-interested calculation leads state actors to relinquish independent decision-making in favor of joint decision-making, proving wrong the proposition "that there simply will not be joint gains for which it is feasible for actors to cooperate."[72]

The international community is witnessing the coming together of variables—knowledge, power, and interest—that may usher in a regime to control the excessive flow and indiscriminate use of small arms and light weapons in the near future. Long ignored by policymakers, the costs of SALW—humanitarian, political, economic, ecological, social, cultural, psychological and spiritual in nature—are simply too great to ignore any longer.

Our approach drew on the conditions for cooperation developed by regime scholars. We showed that knowledge matters, power matters and the ability to overcome self-interests matters. A multivariate analysis allowed a coherent picture to emerge of where we are today with respect to SALW. With greater knowledge of the problem, with a leader, and with countervailing interests adequately addressed, the chances for a global agreement on creating a SALW regime would be greatly improved. Of course, the international community is not quite there yet. It will be a "long, hard road."[73] Overall, however, as we look ahead to the Review Conference in 2006, the outlook is fairly positive. If a regime is realized, curbing the weapons used most often in contemporary violence will be a crucial building block for a sustained global peace.

Acknowledgment

This paper could not have been written without the financial support of the *Fonds pour la formation de chercheurs et l'aide à la recherche* (Fonds FCAR). The author would like to thank Michel Fortmann, Marie-Joëlle Zahar, Edward Laurance and Jean-Philippe Thérien for their encouragement and support.

Notes

1 The terms "small arms" and "light weapons" (SALW) are used here interchangeably. The terms encompass not only small arms in the narrow sense, but also light weapons, ammunition and explosives that can be operated by one or two persons and carried by a pack animal or light vehicle.

2 International Action Network on Small Arms, *The Small Arms Survey 2002: Counting the Human Cost* (Oxford: Oxford University Press, 2002), 163, http://www.iansa-org/documents/2002/small_arms_survey.htm.

3 Keith Krause, "Norm-Building in Security Spaces: The Emergence of the Light Weapons Problematic," http://ww2.mcgill.ca/regis/krause.pdf (accessed 13 January 2004); See also Keith Krause, "Review Essay: Multilateral Diplomacy, Norm Building, and UN Conferences: The Case of Small Arms and Light Weapons," *Global Governance* 8, no. 2 (April–June 2002): 247–63 for a process-tracing approach to the issue.

4 Edward J. Laurance, *Light Weapons and Intrastate Conflict: Early Warning Factors and Preventative Action*, A Report to the Carnegie Commission on Preventing Deadly Conflict (July 1998), http://www.iansa-org/oldsite/documents/research/res_archive/r9.htm.

5 Suzette Grillot, "The Emergence and Effectiveness of Transnational Advocacy Networks" (paper presented at the International Studies Association-Southern-Region meeting, Florida, October 12–14, 2001).

6 See for example Canada, Department of Foreign Affairs and International Trade (DFAIT), *Light Weapons and Micro-Disarmament* (Ottawa: DFAIT, January 1997).

7 See for example Pericles Gasparini Alves and Daiana Belinda Cipoollone, eds., *Curbing Illicit Trafficking in Small Arms and Sensitive Technologies: An Action-Oriented Agenda* (Geneva: United Nations Institute for Disarmament Research Agenda, 1998).

8 See the *Biting the Bullet* series, a collaborative effort by three NGOs: Saferworld, International Alert and the British American Security Council.

9 Michael Renner, *Small Arms, Big Impact: The Next Challenge of Disarmament*, Worldwatch Paper 137 (Washington, DC: WorldWatch Institute, October 1997).

10 See Natalie J. Goldring, "The NRA Goes Global," *Bulletin of Atomic Scientists* 55, no. 1 (January–February, 1999), http://www.bullatomsci.org/issues/1999/jf99goldring.html.

11 Michael Renner, "An Epidemic of Guns," *WorldWatch Institute* (July–August 1999): 26.

12 Stephen D. Krasner, "Structural Causes and Regime Consequences: Regimes as Intervening Variables," *International Organization* 36, no. 2 (Spring 1982): 185.

13 Friedrich Kratochwil and John Gerard Ruggie, "International Organization: A State of the Art on an Art of the State," *International Organization* 40, no. 4 (1986): 759.

14 Andreas Hasenclever, Peter Mayer and Volker Rittberger, "Interests, Power, Knowledge: The Study of International Regimes," *Mershon International Studies Review* 40, no. 2 (1996): 177–228; See also Andreas Hasenclever, Peter Mayer and Volker Rittberger, *Theories of International Regimes* (Cambridge, UK: Cambridge University Press, 1997).

15 For general overviews see Ted Hopf, "The Promise of Constructivism in International Relations Theory," *International Security* 23, no. 1 (Summer 1998): 171–200; and Jeffrey T. Checkel, "The Constructivist Turn in International Relations Theory," *World Politics* 50, no. 2 (January 1998): 324–48. On constructivism and national security, refer to Peter J. Katzenstein, ed. *The Culture of National Security: Norms and Identity in World Politics* (New York: Columbia University Press, 1996).

16 Robert Gilpin, *The Political Economy of International Relations* (Princeton, NJ: Princeton University Press, 1987), 74.

17 Some academics may object to the term "Neo-Liberal" being used to describe this direction of regime study and would prefer "Liberal Institutionalist." I believe that there is very little difference between the two labels and advise, simply, using the name of choice consistently.

18 Ernst B. Haas, "Why Collaborate? Issue-Linkage and International Regimes," *World Politics*, 32 (1980): 357–405.

19 Peter M. Haas, "Introduction: Epistemic Communities and International Policy Coordination," *International Organization* 46, no. 1 (Winter 1992): 14.

20 Richard Elliot Benedick, *Ozone Diplomacy* (Cambridge, MA: Harvard University Press, 1991).

21 Jack S. Levy, "Learning and Foreign Policy: Sweeping a Conceptual Minefield," *International Organization* 48, no. 2 (Spring 1994): 293.

22 Judith Goldstein and Robert O. Keohane, "Ideas and Foreign Policy: An Analytical Framework," in *Ideas & Foreign Policy: Beliefs, Institutions, and Political Change* (Ithaca, NY: Cornell University Press, 1993), 9.

23 Goldstein and Keohane, "Ideas and Foreign Policy," 16–17.

24 For an appraisal of US power, see David A. Charters, *Canada-US Defence Cooperation*, Report for Defence Forum, Fredericton, New Brunswick, April 2000, 2,

http://www.dnd.ca/admpol/org/dg_coord/d_pub/sdf/reports/unb_forum_e.htm (accessed March 28, 2001).

25 See for example Duncan Snidal, "The Limits of Hegemonic Stability," *International Organization* 39, no. 4 (Autumn 1985): 579–615.

26 Peter M. Haas, "Epistemic Communities and the Dynamics of International Environmental Co-operation," in Rittberger, ed., *Regime Theory*, 192.

27 "Tlatelolco Treaty Marks 30th Anniversary," *IAEA Newsbriefs* 12, no. 1 (Jan/Feb 1997), http://f40.iaea.org/worldatom/Press/Newsbriefs/1997/newsv12n1.html#A11.1.

28 Robert O. Keohane and Joseph S. Nye, *Power and Interdependence* (Boston: Harper Collins, 1989), 137.

29 Michael P. Sullivan, *Power in Contemporary International Relations* (Columbia, SC: University of South Carolina Press, 1990), 105.

30 Bob Lawson, "Towards a New Multilateralism," *Behind the Headlines* 54, no. 4 (Summer 1997): 20.

31 Robert O. Keohane, "The Demand for International Regimes," in Stephen Krasner, ed., *International Regimes* (Ithaca: Cornell University Press, 1983), 154.

32 Frederic S. Pearson, *The Global Spread of Arms: Political Economy of International Security* (Boulder, CO: Westview Press, 1994), 85.

33 Peter Wallensteen and Margareta Sollenberg, "Armed Conflict, 1989–98," *Journal of Peace Research* 36, no. 5 (1999): 593.

34 Guy Martin, *Controlling Small Arms Proliferation and Reversing Cultures of Violence in Africa and the Indian Ocean*, Monograph 30 (Pretoria, South Africa: Institute for Security Studies, September 1998).

35 Martin, *Controlling Small Arms*.

36 See Howard Adelman in this volume (chapter 14).

37 Robert Muggah and Eric Berman, *Humanitarianism Under Threat: The Humanitarian Impacts of Small Arms and Light Weapons*, Special Report, Study Commissioned by the Reference Group on Small Arms of the United Nations Inter-Agency Standing Committee (Geneva: Small Arms Survey, 2001), 2.

38 William H. Godnick, "Illicit Arms in Central America," Paper prepared for and international workshop of the British American Security Information Council (BASIC) on "Small Arms and Light Weapons: An Issue for the OSCE," Hofburg Palace, Vienna, 9–10 November 1998, 43, http://sand.miis.edu/research/1998/nov1998/illicit.pdf.

39 Godnick, "Illicit Arms," 43.

40 Godnick, "Illicit Arms," 44.

41 Tara Kartha, "Controlling the Black and Grey Markets in Small Arms in South Asia," in Jeffrey Boutwell and Michael T. Klare, eds., *Light Weapons and Civil Conflict: Controlling the Tools of Violence*, Carnegie Commission on Preventing Deadly Conflict and the American Academy of Arts and Sciences (Lanham, MD: Rowman & Littlefield Publishers, 1999), 50.

42 Edmund Cairns, *A Safer Future: Reducing the Human Cost of War* (Oxford: Oxfam Publications, 1997), 11.

43 See Barbara Cardozo et al., "Mental Health, Social Functioning, and Attitudes of Kosovar Albanians Following the War in Kosovo," *Journal of the American Medical Association* 284, no. 5 (2000): 569–77.

44 "Some Cities See Rise in Homicide Rates," *Boston Globe*, January 14, 2000.

45 Statistics Canada, "Crime Statistics," http://www.statcan.ca/Daily/English/020717/d020717b.htm (accessed December 1, 2002).

46 Dave Grossman, On Killing: *The Psychological Cost of Learning to Kill in War and Society* (Boston, MA: Little, Brown and Co., 1996), 325.

47 Keith Krause, "Description of the Annual *Small Arms Survey*," Programme d'Études Stratégiques et de Sécurité Internationale (PESI) and the Institute Universitaire de Hautes Études Internationales (IUHEI), Geneva, (October 1999), 5.

48 Krause, "Description."

49 *Small Arms Survey: Profiling the Problem* (Oxford: Oxford University Press, 2001).

50 International Action Network on Small Arms, "Founding Document," (11–15 May 1999), 2, http://www.iansa.org/oldsite/mission/nespub/launch/hap.htm (accessed 13 January 2004).

51 International Action Network on Small Arms, "Founding Document," 2.

52 Cairns, *A Safer Future*, 5.

53 Lloyd Axworthy, "Controlling Small Arms: International Action Network Established," *Ploughshares Monitor* (September 1998): 1, http://ploughshares.ca/content/MONITOR/mons98f.html (accessed 13 January 2004).

54 OECD-DAC, *Conflict, Peace and Development Co-operation on the Threshold of the 21st Century*, Development Co-operation Guideline Series (Paris: Organization for Economic Co-operation and Development, 1998).

55 Haas, "Why Collaborate?" 369.

56 Lora Lumpe, "U.S. Policy and the Export of Light Weapons" in Jeffrey Boutwell and Michael T. Klare, eds., *Light Weapons and Civil Conflict: Controlling the Tools of Violence*, Carnegie Commission on Preventing Deadly Conflict and American Academy of Arts and Sciences (Lanham, MD: Rowman & Littlefield Publishers, 1999), 65–88.

57 Rachel Stohl, "Post-Sept.11 Arms Sales and Military Aid Demonstrate Dangerous Trend," http://www.cdi.org/terrorism/military-transfers-pr.cfm (accessed 29 November 2003). Defenders of the country's policy on small arms point out that in many areas, US conduct is to be commended—for example, American weapons-brokering laws are among the most wide-ranging in the world and the US has offered significant technical assistance to help destroy stocks of excess or illicit weapons and improve border security in countries plagued with the problem of illicit trade in small arms and light weapons.

58 Aaron Karp, "Laudable Failure: The UN Small Arms Conference" (paper presented at the International Studies Association-Southern Region, Salem, North Carolina, 12–14 October 2001), 1.

59 Lisa L. Martin, "Interests, Power, and Multilateralism," *International Organization* 46, no. 2 (Autumn 1992), 779.

60 Daniel N. Nelson, "Damage Control," *Bulletin of the Atomic Scientists* 55, no. 1 (January/February 1999), http://ploughshares.ca/content/MONITOR/mons98f.html (accessed 13 January 2004).

61 Belgium had until recently been a contender for leadership until a change in government. Official of Belgian Department of Foreign Affairs, interview with Carolyn Lloyd, Brussels, Belgium, June 23, 2000.

62 Martha Finnemore, *National Interests in International Society* (Ithaca, NY: Cornell University Press, 1996), 11.

63 See Carolyn Lloyd, "Small Arms and Light Weapons: Post-Conference Prognosis," in David Mutimer, ed. *Canadian International Security Policy: Reflections for a New Era* (Selected Proceedings of the International Security Research Outreach Program-York Centre for International and Security Studies Symposium, York University, 2001).

64 See United Nations, Third Session of the Preparatory Committee for the UN 2001 Conference on the Illicit Trade in Small Arms and Light Weapons (19–30 March 2001), A/conf.192/PC/L.4, Revised Draft Programme of Action to Prevent Combat and Eradicate the Illicit Trade in Small Arms and Light Weapons in all its Aspects.

65 Keith Krause, "Review Essay: Multilateral Diplomacy, Norm Building, and UN Conferences: The Case of Small Arms and Light Weapons," *Global Governance* 8, no. 2 (April–June 2002): 247.

66 Krause, "Review Essay: Multilateral Diplomacy," 247–258.

67 Jacques Fomerand, "UN Conferences: Media Events of Genuine Diplomacy?" *Global Governance* 2, no. 3 (September–December 1996): 361–75.

68 Fomerand, "UN Conferences," 367, 371, 372.

69 *Small Arms Survey* 2002, 4.

70 Ken Rutherford, "The Hague and Ottawa Conventions: A Model for Future Weapon Ban Regimes?" *The Nonproliferation Review* 6, no. 3 (Spring–Summer 1999): 37.

71 Rutherford, "The Hague and Ottawa Conventions," 47.

72 Oran Young, "International Regimes: Toward a New Theory of Institutions," *World Politics* 39, no. 1 (October 1986): 118.

73 A refrain from a classic folk song called "Handsome Johnny." The song was made famous by Ritchie Havens and concerns a young boy who marches to every war there ever was across the ages, carrying a different small arm in his hand each time. As history evolves, his weapon changes from a musket to a flintlock, to a carbine, to an M-1, to an M15 and so on...(from Concord, to Gettysburg, to Dunkirk, Korea, to Vietnam, Panama, the Persian Gulf and onwards.)

14 Cultures of Violence

Howard Adelman

WHY DOES ONE PART of a society try to exterminate another part? How and why does such a culture of violence develop? Why do bystanders, particularly agencies charged with the responsibility for stopping such extermination, agencies even founded in part precisely to stop genocide—such as the United Nations—fail to do so? This is a critical question; for if a "Culture of Peace" and a "Culture of Prevention" are to be developed, it is crucial to know why genocide, widely regarded as one of the most heinous, if not the most heinous, form of violence humans perpetrate on one another, develops, and, once started, why it is not stopped. A "Culture of Peace" cannot be developed without understanding the nature of an already established "Culture of War," particularly the epidemic of intrastate wars and ethnic conflicts that at their worst ended up in genocide. A "Culture of Prevention" cannot be created until one understands how a "Culture of Indifference and Inaction to Conflicts" has also developed.[1] This must be the point of departure to any discussion of building sustainable peace.

After all, it is widely agreed that if there was any case where genocide could have been prevented or at least mitigated, Rwanda provides such an example. There were plenty of early warnings that a massive slaughter could have been expected. The perpetrators of the genocide used very low-tech means—largely machetes and clubs—to kill most of the victims. It would have taken a very small, effective force to stop the genocide.[2] There was a UN peacekeeping force present in the country that even kept control of the airport during all the violence. Western forces—namely Belgian, French, and Italian—were dispatched to the country almost immediately after the violence started, but left after rescuing their ex-pats. An American Special Forces unit was nearby that, we have now learned, sent in a reconnoitering mission that reported on the slaughter underway.[3] Later, when the genocide had been well developed, another extremely well armed French force was once again sent into the country in *Opération Turquoise*, but did not take an active role in stopping the genocide and, in fact, has been accused of abetting the escape of the génocidaires.[4]

Further, norms[5] against genocide were well established internationally. The Genocide Convention had been in place for over forty years; the vast majority of states had signed and ratified it. The greatest hit film showing on world screens in the five months preceding the commencement of the massive slaughter of 800,000 Tutsi in Rwanda was *Schindler's List*, a Hollywood movie that went on to win a number of Academy Awards. Virtually anyone who saw that movie about the Holocaust walked out afterwards saying to themselves, "Never Again!" Yet, at the very same time, the country in which the film had been produced, the major hegemonic power in the world, deliberately refused to depict what was happening as a genocide lest it felt obligated to act, indicating at the very least that the antigenocide norm was accepted, had legitimacy and was operative, and even provided a sense of obligation, however weak, to act.[6] This, at the very least, suggests that statements, policies and clear commitments backed even by public support do not determine that a norm will prevail in determining action.

How do antigenocide norms attain preeminence? What institutions help strengthen a norm against genocide? How is it done? These are important questions, but there are even prior ones. How do norms that endorse genocide develop and gain preeminence? How do norms that reinforce inaction and indifference as a response develop? This study focuses on the latter two questions and the various answers provided without attempting to provide a definitive answer. Instead, various interpretations and answers to the questions are analyzed to examine whether cultures shape and define political institutions and socialize the people who work in these institutions, or whether politics and the quest for power and status are the key factors in developing a culture.

In his book on the Rwanda genocide, Mahmood Mamdani argues that there are three types of explanation of the genocide—political, economic, and cultural.[7] Bruce Jones offered a political *synchronic* explanation for the ill-conceived strategic actions of the major players in facilitating peace through planning the integration of the armed forces,[8] creating the broad-based transitional government (BBTG) in Rwanda, and deploying peacekeepers to facilitate the process, strategies that failed to take sufficient account of the real dangers from spoilers and of the capacities and willingness of the various parties to deal with these threats.[9] Mamdani offered a *diachronic* political explanation of the genocide itself rooted in the reification of the racial dichotomy of Hutus and Tutsis by the colonial powers in the political institutions of the state. Prior to colonialism, Rwanda had been a state with a social division of labor divided between pastoralists and cultivators which placed pastoralists, mainly Tutsi, in an elite position, but which also had developed differential structures of social order in which actors from the different social orders operated and came together at different levels so that power was both centralized and diffused through different systems of social control.[10] The reified and centralized system of control that replaced this when the Belgians took over the colony in the 1920s and 1930s and introduced its rigid racial divisions[11] was adopted after the 1959 revolution, the proclamation of a republic in January 1961, the September 1961 plebiscite to end the monarchy, and after independence in 1962, by the postcolonial state that reinforced those identities in the name of justice even while it replaced the autonomous colonial elite with one deeply embedded in the social fabric of the society and its mundane everyday activities. The end result was that it significantly reduced the tensions between the transcendental values and ordinary life for Hutus while it, at the same time, enormously increased the distrust, tensions and violence between Hutu and Tutsi.

Thus, for Mamdani, "Hutu and Tutsi are best understood, not as market based or cultural identities, but as *political identities* reproduced first and foremost through a form of the state."[12] The second Habyarimana republic that took power in 1973 tried to redefine Tutsis in terms of ethnicity rather than race, but did not succeed in destroying the identification of Tutsis as foreign settlers of a different race from the purportedly indigenous Hutus. The racial dichotomy was revived when the Ugandan revolution failed to resolve its own crisis of postcolonial citizenship and exported it back to Rwanda when the Tutsi-dominated Rwandan Patriotic Forces (RPF) invaded Rwanda in October of 1990. The conceptual conditions for genocide had been well institutionalized and historical events served as the catalyst to enact them, for under the threat of war and the perceived reestablishment of the dominance of an alien racial group, the racist extremist faction grew in strength, launched a coup, and began the genocide on 6 April 1994.

Peter Uvin offered the fullest economic explanation of the genocide and documented the social and structural factors developed and reinforced in that society by the international aid community before the violence against the Tutsi broke out during the second republic.[13] In particular, Uvin critiqued the role of the World Bank, the International Monetary Fund (IMF) and the development agencies of various Western countries for their role first in developing an economic system in which the leaders became dependent for their wealth and status on the inflow of external aid. However, when the commodity price of coffee, the main export crop, crashed in 1989, the IMF insisted on restructuring, weakening the state apparatus, creating a motive for corruption, and throwing Rwanda into a crisis that encouraged the RPF invasion. Given the reigning ideology of the international bankers, the IMF insisted on structural adjustment and advocated a reduction in the size of government and the establishment of free-market reforms and norms without taking into consideration the particular circumstances of Rwanda.

Added pressures for democratic reform piled a political crisis on top of the economic one. Once the invasion took place and the Rwandan army was forced to expand immediately, what had been proportionately one of the smallest armies in Africa (Rwanda was famed among development agencies in the 1880s for having the lowest expenditures on the armed forces) grew sixfold. At the same time, the IMF incorporated arms and military reduction targets as a condition of its loans just when the Rwandan government was in the midst of fighting a war. On top of the economic, political and military crisis, the donor governments added pressures to restructure civil society when donor countries such as Canada introduced conditionality to its loans and insisted on strengthening human rights, thus stressing the creation of social capital as a condition of financial aid. Insisting on multiparty democracy, insisting on economic restructuring and government downsizing that created enormous insecurity for a major part of the ruling class, insisting on military downsizing when the country was faced with a civil war, and demanding enhanced attention to human rights all could be virtuous reforms. But at that time and under those circumstances, they weakened those in power who tried to mediate between what Mamdani termed the racist faction and the reformers as the development agencies attempted to strengthen those who advocated a pluralist democratic and ethnic society without discrimination, but without any clout to bring into operation their valued reforms.[14]

Mamdani's diachronous political explanation for the growth and development of racism and genocide, Jones' synchronous political analysis of the weakness of the strategic decisions and actions taken to foster peace, and Uvin's economic structural analysis of the impact of foreign aid in exacerbating the crisis in Rwanda all presume a universal dichotomy of rational and irrational. For Mamdani, it is rational to develop political states in which membership norms are based on residence in the territory of that state and not on ethnicity and particularly not on race. For Jones, rational decisions of leaders must be both coherent and comprehensive in taking into consideration all the factors that might threaten the peace and creating all the necessary and sufficient conditions to foster that peace. For Uvin, it is irrational to impose cookie-cut economic solutions and conditionality for aid after first making the status and security of the leadership class dependent on that aid and then failing to take into account the historical circumstances of the state in question at that time.

The prevalence of a norm of rationality lay behind the reforms of the economic development community, behind Mamdani's historical analysis of the conditions that foster genocide, and behind Jones' analysis of the strategic thinking required to create conditions for conflict management. All these rational approaches deliberately eschew taking into consideration the customs and norms of the local community in question.

Samantha Power, Peter Ronayne, and Michael Barnett offered three types of cultural explanations of why potential interveners failed to intervene and stop the genocide.[15] In all three cases, a culture represents a set of norms and habits, mental and behavioral characteristics of an institution, each institution reflecting its uniqueness and difference from other cultures in the particular set of norms that characterize it and the historical explanation for their predominance. All these notions of culture stand in apparent opposition to culture as an inherited *volkgeist* or spirit presumably characteristic of a nation or ethnic group, or culture as the cultivation of an inner authentic spirituality independent of external norms and influences.

Power's analysis of the US failure documented her country's "consistent policy of nonintervention in the face of genocide" as testimony to a ruthlessly effective system in which, "No US president has ever made genocide prevention a priority, and no US president has ever suffered politically for his indifference to its occurrence."[16] Only the moral courage of the few demonstrated a path to break through this institutionalized indifference. For Peter Ronayne, only strengthening other institutional norms, more specifically the growing anti-genocide norms and values, could challenge the preeminence of state norms based on interests and strategic calculations.[17] In Barnett's attempt to understand the decisions of the UN from within the context of the goals, informal and formal rules and norms, beliefs and expected outcomes of its leaders, that is, from within the bureaucratic culture of the UN, he analyzed how UN officials and member government representatives in the Security Council came to believe that indifference was the correct response. This indifference was rooted in a principled concern for the life of the United Nations as a whole and in the principle of neutrality as well as an accumulation of strategic and expedient steps not offset by cognitive practices that would allow reality to penetrate and challenge the constructed reality created by those institutionalized norms and practices.

In effect, though not motivated by rational calculations of power, UN officers had overwhelmingly become individuals no longer motivated by a search for either truth or justice, but were merely "empty vessels" to ensure the survival of the organization of which they were a part. This affected the mechanisms for interpreting knowledge and the evaluations they made of the institution as well as the mechanisms and processes for making policy, not to mention the policy environment itself.

None of the cultural theorists, however, raised questions (let alone answered them except in the vaguest way) concerning the social processes through which competing sets of norms are mediated, how norms gain preeminence and are institutionalized, and which agents bear the burden of such institutionalization. If the key to dealing with violence cannot be adequately understood through appraising the role and power of culturally embedded norms, the ball is thrown back into the court of the universalists. Is violence and various indifferent and/or inadequate responses to it fostered by incoherent political strategic thinking, or by failing to adopt a political ideal of membership in the state rooted in residency rather than ethnicity or, even worse, race, or by political economic practices that create severe economic strains on the state through trade, monetary and finance problems that foster conflict and corruption in the competition for scarce resources? Before we turn back to the universalists, a more detailed exploration of the cultural models is required.

Whatever the different approaches of Power, Ronayne and Barnett, they all focused on the persistence of norms and practices that not only resisted change,[18] but also deformed the perception of reality deliberately or unconsciously by constructing the depiction of events at odds with the overwhelming evidence. Further, though there are heroic exceptions, these authors suggest that societies and organizations are *existentially* prior to any individual. They do not begin their analysis, as Bruce Jones does, with the assumption that political actors are individual rational decision-makers.

This debate goes back to Hegel and his critique of social contract theory, a position taken up later in the nineteenth century by sociologists such as Wilhelm Dilthey and George Simmel of the German *Geiseswissenschaften* that attempted to understand the formation of the historical world in terms of the interaction between desire and life and the construction of an objectified world. In Dilthey, and in Collingwood in the twentieth century, this process of constructing that objectified world was best grasped through empathetic reenactment, through *verstehen*, through the analysis of the thoughts—the goals, norms, beliefs and anticipated consequences—and decisions of individual political actors. This approach thereby attempted to bridge the gap between methodological individualism and any assumption of a preexisting group mindset, a political identity derivative from cultural identity that Mamdani critiqued.[19] The presumption of a "group mind" was presupposed in the persistence of nationalism of various forms at the base of violent conflict rooted in clashes between cultures in the wars in the Balkans. However, the presumption of a "group mind" was also presupposed in the Second World War in the fight against fascism, in the Cold War fight against communism, and in the current war against international terrorism and Muslim extremism—only these cultural wars were upheld as wars between different views of civilization, or, more often, between civilization and barbarism. A specific culture that upheld the values of democracy and freedom, and that eschewed authoritarianism and dogmatic intolerance, was identified with the higher civilization considered to be the universal *telos* of the international order based on universal rights that could link the fate of an individual with the rest of humankind through scientific and technological progress and the only method that could successfully reign in the excesses of nationalism without oppression.

The heirs to the Dilthey/Collingwood tradition, such as Michael Barnett, while accepting that individuals could be embedded in the *Geist* of the political collectivity to which they belonged, avoided a presumption of a reified group mind and insisted that the individual was *ontologically* prior to the collectivity even if the collectivity was *existentially* prior to the individual. However, for Mahmood Mamdani, such thinkers fell into another error. In their insistence on recognizing the sovereignty of the individual mind over the social situation, in their effort to understand the mind *sub specie internitatis*, in the name of history and understanding decision-making in terms of its time and place, they gave short shrift to the historical process (of state formation for Mamdani) that led to and altered political identities. For critics such as Mamdani, culture was derivative of this historical process and not the main determinant of it.

If the development of a group mind must be grasped, both as an historical product of a political process and as a process that is the expression and articulation of minds overwhelmingly constituted and shaped by the norms and values and priorities of the collectivities of which the individuals are members, we have to go back to the Hegelian roots before the schism between these two premises took place—the split between the Dilthey/Collingwoodian subjective idealists of the empathetic school and the historicism of thinkers such as Mamdani who place such a strong emphasis on political historical processes and the competition for power that shapes our outlooks.

If we have to go back to the roots of the schism between the historicity of subjective idealism and the historicism of the dynamics of power (and money, I would add), then we must once again examine the dialectic of desire and life in the analysis of the relationship of lord and bondsman in Hegel's *Phenomenology of Spirit*.[20] There are two basic interpretations of this dialectic. In one popularized in the twentieth century by the Hungarian/Parisian Marxist intellectual, Alexandre Kojève, who had such a powerful influence on the post WWII intellectual tradition, conflict is rooted in the clash of power *and the quest for recognition of that power* via an interpersonal expression of deference.

Two knights cross paths. Each demands of the other that he be recognized as dominant. Each refuses to give that recognition. They clash, each willing to risk his life to gain the recognition of the other. If one kills the other, though he wins, he also loses for he forfeits obtaining the recognition that he sought. So in the desire to be as a god *vis-à-vis* the other, both in the expression of greater power and as a giver of life, the victor allows the other to live so long as the other agrees to be his servant. The loser, willing to surrender his desire for recognition to be a god to another in the name of life and survival, agrees. He becomes a bondsman to the other as lord. The lord achieves his desire to be recognized as a god and lord of all he surveys at the same time as he is relieved from the tedium of tending to his own material survival for he now has a servant to provide the necessities of life. The defeated one survives as a servant and surrenders his desire for power, but has the satisfaction of knowing that the lord is dependent on him both for recognition and for his material sustenance. This is the version of the tale of the lord and the bondsman that directly leads to the historicism of power in accounts of genocide such as in Mahmood Mamdani. The objectified world is a product of replaying clashes of power arising out of a particular past, and set of historical circumstances, in the search for identity and recognition in the real world; though the replay does not imitate the original process of colonial enslavement.[21]

In the other version of the tale of the lord and bondsman—one that claims to reveal the deeper sources of the human intellect and spirit beneath any quest for power and recognition—the clash occurs between two mortals who recognize they are mortal but who desire divine recognition for their way of life. Here prestige and recognition are not the means to gain deference or even, more instrumentally, money or power, though these may be byproducts, but is the very basis for determining social stratification and value priorities in society by creating a hierarchy of different lifestyles originally tied to the means of production. It is the clash between Cain and Abel. Each represents a different culture and one must be recognized as having priority. The cowboy and the farmer can't be friends. One requires the open range. The other needs fences and enclosed land. One is a herdsman such as the archetypal Tutsi (as distinct from the historically real one) who sacrifices the best of his animals to earn the recognition as God's chosen one on earth. The farmer, the archetypal Hutu, offers the best of his grain to demonstrate that desire for divine recognition is more important than the material production in which he is engaged to sustain life. The divine power of the imperial realm accepts the sacrifice of the herdsman and gives His recognition to the Tutsi to be his loyal servant. In a rage, the Hutu lashes out and slays the Tutsi. Two cultures, rooted in two different economic ways to sustain life, clash materially, but, more importantly, clash in the quest for historical recognition for which way of life has priority in the divine scheme.

The first tale roots the genesis of violent conflict in an atheistic vision of a desire for humans to be recognized by other humans as god, as having superior power, and willing to risk life for that recognition. In the master-servant relationship that results from such a clash, the master from his upstairs perspective sees the servant as protected by him and dependent on him for his survival. The servant from his downstairs perspective sees the master as dependent on him for his survival. Further, whereas the servant knows everything about the master's world, the world of the servant remains a total mystery to the master so that the servant sees his cognitive realm as more comprehensive and objective than the construction of reality created upstairs.

In the second tale, two mortals clash who represent two different ways of material life and two different cultures clash. Each is willing to sacrifice the best of his way of life in service of the divine and for divine recognition. They do not begin as warriors but as peaceful human beings intent on doing their best to survive in this world, but also driven by a desire to gain recognition for their effort. Violent conflict is primarily a product of cultural conflict and not of a quest for power in this world. The violence does not end with one culture ruling over the other, but with the supercession of both cultures in a new way of life.

In one version, the history of power conflicts leads to the construction of a version of objective reality. In the other, our construction of the objectified world is a result of tradition shaping our norms, beliefs and even character, norms that lead either to clashes with others who construct the objectified world differently, or to passivity in the face of such clashes. In each perspective, there are really three different realms. The first is the realm of life and the quest for survival that results in an economic way of life that in its most basic form entails the production and consumption of food and the territorial mode of life and technology that goes with it. The second is the realm of desire and creativity in the quest to demonstrate that the human spirit is not restricted by the demands of the material world, a realm that leads to constructing, comprehending and understanding the world in a specific way and produces a specific form of rationality. The third realm is the real world, the world in which different ways of life and different rational constructions clash, indicating the existence of an objective realm independent of the subject.

Thus, as well as the inclusive culture of a particular form of master and servant, we have the creation of class cultures. In the cultural version of the interaction of these different realms within and between cultures, conflicts between different forms of master-servant culture and within each one lead to violence and challenges to the rational order that has been constructed. In the historical version of the interaction of these different realms, the system of restricting membership and access to power within each master-servant system, and between and among ways of defining and distributing power, produces violence that reveals the limitations on the way systems allow access to membership. One of the virtues of this perspective is that culture is viewed as a protean product of history and human agents who both inherit and have an impact on its development by their actions in pursuit of power. Culture is not reified, identified with established patterns, customs or norms, or considered homogeneous in any one society. Nor is there a presumption that all members of a society share the same sense of culture. Ironically, however, the analysis leaves a reader with the conviction that the power of a culture (such as the view of the other as a race of foreign interlopers) can be dominant in a society in response to changing circumstances and crises.

In the political theories, two utopian solutions are envisioned. In one, there is equality of membership within each political construction. People are not divided into different groups by ethnicity or race. Each individual has equal and full membership rights. As a by-product, it is held that these different democratic systems will not war with one another. In the second utopian scheme that gives priority to the economic over the political sphere, the stress is on cosmopolitan membership that does away with territorial political constructions and has as its ideal a world in which there are no class divisions. One envisions the construction of a world made up of equal states, each with equality of political membership within each without privileging a particular ethnicity or discriminating on the basis of race. The other envisions the construction of a single political world without class divisions. The individualist rational school (represented by Bruce Jones) presumes that individuals already are capable of detached instrumental rational calculation and do not need to create political or economic utopias to avoid violent conflict. The last is rooted in a basic presumption about the congruity of the material pursuit of survival or a life force and reason that has its intellectual heir in René Descartes. It contrasts with a rational system rooted in the pursuit of interests whose intellectual ancestor is John Locke, and a rational system of power relations whose modern founder is Thomas Hobbes.[22]

Once the belief in the benevolence of nature was discarded, that is, that nature existed to serve human ends, and the belief was adopted that knowledge had to be based on certainties arrived at by a rational method, then species and classes, correlations and laws became constructs rather than mirrors of a natural order, and reason itself became simply an instrument for security, for survival, or for power in a world of atomic individuals who only belong to wholes they themselves construct.

All of the above three ways of dealing with overcoming conflict and violence are rooted in the common enlightenment presumption that individual political human autonomy is best achieved by the pursuit of human happiness without a *telos*, a final cause or end in which reason functions as an instrument of the passions, whether it be a passion for power or for pursuing material acquisitiveness, or even for the pursuit of the divine omniscience of comprehensive knowledge. Human freedom and the pursuit of happiness is just a self-serving project.

At the other pole are the cultural theorists who presume that there will always be cultural clashes. The way of ensuring that these do not become violent entails putting in place institutional mechanisms for allowing our constructed intellectual versions of the world to be challenged by a reality and/or morality independent of those constructions. Cultural theorists tend to be anti-utopian both with respect to any ideal of a perfect detached rational calculation or concerning any political or economic system that can overcome and prevent violence. The best we can do is to manage and mitigate conflict to prevent and limit violence as much as possible. Contrary to the presumption that identifies these theorists with a utopian idealism, these various versions of subjective idealism already presume that an individual belongs to some higher (and, in some sense, sacred) transcendent order that obligates individuals to pursue goals not simply dictated by self-service and this saves them from utopianism. Instead, humans pursue a wholeness that is with them from the start.

The two radically different interpretations of life, desire and the lordship/bondage relationship are often distinguished as the "scientific" atheistic approach that stresses the inherent logic of development independent of any higher order, and the "hermeneutic" approach that interprets the science of experience itself as a sequence of illusory visions that the absolute that is with us from the start is also realizable in human historical time, for the absolute is always a beyond to which we belong but which we can never fully inhabit. Having lost faith in either an immediate or a mediated knowledge of the highest ground of being, and driven by the failure to establish any certainty about the human good, enlightenment thought first begins with systematic doubt and skepticism in the attempt to find a solid foundation in reason itself and then turns to human power or interests.

We will have to return to the issue of whether any process can overcome the fundamental divisions in understanding between enlightenment universal schools for understanding modernity and cultural approaches, but we must first expand our comprehension of those cultural approaches.

Though all cultural schools are anti-utopian, they can be divided into three groups, depending on the realm they rely upon to rescue us from our limited constructed worlds. For a scholar such as Power, the source of salvation rests in the life world that also maintains a fundamental human moral sensibility that allows humankind not only to rise above the pattern of institutional restrictions, but provides the criteria—human rights norms—for measuring the limitations of any institutional constructions. It is the one cultural school (and for that matter, the only school, including the three universalistic rational schools) that adopts an overt cosmopolitan approach that insists that all humans ultimately belong to a common human culture of rights and freedoms. The antidote to intrastate and interstate rivalries and hatreds is neither a common and heightened use of reason, nor the pursuit of economic self-interest within a framework of fair and just norms not dictated by either ideology or paternalism, nor even a system of democratic states that eschews ethnic nationalism or racial jingoism but treats all its residents as equal citizens under the law. Nor, for that matter, is salvation to be found in a critical rationality that ensures that we can cut through our cultural prejudices and fixed patterns of giving shape to reality.

Even developing and strengthening international legal norms, such as the genocide convention, and ensuring that they have teeth, is not the direction that needs to be stressed. Instead, we must strengthen the relations among nations by developing an extant global culture already present within those states that recognize and protect human rights, rights that must be protected universally through cross-national cooperation and transnational efforts backed by the power of those states. Such a program is not to be confused with its weak sister that works towards creating mutual human understanding by simply relying on cultural internationalism in which international cooperation is fostered through the exchange of ideas and persons through scholarly, artistic, and interstate cultural and athletic exchanges. Rousseau, as the "discoverer" of a "natural" wholeness presupposed to lie beneath the harsh realities encountered, was not so naïve. Though relying on a pre-cognitive sentiment rather than intellectual apprehension, freedom had to rest on a human capacity common to us all, but progress could only be made through the battle between those with human and poetic sensibilities and the political-military giants that ruled the world.[23]

For a scholar such as Barnett, the source of salvation is not to be found in an inner moral and spiritual excellence sensitive to the natural needs of all humans, but in the norms that regulate human society. However corrupted those norms have become in fostering self-service and hypocrisy, salvation resides in the realm of intellectual creativity that at once allows us to create a second order constructed reality and to develop intellectual institutions that allow that very same constructed reality to be tested and challenged. In Barnett, culture stresses social and cognitive processing more than institutional patterning.[24] For Ronayne, who belongs to a third cultural school, the moral sensitivities that Power relies upon and the intellectual creativity that Barnett requires have already led to the creation of countervailing cultural norms and institutions within the system. The culture is not monolithic. What is required is to strengthen those cultural institutions and norms that reflect this moral sensitivity and more comprehensive intellectual frame, and to allow the limitations of the predominant cultural norms to be overcome.

One of the most glaring ironies of the difference between the cultural and the universalist schools is that the universalist schools end up distinguishing between irrational and rational cultures (ethnic and racial cultures versus states based on equal membership of everyone within a territory; a culture based on inaccurate and inadequate observations and analysis versus a clear and farsighted culture of rational wise observers, analysts and decision-makers; a global economic system based on dependency that corrupts the soul and the institutions of any state versus one that encourages independence and integrity). At the same time, the cultural schools find salvation in that which provides a unitary basis for all humans either in a common sensibility, a common mode of grasping objective reality independent of the institutionally-created blinkers we wear for constructing reality, or in already extant norms that represent the human rather than the parochial spirit of humans. It would appear that the universalist cannot escape culture and the cultural theorists cannot avoid grasping for a universal realm that allows humans to emancipate themselves from the actual.

I contend that the tension between various communitarian cultural presuppositions and universalist presumptions cannot be avoided. The two radically different ways of interpreting the lordship/bondage narrative are but two *gestalt* images that depend on the perspective adopted. The two cannot be seen at the same time, nor can one be reduced to the other. We can simply flip back and forth from one image to the other. The tension between the two always reemerges in new forms. But both sets of ways and their subdivisions represent themselves in new forms. However, whatever the form, they all oppose oppression.

The difference between the roots of freedom and escape from violence espoused by the universalists and the culturalists (both in opposition to authoritarian modes), can best be exemplified in three versions of the origin of sin as interpreted through the story of Adam and Eve. In one version, the source of evil is found in disobedience to divine authority. Adam and Eve did not obey a divine commandment not to eat of the Tree of Knowledge. Blind obedience to what is held to be divine or divinely-inspired orders is intended to root out violence, though one should not be surprised to learn that while successful domestically, the shift in the expression of violence targets dissidents and outsiders driven by alternative visions of the divine order.

In a second interpretation, the source of sin is surrendering to temptation. Eve listens to the entreaties of the sensuous snake and then seduces Adam. Erotic passion is the problem and passions must be ruled by reason, for human reason imitated and expressed the divine and perfect intelligence that animated the universe. In a third interpretation, God said that if you eat of the Tree of Knowledge, you will surely die. This conditional assertion is misread as a commandment. The real story is one of Adam so caught up in his belief that his ability to reason and classify and order the realm of nature is what makes him imitate the creativity of God, that he does not even know he feels lonely. He sees himself as a pure intellect without a body that will die. Though man is born of woman and the original man and woman are created equal in God's eyes, Adam projects his material self onto another and in his imagination sees woman as the projection of his own flesh while denying that his own flesh has any connection with his essential being. Even his penis is projected as other as a talking erect serpent that seduces Eve. His erotic body is other, as is Eve, whom he can then blame for seducing him.

Eve, the original and authentic expression of spontaneity, individuality and oneness with nature, saw the function of sex clearly; if you are going to obey God's natural commandment to be fruitful and multiply, then sex and bearing children must take place even if it means coming to the recognition that humans are mortal and must die. The source of sin is not eros or passion, but the blindness of reason to the materiality of humankind. Adam, not Eve, is the original sinner. Eros, rooted in culture, is the foundation for a prerational unity and the basis for the peaceful pursuit of happiness rather than a civilization based on a self-centered rational pursuit of justice that in fact domesticates man, repressing his creative spirit, and subjecting him to the reign of the common and the calculable.[25] Established norms only have merit if they reflect and express this unity rather than serve as vehicles for repression.

On the other hand, established norms are part of our cultural heritage that instills in each of us enduring traits that influence both our social structures and our responses to historical challenges. The problem, as George Simmel phrased it, is that, "[i]t is the paradox of culture that subjective life which we feel in its continuous stream and which drives itself toward inner perfection cannot by itself reach the perfection of culture."[26]

If we are not to fall into a system constructed on blind obedience to a higher authority, then we must check the pride of ostensible reason as an infallible source of truth through reason's critique of itself or by relying on sensibilities outside the realm of reason's jurisdiction in an original form or as already exemplified in some institutional norms. The fault lies in our culture and must be corrected to create a new culture. Alternatively, it is passion that must be checked and ruled by reason in the quest to develop a civilization free of oppression and irrational desire that gives rise to such oppression.[27]

None of the analyses of solutions are wrong. They are either too ambitious or just inadequate and reductionist. Restructuring the world economic order might prevent genocide, but the rarity of the latter seems insufficient to motivate the all-encompassing solution of the former. In Mamdani's envisioned solution, we do need a system of states that guarantee everyone protection so that no individual lacks a political home that guarantees him/her protection. However, solving the problem by insisting that anyone resident within the territory of a state should have citizenship merely provides an incentive for irregular migrants to seek residency in the most prosperous states. Further, ethnic identification within a state need not be a source of interethnic conflict but can be a source of interethnic recognition and respect.

Nor is the problem resolved by finding and constituting a group that is wise and all-knowing to devise strategies for preventing and mitigating violence. Perceptual and analytic capacities are insufficient. Tough choices have to be made based on limited knowledge and an inability to forecast changing geopolitical circumstances. Do you put in sufficient force to neutralize the spoilers? Or do you try to co-opt the spoilers through inclusion and thus risk giving them more power and leverage? Or do you try to muddle through, exclude the spoilers, and hope the political solution will be in place to offset the need for a military solution? And when circumstances tend to dictate one choice rather than the other and that choice proves to be calamitous, then hindsight will fault you for lack of vision.

If the universalist solutions are too grand, the cultural solutions are too limited. Humanitarian sensibilities are both unreliable and historically inadequate. Institutionalized systems for reality checks on our constructions of reality are necessary and helpful, and may lead to different decisions in certain circumstances, but in themselves are unlikely to do so. Strengthening the identification of crimes like genocide and the enforcement mechanisms offer a worthy long term goal, but the question remains concerning how to get there from here. Further, any of these solutions by themselves are unlikely to work and will generally require the others as well.

Anthony Giddens heroically but unsuccessfully, I believe, tried to bridge the gap between cultural and universalist approaches by stressing the role of human factors that enabled as well as constrained human action in his structuration approach.[28] It is an approach that tries to overcome the reification of the traditional structural-functional approach towards culture with its emphasis on the constraints of norms and values and its propensity for reification by showing how change takes place in specific temporal and spatial frameworks. Others introduced concepts such as "social capital" that are now standard in international studies as an indicator to show how objective structures and subjective meaning clash and interact to facilitate and inhibit social change.[29] Other studies emphasized that the cooperative and synergistic relations of political economy and culture are interactive, sometimes in tension and more often mutually reinforcing, such as in Richard Swedburg's plea for socioeconomics.[30]

However useful and insightful these efforts to unite studies of power and interest relations with studies of norms of legitimation concerning the premises and patterns of different cultural systems, my analysis suggests any effort at an overall synthesis is doomed and just as prone to reductionism of one kind or another. Either culture becomes an epiphenomenona of power or, alternatively, the roles of individual actors and of states are neglected.

We do need an image of a global political and economic order that is both realistic while at the same time overcoming the problems that contribute to making conflicts violent in the current order. We do need leaders who can work together both to alter the present system in that direction while creating an institutional mechanism for anticipating threats to the development of that order, and develop strategies and institutional mechanisms for dealing with those threats on the basis of norms backed by enforcement powers that, based on a humanitarian sensibility, give respect *and protection* for all humans. To facilitate the development of a "culture of peace" and a "culture of conflict prevention" in an attempt to build sustainable peace, we need to develop not only an understanding of the nature of already established war cultures, but we have to develop institutions that check our constructions of reality and translate analyses of potential violent ethnic conflicts that can end up in genocide into possible alternative scenarios and action responses. We have to know where we are going, where we are coming from, and how to get from here to there.

We need a comprehensive approach that takes into account both a vision of a civilized society and the various cultures and the degree to which they manifest and contribute to the realization of such a society, while trying to remain in touch with the traditional characteristics of these cultures. Most of all, we must recognize that these radically different approaches, one based on overt and covert strategies to deal with money and power, and the other based on norms and values and, in the end, a sensitivity to the unique individuality of every individual and culture while trying to develop norms that embrace all of humanity, are approaches that cannot be coherently integrated but must be perceived from shifting, opposed and paradoxical *gestalt* perspectives in order to grasp a larger truth that neither of the perspectives are capable of doing on their own.

Author's Note

I use the term culture in the plural for two reasons. First, culture is an equivocal term with many meanings. Although there are a number of meanings that are not used in this essay, such as the use of the term "cultured" to refer to cultivation of manners and a specific aesthetic sensibility, or to refer to the media and magazines and television that are part of "popular culture," there are many meanings that are relevant in this context. Matthew Arnold said that his society associated culture with "frivolous and unedifying activity" (*Culture and Anarchy*, 43), whereas he preferred to use culture in two different senses: to identify the fruits of the passion of a curious mind determined to see things as they really are as the foundation for augmenting the excellence of human nature; and, in a second sense, not as the collection of products of a curious mind, but as originating in the love of perfection and a moral and social passion for doing good that results in benevolent actions and love of neighbor—in this context, in the desire to eliminate the scourge of genocide. Thus, for Matthew Arnold, the curiosity to understand both genocide and the indifferent response to it as well as the desire to do something about it are both motives that produce culture. In that sense, this essay is a contribution to culture. However, whatever the motives for producing culture, and without the evaluative associations of Matthew Arnold, "culture" has come to stand for the mental predispositions shared by a group or community that either provide the schema of interpretation for the way they view the world or that shape their evaluations of that world through the values and norms of a specific culture, or that include both cognitions as well as values and norms. Some would go even further and include in culture the actions that follow from these predispositions and from which the predispositions can be read. Even further, studies of culture often include the institutions that are a product of those actions, that embody those mental predispositions and that, in turn, reinforce them either through the means they provide for interpreting the world or through the bonds they build within groups and in societies, or both. Thus, given these different senses, there are different cultures of violence. Second, I do not presume that there is only one culture—whatever meaning is given to the term—that results in violence. I leave it as an open possibility that there may be several cultures of violence.

Notes

1 See Gabriel A. Almond, "The Study of Political Culture," in Lane Crothers and Charles Lockhart, eds., *Culture and Politics: A Reader* (New York: St. Martin's Press, 2000), 5–20, where he argues that these same questions with respect to WWII and the Holocaust gave rise to the revival of the modern study of political culture as an effort to solve these tragic historical puzzles. The development of survey research methodology had a tremendous impact on structural-functional sociology, social psychology and psychoanalytic sociology and placed values, affects and beliefs at the center of the study of social and political structures.

2 General Roméo Dallaire, the Force Commander of the peacekeeping forces in Rwanda (UNAMIR), claimed that at the beginning of the genocide, 5,000 troops would have been sufficient. An international panel of military officers, convened by the Carnegie Commission on Preventing Deadly Conflict, the Institute for the Study of Diplomacy at Georgetown University, and the US army, confirmed that such a force (made effective with air support, logistics and communication) could have stopped the genocide at little risk during the window of opportunity that existed between 6–21 April. See Scott R. Feil, *Preventing Genocide: How the Use of Force Might Have Succeeded in Rwanda* (New York: Carnegie Commission on Preventing Deadly Conflict, 1997). The report also includes the details of Dallaire's three-phased plan. For a contrary view, see Alan J. Kuperman, "Rwanda in Retrospect," *Foreign Affairs* 79, no. 1 (January /February, 2000), 94–118.

3 Samantha Power, *A Problem from Hell: America and the Age of Genocide* (New York, NY: Basic Books, 2002), 354.

4 Mahmood Mamdani, *When Victims Become Killers: Colonialism, Nativism, and the Genocide in Rwanda* (Princeton, NJ: Princeton University Press, 2001), 254–55, and Linda R. Melvern, *A People Betrayed: The Role of the West in Rwanda's Genocide* (London: Zed Books, 2000), 214, describe France as creating protective corridors that allowed those politically responsible for the genocide to escape and re-establish themselves in Zaire.

5 The term "norms," as used in this chapter, stands for conceptualized collective internalized values that shape positive and negative attitudes; they are expressed in rational language as regulative rules directed at making decisions and determining subsequent actions that follow from such decisions and the corresponding regulative norms. However, norms need not be explicitly consensual and may only be derived by abstracting from actual behavior. Norms may be constituted as a system of values based on a limited number of guiding principles and may be used to determine modes and conditions that govern separate decisions—as in the interpretations of the rules of engagement sent to General Dallaire by the Secretariat in New York that commanded Dallaire not to take a proactive role in uncovering hidden arms in Kigali.

6 Peter Ronayne, *Never Again? The United States and the Prevention and Punishment of Genocide since the Holocaust* (Lanham, MD: Rowman & Littlefield Publishers, Inc., 2001), 188–89.

7 Mamdani, *When Victims Become Killers.*

8 Bruce Jones, *Peacemaking in Rwanda: The Dynamics of Failure* (Boulder, CO: Lynne Reinner, 2001).

9 As Jon Elster characterizes this dichotomy in the instrumental rationality paradigm, future rewards (or fear of losses) "pull" decisions forward, while in cultural theory dictated by social norms, behavior is "pushed" from behind by quasi-inertial forces. In the former, opportunistic decision-making is operative in the attempt to adapt to changing circumstances. The latter, in contrast, tends to be insensitive to dramatic changes. See Jon Elster, *The Cement of Society* (Cambridge: Cambridge University Press, 1989).

10 For a more general study of the African state along these lines, see S.N. Eisenstadt, M. Abitbol, and N. Chazan, eds., *The Early State in African Perspective: Culture, Power, and Division of Labor* (Leiden: E. Brill, 1987).

11 The concept of race and its science was itself rooted in nineteenth century culture and the newly discovered emphasis on evolution and progress. It posited a view of culture that included knowledge, beliefs, morals, laws, customs and habits characteristic of a society, with various societies reflecting simple or more complex combinations, so that societies could be ranged from primitive to highly civilized. See Edward Tylor, *Primitive Culture* (1870), mentioned in Kevin Avruch, *Culture and Conflict Resolution* (Washington, D.C.: United States Institute for Peace 1998), 6.

12 Mahmood Mamdani, *When Victims Become Killers*, 59.

13 Peter Uvin, *Aiding Violence: The Development Enterprise in Africa* (West Hartford, Conn.: Kumerian Press, 1998).

14 A cultural explication of this same phenomenon might focus on the prevalence of low levels of trust in societies constructed on the basis of patron-client relations and the prevalence of relatively high levels of trust characteristic of developed societies and economic international organizations, in which clientelistic relations are peripheral rather than marginal in the organizational structure and in which instrumental universalist norms are central. Relatively high trust institutions thus prove to be naïve when dealing with low trust ones in which patron-client relationships are central; low trust institutions, when threatened and under stress, tend to toss overboard the ballast of universalist norms adopted under pressure of their international patrons in order to preserve and even strengthen the prevalence of patron-client relationships domestically. For examples of such an approach, see S.N. Eisenstadt and L. Roninger, *Patrons, Clients, and Friends* (Cambridge: Cambridge University Press 1984). In *Center and Periphery* (Chicago: University of Chicago Press, 1975, 3–17) Edward Shils expands on Eisenstadt's earlier conceptualization of center-periphery relations (see Eisenstadt's *Political Systems of Empires* [Glencoe, IL: Free Press, 1963]). Shils argues that Eisenstadt's conceptualization could also be used to show that, in addition to empire's exemplifying a social division of labor between center and periphery (previously perceived to be the central focus for constructing the social order), Max Weber's notion of charisma could be operative as an instrument of change. Although, for Weber, culture is a major determinant of behavior in face-to-face relations, groups and organizations (as well as macrosocial and cultural frameworks and individuals) enjoy limited freedom and few opportunities for creative input. Change therefore generally occurs through imperceptible small accretions in the periphery, and charisma may be the operative that allows great

dramatic innovations in societies and cultures. These dramatic innovations are not always creative; if key leaders in the periphery exhibit manifestations of significant alienation, they may express themselves in a nihilistic and destructive fashion by exhibiting extreme hatred towards the initiators of change. One of the implications of borrowing from such an analysis for the study of violent and genocidal phenomena would be a shift away from the traditional structural-functional sociological school's study of culture and emphasis on values and norms (such as exhibited by the cultural theorists of the Rwanda genocide and analyzed in this chapter) to adopting the symbolic interactionist models suggested by theorists like Clifford Geertz (*The Interpretation of Cultures*, New York: Basic Books, 1973), in which culture is viewed not so much as first order customs, habits, values and attitudes formulated as norms, but as second order process rules for governing behavior. However, that would push the analysis into a *gestalt* switch to the universalists where the state and autonomous individual actors again are critical and central elements.

15 Samantha Power, *A Problem from Hell*, 329–390; Peter Ronayne, *Never Again*, 196; and Michael Barnett, *Eyewitness to a Genocide: The United Nations and Rwanda* (Ithaca, NY: Cornell University Press, 2002).

16 Power, *A Problem from Hell*, xxi.

17 Ronayne instantiated a wider perspective on culture that focused on social change in terms of competing sets of norms of structural-functional models that study immigrant norms in confrontation with the dominant norms of the society into which they were resettling, or youth groups as manifestations of the tension between family values and the broader purportedly universalist norms governing behavior in the institutions of society, or the world systems theory and symbolic structuralism studies of cultures, states and empires as they developed systemic values and norms embedded in their organizations and institutions (especially bureaucracies in developed states and organizations) to preserve their institutional boundaries against external challenges and competing norms. These cultures ended up generating internal conflicts between rulers who gained their positions by mastering the exercise of power and creatively interpreting inherited norms, and traditional authorities that were charged with legitimizing "proper" interpretations. Culture then emerges as the realm of symbolic interaction in the power struggles between the deep structures and values of a community and the negotiated political compromises that challenge those deep structures and values. These varieties of approaches to normative change within institutions, as well as the reification of norms within institutions, all stood at odds with rational choice models that argued against explaining social behavior in terms of roles and, instead, insisted on understanding change in terms of interactions between and among rational individual social actors who might represent states but who based their recommendations and decisions on utilitarian instrumental calculations that relied on the optimization of utilities using offers of rewards or threats of deprivation to induce conformity to their recommendations. The cultural theorists, however, found that the power theorists (or rational choice models) could never account for the adoption of non-utilitarian goals or ends or ultimate values in terms of any instrumental calculation and failed to develop a basis for adopting second order or ground rules.

18 Since cultural theories make political continuity the norm, the corollary is that societies or groups confronted by large-scale changes and radically new and unexpected situations will respond either with knee-jerk responses or with incoherent and fragmented reactions, since their culture-bound propensities do not allow them to adapt readily. Harry Eckstein emphasizes the point in his essay, "A Culturalist Theory of Social Change," *American Political Science Review* 82, no. 3 (1988): 789–804.

19 Mamdani, *When Victims Become Killers*, 21.

20 Georg Wilhelm Friedrich Hegel, *Phenomenology of Spirit: Selections*, trans. and ann. Howard P. Kainz (University Park, PA.: Pennsylvania State University Press, 1994).

21 Note that "leads to" is the operative phrase. The master/slave struggle is not the same as the racial conflict between Hutu and Tutsi, though the latter is derivative from it. This should be obvious since the Hutu racist extremists did not believe in preserving the lives of the Tutsi as slaves who did the material work and in turn recognized the Hutu as their masters. The Hutu extremists sought to exterminate the Tutsi. However, the roots of this racism is to be found in master/slave settler societies in which the indigenous population is defeated and given protection so that they can both work the land on behalf of their masters and recognize the settlers as lords and masters of the universe. Rwanda was a unique settler society in Africa—a mixture of direct and indirect rule that used a part of the indigenous population, the Tutsis, and transmogrified them into a quasi-white race that had migrated to Rwanda, conquered the local population, and thus were suited to implement the rule of the colonists. That is why the origin of the conflict dates from the Belgian reification of Hutus and Tutsis as dichotomous races. Mahmood Mamdani posits another position on this matter. He believes that Tutsis were once an ethnic group but that Hutus are a totally constructed entity collecting together various conquered populations. After the slaves revolt, after their masters are overthrown, and if the masters are viewed as aliens, then in the justice of the victims turned victors, the former masters can be expelled or even exterminated if they pose a threat of resuming their rule over the local population.

22 Hobbes defined power as a means to achieve a future *apparent* need; in this interpretation of Hegel, the need for recognition appears first in the quest for power over another. Culture does not define what those needs are.

23 It is easy enough to put a high value on poetic sensibility and humanitarianism. However, when one recalls that Martin Heidegger, in the tradition of Rousseau, also sought out a precognitive, prediscursive hidden ground in Being and was a Nazi supporter of Hitler who was silent, if not complicit, in the dismissal of his Jewish colleagues and mentors, one can become wary of idealizing any poet-philosopher who rails against the violence of tech-speak and science. When respected humanitarian organizations wail about the hundreds of thousands of missing (and presumably dead) Hutu refugees in Zaire in 1997 (a charge dismissed by US air force surveys and more accurate counts of the refugees actually in the camps in contrast to the official counts), and when even more respected human rights organizations like Amnesty International and Human Rights Watch denounce the massive slaughter of an estimated 500 Palestinian civilians by

Israeli soldiers in the Jenin refugee camp (when it was later established by a UN Commission of inquiry that 52 died, most of whom were militants), it reinforces a wariness about relying on sensibilities that create phantom refugees and phantom deaths, rather than on objectively and scientifically observed facts.

24 Kevin Avruch generalizes this approach. However, unlike Barnett, Avruch takes a heterogeneous approach to culture. Rather than viewing one institution such as the UN sharing a coherent singular culture, "individuals reflect or embody multiple cultures and that 'culture' is always psychologically and socially distributed in a group" (Avruch, *Culture and Conflict Resolution*, 5).

25 See Richard L. Velkey, *Being after Rousseau: Philosophy and Culture in Question* (Chicago: University of Chicago Press 2002), esp. ch. 1, "The Tension in the Beautiful: On Culture and Civilization in Rousseau and German Philosophy."

26 George Simmel, *The Conflict of Modern Culture and Other Essays*, trans. K Peter Etzkorn (New York: Teachers College Press, 1968), 30.

27 In *Totem and Taboo: Resemblances between the Psychic Lives of Savages and Neurotics* (trans. J. Strachey [New York: Norton, 1950], 198–224), Sigmund Freud viewed culture itself as originally emerging through the repression of desire. Through the combination of Oedipal desire and (imagined?) patricide, as well as guilt over that murder, males inculcate a superego through the father with whom they identify. This superego becomes the basis for the sets of prohibitions and aspirations that are organized into social institutions that either repress desire or displace its gratification through substitutes.

28 Anthony Giddens, *The Constitution of Society: Outline of the Theory of Structuration* (Oxford: Polity Press, 1984).

29 See Robert D. Putnam, "Bowling Alone: America's Declining Social Capital," *Journal of Democracy* 6, no. 1 (1995): 65–78. Putnam identifies social capital with civil society and argues that it was in decline, thus leading to the erosion of social trust. The relationship between social capital and social trust can be correlated with Eisenstadt's work, where he found a correlation between clientelism and low trust societies, whereas high trust societies pushed patron-client relations to the periphery and emphasized merit (see n.7).

30 Richard Swedberg "Socioeconomics and the New "Battle of Methods": Toward a Paradigm Shift?" *Journal of Behavioral Economics* 19, no. 2 (1990): 381–92.

15

Joseph Masciulli

From a Culture of Violence to a Culture of Peace

EVOLVING COSMOPOLITAN POLITICS AND ETHICS

SIMPLIFYING—though not oversimplifying—the complex theoretical debates occurring in international relations and global politics today, one may affirm that "the study of international affairs is best understood as a protracted competition between the realist, liberal, and radical traditions. Realism emphasizes the enduring propensity for conflict between states; liberalism identifies several ways to mitigate these conflictive tendencies; and the radical tradition describes how the entire system of state relations might be transformed."[1] I will argue from an idealist-liberal and just war perspective against Huntington's realist theory of the clash of civilizations, and against moralistic abolitionist pacifism—a seemingly laudable, but extreme, utopian, and problematic notion of nonviolence. It is a seductive ideal that many participating in peace movements and United Nations conferences and organizations have adopted and advocated as a response to cultures of violence.

"Wherever human beings form communities, culture comes into existence," from the village level to the global level.[2] As a working analytical-empirical definition of the term "culture," let us say that a "culture" refers to "structures of meaning, including memory, ideology, emotions, life styles, scholarly and artistic works, and other symbols."[3] These "set[s] of meanings and values that inform...

a way of life," may be macro or micro in their inclusiveness and extensiveness, remain relatively unchanged for ages, or may be in the process of slow or rapid development or dissolution.[4] This broad, empirical notion of a plurality of cultures or civilizations is developed in opposition to the normative notion of classicist culture or civilization versus barbarism.[5]

One should stress[6] that "culture transcends [political] ideology [though it may include it as one of its elements], and is about the substance of identity for individuals in a society. ...[Moreover, it involves an] awareness of a common language, ethnicity, history, religion, and/or landscape [which] represent the building blocks of culture."[7] It is generally accepted in the literature that "the broadest construction of cultural identity is the civilization" and that today "a number of civilizations clearly exist, notably, the Western, Islamic, Indian, and Chinese," though it is more difficult to classify other peoples' cultures in macro categories because they are not sufficiently united around distinct cores or split between civilizations or of small size.[8]

In contrast, there is also a normative notion of culture. One version is that there is a classicist culture that embodies the best thinking and artistic achievements of the past; the uncultured become cultured by aspiring to the ideals and norms of the classics and mastering their performances.[9] A variant notion of normative culture is the notion of "civilization" in the singular, in opposition to "barbarism" or some such opposite. To be civilized is good, to be uncivilized is bad. Eighteenth-century French thinkers proposed this idea of civilization in opposition to the concept of "barbarism" or "primitivism"—a settled, urban, and literate society in contrast with a barbaric society that lacked these features. This ideal of civilization versus barbarism was used ideologically in the pursuit of European colonialism and to exclude the colonized from being accepted as equals in the European-dominated international system.[10]

Few consistently peaceful societies and cultures exist or have existed historically, and clearly none that has been a macro culture or civilization. Anthropological investigations have revealed the existence of societies that experience conflict but consistently employ nonviolent modes of conflict resolution: the Semai people of Malaysia, and at least another ten known nonmodern societies. Switzerland, The Netherlands, Sweden, Costa Rica, and a few other countries have more or less dropped out of the warfare system.[11] The question is still open about the biological basis of aggressive violence, though socialization, as Adelman points out, clearly plays a dominant role in learning such behaviors.[12] Some psychological literature about primates points to the conclusion that male bonding and violence against targeted outside groups occur cross-culturally. The genetic potential for disemboweling one's enemies has been constant in humanity's history and continues to be operative in masses of people.[13] Nonetheless, group cultural norms (from the family to the national and international levels) can reinforce, channel, or deflect aggressive-violent desires (*i.e.*, capacities) to dominate others or to strike out at those believed to be the source of one's frustrations, deprivations, or a threat to one's identity.[14]

For, indeed, "the detrimental values ingrained in our culture include violence, aggression, the urge to dominate or conquer, individualism, and materialism. They are consistent with armament growth, the preparation for war, and the conducting of war. These values are representative of the rubric of social Darwinism, where through struggle, only the fittest survive," and this "Darwinian version of evolution postulating variation and selection premised on self-interested needs" effectively and prominently exists in most societies today, despite states' declaratory policies that accept the United Nations Charter and the United Nations Declaration of Human Rights (UNDHR) as aspirations and standards to be realized in national and international institutions. Indeed, survivalist perspectives based on militarism and lifeboat ethics, for example, are explicitly or subtly embodied in "child rearing, family life, interpersonal relationships, games, relationships with foreign countries, legends, and especially television."[15]

More generally, peace education analyses of current cultures has led some researchers to conclude that most cultures are pathological, and to declare that "the challenge of peace education" is "replacing cultures of militarism" with "a new kind of paradigm for perceiving the world. In this new perception, humankind is experienced as a unity, people are seen as children of the same Mother Nature, and one and the same universal life manifests itself in each individual human life. ...[A]ll the world's creatures have a value an sich." Moreover, "peace education aims to create a new male culture.... The violent, domination, and possessive macho image propagated by militaristic culture appears ridiculous and dangerous in this new male culture. In this new culture, courage is the ability to find peaceful means to resolve conflicts, and it is possible to take off the straitjacket of competition without threatening this healthy and self-confident masculinity."[16] Whatever the normative merits of this perspective, it does underline what does not generally exist today at the macro, global level, despite some ongoing changes towards nonviolent modes of thinking and acting in some local, national, and international cultural settings.

The historical facts remain startling no matter how many times we reflect on them. Over one hundred and ten million people have been killed in wars[17] in the twentieth century; and there have been over one hundred and twenty wars since the end of WWII in 1945.[18] The last century invented the gas chambers, total war, state-sponsored genocide and extermination camps, brainwashing, state security apparatuses, and "the panoptic surveillance of entire populations." It generated more victims, dead soldiers, murdered civilians, displaced minorities, torture, political prisoners and refugees, and more dead from cold, hunger, maltreatment "than ever could have been imagined. The phenomena of violence and barbarism [some have concluded] mark the distinctive signature of the age."[19] By the end of the century wars within states (Bosnia, Chechnya, Rwanda, Kosovo, East Timor, among others) seem to be replacing wars between states. "War lovers" or "someone who launches aggressive war against another nation and will do so again and again until he is brought down," as well as tyrants who exterminate their own people, have been and remain a constant feature of global politics (Hitler, Stalin, Mao, Idi Amin, Pol Pot, Saddam Hussein, Slobodan Milosevic, etc).[20]

Moreover, terrorism—"the deliberate killing of innocent people, at random, in order to spread fear through a whole population and force the hand of its political leaders"—promises to continue into the indefinite future as the prevalent mode of conflict.[21] It will be "sometimes in its pure form [the direct targeting and destruction of innocent civilians for political ends], sometimes within the framework of civil war or general lawlessness."[22] There is a growing hiatus between past military strategies—from Thucydides to Powell/ Schwartzkopf—and present and future ones. The distinction between innocent civilians and military combatants almost totally collapses with Mutually Assured Destruction and Nuclear Utilization Theory as deterrence and warfare strategies in the context of nuclear terror. As well, preparations to defend against and respond to attacks by biological and chemical weapons of mass destruction give rise to new dilemmas.

State terrorism has sought to make domestic political opposition impossible (used by authoritarian and totalitarian regimes against their own people—for example, the Argentinean "disappearances" in the 1980s and Saddam Hussein's terrorist repressions of his own people). War terrorism has sought to kill civilians in such a large number as to force a government to surrender (for example, Truman's decision to drop atomic bombs on Hiroshima and Nagasaki). Such massive, indiscriminate uses of force have been, prevalently, a part of national military strategies in the twentieth century, and continue to be "on the books."[23]

We cannot adequately understand contemporary and future state-sponsored and nonstate terrorism without much radical rethinking of terrorist acts of the past. Certainly, we cannot use as our guide for the future, the type of past terrorism that was "buttressed by the existence of oppression and social conflicts to which violence seemed the only effective response"; and that was carried out mostly by "idealistic, courageous young patriots and social revolutionaries driven to desperate actions by intolerable conditions, oppression, and tyranny."[24] Such terrorists—though they use evil means—were and are generally committed patriots and ideological revolutionaries (freedom fighters) with limited political goals. The current trend is in the direction of national and religious fanaticism and extremism—a mode of terrorism coeval with written history, but one that was secondary or marginal or restricted for much of our known past. Ultranationalism and religious fanaticism today have become coupled with weapons of mass destruction as a usable form of terrorist power, and nihilistic and suicidal motivations—"the genocidal mentality"—to carry out apocalyptic visions.[25]

In addition to extremist syncretic religious sects such as the Japanese Aum Shirinkyo, no major religion lacks its extremists who are in contention with moderate, inclusive, and truly pious members. The creative, bold, and well-organized terrorist attacks on 11 September 2001 that killed over three thousand innocent civilians in the United States and shocked its entire political and economic systems—with global reverberations—set a new standard for lethal and effective terrorism. In the future, terrorist individuals and groups of all sorts will seek to emulate and surpass the 9-11 model of terrorist hard (physically destructive) power that resulted in notable support among some mass publics and influential elites who thought the United States of America "had it coming!" and "deserved it."

It is possible that nationalism, religious extremism and fanaticism might recede in the foreseeable future and, for example, violent interpreters of "jihad" may become discredited among most of their coreligionists, and the moderate Islamists win out against the extremists in different countries. However, "the sad truth is that candidates for the new [indiscriminate, mass-destructive] terrorism may appear on the fringes of any extremist movement at any time."[26] Moreover, the temptation exists today in democracies and rights-respective regimes, and may become more overwhelming in the future, for police, military, and intelligence personnel engaged in counterviolence and counterterrorism activities to adopt amoral consequentialism and a neo-Darwinian perspective in practice, whatever their governments' public declarations may be about protecting people's civil liberties and human rights. But such strategic and tactical responses to terrorism that discard the just war principle that innocent noncombatants ought not to be harmed in fighting one's enemies would itself be a form of terror.[27]

The UNESCO charter insists that war begins in the minds of men and women. Radical abolitionist pacifists insist, "It can end there as well." Peoples and leaders, they argue, must become enlightened, and see that war is a human, historical institution that is disgusting, ridiculous, unwise, repulsive, futile, and costly.[28] They argue that in the last three centuries, peace advocates have succeeded in slowly convincing people of the terminal disrepute of war because of its lack of all value, and in the developed world since WWII there has been a widespread acceptance of this abolitionist viewpoint by peoples and leaders. Major war, indeed, can be considered as obsolete in the developed world, despite its threat and actuality in developing countries. Though war cannot be un-invented and made strictly impossible, because the ability and knowledge to make war will persist, this is no different than the human "ability or knowledge to institute slavery, eunuchism, crucifixion, or human sacrifice."[29]

Radical pacifists and peace advocates differ in many respects, but generally use slavery as the pertinent paradigm for the abolition of war and organized violence and the triumph of nonviolent modes of conflict resolution in modern societies. A century-and-a-half ago, slavery was endemic in United States society. In the eighteenth century and before there were no major social and political movements that directly advocated the abolition of slavery, though there were enlightened moral elites doing so.[30]

John Mueller—a minimalist among abolitionist pacifists—contends that unlike breathing, eating, or sex, war is not something that is somehow required by the human condition, by the structure of international affairs, or by the forces of history. Accordingly, war can shrivel up and disappear, and this may come about without any notable change or improvement on any of the level-of-analysis categories.[31] More demanding abolitionist pacifists insist for a full "conversion" in consciously held and practiced values at the individual, state-society, and international systemic levels of global politics. But the major weaknesses in Mueller's minimalist version of abolitionist pacifism, as we will see below, would characterize more maximalist and holistic versions as well.[32]

Huntington's general notions of "culture" and "civilization" are in the analytical-empirical mode and descriptively and explanatorily helpful, though one rightly can call into question his use of data to stress inter-civilizational conflicts over intra-civilizational fissures.[33] He says that "civilization and culture both refer to the overall way of life of a people, and a civilization is a culture writ large," or "a civilization is the broadest cultural entity."[34] Huntington's overall "realist" and rather pessimistic theory of the clash of civilizations and the remaking of world order[35] is premised, in part, on distinctiveness theory of social psychology. Huntington contends, "people define themselves by what they are not. As increased communications, trade, and travel multiply interactions among civilizations, people increasingly accord greater relevance to their civilizational identity." And "globalization theory produces a similar conclusion: 'in an increasingly globalized world—characterized by interdependence and widespread consciousness thereof—there is an exacerbation of civilizational, societal and ethnic self-consciousness.' The global religious revival, 'the return to the sacred' is a response to people's perception of the world as a 'single place'."[36]

Huntington's overall conclusion is that under conditions of globalization (modernity's latest phase) what is likely to result is not a universal civilization centered and based on common interests and basic moral principles and ideals, but rather a clash of civilizations. The idea of a universal civilization, he says, is based on the notion that the demise of communism would result in the universal victory of liberal democracy (the single alternative fallacy). In fact, however, Huntington stresses that there are many forms of authoritarianism, nationalism, corporatism, and market communism (as in China) that are contenders to liberal democracy today. More importantly, though, "in the modern world, religion is a central, perhaps the central, force that motivates and mobilizes people. It is sheer hubris to think that because Soviet communism has collapsed, the West has won the world for all time and that Muslims, Chinese, Indians, and others are going to rush to embrace Western liberalism as the only alternative. The Cold War division of humanity is over. The more fundamental divisions of humanity in terms of ethnicity, religions, and civilizations remain and spawn new conflicts."[37] Thus, the new multipolarity is also civilizational pluralism, or multi-civilizational multipolarity.

Moreover, economic, social, and cultural globalization will not create a homogeneous, universal civilization based on peace, common feelings, secularism, a culture of human rights, market capitalism, and liberal democracy. Such increased interaction among people—trade, investment, tourism, media, and electronic communications generally—far from generating a common world culture, is likely to result in greater conflict, and "[t]he evidence simply does not support the liberal, internationalist assumption that commerce promotes peace."[38]

The best that can be done, according to Huntington, is for the West to prepare for the worst-case scenarios by military, moral, and political rearmament. A third world war is possible between the West and China and/or Islam, and the West is not ready (in 1995). Alternatively, he argues, members of all civilizations should engage in cooperative strategies: seeking to uphold the principles of noninterference in the spheres of other civilizations, strengthening the United Nations' capacity to mediate conflicts resulting from direct and indirect civilizational struggles, and seeking commonalities between and among civilizations.

Mueller's uni-causal explanation[39] is that war is becoming obsolete in the developed world simply because "many people [have] come to find it obnoxious," and that it can become unfashionable and thus obsolete everywhere, like slavery and dueling have become. What is needed is that more and more people come to view it as an undesirable, irrational (from a cost-benefit analysis), and even a ridiculous policy.[40] He goes on to stress that major war is becoming obsolete "without [the improvement] or the competence or moral capacity of political leaders" or, in another formulation, without "a notable improvement in the competence of political leaders," or without a reduction "in the world's considerable store of hate, selfishness, nationalism, and racism; without [an] increas[e] in the amount of love, justice, harmony, cooperation, good will, or inner peace in the world."[41]

In contrast, one discerns an improved competence and moral capacity among key leaders in democracies in the developed and developing worlds and in international organizations in the recent history of international affairs, particularly after the Cold War. Mandela, Havel, Walesa, Carter, Blair, Aung San Suu Ky, Clinton, Boutros-Boutros Ghali, and Annan, for example, all have demonstrated political toughness and creativity while advancing policies dedicated to democratization and human rights. Leadership by NATO, the UN, Clinton, and Blair resulted in the implementation of the peace accords in Bosnia from 1996 onwards, in prosecuting the Kosovo War of 1999 against ethnic cleansing, and in the UN enforcement-intervention in East Timor in 1999. To be sure, there have been notable inconsistencies resulting in the failure of the international community to intervene in the Rwandan genocide in 1994, and in its double standard over China's human rights violations.

Moreover, a spiritual climate of cooperation is being fostered through the United Nations, the European Union, and soft power-oriented countries such as Canada, South Africa, Norway, Sweden, and the Netherlands. The successful launching of the new International Criminal Court (ICC) through their international leadership is dramatically changing the perception of the efficacy of international human rights law. Their leadership, moreover, is strengthening effective security communities, beginning a just response to unfair aspects of globalization, and continuing to stress the indispensable value of arms control and arms reduction agreements.

In addition to missing the continuing centrality of idealistic international leadership using hard and soft power to oppose massive human rights violations and to strengthen the rule of law globally, Mueller and other abolitionist pacifists inadequately use the abolition of slavery as an analogy for the elimination of war. The analogy with slavery is thought-provoking. Individual pacifists (Erasmus, Tolstoy) and small groups of pacifists (Quakers, Mennonites) have existed throughout history. As an organized peace movement, however, activists and advocates have been significantly on the world stage only since 1815; then "peace advocates were a noisy gadfly minority by 1900 [when] they had established a sense of momentum."[42] They were rejected and derided by the majority with the traditional wisdom that war was noble and for many people a desirable way of settling international disputes. However, the holocaust of WWI "fumed peace advocates into a pronounced majority in the developed world and destroyed war romanticism,"[43] and Japan only got the lessons after WWII, which most Europeans learned from WWI. Thus, the intensity of moral revulsion at warfare continues today, and will grow stronger.

However, Mueller seems to grant that war cannot be abolished sector by sector, as slavery was; it would have to be abolished all at once, for otherwise the abolitionists would be at the mercy of those who keep aggressive war in their repertoire. And yet he comes close to saying that in fact war can be abolished sector by sector. For the widespread psychic and physical costs of war would seem to make it more costly than dueling or slavery—all things considered—making it understandable that war has started to succumb to the forces of rational calculation and moral revulsion. The developed world's aversion to warfare may transform attitudes still favorable to war in the rest of the world, but even if this does not occur, the vanishing of war elsewhere would not be negated (as slavery continued in Brazil after it had been abolished elsewhere).[44]

Clearly, radical abolitionist pacifist adherents of peace movements constitute an influential strand of international civil society that is coherent and in many ways inspirational. For many of us, the dilemma is that though we would like to believe that warfare states could be abolished as slavery was, we cannot do so in the end. For slavery is absolutely evil, whereas defensive wars against unprovoked aggression may be relatively or overwhelmingly just. Generally, abolitionist pacifists are single-issue advocates who make a morality of human dignity and human rights and duties into the sole criterion for human action. They unapologetically ignore the relative independence of law, economics, and politics in relation to moral principles. This requires the judgments of those expert or experienced and involved in these spheres of social being to work out long-term strategies in view of moral principles.

In our complex global information age, what we need is not the elimination of defensive wars, but making them more just. The elimination of defensive wars would free aggressors, genocidal fanatics, terrorists, and human rights violators to reconstruct the planet as a "failed global system." However, we ought to strive to make defensive wars the least frequent possible and only the very last resort after all nonviolent forms of conflict resolution have been tried to counter aggression abroad or massive human rights violations at home. We ought to try to make defensive wars less destructive, more focused and surgical, more electronic and robotic, and keep on searching for nonlethal uses of defensive force at the micro and macro levels. Most importantly, we ought to strive to make defensive wars more just by greater adherence to the proportionality principle, the protection of innocent noncombatants, and the accumulated civilizing matrix of the laws of war as represented most clearly in the Geneva Convention.

The above position would most likely be dismissed out of hand by pacifists whose strong moralistic position closes off any possibility of engaging in any type of warfare—even the kind that targets defectors of international law. However, as King reminds us, "[m]oralism manifests itself in a one-sided and penetrating insistence on particular moral positions...which makes a rational dialogue with those of other conditions impossible."[45] For example, "the goal [of the peace research community begun at the University of Groningen, Netherlands, in 1967] is now, as it was then, to render obsolete the field of security studies based on the military defense of nation states."[46] That position does not leave much room for dialogue about the right of self-defense and transforming weapons systems to accord more with just war criteria. In the post 9-11 world, more than ever, military personnel and civilians, as well as leaders need to engage in this dialogue.

In fact, whether or not its specific terminology is adopted, just war theory has always played and continues to play a constitutive, major part in official and unofficial arguments about war. Michael Walzer, one of the foremost theorists of just war and terrorism, contends "no political leader can send soldiers into battle, asking them to risk their lives and to kill other people, without assuring them that their cause is just—and that of their enemies unjust."[47] He admits that the revival of just war theory and its increasing use in public discussions and by political and military leaders is a dangerous moment: "Think of the perverse if exhilarating effects upon religion whenever the language of holiness is taken over by politicians. Of course, politics and war are never holy—not, at least, as I understand holiness—while they are sometimes, or to some degree, just. But only sometimes and to some degree, and when more blanket justifications are claimed, the theory is rendered suspect."[48] Walzer helpfully concludes with an overall methodological orientation: it is important that we not give up just war theory simply because it can be misused and exploited by lying leaders, for in "the complex structure of their hypocrisy" we discover "the tribute that vice pays to virtue. ...The point of the theory is to help us make distinctions, to prepare us for political decision-making or for the more ordinary work of criticizing or supporting this or that war or wartime decision."[49]

Huntington's clash of civilizations theory may turn out to have some fundamental predictive power as a macro-theory about possible severe present and future clashes between Islam and the West, or Confucian, nationalistic China and the West, or Islam and Hindu India, or India and China.[50] Huntington's theory stands or falls by its subtheory of identity formation: identity-formation occurs dialectically in opposition to another who is not who and what we are. One's several identities must be arranged hierarchically according to cultural comprehensiveness, with a plurality of civilizations as the most comprehensive level of identities available to humans ("we" are New Yorkers, Americans, Westerners; "we" are Shanghaians, Chinese).[51] Mass publics, it is true, for the most part, still follow this pattern,[52] but in our turbulent era, publics are differentiating and elites proliferating, as we shall see below.[53]

Huntington unpersuasively dismisses the significance of clashes within civilizations—because of nationalism, for example—to stress inter-civilizational clashes at the fault lines where they meet. He is very likely wrong in underestimating the power of secularism (the separation of religion, science, and politics by way of the principles of religious, associational, press, and academic freedom) in countries such as India, and in developing countries as a whole.[54] In addition, he unpersuasively de-emphasizes the subtleties of elite economic and political interactions between civilizations, such as the "Davos economic forum culture." For example, he says that the Davos phenomenon does not represent a new universal civilization, even though they use English as their working language, for they lack a common religion and are not representative of the mass publics they come from.[55] However, though the Davos culture is not a new universal civilization transcending the established ones, it is part of a growing global, thin network of elites and selective publics that is diverse and in turbulence. It includes not only executives of multinational corporations, but also intergovernmental representatives from the city to the national and international levels.

Members of movements and nongovernmental organizations in international civil society are using the Internet and air travel to organize virtual and physical communities.

Indeed, professors, teachers, students, scholars in research institutes, writers, religious leaders, human rights activists, peace researchers and activists, lawyers, judges, media specialist of all types, entertainment celebrities, athletes, demographers, computer programmers, commercial pilots, members of United Nations associations[56] are learning to communicate with each other electronically. They are committed, in different value mixes, to science and technology, the rule of law, reciprocity, secularism in public affairs, religious freedom in private matters, minimal economic justice, and democracy (however understood).[57] Most significantly, these internationalizing elites and publics are not as manipulable by nationalist, religious, cultural, and civilizational extremists as traditional mass Internet-illiterate publics were and are.[58]

Members of this thin but proliferating multidimensional network do experience multiple identities, but not as organized hierarchically according to Western, Chinese, Islamic, Hindu, etc. super-identities. Rather, they experience them in tension, if not contradiction, with one another. They are "divided selves,"[59] caught in paradoxical situations, realizing that safety and justice require them to care at the same time for several levels of governance, for narrower and wider, thinner and thicker, cultures and communities. To the extent there is a hierarchy in multiple, divided selves, it is a problematical hierarchical ordering of commitments. It is the acceptance of global order, peace, economic justice, cultural pluralism, and the universal protection of individual rights as primary,[60] based on the insight that the attainment of their individual, local, and national interests and values depends on the prior securing of global interests and values[61] through the United Nations, the International Criminal Court, and other universal international and global institutions.

The conscious experience of multiple identities, however, requires habituation in dealing with complexity, ambiguity, and a high degree of uncertainty. Reinvigorated ethnic consciousness, nationalism, and civilizational identity tied to consciousness of territoriality and civilizational difference is ready to provide a much greater sense of certainty.[62] And globalized consumerism and high technology, with its simple, universal hedonistic attractiveness, can be combined with a hierarchical civilizational identity.

The members of these elite groups and selective publics, then, do not constitute a universal civilization in either the empirical or normative senses of the term. However, they are open to a cosmopolitan perspective. Cosmopolis means "city" of the "world," and it generally functions today as an ideal tied to cosmopolitan human rights enforcement across borders, and cosmopolitan citizenship and democracy stressing environmental and globalization issues.[63] Cosmopolitan theorists and activists, following in the footsteps of Rousseau and Kant, envisage a humane global ethic and international law applied by the new International Criminal Court, and other global tribunals, that will make international law applicable to all human individuals across borders and national legal systems. All advocate some form of global governance—some desiring global federal, democracy beginning with the European Union model. Others advocate, as politically and ethically preferable, strengthening the United Nations, global civil society, and regional federations, but going no further in the direction of world government because of the fallibility of human nature that could result in global tyranny.[64]

In a constructivist perspective, one might view cosmopolis as a future "emancipatory culture" devoted to the simple formula: "Fidelity to the project of questioning ...[whose positive task is]... through persuasion and example, to appeal to the latent openness of individuals and groups, to support the struggle for authenticity, to tap the psychic energy of awe and wonder—in a word, to promote self-transcendence."[65]

Preparatory conditions are required for the elimination of various forms of individual and group bias that constitute the darker side of reflection, thinking, and communication in global interactions today. Cosmopolis would express the central cultural value of a collaborative and communicative process of open and honest conversation about what is most significant for human living.[66] Most significantly, "redefining culture has itself been a cultural activity" and is characteristic of cultural internationalism, which would also be an element of cosmopolis.[67]

In the cosmopolitan mode, we can envisage a core humane morality that is elaborated differently in different cultures and that the global ethic movement and the United Nations Millennium Declaration are affirming today. Such a global ethic is a "minimal basic consensus relating to binding values, irrevocable standards, and moral attitudes which can be affirmed by all ["open" representatives of] religions and [nondogmatic] non-believers."[68] In particular, this global ethic accepts "a culture of non-violence and respect for life." In this culture, "persons who hold political power must work within the framework of a just order and commit themselves to the most non-violent, peaceful solutions possible," but the global ethic also clearly affirms that "the international order of peace...itself has need for protection and defence against perpetrators of violence."[69]

The other elements of evolving cosmopolitanism would include a rejection of apocalyptic terrorism and all forms of wars of mass destruction, even if in retaliation; and cross-civilizational and cross-ideological dialogue with those others who are not exclusivists or terrorists (state or nonstate actors). Lastly, it includes a basic commitment to decent politics that transcends moral systems and cultures, as a politics that is "intelligent, responsible, morally nuanced."[70] To be intelligent and responsible, minimally, means to use intelligent foresight to avert future harm, to avoid evil and prevent things from becoming worse than they are. To be morally nuanced means to seek relative justice in the midst of crises and turbulence, and not demanding perfection in moral behavior. It also means being willing to act according to the principle of reciprocity, both as an ethical principle and as a prudential strategy to avoid escalation of conflicts into major incidents or wars and victimization of oneself at the same time.

In conclusion, then, cosmopolis rejects the notion "that there is no middle way between being wertfrei and being biased."[71] Those who enter its "frontier"[72] agree to advance reasonable grounds for their evaluations and justifications for their preferences, without the use of hard power in those dialogues, and an honest disclosure of their soft power resources. The spirit of cosmopolis is "a measured and critical recognition of values"[73] and a measured and critical set of insights into the best secular scientific, technical, and sociocultural knowledge available in one's era.[74]

This cosmopolitan ethical and political vision accepts the complexity of moral-political judgments and the pluralism of values and perspectives that will always be part of global politics. Perpetual and complete global peace that would result from the elimination of war is neither realizable nor desirable. It is not realizable in the real world of fallible and corruptible human beings, a world in which spiritual and material goods are limited and conflicts endemic—even in an era of advanced technology. Perpetual and complete peace is not desirable if it is to be attained by excluding justice, because defensive war against unprovoked aggression and human rights violations is just, if conducted in a manner that would as much as possible not negate other goods and values.

We can effectively and ethically strive to attain the ideal of an incomplete, yet relatively just peace that would prevent major world and regional wars, but coexist with forms of limited and transformed warfare in the future. I would argue that we need this cosmopolitan just war ethical perspective combined with political imagination, creativity, dialogue, and pluralism. What must be avoided are attitudes and perspectives characteristic of political holiness, one-dimensional, absolute moralism, and uncontextualized legalism. The attempt to abolish discerning politics and the just use of defensive force in global politics and replace them with nonpolitical moralism and legalism is flawed.[75] Such attitudes and behaviors—resulting from "the seductiveness of moral disgust"—would themselves facilitate the hell of total war and apocalyptic terrorism breaking through a world constituted by consciences and institutions that sought to abolish politics. Political leadership, democratic citizenship, political dialogue and compromise in the face of global conflict and turbulence all need to be relearned in the context of our evolving high-technology global system. War and advanced weapons of war cannot be abolished, but they can be partially transcended and replaced with limited and just uses of force, guided by a decent politics that is inspired by the evolving construction of a global cosmopolitan culture and world polity.

Notes

1 Stephen M. Walt, "International Relations: One World, Many Theories," *Foreign Policy*, 110 (1998): 30.

2 Simon Murden, "Cultural Conflict in International Relations," in John Baylis and Steve Smith, eds., *The Globalization of World Politics*, 2nd ed. (New York: Oxford University Press, 2001), 456.

3 Akire Iriye, *Cultural Internationalism and World Order* (Baltimore and London: The Johns Hopkins University Press), 3.

4 Bernard Lonergan, *Method in Theology* (New York: Herder and Herder, 1972), xi.

5 Samuel Huntington, *The Clash of Civilizations and the Remaking of World Order* (New York: Simon & Schuster, 1996), 41.

6 The following general definition of culture and civilization have, in fact, been put forward by UNESCO; it defines culture as "the whole complex of distinctive spiritual, material, intellectual and emotional features that characterize a society or a social group. It includes not only arts and letters, but also modes of life, the fundamental rights of the human being, value systems, traditions and beliefs," (http://www.unesco.org).

7 Murden, "Cultural Conflict in International Relations," 458.

8 Murden, "Cultural Conflict in International Relations," 458.

9 Lonergan, *Method in Theology*, xi.

10 Huntington, *The Clash of Civilizations*, 40–41.

11 Seyom Brown, *The Causes and Prevention of War* (New York: St. Martin's Press, 1994), ch. 1. However, as Brown explains, it is certainly safe to conclude from psychology and biology that most humans are quite capable of behaving violently towards other humans, especially when involved in intense conflicts over seemingly indivisible objects. The typical human being is not strongly inhibited about killing other humans—without it being strictly an instinct or need for violence; humans do not have an instinct for peace and human violence can be easily provoked (22–23).

12 See Adelman in this volume (chapter 14).

13 Francis Fukuyama, "Women and the Evolution of World Politics," *Foreign Affairs* 77, no. 5 (Sept–Oct. 1998): 27; Walter Laqueur, "Terror's New Face: The Radicalization and Escalation of Modern Terrorism," in Charles W. Kegley, Jr. and Eugene Wittkopf, eds., *The Global Agenda: Issues and Perspectives*, 6th ed. (New York: McGraw-Hill, 2001), 83.

14 Riitta Wahlstrom, "The Challenge of Peace Education: Replacing Cultures of Militarism," in Elise Boulding, ed., *New Agendas for Peace Research: Conflict and Security Reexamined* (Boulder, CO and London: Lynne Reinner, 1993), 178–79.

15 Gary Spraakman, "Values for peace," in Paris Arnopoulos, ed., *Prospects for Peace* (Montreal: Gamma Institute Press, 1986), 44–45.

16 Riita Wahlstrom, "The Challenge of Peace Education," 178–79.

17 War is defined here as a conflict that involves at least one government and at least 10,000 battle deaths per year of conflict.

18 M.V. Naidu, *War, Security, Peace* (Brandon, Manitoba: M.I.T.A. Press, 1996), 11.

19 Jurgen Habermas, The Post-national Constellation (Cambridge, MA: MIT Press, 2001), 45.

20 John Stoessinger, *Why Nations Go to War* (New York: Wadsworth, 2001), 262.

21 Michael Walzer, "Five Questions About Terrorism," *Dissent* 49, no. 1 (Winter 2002), 5.

22 Laqueur, "Terror's New Face," 82.

23 Walzer, "Five Questions About Terrorism," 5.

24 Laqueur, "Terror's New Face," 82.

25 Laqueur, "Terror's New Face," 82.

26 In the future, even if radicals become more moderate, individuals will still embrace Mephisto's credo of "Alles was entsteht, ist wert, class es zugrunde geht" (all that comes into being is worthy of destruction [Laqueur, "Terror's New Face," 87–88]).

27 Michael Walzer, "Five Questions About Terrorism,"; Noam Chomsky, *9-11* (New York: Seven Stories Press, 2001).

28 See, for example, John Mueller, who writes: "War is merely an idea. It is not ... a natural calamity, or a desperate plot contrivance dreamed up by some sadistic puppeteer on high" ("The Obsolescence of Major War," in Charles W. Kegley, Jr. and Eugene Wittkopf, eds., *The Global Agenda: Issues and Perspectives*, 6th ed. [New York: McGraw-Hill, 2001], 65).

29 Mueller, "The Obsolescence of Major War," 65. Non-slavery philosophies and theologies certainly influenced intellectual life in the West (the natural law tradition, liberalism, Christianity, Judaism), but application to real life was short-circuited by ideological bias.

30 Mueller, "The Obsolescence of Major War," 65.

31 In Mueller's war-abolitionist way of thinking, the usual frameworks for understanding organized politically-directed violence should be discarded: Waltz's human nature, nature of state and society, and the nature of the international system causality; or Levy's decision-making process, nature of the state and society, and the systemic level. Mueller argues that these frameworks should be discarded in favor of the view that "war is merely an idea, an institution, like dueling or slavery, that has been grafted onto human existence" (Mueller, "The Obsolescence of Major War," 58).

32 Mueller, "The Obsolescence of Major War," 64–65: For Mueller, the essential point is that the more people find life minimally satisfying, the more dramatically horrible they think an experience like WWII would be, whether conventional or nuclear-enhanced. After the Cold War, the vast majority of people in all developed countries are "questing after prosperity and a quiet, normal international situation. Peace facilitates more trade, interdependence, and economic growth; peace ought to be viewed as an independent, not a dependent variable. An international government or police force would not be necessary, nor in fact desirable, because of its poor economic consequences; ad hoc arrangements would suffice in this new atmosphere of horror regarding warfare and the desire for prosperity and economic and technological creativity."

33 See Hans Kung, *A Global Ethic for Global Politics and Economics* (New York: Oxford University Press, 1998): 82–83.

34 Huntington, *The Clash of Civilizations*, 43.

35 Huntington, *The Clash of Civilizations*, 68.

36 Huntington, *The Clash of Civilizations*, 66–67.

37 Huntington, *The Clash of Civilizations*, 66–67.

38 Huntington, *The Clash of Civilizations*, 310–21.

39 John Mueller, "The Obsolescence of Major War," 58. Mueller concludes that major war "is apparently becoming obsolete, at least in the developed world"; a conviction has become widespread that war would now be "intolerably costly, unwise, futile, and base," when not so long ago war was often "casually seen as beneficial, noble, and glorious, or at least as necessary or inevitable." For Mueller, both "war" and "peace" have been taken too seriously in a way; peace is simply the opposite of war, and should not be given further content, such as a condition of love, justice, harmony, cooperation, brotherhood, and good will. People still remain contentious and there still remain substantial conflicts of interest. The difference is that they no longer resort to force to resolve their conflicts.... Mueller would be a minimalist among radical abolitionists because he does not link up peace with justice (as do most peace advocates and movements within the UN system or collaborating with it), nor does he advocate a global government to prevent a recurrence of major war (58, 65–66).

40 Mueller, "The Obsolescence of Major War," 59.

41 Mueller, "The Obsolescence of Major War," 61.

42 Mueller, "The Obsolescence of Major War," 64–65.

43 Hans Kung, *A Global Ethic*, xiv.

44 Mueller, "The Obsolescence of Major War," 64–65

45 Hans Kung, *A Global Ethic*, xiv.

46 Elise Boulding, introduction to *New Agendas for Peace Research*, 2.

47 Michael Walzer, *Just and Unjust Wars*, 2nd ed. (New York: Basic Books, 1992): xi–xii.

48 Walzer, *Just and Unjust Wars*, xi–xii.

49 Walzer, *Just and Unjust Wars*, xii.

50 I would argue that we ought to set aside as analytically unhelpful Huntington's more precise definition of "civilization": "A civilization is thus the highest cultural grouping of people and the broadest level of cultural identity people have short of that which distinguishes humans from other species" (*Clash of Civilizations*, 43). As Huntington admits later, this formulation of the concept of civilization by definition disallows the notion of a universal civilization. Indeed, Huntington has to "relax that definition to allow the possibility of peoples throughout the world identifying with a distinct global culture which supplements or supplants civilizations in the Western, Islamic, or Sinic sense" (57). Huntington relaxes that definition so that he can argue that there is no empirical entity called a universal or global civilization, for "the central elements of any culture or civilization are language and religion. If a universal civilization is emerging, there should be tendencies toward the emergence of a universal language and religion" (52–66). He concludes that this is not the case.

51 Huntington, *Clash of Civilizations*, 32–33, 43.

52 William Bloom, *Personal Identity, National Identity and International Relations* (Cambridge, England: Cambridge University Press, 1990), 128–63.

53 James Rosenau, *Turbulence in World Politics* (Princeton, NJ: Princeton University Press, 1990).

54 See Stephen M. Walt, "Building Up a New Bogeyman: Review of Huntington's *The Clash of Civilizations and the Remaking of World Order*," *Foreign Affairs* 76, no. 3 (1998): 132–39; Fouad Ajami, "The Summoning," *Foreign Affairs* 72, no. 4 (September/October 1993): 2–9.

55 Huntington, *Clash of Civilizations*, 57–58.

56 See Benjamin Barber, *A Place for Us: How to Make Society Civil and Democracy Strong* (New York: Hill and Wang, 1998).

57 Rosenau, *Turbulence*, ch. 12 and 13.

58 Rosenau, *Turbulence*, 316–19; 364–387.

59 Michael Walzer, *Thick And Thin: Moral Argument at Home and Abroad* (Notre Dame, Indiana: University of Notre Dame Press, 1994): 85–104.

60 See Michael Walzer, "Governing the Globe: What is the Best We Can Do?" *Dissent* 47, no. 4 (Fall 2000): 44.

61 Seyom Brown, "World Interests and the Changing Dimension of Security," in Michael T. Klare and Yogesh Chandrani, eds., *World Security* (New York: St. Martin's Press, 1998), 16.

62 Benjamin Barber, *Jihad vs. McWorld* (New York: Ballantine Books, 1996).

63 See Thomas McPartland, "Lonergan and Cosmopolis," The Lonergan Center, Santa Clara, University of California, 12th Eleanor Giuffre Lonergan Conference (March 1994), 1; Jack Donnelly, *International Human Rights* (Boulder, CO: Westview, 1998), 28–29; Richard Falk, Human Rights Horizons (New York and London: Routledge, 2000), 149; David Held, *Democracy and the Global Order: From the Modern State to Cosmopolitan Governance* (Stanford CA: Stanford University Press, 1995), 231–35.

64 Michael Walzer, "Governing the Globe," 52.

65 McPartland, "Lonergan and Cosmopolis," 6. However, McPartland goes on to say, "cosmopolis must always recognize limitation, always address the meaningful concreteness of the historical situation, the particular configuration of particular social reality, the affectivity of incarnate consciousness, always speak to the heart as well as to the mind. Thus cosmopolis in its positive task is not restricted ...to philosophy narrowly conceived and science—but embraces necessarily art, the media, and historiography. The blocking of the possibility of independent inquiry and open communication in scholarly and popular modes lays down the seeds of various forms of totalitarianism and cycles of decline."

66 McPartland, "Lonergan and Cosmopolis," 7.

67 Iriye, *Cultural Internationalism*, 4.

68 Hans Kung, *A Global Ethic*, 111. Or we can think of cosmopolis as resulting from "thick" moralities (the major cultures and civilizations) discovering commonalities in specific purposes—a "thin expression" through processes of reiteration—of what justice, truth, and freedom mean? See also Michael Walzer: "We march vicariously with people in trouble [for "truth" and "justice"] wherever they are; and we have our own parade" (*Thick and Thin*, 8).

69 Hans Kung and Karl-Josef Kuschel, *A Global Ethic: The Declaration of the Parliament of the World's Religions* (New York: Continuum, 1994), 16.

70 Michael Walzer, "Can There Be a Decent Left?" *Dissent* 49, no. 2 (Spring 2002): 19.

71 Maurice Cranston, *The Mask of Politics* (London: Allen Lane, 1976), 24.

72 See James Rosenau, Along the Domestic-Foreign Frontier (Cambridge, England: Cambridge University Press, 1997) on past-transcending trends in our turbulent bifurcated world with its multicentric and state-centric subsystems. See also Richard B. Day, Ronald Beiner and Joseph Masciulli, eds., *Democratic Theory and Technological Society* (Armonk, NY: M.E. Sharpe, 1988).

73 Cranston, *The Mask of Politics*, 24.

74 See John Ruggie, *Constructing the World Polity* (London: Routledge, 1998), Introduction and chapter 3.

75 Michael Ignatieff, *The Warrior's Honor* (New York: Henry Holt and Company, 1998), 72–108.

Conclusion

W. Andy Knight

PEACEBUILDING THEORY AND PRAXIS

THE PRACTICE OF PEACEBUILDING has been running ahead of peacebuilding theory. As the world watches the extensive peacebuilding efforts underway in Afghanistan, Iraq and Sierra Leone, among others, it is evident that peacebuilding is an enormously complicated task. This volume is a critical reflection on peacebuilding praxis with a view to understanding the complexities and intricacies of this relatively new phenomenon and to melding the practice with the theory. It is hoped that the individual contributions, along with this concluding reflection, will at the very least provide readers with a better knowledge and a more critical appreciation of what has become widely known as peacebuilding.

As the title of the book suggests, contributors to this volume are interested in drawing out from the accumulating data and experience of peacebuilding operations those elements and recommendations that can assist policy makers in advancing sustainable peace in war-ravaged states. However, the book is also designed with academics in mind. As such, care and attention was given to conceptual and theoretical aspects of peacebuilding. This final contribution summarizes some of the main findings of the study in an attempt to bridge the gap between theory and practice, between concept and reality. It also offers a critical reflection on peacebuilding while identifying some of the more interesting proposals for enhancing the effectiveness of peacebuilding.

What can be gleaned from the individual contributions about how peacebuilding and sustainable peace are conceived? Why has peacebuilding risen in prominence internationally since the end of the Cold War, and why has it become such an urgent matter for the global community? Where is sustainable peace most needed? Who is expected to provide it? When is it needed and how should such a peace be built? How do we know when peacebuilding is successful/unsuccessful? What lessons can be learned from specific attempts at peacebuilding? These are some of the main questions addressed in this conclusion.

The concept of peacebuilding represents a noticeable advance over concepts such as "peacekeeping" and "conflict management" in the sense that it embodies more than simply band-aid and reactive solutions to dealing with violent conflicts. Indeed, it embraces immediate, short, and longer-term policy approaches to laying the foundation upon which peace can thrive. There is a clear preference amongst the contributors to this volume for peacebuilding to address underlying and structural causes of conflict, rather than simply to focus on relief efforts. This raises the issue of the definition of peacebuilding and its link to the notion of sustainable peace.

As Bush noted, any critical discussion of peacebuilding must necessarily begin with a revisiting of the vocabulary we use to describe the phenomenon. Language is the basis for action, therefore it is important to begin with an understanding of how the concept of peacebuilding developed and what it has come to mean. With its widespread use today, there is no longer any reason for conceptual fuzziness with regards to peacebuilding. But we need to determine whether and how the concept may be evolving if we are to make a contribution to the way it will be used in the future. We need also to examine critically the ways in which the concept has developed since Boutros-Ghali first brought it into the mainstream of international relations thinking.

Tom Keating and I noted in the introduction that the genealogy of peacebuilding can be traced to fairly radical origins found in the works of such peace researchers as Galtung and the Bouldings. Their "critical" usage of the term indicates that peacebuilding ought to address underlying structural causes of conflict through bottom up processes and decentered socioeconomic and political structures. As defined by Adelman and Masciulli, peacebuilding is no less than a radical transformation of society away from cultures of violence to embedded cultures of peace. There is another version of peacebuilding that promotes, in essence, reactive or band-aid solutions to existing conflicts. This second, "problem-solving" concept of peacebuilding continues to resonate in the contemporary period, despite the best efforts to promote the former concept.

Many of the authors in this volume support a third concept of peacebuilding that combines both problem-solving and critical approaches. This third concept recognizes and accepts the view that something must be done to address the immediacy of the breakdown in societal structures. It also recognizes the limitations imposed by political and economic exigencies. It also realizes that it would be futile to pour resources and personnel into every problem associated with complex humanitarian emergencies and violent outbreaks if the peace that results cannot be sustained. "Sustainable peacebuilding" captures the spirit and essence of the contributions to this book.

Conflict prevention through development and social transformation is central to the concept of sustainable peace. Beer, drawing on Brinkerhoff, defines sustainability as a program's ability to produce outputs and benefits that are valued highly enough to command continued resources and attention and thus ensure continued outputs. Implied in this definition is the notion that both donors and recipients must accept the value of the activity and commit to maintaining it for an extended period of time. When applied to peacebuilding, sustainability refers to the long-term commitment to peace and to doing all that is necessary to build and maintain the architecture of peace. Thus, conflict prevention and peace maintenance become essential building blocks of the peacebuilding concept and operation. However, the focus should be on those long-term development projects that build indigenous capacity and peaceable interactions in states generally prone to violent conflict. The whole idea is to nip conflicts in the bud before they erupt into violent ones, rather than wait until the violence erupts before taking measures to quell it.

For us, then, peacebuilding must have the long-term objective of bringing about a fundamental transformation of conflict-ridden societies. But that long-term objective must be concretized by developing specific medium and short-term programs, policies and practices that can be employed to resolve civil conflicts in various regions of the world and support norms of conflict prevention and cultures of peace. This ensures that peacebuilding becomes more than just a lofty idea; it will be grounded in concrete action and policy and provided with a road map to get from violent conflict to sustainable peace.

The above definition of sustainability also allows us to develop measurement criteria for successful peacebuilding operations (*i.e.* those peacebuilding operations that are sturdy enough to maintain the long term objective of continually addressing root causes of conflict and of ensuring that violent conflict is not resorted to as a mechanism for conflict resolution).

Finally, there is another way of conceiving peacebuilding—as a twofold process: (1) *deconstructing* the structures of violence, and (2) *constructing*, or *reconstructing* the structures of peace.[1] These, according to Bush, are interrelated but separate activities that have to be undertaken simultaneously. In his view, the instruments required for peace construction (*e.g.* confidence building between formerly warring factions) are different from those required for deconstruction (such as disarmament, demobilization, and the demilitarization of society, economy and polity). Peacebuilding then utilizes tools of conflict prevention and conflict resolution to facilitate change and transformation in a target society. These tools are used to strip away the conflict nurturing and dysfunctional institutions, norms and practices and to help build or rebuild those fundamental institutions of a society that support tolerance, stability, socioeconomic development and enduring peace. The process involved is quite likely to be a lengthy one, as Bush, Daudelin, and Das remind us. They also point out that few states or agencies are willing to make such commitments unilaterally. Yet it is clear that bungee cord intervention into theaters of conflict simply cannot count as peacebuilding. Therefore any notion of predetermining exit-timing strategies for peacbuilding operations ought to be viewed with a fair amount of skepticism.

Peacebuilding's ultimate goal is to prevent and/or resolve violent conflicts, create or restore peaceful conditions and lay the foundation and building blocks for an enduring peace through the strengthening of institutions of governance. This involves both social engineering and the transformation of a society from a culture of violence to a culture of peace. However, peacebuilding also has operational goals, *i.e.* specific programmatic steps in constructing the edifice leading to the ultimate goal of sustained peace. Examples of these subgoals include: restoring order and stability; disarming warring factions; separating armed groups; decommissioning weapons; de-mining; repatriating refugees and displaced persons; reintegrating soldiers into civilian life (including child soldiers and bush brides); creating and rebuilding administrative, court and judicial systems, police forces, and custom agencies; reforming the security sector; advancing the protection of human rights; providing technical assistance and economic development; promoting formal and informal participation in the political decision-making process; reforming and strengthening institutions of governance; and monitoring elections.

The peace dividend that was supposed to result from the thawing of the Cold War never really materialized. For one thing, conflicts that had been more or less frozen during the East-West tension seem to percolate out of the thawing conditions of the immediate post–Cold War period and neither the US nor the dismantling Soviet Union seemed interested, initially, about doing much about them. Beer cites estimates that indicate that there were approximately 93 conflicts around the world in the first half of the last decade of the twentieth century, 5.5 million people were killed and 75 percent of those were civilians. Almost all of these conflicts were intrastate ones, thus explaining the disproportionate number of civilian casualties. The majority of these conflicts were found in the poorest corners of the globe, particularly on the African continent but also in parts of the Middle East, Central Asia, Eastern Europe, and parts of the former Soviet Union.

The debacle in Somalia, the Rwandan genocide, the at times indiscriminate but politically motivated slaughter in the Congo, Sierra Leone, Liberia, Mozambique, and the continued violence in other places such as the Middle East, Asia, Chechnya, and Latin America all indicated a persistent adherence to a culture of violence. Many of these human tragedies and gross human rights violations occurred in so-called "failed states" where the absence of effective governance meant that civilians were particularly vulnerable to wanton violence. Millions of innocent people became refugees and displaced persons and billions of dollars worth of destruction to national infrastructures and to governmental and societal institutions have been caused by internecine violence during the post–Cold War period. The problem of failed states reached the highest levels of national security planning after the terrorist attacks on the United States in September 2001. US officials identified failed states as a major source of terrorist activity and identified these states as the principal targets of concern in their National Security statement in September 2002.

This new dimension of insecurity was added to the long-standing and continuing problems of unchecked population growth, crushing debt burdens, barriers to trade, drugs trafficking, the trafficking in women and children, and a growing disparity between rich and poor. Poverty, disease, famine, natural and manmade disasters, oppression and despair compounded the problems.

It became evident that the sources of many of these conflicts were so pervasive and deep that to address them successfully, the international community would have to harness its resources to tackle the underlying factors that perpetuated these conflicts. The UN and others applied familiar tools of diplomacy, ceasefire monitoring, observer missions, peacekeeping and peacemaking with varying degrees of success. What became clear is that the "new" conflicts required new tools to deal with them. Thus began a period of experimentation with the modification of existing tools, such as second-generation peace operations, peace enforcement, and preventative deployment. Boutros Ghali introduced the concept of peacebuilding to complement peacemaking, peacekeeping and preventive diplomacy. In his own words, he felt that if the UN was to be successful in dealing with these new conflicts it would have to develop "comprehensive efforts to identify and support structures which will tend to consolidate peace and advance a sense of confidence and well-being among people."[2]

As Abiew and Keating note, the prevalence of civil conflict generated "too many opportunities for postconflict peacebuilding operations." In addition, growing interest and concern for human/individual security prompted a flurry of peacebuilding activity around the globe, especially on the African continent where there seemed to be a demonstrated link between poverty, underdevelopment and conflict. Concerns about terrorist threats emerging from these "states of insecurity" have only increased the interest and involvement of certain major powers in peacebuilding.

Sustaining peace, however, has not been easy. As the concept and practice of peacebuilding evolved, the challenges became more daunting. Clearly, the chapters in this volume describe the difficulty and complexity of remodeling dysfunctional structures in countries torn apart by war. The chapters also show that peacebuilding is a multidimensional exercise involving multiple tasks, many tools, and a variety of actors that address both the proximate and structural causes of conflict.

In the introduction, the analogy of an orchestra was used to describe peacebuilding. A full orchestra is comprised of several diverse instruments and musicians. Each individual instrument has a particular role to play in the musical production. These instruments, however, must be finely tuned so that there is coherence to the music being produced. At the same time, the musicians must have a good knowledge of the instruments they are using, and it also helps if they have at least an appreciation of the instruments that are not their own. Naturally, it helps as well if all the players are using the same sheet of music, with clearly delineated notations that reveal to each musician not only what part s/he ought to be playing but also at what time s/he would need to enter or leave particular passages of the musical piece. While a sophisticated orchestra with excellent players can get by without a conductor, there is a much better chance that cacophony will be avoided if a maestro is leading, using the baton to coordinate the players, keep the tempo, manage the entrances and exits, build towards a crescendo, lengthen a specific note, or bring the entire piece of music to satisfying resolution. As with the orchestra, peacebuilders must learn to work in concert in order to produce anything resembling a coherent approach to postconflict reconciliation, conflict prevention and sustainable peace.

The authors in this volume note that peacebuilding tasks vary from the mundane to the sophisticated, the simple to the complex, and the immediate/medium to the long term. The objectives may be disarming warring parties, decommissioning and destroying weapons, de-mining or repatriating refugees. But some of the objectives may be of a different order, for example, restoring law and order, creating or rebuilding justice systems, providing long term technical assistance and sustained economic development, advancing human rights, strengthening civil society institutions, or revamping governance structures. In the long run, for peace to be sustained, the underlying objective of peacebuilding efforts ought to be transforming a society from a culture of violence to one of conflict prevention and peace.

Central to peacebuilding is the notion of dispute resolution. No peace can be initiated or sustained unless mechanisms are in place for resolving potential, incipient and actual conflicts. Thus, it is incumbent upon those who devise peacebuilding operations to bear in mind that mechanisms of negotiation, early warning, enquiry, mediation, conciliation, arbitration, judicial settlement and resorting to regional agencies or arrangements, among others, ought to be considered and used in building the foundation for peace. These particular instruments are designed primarily to forestall violent conflicts. In other words, they are considered tools of conflict prevention and resolution. However, we are reminded by several of the authors in this volume that there are times when the use of coercive tools might be required to abate threats designed to unravel a peace. In such cases, peacebuilders may have to consider the utilization of measured armed force to ensure that a stable climate is created for nourishing peace initiatives, or for beating back the destructive forces that are determined to dismantle the architecture of peace.

Building sustainable peace may require, in some cases, the use of such measures as the complete or partial interruption of economic relations and of rail, sea, air, postal, telegraphic, radio, and other means of communication, and the severance of diplomatic relations. It may also demand the employment of economic sanctions or arms embargoes, military demonstrations, blockades, or as a last resort, coercive military interventions. As Masciulli starkly put it, even though our long-term objective is the creation of a culture of peace, "defensive war against unprovoked aggression and human rights violations is just." Ankersen furthers the argument when he says: “no one can distribute food or construct democratic institutions under a hail of gunfire. The conditions for success must be achieved first. For this task, there is no one else. Military forces alone have the expertise and the hardware to create and maintain order. It so happens that they also have a great deal to offer in the creation of peace as well.”

Labonte makes it clear that for the foreseeable future, the development of robust norms of peace and conflict prevention will no doubt have to include at least the possibility of the use of force, in some instances. As she puts it: “Even in the most forward-looking operational frameworks of conflict prevention and peacebuilding, the option to employ preventive action in the form of military or armed humanitarian intervention will inevitably be featured.” One of necessary conditions for any successful peacebuilding operation is the restoration and maintenance of political and social stability. This requires, at minimum, the termination of military hostilities (as argued by Adebajo, Adelman, Ankersen, Das, Daudelin, and Gebremariam) and the control of weapons (as pointed out by Lloyd).

The linkage of political and social stability to the cessation of military hostilities thus leaves open the prospect of the use of armed force as an optional tool in pursuit of that goal. To think otherwise would be tantamount to putting on conceptual blinkers. In many postconflict theaters there are “low intensity” civil conflicts that can spiral out of control unless a credible deterrent force is present. One only has to look at the conditions that exist in such war-torn countries Afghanistan, Angola, Burundi, Congo (Zaire), Haiti, Lebanon, Liberia, Rwanda, Sierra Leone, Somalia, and Sudan to recognize the potential need for a military insurance policy that can positively influence local conflict dynamics so as to enhance the effectiveness of humanitarian operations and create the necessary conditions for sustainable peace. Adebajo, as well as Das, noted the brief British military intervention in Sierra Leone between May-June 2000 that not only helped to stabilize the situation in Freetown and its environs but also helped to save the UN's effort to set up the conditions for peacebuilding in that country.

However, as Ankersen points out, the military tool can also be modified to deal with some of the non-coercive elements in peacebuilding operations. For instance in the vacuum of civil authority in Kosovo, soldiers assumed functions of the police. They responded to occurrences of domestic violence, sexual abuse, theft, and impaired driving—functions that would normally be undertaken by civilian police forces. In the temporary absence of a judicial system in Kosovo, the NATO military commanders filled in by running a detention facility and acting as jailor, judge and jury. Other activities undertaken by military forces in missions such as Kosovo have included offering humanitarian relief; providing emergency shelter delivery, critical medical care, and food; helping local doctors establish practices in areas of mixed ethnicity; rebuilding bridges, road, houses, schools, churches and mosques; and guarding mixed ethnic schools so that children in fragile peace situations could still get an education. These were not military tasks but were accomplished by the military instrument.

Having said this, we need to bear in mind the words of caution that echo through Bush's contribution. He admits that there are often clear military security tasks in "postconflict" settings that are best undertaken by military actors. However, he warns of the danger of casting "military activities as the cardinal referent from which all other activities take their bearing." In other words, Bush is weary of attempts at militarizing peacebuilding. He sees peacebuilding as essentially a "developmental initiative with a crucial security component," not the other way around. It therefore should not be driven by "military-security logic." The problem is that military-led approaches are generally top-down and tend to minimize local inputs. They are also task-oriented, short-term and dependent on a top-down command structure and elaborate institutional support. In opposition to arguments made by Ankersen and Labonte, Bush asserts that the military does not possess the necessary skill required to play effective nonmilitary roles. Further, he argues that the "privatization of security" at the international level helps to erode the legitimacy of the state as an institution and the idea of the state as the sole actor with legitimate recourse to the use of armed force.

This trend towards gun-based authority structures in peacebuilding situations may even result in a remilitarization of a subdued conflict environment and would most likely contribute more to a culture of violence than one of peace. Militarization as well as the development of a war economy is basically an unintended negative consequence of some peacebuilding. As we write, developments in both Afghanistan and Iraq reinforce this position as militarization impedes the provision of other necessary services. The arguments against the militarization of peacebuilding are strengthened by Nakaya's analysis of the situation in Somalia prior to the departure of UNOSOM II, although it is not restricted to that operation. As she puts it, the injection of foreign troops into that country "had a destabilizing effect on the local economy," exacerbating the "economy of war." It also created a false economy that had devastating effects on women and children once the foreign military forces left that country. This is a general observation that is applicable to many peacekeeping and peacebuilding environments (most notably those in Cambodia and East Timor).

What is evident in this volume is that the players involved in peacebuilding are as varied as the tasks and tools of this concept and practice. These players range from actors in military and police establishments, civil society and nongovernmental organizations, governments, international and regional organizations, *ad hoc* criminal tribunals (and potentially the International Criminal Court), departments of justice, intelligence agencies, criminal investigative agencies, drug enforcement agencies, to those on truth and reconciliation commissions.

Several authors have pointed out the important role that humanitarian bodies, medical groups (like Médicins sans Frontières), aid agencies (like USAID, CIDA), engineers, and international and regional economic and financial institutions have been playing recently in peacebuilding efforts. Certainly we cannot overlook the important peacebuilding roles of the United Nations and its specialized agencies (especially the Security Council, the WFP, UNICEF, UNIFEM, UNDP, UNHCR, UNCIVPOL, and UN special representatives), the Bretton Woods institutions (the World Bank, the IMF, the IDA), transregional organizations (*e.g.* NATO, the Group of 7/8, the Commonwealth and La Francophonie), regional organizations (like the OSCE, the EU, the OAU, ASEAN, the OAS), subregional bodies (like ECOWAS and IGADD) and regional development banks (*e.g.* the Asian Development Bank's role in East Timor). However, as we learn from Adebajo, Gebremariam, and Narine, regional bodies often lack the resources and capacity and/or the political will to perform many of the tasks needed for peacebuilding.

States are also heavily involved in peacebuilding activities, either individually or collectively. Major powers like the US, the UK and Russia can provide substantial material support for peacebuilding (note the African Crisis Response Initiative by the US in Africa or Washington's International Military Education and Training Programmed in Africa). Daudelin points out that given the scope and costs of some peacebuilding operations, as well as the logistical capacity they may require, only the rich and materially-endowed "West" can "arm, organize, and finance them." However, there is a tendency at times for these powers to be self-interested, media driven, ethnocentric, and heavy handed in their approaches to peacebuilding. For these reasons, these powers have been accused by some of being inconsistent, biased and unfair in the operationalization of their peacebuilding policies.

Middle range powers like Australia, Canada, Japan, the Netherlands, Switzerland, Sweden, and Norway are also able to provide material support for peacebuilding efforts but are generally better known for their active involvement in development projects that can nurture peace, even though, as Beer reminds us, they can also be driven by self-interest and bias. Regional powers such as Nigeria and South Africa are also becoming involved in peacebuilding activity. However, the quest for regional hegemony, as Daudelin charges, may unfortunately be one of the powerful motivating factors for this involvement. Former colonial powers such as the UK, France, and Belgium have played significant roles in recent peacebuilding operations. But their motivations for doing so are questioned primarily because of their exploitative colonial past.

International NGOs are generally at the center of most peacebuilding operations. Part of the reason for this, particularly over the past decade or so, has been the tendency of states and state-based international organizations to contract out certain elements of peacebuilding operations to NGOs. Abiew and Keating as well as Labonte write of the peacebuilding tasks performed by NGO in postconflict reconstruction. These tasks are usually seen in the context of ongoing development work by these bodies. It is the nature of their on-going development activities that generally place NGOs in situations where multilateral peacebuilding operations are active. In other words, peacebuilding is generally viewed by NGOs as a natural extension of their development work. NGOs are generally on the ground in states coming out of conflict long before IGOs and external state actors.

It has been suggested that NGOs also possess certain comparative advantages in terms of their capacities *vis-à-vis* states and IGOs. These advantages included their ability to reach the poorest and most needy in war-ravaged states and to get to remote areas; a capacity to promote local participation and to implement programs in direct collaboration with target beneficiary groups; and a capacity to operate on low costs; a capacity to strengthen local institutions and to facilitate the empowerment of marginal groups. Added to these qualities, is the fact that NGOs are generally more flexible and pragmatic than most governments and are not encumbered by such weights as "sovereignty" and "nonintervention" principles that IGOs at both international and regional level are constitutionally bound by. These sovereignty-free actors of civil society provide a people-to-people approach and can be less partial than state and state-based actors in their delivery of services. Their comparative lack of bureaucracy and the commitment and dedication of the usually young staff of these NGOs are other obvious reasons why these players are highly valued in peacebuilding operations.

Another reason why NGOs have been so heavily involved in peacebuilding operations is that in difficult internal situations, target governments are often unwilling to accept intergovernmental involvement, be it by the United Nations, regional organizations, or other states, because of the legitimacy such action may bestow on insurgents or opposition groups. But as Abiew and Keating note, parties to the conflict sometimes use NGOs for their own political purposes more effectively than other institutions and foreign governments and thus prefer their involvement because of their perceived manipulability.

Finally, the main reason why NGOs have undertaken peacebuilding activity has to do with the tendency of governments and IGOs to subcontract elements of peacebuilding to these nonstate actors. Decreases in government's ODA have been mirrored by increases in government allotments to NGOs for peacebuilding work in developing countries. Many NGO's have gone well beyond providing relief during complex humanitarian emergencies to being increasingly asked to perform more politicized roles such as monitoring human rights violations, assisting with conflict resolution, and monitoring elections. Some have even taken over state-type functions in areas like health, education, water and sanitation systems, and agricultural extension services. In many ways, NGO activity can thus be seen as filling a vacuum left by the state—both the target state and the donor state. NGO representatives have often made references to their operations "as comprising a continuum of relief efforts, rehabilitation, reconstruction, and sustainable development"—these are component parts of peacebuilding.

Nakaya notes the role that the Catholic Church played in support of peacebuilding effort in Mozambique. Adebajo notes the work of the US-based Carter Center in Liberia in observing and monitoring elections as well as the support provided by the US-based National Democratic Institute and the UK-based Westminster Foundation for Democracy to strengthening political parties in Sierra Leone.

Local groups are also partners in the peacebuilding process. Some of these local groups are former enemies who have benefited from the creation of a new climate due in large part to peacebuilding activity. One such example is the relationship that has developed between FRELIMO and RENAMO in Mozambique. Women's groups have played interesting and important peacebuilding roles in Somalia and Mozambique. Nakaya reports how women's groups in Somalia contributed to peacebuilding by initiating inter-clan dialogue for peace. They were able to do so because through marriage many of them developed cross-clan connections; as daughters they belong to the clan of their fathers, but as wives they also belong to the clan of their husbands. Nakaya concluded that by linking gender-specific roles in clan-based systems, those women were in a position to influence the structural base of power relations and use it to facilitate peacebuilding activity.[3]

Adebajo also points to important work done by local civil society groups like Liberia's Interfaith Mediation Committee and Sierra Leone's Inter-Religious Council to try to break the warlords' grip on the societies in these respective countries, even though their efforts were not always successful. Chopra and Hohe describe the importance of national, district, subdistrict and village councils to the peacebuilding process in East Timor.

Individuals are also important partners in the peacebuilding process. Gebremariam notes the role that eminent persons, such as Heads of State or Special Representatives of the UN Secretary-General can play in peacebuilding. Indeed, the tributes paid to Sergio de Mello, the UN Secretary General's Special Representative for Iraq, after his untimely death in the bomb blast in Baghdad in August 2003 revealed the important role that individuals like him play in peacebuilding.

There is also a role for local clan leaders who may have a tremendous amount of influence in their societies. Gebremariam acknowledges the importance of the wisdom of the Council of Elders in Somali, known as the Guurti, which represented various clans in national peace conferences and other peacebuilding-type initiatives. Chopra and Hohe also recognized the significant contributions that village chiefs can and should make to the peacebuilding process. Attempts by outside agencies to skirt these important societal actors are foolhardy. Based on the analysis of Chopra and Hohe, it is evident that outside agencies' authority with respect to local perceptions could be greatly enhanced if there is a clear attempt to involve village chiefs and other significant local leaders at every stage of the peacebuilding effort.

Das also reminds us of the importance of individuals such as doctors, police officers, nurses, teachers, engineers, lawyers, waterworks builders, judges, civil administrators and garbage collectors to rebuilding a normal life in any postconflict society. This is something we, living in more peaceful and stable environments, take for granted. However, these individuals are important cogs in the wheel of peacebuilding activity.

The need for partnership amongst all of these players is one of the important lessons of multidimensional peacebuilding. The complexity of this activity requires the coordination and collaboration of many players. Implicit in the concept of peacebuilding, therefore, is the idea that partnerships, including the participation of the recipient state and local civil society actors, must emerge to address these broad challenges. The dynamics of any partnership further complicate the peacebuilding process as consensus, cooperation, coordination, and competing interests, and varying human and financial resources potentially muddy common goals and the experience of the myriad actors involved. As Beer and other contributors attest, perhaps most significant in all of this is the extent to which the recipient state and local civil society is open and receptive to peacebuilding.

There are a number of important lessons to be gleaned from the analysis and evaluation of past experiences with peacebuilding. The first lesson is that peacebuilding operations must take into consideration the history and culture of the target country and its people. The first point to make is that conflicts are *sui generis* in nature. This means that there are several different possible actions that can be taken to bring them to an end and to sustain peace over a long period. One can agree with Beer when he states that peacebuilding should involve a common vision of the future. But that vision must be one that sees peacebuilding as a complex and multidimensional phenomenon. It must also be a vision that is largely defined by local actors. The complexity of the exercise ought to be acknowledged, and if the challenges are to be overcome successfully it will require a singularity of focus and a unity of action—something that has not always been present among the various actors and partners in peacebuilding operations.

Bush states that peacebuilding entails strengthening or creating those structures and processes that are democratic, fair and responsive to the needs and concerns of an entire population, from the weakest members to the most powerful. Unfortunately, many peacebuilding operations have strayed substantially from this ideal. In fact, most peacebuilding interventions by Western (or Northern) actors can be accused of being ethnocentric and "top-down" in the sense that they try to impose external values on the target society within which the peacebuilding initiative is being undertaken.

A second lesson is that peacebuilders need to assess more thoroughly the impact of their efforts. Better analysis needs to be done by external actors before embarking on a peacebuilding mission. In addition, an evaluative criterion should be devised to guide the actions of peacebuilders. Many peacebuilding initiatives from the North have done harm in the name of good. We learn from Bush that in Kosovo reconstruction would have been put on a more solid foundation if it had been built around civil society instead of humanitarian commodities and services.

The massive concentration of international aid had devastating impacts on that society, created a false economy and probably did more harm than good. He also implores the international community to avoid the "conflict-nurturing impacts" of certain so-called peacebuilding activities (and the commodification and militarization of peacebuilding). Some peacebuilders, in their attempt to be impartial, may actually strengthen the hand of groups within the target society that are most responsible for the violence. Bush provides an example in which outside peacebuilders simply reinforced the "apartheid geographies" sought and achieved by the Balkan genocidiers. Daudelin echoes the advice of Noam Chomsky who admonished external actors to "do no harm," and if they can't find a way to adhere to this elementary principle, then they should simply "do nothing." Yet, doing nothing, in the case of Rwanda, resulted in close to a million deaths. Evaluative measurement of peacebuilding activities and initiatives should be based on whether on not such programs support sustainable structures and processes that strengthen prospects for peaceful coexistence and decrease the likelihood of an outbreak of violence.

A third lesson is the importance of distinguishing among those peacebuilding activities that are short term, those that are medium term and those that are long term and recognizing that many such tasks will fall into the last category. Peacebuilders must be prepared to be present in the target country for lengthy periods of time, or until the local community can take over the functions of governance. Daudelin decried those bungee cord-type humanitarian efforts that plan their exit strategies before completing the peacebuilding tasks. But there may be some elements of peacebuilding activity that require certain peacebuilding actors to be present in the target country for a brief period of time and then hand over the remainder of the operation to other actors. The actors involved at each stage should be aware of the role they are playing and the time and resources it will take to get the job done.

For instance, the military can play an important role at the initial stages of a peacebuilding operation. As Ankersen shows, in an absolute vacuum of civil authority, the military may assume temporarily the functions of the police. It may also take on some of the governance roles until an authority (either international or local) is put in place. And, certainly, in unsafe settings, humanitarian relief groups depend on the military to escort them into areas where their assistance is most needed. But soldiers are also trained to carry out roles that are strictly speaking nonmilitary ones. In addition, as Ankersen has argued, the same capacity that is developed to fight wars can be used to build peace. Peacebuilding is not a unilinear activity. There can be some backsliding by formerly belligerent groups. It helps if there is at least some military presence to ensure that such a situation does not get out of hand and that a secure and stable environment is maintained for the other functions of peacebuilding to proceed uninterrupted. However, it must also be realized that while the military may be necessary, it is not sufficient.

Another lesson identified in the preceding contributions is that military instruments cannot provide sustainable solutions to the political, economic and social root causes of violence. The militarization of peacebuilding should be avoided. Peacebuilding is essentially involved in directing societies away from military solutions to conflict. The military can play an important role in providing security initially. They can help create the conditions of stability so that civilian peacebuilders can get on with their jobs. However, it would be much better if local conflict management mechanisms were developed rather than try to insert armed forces or mercenaries to fight their way into situations. The use of private armies in peacebuilding is a dangerous practice. It erodes the legitimacy of fledgling states that are trying to reassert themselves and control the use of force within their boundaries and there is no accountability mechanism at the international or regional levels to ensure that these private militaries follow specific codes of conduct. Additionally, such armies help legitimate gun-based authority structures that can only lead to a further embrace of the norms and cultures of violence.

There needs to be a concerted effort to improve the relationship between the military, IGOs and NGOs in the theaters of peacebuilding. Ankersen suggests that the best way of dong this is to establish joint coordination centers replete with liaison officers and advisors. These centers would be used as clearinghouses where information can be shared amongst the various partners in the peacebuilding operation.

Additionally, international NGOs have to be careful not to alter in a negative way the balance of domestic forces in the societies in which they are carrying out peacebuilding activity. While the role of NGOs has been viewed mostly positively by the authors in this volume, some concerns were raised about their lack of accountability, their inability at times to get along with the military units brought in to protect them, their tendency at times to bypass local NGOs in their delivery of aid, and about the motivations behind their involvement in peacebuilding activity. Abiew and Keating recommend that NGOs need to develop a code of conduct in an effort to make them more accountable. These authors also agree with Prendergast that any form of aid that ignores the local context is potentially destabilizing. They should implement programs that support those local people who seek alternatives to conflict and to build the necessary indigenous capacity so that the locals can address the root causes of conflict eventually on their own. Their role in peacebuilding should be supportive rather than dictatorial.

Local actors, talent, and wisdom ought to be drawn upon at every stage of the peacebuilding process. Long-term transformation in postconflict societies may be highly dependent on designing mechanisms that could allow for genuine popular participation and local input into peacebuilding decisions. Chopra and Hohe are critical of the intrusive UN transitional administration in East Timor because it failed to solicit direct participation of the local communities. These kinds of asocial peacebuilding initiatives are bound to run into difficulties. They are certainly not amenable to building sustainable peace. Indeed, participatory peacebuilding should be the next phase of international peace operations aimed at developing a culture of peace and constructing sustainable governance structures. Peacebuilding thus ought to be, whenever possible, a bottom up process. After all, those people most affected by the peacebuilding initiatives should have a say in their outcomes.

Nakaya makes it clear that one important lesson to be learned is that all international approaches to peacebuilding "need to involve gender analysis as part of structural reforms toward equality." The mainstreaming of a gender perspective in peacebuilding is absolutely essential to the future success of these efforts. The role of women in peacebuilding must be given prominence of place. Nakaya points out that the 1995 Beijing Platform of Action called for increased participation of women in conflict resolution at decision-making levels. The UN Security Council has also made a similar demand and it called on those involved in peace operations to pay particular attention to the needs of women and to their plight. UNIFEM has commissioned independent experts to assess the impact of armed conflict on women and the role of women in peacebuilding.

There is a sense that women have a specific perspective to offer on these matters that ought not to be ignored. In addition, as Nakaya ably demonstrates, the sustainability of peace may well depend on the extent to which women are on board in terms of supporting peacebuilding efforts. But to do so may require affirmative action and structural reform to the decision-making, constitutional, legal and governance mechanisms.

Regional actors must also be prepared to do more when it comes to peacebuilding in countries in their region. Adebajo noted that it took the growing indifference of external actors to African conflicts for regional actors like Nigeria and South Africa to play a greater role in peace operations, including peacebuilding, on the continent. ASEAN, a regional actor, is reluctant to become involved in peacebuilding if this requires it to undermine in any way the sovereign integrity of its members. This may have much to do with the fact that most states in that region are relatively weak states that are in the process of state-building. However, ASEAN may be helping to contribute to the development of a culture of conflict prevention amongst its member countries because its member states disavow violence in their dealing with each other. To the extent that this is so, Narine argues that ASEAN is in fact contributing to an element of peacebuilding in the South East Asia region.

Not all regional organizations can contribute in the same way to peacebuilding. Subregional bodies like ECOMOG and ECOWAS, as well as the main regional body in Africa—the OAU/AU—worked in partnership with UNOMIL in Liberia and UNAMSIL in Sierra Leone. But regional players often lack the resources needed to take on peacebuilding tasks on their own. Gebremariam acknowledges that the OAU's Mechanism for Conflict Prevention, Management and Resolution is confronted with major limitations, not the least of which are a shortage of human resource capacity and a paucity of financial commitment from OAU member states.

Adebajo provides us with five observations based on his analysis of two peacebuilding operations in the African region: Sierra Leone and Liberia. These are: (1) regional and subregional organizations must be provided with logistical and financial resources to assist them in peacebuilding efforts; (2) the role of regional hegemons, while important to the peacebuilding effort, should be considered and weighed carefully; (3) peacebuilding efforts should adopt a subregional approach especially in cases where the effects of the conflict has spilled over to several countries in the subregion; (4) regional action in peacebuilding must be supplemented by that of the UN and international NGOs; and, (5) donor conferences which provided crucial electoral and postconflict assistance in Liberia and Sierra Leone must continue to mobilize resources in support of peacebuilding in both countries.

Adebajo's policy recommendations boil down to a single point (one also made by Das) that becomes another lesson to be learned: the international community needs to dig deeper into its pockets and commit substantially greater funds and resources to peacebuilding exercises. Peacebuilding is not cheap.

Yet another lesson is to acknowledge the importance of the rather mundane aspects of peacebuilding that tend to go unnoticed and to recognize how many diverse activities can contribute to the peacebuilding process. For instance, Bush draws attention to national immunization campaigns that helped to expand the peacebuilding space in the Democratic Republic of the Congo, Sri Lanka, Cambodia, El Salvador, Lebanon, and the Philippines. He also alerted us to similar examples in Sri Lanka where a USAID-sponsored water management project generated both development and peacebuilding benefits to the community. The Gal Oya project resulted in the construction of *ad hoc* institutions of inter-communal cooperation beyond the scope of the water management project—converting zero-sum into positive sum games—even though it was not consciously developed as a peacebuilding project. It also supports Chopra and Hohe's notion of participation as being essential to successful peacebuilding operations. Any activity that helps to cement and sustain the peace ought to be considered under the rubric of peacebuilding, even if this has traditionally not been the case.

Greater attention must also be paid to the reform of justice and policing systems in countries where peacebuilding efforts are being undertaken. Beer's case study of the situation in Haiti is instructive in this regard. It does not make sense to develop one part of the justice system in a country emerging out of conflict without addressing the weaknesses in other parts of that system. As Beer observed: "The absence of parallel and overlapping development in the three sectors of justice (the police, the judiciary, and the prison system), is now recognized as a significant problem in justice development in Haiti." Worse yet, the international assistance provided to strengthen the police force in Haiti, at the expense of the other two judicial sectors, served only to boost an institution that has long been responsible for human rights abuse in that country. The lesson here is clear: all actors involved in peacebuilding must find a way to coordinate their activities so that all aspects of the justice system in the target state are being addressed simultaneously.

Finally, but not unimportantly, it is evident that peacebuilding will be most successful when it receives proper political and economic support. Critically important, given its hegemonic position, is the US government's support for peacebuilding and related activities. For example, sustainable peace cannot be obtained unless small arms and light weapons proliferation is brought under control. As Lloyd argues, prospects for an international SALW regime have improved as attention has been focused on this problem. However, the main obstacle to the further development of that regime may come from the US, which has refused to endorse the idea. The activity may continue without the US, but it would be much better if peacebuilding efforts have the endorsement of the world's greatest power. At the same time, given the diversity of the tasks and the necessity of the substantial costs and commitments required, and the need for local buy-in, the US cannot and should not act alone. Effective peacebuilding requires a multilateral commitment from the international community, including the active support of the major powers.

The challenge for the scholars and practitioners involved in either observing or carrying out peacebuilding activities is to stand back from the prevailing understandings of what peacebuilding ought to be and critically assess the burgeoning activities which fall under the label of peacebuilding. It is also important to go beyond the anecdotal knowledge of the issue and begin to aggregate and learn from the accumulating experiences of peacebuilding activity. The authors in this volume have begun this process and have striven to link the theory and praxis of peacebuilding.

The preceding contributions have provided a clear and thorough assessment of a variety of peacebuilding operations. The analyses point to the exceptional complexity and difficulty involved in peacebuilding. The record of success to date has not been as impressive as one would like. Indeed, the litany of problems experienced up to this point might be sufficient to scare many away from future attempts. On the other hand, it is absolutely clear that the demand, let alone desperate need, for effective peacebuilding continues to grow. The threats posed by civil conflicts and failed states not only to the civilians attempting to survive in the midst of pervasive insecurity but also to regional and more global interests have become more starkly evident in the days since the terrorist attacks on the United States. Concern among states and civil society actors for human security also continue to expand. Peacebuilding remains the most viable international response to addressing these persistent sources of insecurity and oppression.

If we are to facilitate a transition from a culture of violence to a culture of peace, then we need to have a clear understanding not only of the nature of already established war cultures, but also of the cultural presuppositions we bring to the understanding of those cultures. Adelman provides a framework that enables us to be self-critical of our own analyses of the presuppositions and proposals we bring to peacebuilding. Many of today's violent conflicts are exacerbated by the absence of coherence that peacebuilders and analysts of peacebuilding bring to the issue, thereby exacerbating conflict.

It is our position that peacebuilding operations should aim to address underlying causes of conflict if they are to construct an architecture of peace that will withstand the test of time. If there will always be conflicts, one way to ensure that such clashes do not become violent is to set up functional institutions to mitigate such violence. As was noted earlier, peacebuilding tools can be used to deconstruct dysfunctional institutions and norms and to construct institutions and norms that support sustainable peace. However, we want to make clear that this is a complex issue and that the answers are not always as clear cut as some would want us to believe.[4] Furthermore, this volume raises fundamental questions not only about what to reconstruct but also about how to do so in order not to recreate the unsustainable institutions and structures that originally contributed to violent conflict.

This still leaves room for the embrace of a cosmopolitan theory, similar to the one put forward by Masciulli. He argued that if societies can embrace a humane global ethic, we will be in a better position to witness a transformation of those societies from ones embedded in a culture of violence to ones in which a culture of peace will be prevalent. Along with Masciulli, I would emphasize that cultures are not static entities, but are always undergoing transformations. Prevalent global cultures need to change and undergo a parametric transformation from (honorable and dishonorable) warrior violence, to institutionalized "postwarrior" peaceful conflict resolution. Cosmopolitan ethics, unlike divisive warrior ethics, appeals to what is reasonably and creatively best in every culture, pointing to a new world in which, for the most part, conflict and competition would be conducted nonviolently, humanely, decently, and honorably. In the end, this is ultimately what peacebuilding hopes to achieve.

Notes

1 Admittedly, the influence of a structural constructivist perspective built on a universalist rationalist instrumental is evident in my work. However, this volume can be seen as an attempt to straddle the fence that separates universalist and varied local positions.

2 Boutros Boutros-Ghali, "An Agenda for Peace: Preventative Diplomacy, Peacemaking and Peace-keeping. Report of the Secretary-General Pursuant to the Statement Adopted by the Summit Meeting of the Security Council on 31 January 1992, A/47/277–S/24111 (17 June 1992), section VI, para 55.

3 Nakaya reaches this conclusion even though in the end Somali women abandoned this approach at the peace conference and conformed to clan-based allocation of the transitional national assembly seats that included seats for women themselves (25 seats for women were allocated according to clans). This institutional arrangement therefore preserved the existing social categories instead of influencing the structural base of power. As a result, unfortunately, women in Somalia are not allowed to participate effectively in peacebuilding at the national or clan levels.

4 The complexity of this issue is well documented in a recent book, Antonio Donini, Norah Niland, and Karin Wermester, eds., *Nation-Building Unraveled? Aid, Peace and Justice in Afghanistan* (Bloomfield, CT: Kumarian Press, 2004).

Bibliography

Aall, Pamela. "Nongovernmental Organizations and Peacemaking." In Chester Crocker, Fen Osler Hampson and Pamela Aall. *Managing Global Chaos: Sources of and Responses to International Conflict*, 433–43. Washington DC: United States Institute of Peace, 1996.

Abdullah, Ibrahim and Patrick Muana. "The Revolutionary United Front of Sierra Leone: A Revolt of the Lumpenproletariat." In Christopher Clapham, ed. *African Guerrillas*, 172–94. Oxford: James Currey / Kampala: Fountain Publishers / Bloomington: Indiana University Press, 1998.

Abiew, Francis Kofi. *The Evolution of the Doctrine and Practise of Humanitarian Intervention*. The Hague: Kluwer, 1999.

Abiew, Francis and Tom Keating. "NGOs and UN Peacekeeping Operations: Strange Bedfellows." *International Peacekeeping* 6, no. 2 (1999): 90–105.

Aboagye, Colonel Festus. ECOMOG: *A Subregional Experience in Conflict Resolution, Management and Peacekeeping in Liberia*. Accra: Sedco Enterprise, 1999.

Acharya, Amitav. *An Arms Race in Post-Cold War Southeast Asia? Prospects for Control, Pacific Strategic Paper No. 8*. Singapore: Institute of Southeast Asian Studies, 1994.

——. *Constructing a Security Community in Southeast Asia*. London: Routledge, 2001.

——. "Ideas, Identity and Institution-building: from the 'ASEAN way' to the 'Asia-Pacific way'?" *The Pacific Review* 10, no. 3 (1997): 319–46.

——. "Imagined Proximities: The Making and Unmaking of Southeast Asia as a Region." *Southeast Asian Journal of Social Science* 27, no. 1 (1999): 55–77.

——. *The Quest for Identity: International Relations of Southeast Asia*. Singapore: Oxford University Press, 2000.

Adebajo, Adeke. *Economic Agendas in Civil Wars. A Conference Summary*. New York: International Peace Academy, 1999.

——. *Building Peace in West Africa: Liberia, Sierra Leone and Guinea-Bissau*. Boulder, CO: Lynne Reinner, 2002.

——. *Liberia's Civil War: Nigeria, ECOMOG and Regional Security in West Africa*. Boulder, CO: Lynne Reinner, 2002.

Adebajo, Adekeye and Chris Landsberg. "Back to the Future: UN Peacekeeping in Africa." In Adekeye Adebajo and Chandra Lekha Sriram, eds. *Managing Armed Conflicts in the 21st Century*, 161–88. London and Portland: Frank Cass, 2001.

Adibe, Clement E. "Accepting External Authority in Peace-Maintenance." *Global Governance* 4, no. 1, (January–March 1998): 107–22.

——. "The Liberian conflict and the ECOWAS-UN partnership." *Third World Quarterly* 18, no. 3 (1997): 471–88.

Advisory Council on International Affairs. *Humanitarian Intervention*. The Hague: Advisory Committee on Issues of Public International Law, 2000.

"After the horror, a new beginning." *The Economist*, 45–46. 18 May 2002.

Africa Confidential. 16 December 1994.

Africa Confidential. 5 January 1996.

Africa Confidential. 17 May 1992.

Africa Research Bulletin 32, no. 2 (28 February 1995): 1174–75.

Ajami, Fouad. "The Summoning." *Foreign Affairs* 72, no. 4 (September–October 1993): 2–9.

Alao, Abiodun, John Mackinlay and Funmi Olonisakin. *Peacekeepers, Politicians, and Warlords: The Liberian Peace Process*. Tokyo, New York and Paris: United Nations University Press, 1999.

Alger, Chadwick F. "The Emerging Role of NGOs in the UN System: From Article 71 to a People's Millennium Assembly." *Global Governance* 8, no. 1 (2002): 93–118.

Almond, Gabriel A. "The Study of Political Culture." In Lane Crothers and Charles Lockhart, eds. *Culture and Politics: A Reader*, 5–20. New York: St. Martin's Press, 2000.

Alves, Pericles Gasparini and Diana Belinda Cipollone, eds. *Curbing Illicit Trafficking in Small Arms and Sensitive Technologies: An Action-Oriented Agenda*. Geneva: UNIDIR, 1998.

"America's Chinese Puzzle." *The Economist*, 25 May 1996.

Amnesty International. "Sierra Leone: Human Rights Abuses in a War Against Civilians." *AI Index* (13 September 1995).

Anderson, Jon Lee. "The Devil they Know." *New Yorker*, July 27, 1998. http://www.newyorker.com/archive/content/?30728fr_archive01.

Anderson, Mary B. *Do No Harm: How Aid Can Support Peace—or War*. Boulder, CO: Lynne Reinner, 1999.

——. "Humanitarian NGOs in Conflict Intervention." In Chester Crocker, Fen O. Hampson, and Pamela Aall, eds. *Managing Global Chaos: Sources and Responses in International Conflict*, 343–54. Washington, DC: United States Institute of Peace, 1996.

Ankomah, Baffour. "Knives out for Taylor." *New African Magazine*, September 1998. http://www.africasia-com/newafrican/na-php?ID17&back_month=06.

Annan, Kofi. *Facing the Humanitarian Challenge: Towards a Culture of Prevention*. New York: United Nations, 1999.

——. "Peacekeeping, Military Intervention, and National Sovereignty in Internal Armed Conflicts." In Jonathan Moore, ed. *Hard Choices: Moral Dilemmas in Humanitarian Intervention*, 55–70. Lanham, MD: Rowman and Littlefield, 1998.

——. *Renewing the United Nations: A Programme for Reform, Report of the Secretary-General*. New York: United Nations, 1997.

Antolik, Michael. *ASEAN and the Diplomacy of Accommodation*. Armonk: M.E. Sharpe, 1990.

Anwar, Dewi Fortuna. "The Rise in Arms Purchases: Its Significance and Impacts on South East Asian Political Stability." Unpublished paper. University of Toronto. April 1993.

Aoul, Samia Kazi, Emilie Revil, Bruno Sarrasin, Bonnie Campbell and Denis Tougas. *Vers une spirale de la violence? "Les dangers de la privatisation de la gestion du risque des investissements en Afrique." Les activités minières det l'emploi de compagnies privées de sécurité.* Montréal: Table de concertation sur les droits humains au Congo / Kinshasa: Organisation Catholique Canadienne pour le développement et la paix, 2000.

Apthorpe, Raymond. "Was International Emergency Relief Aid in Kosovo 'Humanitarian'?" Humanitarian Practice Network. Overseas Development Institute, London. http://www.odihpn.org/report.asp?ID=2417.

Arbour, Louise. "Opening Comments to the Symposium on Peacebuilding." University of Alberta, 10 March 2000.

Arnold, Matthew. *Culture and Anarchy.* Edited with an introduction by J. Dover Wilson. Cambridge: Cambridge University Press, 1960.

Art, Robert J. and Kenneth N. Waltz, eds. *The Use of Force: Military Power and International Politics.* 3rd ed. Lanham, MD: Rowman and Littlefield, 1999.

"ASEAN's commitment to new nation tested." East Timor Action Network. http://www.etan.org/et2000a/january/22-31/31ASEAN.htm.

Austin A., Fischer M. and N. Ropers, eds. *Berghof Hand Book for Conflict Transformation.* Berlin: Berghof Research Centre for Constructive Conflict Management, 2003. http://www.berghof-handbook.net.

Avruch, Kevin. *Culture and Conflict Resolution.* Washington, DC: United States Institute for Peace, 1998.

"Axworthy Launches International Commission on Intervention and State Sovereignty." News Release No. 233. Ottawa: Department of Foreign Affairs and International Trade, 2000.

Axworthy, Lloyd. "Canada and Human Security: The Need for Leadership." *International Journal* 52, no. 2 (1999): 183–96.

——. "Controlling Small Arms: International Action Network Established." *Ploughshares Monitor.* September 1998. http://ploughshares.ca/content/MONITOR/mons98f.html.

——. "Human Security and Global Governance: Putting People First." *Global Governance* 7, no. 1 (January–March 2001): 19–23.

——. "Notes for an Address by the Honourable Lloyd Axworthy, Minister of Foreign Affairs, at the New York University School of Law." *The Hauser Lecture on International Humanitarian Law: Humanitarian Interventions and Humanitarian Constraints.* New York, February 10, 2000. Ottawa: Department of Foreign Affairs and International Trade, 2000. http://www.un.int/canada/html/s-10feb2000axworthy.htm.

Baden, Sally. *Post-Conflict Mozambique: Women's Special Situations, Issue and Gender Perspectives to be Integrated into Skills Training and Employment Promotion.* Geneva: International Labor Organization, 1997. www.ilo.org/public/english/employment/skills/training/publ/pub7.htm.

Bailey, Michael, Robert Maguire, and J. O'Neil G. Pouliot. "Haiti: Military-PolicePartnership for Public Security." In Robert B. Oakley, Michael Dziedzic and Eliot M. Goldberg, eds. *Policing the New World Disorder,* 215–34. Washington, DC: National Defence University Press, 1998.

Baitenmann, Helga. "NGOs and the Afghan War: The Politicisation of Humanitarian Aid." *Third World Quarterly* 12, no. 1 (1990): 62–85.

Barber, Benjamin. "Feeding Refugees, or War? The Dilemma of Humanitarian Aid." *Foreign Affairs* 76 (July–August 1997): 8–14.

——. *Jihad vs. McWorld*. New York: Ballantine Books, 1996.

——. *A Place for Us: How to Make Society Civil and Democracy Strong*. New York: Hill and Wang, 1998.

Barnett, Michael. *Eyewitness to a Genocide: The United Nations and Rwanda*. Ithaca, NY: Cornell University Press, 2002.

Barnett, Michael and Martha Finnemore. "The Politics, Power, and Pathologies of International Organizations." *International Organization* 53 (Autumn 1999): 699–732.

Barry, Jane and Anna Jeffreys. "A Bridge too Far: Aid Agencies and the Military in Humanitarian Response." *Humanitarian Practice Network*. Network Paper Number 37. London: Overseas Development Institute, 2002.

Beauvais, Joel C. "Benevolent Despotism: A Critique of U.N. State-Building in East Timor." *New York University Journal of International Law and Politics* 33, no. 4 (Summer 2001): 11–26.

Beigbeder, Yves. *The Role and Status of International Humanitarian Volunteers and Organizations: The Right and Duty to Humanitarian Assistance*. Dordrecht: Martinus Nijhoff Publishers, 1991.

Bell, J. Bowyer. "Strategic Implications of the Soviet Presence in Somalia." *Orbis* 19, no. 2 (1975): 402–11.

Benedick, Richard Elliot. *Ozone Diplomacy*. Cambridge, MA: Harvard University Press, 1991.

Bennet, J. and Mark R. Duffield, eds. *Meeting Needs: NGO Coordination in Practice*. London: Earthscan Publications, 1995.

Berman, Eric G. and Katie E. Sams. *Peacekeeping in Africa: Capabilities and Culpabilities*. Geneva: UN Institute for Disarmament Research / Pretoria: Institute for Security Studies, 2000.

Bettati, M. and Bernard Kouchner, ed. *Le devoir d'ingérence*. Paris: Denoël, 1987.

Betts, Richard K. "The Delusion of Impartial Intervention." In Chester A. Crocker and Fen Osler Hampson and Pamela Aall, eds. *Managing Global Chaos*, 333–41. Washington, DC: United States Institute of Peace Press, 1996.

Biersteker, Thomas J. and Cynthia Weber. *State Sovereignty as Social Construct*. Cambridge: Cambridge University Press, 1996.

Björkdahl, Annika. *From Idea to Norm: Promoting Conflict Prevention*. Lund: Lund University, 2002.

Blair, Tony. "Doctrine of the International Community." Speech by the Prime Minister of Britain, Tony Blair, to the Economic Club of Chicago, Hilton Hotel, Chicago, USA, 22 April 1999. http://www.fco.gov.uk/news/speechtext.asp?2316.

Bland, Douglas. "Canada and Military Coalitions: Where, How, and with Whom?" *Policy Matters* 3, no. 3 (2002): 1–52.

Bloom, William. *Personal Identity, National Identity and International Relations*. Cambridge: Cambridge University Press, 1990.

Boulding, E., ed. *New Agendas for Peace Research: Conflict and Security Reexamined*. Boulder, CO and London: Lynne Reinner, 1993.

Boulding, E. and K. Boulding. *Building a Global Civic Culture*. New York: Columbia University Press, 1998.

——. *Cultures of Peace: The Hidden Side of History*. New York: Syracuse University Press, 2000.

——. *The Future: Images and Processes*. Thousand Oaks, CA: Sage Publications, 1995.

Boutros-Ghali, Boutros. "An Agenda for Peace: Preventative Diplomacy, Peacemaking and Peace-keeping. Report of the Secretary-General pursuant to the Statement Adopted by the Summit Meeting of the Security Council on 31 January 1992." A/47/277-S/24111. 17 June 1992.

——. *An Agenda For Peace*. New York: United Nations, 1992.

——. *An Agenda for Peace*. 2nd ed. New York: United Nations, 1995.

Brinkerhoff, Derick W. *Improving Development Program Performance*. Boulder, CO: Lynne Reinner, 1991.

Brinkerhoff, Derick W. and Jean Claude Garcia-Zamor. *Politics, Projects and People-Institutional Development in Haiti*. New York: Praeger, 1986.

Brown, Gillian, Sarah Cliffe, Scott Guggenheim, Markus Kostner and Susan Opper. "A Tale of Two Projects: Community-Based Reconstruction in East Timor and Rwanda." *Social Funds Innovation Update* 2, no. 4 (July 2002). www.worldbank.org/sp.

Brown, Seyom. *The Causes and Prevention of War*. New York: St. Martin's Press, 1994.

——. "World Interests and the Changing Dimension of Security." In Michael T. Klare and Yogesh Chandrani, eds. *World Security*, 1–17. 3rd ed. New York: St. Martin's Press, 1998.

Bryans, Michael, Bruce D. Jones and Janice Gross Stein. *Mean Times: Humanitarian Action in Complex Political Emergencies—Stark Choices, Cruel Dilemmas*. University of Toronto: Program on Conflict Management and Negotiation Centre for International Studies, 1999.

Bull, Hedley. *The Anarchical Society*. London: Macmillan, 1977.

Bush, Kenneth D. "Beyond Bungee Cord Humanitarianism: Towards a Democratic Agenda for Peacebuilding." In "Governance, Democracy and Human Rights." Special Issue, *Canadian Journal of Development Studies* (1996): 75–92.

Bush, Kenneth. *From Putty to Stone: Report of a Mission Investigating Human Rights Programming Opportunities in Sri Lanka*. Colombo, Sri Lanka: UK Department for International Development (DFID) Sri Lanka, 2002.

——. "A Measure of Peace: Peace and Conflict Impact Assessment (PCIA) of Development Projects in Conflict Zones." *Working Paper #1*. Ottawa: International Development Research Centre, 1998. http://www.idrc.ca/peace/p1/working_paper1.html.

——. "Towards a Balanced Approach to Rebuilding War-Torn Societies." *Canadian Foreign Policy* 3, no. 3 (1995): 49–69.

Busse, Nikolas. "Constructivism and Southeast Asian security." *The Pacific Review* 12, no. 1 (1999): 55–77.

Byman, Daniel L. "Uncertain Partners: NGOs and the Military." *Survival* 43, no. 2 (2001): 97–114.

Byrne, Bridget Rachel Marcus and Tanya Powers-Stevens. *Gender, Conflict and Development: Volume II: Case Studies: Cambodia, Rwanda, Kosovo, Algeria, Somalia, Guatemala and Eritrea*. Brighton: Institute of Development Studies, July 1996.

Cahill, Kevin M. *Preventive Diplomacy: Stopping Wars Before They Start*. New York: Basic Books, 1996.

Cairns, Edmund. *A Safer Future: Reducing the Human Cost of War.* Oxford: Oxfam Publications, 1997.

Calhoun, Craig. *Critical Social Theory: Culture, History and the Challenge of Difference.* Massachusetts: Blackwell Publishers, 1995.

Call, Charles and Michael Barnett. "Looking for a Few Good Cops: Peacekeeping, Peacebuilding and CIVPOL." In Tor Tanke Holm and Espen Barthe Eide, eds. *Peacebuilding and Police Reform*, 43–68. London: Frank Cass, 2000.

Call, Charles and Susan E. Cook. "On Democratization and Peacebuilding." *Global Governance* 9, no. 2 (2003): 233–47.

Call, Charles and William Stanley. "Civilian Security." In Stephen John Stedman, Donald Rothchild and Elizabeth Cousens, eds. *Ending Civil Wars: The Implementation of Peace Agreements*, 303–26. Boulder, CO: Lynne Reinner, 2002.

Canada. *Debrief the Leaders Report: Officers.* Ottawa: Department of National Defence, 2001.

Canada. Department of Foreign Affairs and International Trade (DFAIT). *Light Weapons and Micro-Disarmament.* Ottawa: DFAIT, January 1997.

Cardozo, Barbara, Alfredo Vergara, Ferid Agani and Carol Gotway. "Mental Health, Social Functioning, and Attitudes of Kosovar Albanians Following the War in Kosovo." *Journal of the American Medical Association* 284, no. 5 (August 2000): 569–77.

Carnegie Commission on Preventing Deadly Conflict. "Executive Summary." *Preventing Deadly Conflict, Final Report.* New York: Carnegie Commission on Prevention of Deadly Conflict, 1997. http:///www.wilsoncentre.org/subtitles/frpub.htm.

——. *Preventing Deadly Conflict, Final Report.* Washington, D.C.: Carnegie Commission on Preventing Deadly Conflict, 1997.

Chandler, David. "The People-Centred Approach to Peace Operations: The New UN Agenda." *International Peacekeeping* 8, no. 1 (2001): 1–19.

Charters, David A. *Canada-US Defence Cooperation.* Report on Defence Forum, Fredericton, New Brunswick, April 2000. http://www.dnd.ca/admpol/org/dg_coord/d_pub/sdf/reports/unb_forum_e.htm.

Checkel, Jeffrey T. "The Constructivist Turn in International Relations Theory." *World Politics* 50, no. 2 (January 1998): 324–48.

Chomsky, Noam. *9-11.* New York: Seven Stories Press, 2001.

——. *The New Military Humanism, Lessons from Kosovo.* Vancouver: New Star Books, 1999.

Chopra, Jarat. "Building State Failure in East Timor." *Development and Change* 33, no. 5 (2002): 979–1000.

——. "Introducing Peace Maintenance." *Global Governance* 4, no. 1 (1998): 1–18.

——. *Peace-Maintenance: The Evolution of International Political Authority.* London: Routledge, 1999.

——, ed. *The Politics of Peace-Maintenance.* Boulder, CO: Lynne Reinner, 1998.

Chopra, Jarat, Åge Eknes and Toralv Nordbø. "Fighting for Hope in Somalia." *Journal of Humanitarian Affairs* (1995). www.jha.ac/articles/a007.htm.

Clark, Wesley. *Waging Modern War.* New York: Public Affairs Publishing, 2001.

Clarke, Michael and Steve Smith. "Perspectives on the Foreign Policy System: Implementation Approaches." In Michael Clarke and Brian White, eds. *Understanding Foreign Policy: The Foreign Policy Systems Approach*, 163–84. London: Elgar, 1989.

Cohen, Roberta and Francis M. Deng. *Masses in Flight: The Global Crisis of Internal Displacement.* Washington, DC: Brookings Institution Press, 1998.

"Consensual Democracy" in Post-Genocide Rwanda: Evaluating the March 2001 District Elections. ICG Africa Report No. 34. October 2001.

Cooper, Andrew F., John English and Ramesh Thakur, eds. *Enhancing Global Governance: Towards a New Diplomacy?* Tokyo: United Nations University Press, 2002.

Cortright, David, ed. *The Price of Peace: Incentives and International Conflict Prevention.* Lanham, MD: Rowman and Littlefield, 1997.

Council of Europe. *Gender Mainstreaming: Conceptual Framework, Methodology and Presentation of Good Practice.* Final Report of Activities of the Group of Specialists on Mainstreaming. EG-S-MS 98, 2. Strasbourg, May 1998.

Cousens, Elizabeth and Chetan Kumar. *Peacebuilding as Politics: Cultivating Peace in Fragile Societies.* Boulder, CO: Lynne Reinner, 2000.

Cranston, Maurice. *The Mask of Politics.* London: Allen Lane, 1976.

Crisp, Jeff. "Mind the Gap! UNHCR, Humanitarian Assistance and the Development Process." *Journal of Humantiarian Assistance.* Working Paper 43. 11 November 2001. http://www.jha.ac/articles/u043.htm.

Crocker, Chester. "A Poor Case for Quitting. Mistaking Incompetence for Interventionism." *Foreign Affairs* 79, no. 1 (January–February 2000): 183–87.

Crocker, Chester, Fen Osler Hampson and Pamela Aall, eds. *Managing Global Chaos: Sources of and Responses to International Conflict.* Washington, DC: USIP Press, 1996.

Crozier, Brian. "The Soviet Presence in Somalia," 1–20. Occasional Paper. London: Institute for the Study of Conflict, 1975.

Cuny, F.C. "Dilemmas of Military Involvement in Humanitarian Relations." In Thomas G. Weiss and Leon Gordenker, eds. *Soldiers, Peacekeepers and Disasters,* 52–81. London: Macmillan, 1991.

Daalder, Ivo and Michael O'Hanlon. "Unlearning the Lessons of Kosovo." *Foreign Policy* 116 (Fall 1999): 128–41.

Dallaire, Roméo. "The Changing Role of UN Peacebuilding Forces: The Relationship between UN Peacekeepers and NGOs in Rwanda." In Jim Whitman and David Pocock, eds. *After Rwanda: The Coordination of United Nations Humanitarian Assistance,* 205–18. London: Macmillan Press, 1996.

——. "The End of Innocence: Rwanda 1994." In Jonathan Moore, ed. *Hard Choices: Moral Dilemmas in Humanitarian Intervention,* 71–86. Lanham, MD: Rowman and Littlefield, 1998.

Das, Sukanya Mohan. "Process Issues: An Argument for Inclusion of Grass-Roots Communities in the Formulation of National and International Initiatives in Re-building Afghanistan." *Journal of Humanitarian Assistance* (2 February 2002). www.jha.ac/articles/a076.htm.

Davies, John L. and Ted Robert Gurr, eds. *Preventive Measures: Building Risk Assessment and Crisis Early Warning Systems.* Lanham, MD: Rowman and Littlefield, 1998.

Day, Richard B., Ronald Beiner and Joseph Masciulli, eds. *Democratic Theory and Technological Society.* Armonk, NY: M.E. Sharpe, 1988.

De Soto, Alvaro and Graciana Del Castillo. "Obstacles to Peacebuilding." *Foreign Policy* (Spring 1994): 69-83.

Delaney, Douglas E. "CIMIC Operations During Operation 'Kinetic'." *Canadian Military Journal* (Winter 2000–2001): 29–34.

DeMars, William. "War and Mercy in Africa." *World Policy Journal* 17, no. 2 (Summer 2000): 1–26.

Deng, Francis M., S. Kimaro, T. Lyons, D. Rothchild and William I. Zartman, eds. *Sovereignty as Responsibility: Conflict Management in Africa.* Washington, DC: Brookings Institution, 1996.

Deng, Francis and I. William Zartman, eds. *Conflict Resolution in Africa.* Washington, DC: Brookings Institution Press, 1991.

Department of Foreign Affairs and International Trade. Canada. *Human Security: Safety for People in a Changing World.* Ottawa: Department of Foreign Affairs and International Trade, April 1999.

DeSombre, Elizabeth R. *Domestic Sources of International Environmental Policy: Industry, Environmentalists, and U.S. Power.* Cambridge: MIT Press, 2000.

DeWaal, Alex. *Famine Crimes.* New York: St. Martin's Press, 1998.

Dhanapala, Jayantha. *Statement before the First Committee of the General Assembly.* New York: United Nations, 8 October 2002. http://disarmament.un.org/speech/08oct2001.htm.

Diehl, Paul F., ed. *The Politics of Global Governance: International Organizations in an Interdependent World.* Boulder, CO: Lynne Reinner, 1997.

Donini, Antonio, Norah Niland, and Karin Wermester, eds. *Nation-Building Unraveled? Aid, Peace and Justice in Afghanistan.* Bloomfield, CT: Kumarian Press, 2004.

Donini, Antonio. "Asserting Humanitarianism in Peace-Maintenance." *Global Governance* 4, no. 1 (1998): 81–96.

——. "Asserting Humanitarianism in Peace-Maintenance." In Jarat Chopra, ed. *The Politics of Peace-Maintenance*, 81–86. Boulder, CO: Lynne Reinner, 1998.

——. "Surfing on the Crest of the Wave until it Crashes: Intervention and the South." *Journal of Humanitarian Assistance* 3 (October, 1995). http://www.jha.ac/articles/a006.htm.

Donnelly, Jack. *International Human Rights.* Boulder, CO: Westview, 1998.

Duffey, Tamara. "Cultural Issues in Contemporary Peacekeeping." *International Peacekeeping* 7, no. 1 (2000): 142–69.

Duffield, Mark. "NGO Relief in War Zones: Toward and Analysis of the New Aid Paradigm." In Thomas G. Weiss, ed. *Beyond UN Subcontracting: Task-Sharing with Regional Organizations and Service-Providing* NGOs, 139–59. London: Macmillan Press, 1998.

——. "The Political Economy of Internal War: Asset Transfer, Complex Emergencies, and International Aid." In Joanna Macrae and Anthony Zwi, eds. *War and Hunger: Rethinking International Responses to Complex Emergencies*, 50–69. London: Zed Books, 1994.

Dunne, Tim. *Inventing International Society: A History of the English School.* New York: St. Martin's Press, 1998.

Dupont, Alan. "ASEAN's Response to the East Timor Crisis." *Australian Journal of International Affairs* 54, no. 2 (2000): 163–70.

E.T. Jackson and Associates, Ltd. *Learning for Results: Issues, Trends and Lessons Learned in Basic Human Needs.* Ottowa: CIDA, June 1996. http://www.acdi-cida.gac.ca/cida_ind.nsf.

Eckstein, Harry. "A Culturalist Theory of Social Change." *American Political Science Review* 82, no. 3 (1988): 789–804.

ECOWAS. *Meeting of ECOWAS Ministers of Foreign Affairs, Final Communique*. Lomé, 24–25 May 1999.
——. *Protocol Relating to the Mechanism For Conflict Prevention, Management, Resolution, Peacekeeping and Security*. Abuja: ECOWAS Secretariat, 1999.
Eisenhour, John Howard and Edward Marks. "Herding Cats: Overcoming Obstacles in Civil-Military Operations." *Joint Force Quarterly* (Summer 1999): 86–90.
Eisenstadt, S.N. *The Political Systems of Empires*. Glencoe, IL: Free Press, 1963.
Eisenstadt, S. N., M. Abitbol and N. Chazan, eds. *The Early State in African Perspective: Culture, Power, and Division of Labor*. Leiden: E. Brill, 1987.
Eisenstadt, S.N. and L. Roninger. *Patrons, Clients, and Friends*. Cambridge: Cambridge University Press, 1984.
Eliasson, Jan, "Establishing Trust in the Healer." In Kevin M. Cahill, ed. *Preventive Diplomacy—Stopping Wars Before They Start*, 318–43. New York: Basic Books, 1996.
Ellis, Stephen. *The Mask of Anarchy*. London: Hurst and Company, 1999.
Elster, Jon. *The Cement of Society*. Cambridge: Cambridge University Press, 1989.
Elwood-Dunn, D. "Liberia's Internal Responses to ECOMOG's Intervention Efforts." In Karl Magyar and Earl Conteh-Morgan, eds. *Peacekeeping in Africa: ECOMOG in Liberia*. London: Macmillan / New York: St. Martin's Press, 1998.
Engendering the Peace Process. A Gender Approach to Dayton—and Beyond. Sweden: The Kvinna till Kvinna Foundation, June 2000.
Eriksson, Par. "Civil-military Coordination in Peace Support Operations—an Impossible Necessity." *Journal of Humanitarian Assistance* (2000). http://www.jha.ac.uk/articles/a061.htm.
Ero, Comfort. *Sierra Leone's Security Complex*. Working Paper no. 3. London: Centre For Defence Studies, June 2000.
European Parliament. Resolution on the Participation of Women in Peaceful Conflict. Resolution 2000/2025 (INI). http://www3.europarl.eu.int.
Evans, Grant and Kevin Rowley. *Red Brotherhood at War: Vietnam, Cambodia and Laos since 1975*. London: Verso, 1990.
Falk, Richard. *Human Rights Horizons*. New York and London: Routledge, 2000.
Federation of South African Women. "Women's Struggle in the African National Congress." Women's Charter. http://www.anc.org.za/ancdocs/history/women/wcharter.html.
Feil, Scott R. *Preventing Genocide: How the Use of Force Might Have Succeeded in Rwanda*. New York: Carnegie Commission on Preventing Deadly Conflict, 1997.
Ferris, Elizabeth G. *Beyond Borders: Refugees, Migrants and Human Rights in the Post–Cold War Era*. Geneva: World Council of Churches Publications, 1993.
Findlay, Trevor. *Challenge of the New Peacekeeper*. New York: Oxford University Press, 1996.
Finnemore, Martha. "Emerging Norms of Humanitarian Interventions." In Peter Katzenstein, ed. *The Culture of National Security*, 153–86. New York: Columbia University Press, 1996.
——. *National Interests in International Society*. Ithaca, NY: Cornell University Press, 1996.
Fomerand, Jacques. "UN Conferences: Media Events of Genuine Diplomacy?" *Global Governance* 2, no. 1 (September–December 1996): 361–75.
France. Assemblée Nationale, *Rapport d'information déposé par la Mission d'information de la Commission de la défense nationale et des forces armées et de la Commission des affaires*

étrangères, sur les opérations militaires menées par la France, d'autres pays et l'ONU au Rwanda entre 1990 et 1994. Paris, 15 décembre 1998.

Freud, Sigmund. *Totem and Taboo: Resemblances between the Psychic Lives of Savages and Neurotics*. Trans. J. Strachey. New York: Vantage Books, 1946.

Frye, Alton. *Humanitarian Intervention: Crafting a Workable Doctrine*. New York: Council on Foreign Relations, 2000.

Fukuyama, Francis. "Women and the Evolution of World Politics." *Foreign Affairs* 77, no. 5 (September–October 1998): 24–41.

"G8 Miyazaki Initiatives for Conflict Prevention." http://www.auswaertiges-amt.de/www/en/infoservice/download/pdf/friedenspolitik/miyazaki_konfl.pdf.

Galtung, Johan, Carl G. Jacobsen, Kai Frithjof Brand-Jacobsen and Finn Tschudi. *Searching for Peace: The Road to TRANSCEND*. London: Pluto Press, 2000.

Garba, Joseph. *Diplomatic Soldiering: Nigerian Foreign Policy, 1975–1979*. Ibadan: Spectrum Books, 1987.

Garfinkle, Adam. "Strategy and Preventive Diplomacy." *Orbis* 45, no. 4 (2001): 503–18.

Geertz, Clifford. *The Interpretation of Cultures*. New York: Basic Books, 1973.

George, Alexander. *Forceful Persuasion: Coercive Diplomacy as an Alternative to War.* Washington, DC: USIP Press, 1992.

George, Alexander and Jane E. Holl. *The Warning-Response Problem and Missed Opportunities.* Washington, DC: Carnegie Commission on Preventing Deadly Conflict, 1997.

Getting it Right? A Gender Approach to UNMIK. Sweden: The Kvinna till Kvinna Foundation, 11 May 2002.

Giddens, Anthony. *The Constitution of Society: Outline of the Theory of Structuration.* Oxford: Polity Press, 1984.

Gilpin, Robert. *The Political Economy of International Relations*. Princeton, NJ: Princeton University Press, 1987.

Glennon, Michael J. "The New Interventionism: The Search for a Just International Law." *Foreign Affairs* 78, no. 3 (May–June 1999): 2–8.

Godnick, William H. "Illicit Arms in Central America." Paper prepared for and international workshop of the British American Security Information Council (BASIC) on "Small Arms and Light Weapons: An Issue for the OSCE." Hofburg Palace, Vienna, 9–10 November 1998. http://sand.miis.edu/research/1998/nov1998/illicit.pdf.

Goldring, Natalie J. "The NRA Goes Global." *Bulletin of Atomic Scientists* 55, no. 1 (January–February, 1999). http://www.bullatomsci.org/issues/1999/jf99goldring.html.

Goldstein, Judith and Robert O. Keohane, eds. *Ideas and Foreign Policy: Beliefs, Institutions, and Political Change*. Ithaca, New York: Cornell University Press, 1993.

Good, Robert. "Changing Patterns of African International Relations." *American Political Science Review* 58, no. 3 (1964): 632–41.

Goodhand, Jonathon and David Hume. "From Wars to Complex Political Emergencies: Understanding Conflict and Peace-building in the New World Disorder." *Third World Quarterly* 20, no. 1 (1999): 13–27.

Gordenker, Leon and Thomas G. Weiss. "NGO Participation in the International Policy Process." *Third World Quarterly* 16, no. 3 (1995): 543–56.

———. "Pluralizing Global Governance: Analytical Approaches and Dimensions." In Thomas G. Weiss and Leon Gordenker, eds. *NGOs, the UN, and Global Governance*, 17–47. Boulder, CO: Lynne Reinner, 1996.

——, eds. *Soldiers, Peacekeepers and Disasters*. London: Macmillan, 1991.

Gordon, Stuart. "Understanding the Priorities for Civil-Military Cooperation (CIMIC)." *Journal of Humanitarian Assistance* (2001). http://www.jha.ac/articles/a068.htm.

Gourevitch, Philip. *We Wish to Inform you that Tomorrow We will be Killed with our Families*. New York: Picador, 1999.

Gowon, Yakubu. "The Economic Community of West African States: A Study of Political and Economic Integration." Ph.D. diss., Warwick University, 1984.

Green, Michael J. and Benjamin L. Self. "Japan's Changing China Policy: From Commercial Liberalism to Reluctant Realism." *Survival* 38, no. 2 (Summer 1996): 35–59.

Green, Reginald Herbold and Ismail I. Ahmed. "Rehabilitation, Sustainable Peace and Development: Towards Reconceptualisation." *Third World Quarterly* 20, no. 1 (1999): 189–206.

Greenaway, Sean. "Post-Modern Conflict and Humanitarian Action: Questioning the Paradigm." *Journal of Humanitarian Assistance* (2000): 1. http://www.jha.ac.uk/articles/a053.htm.

Griffiths, Ann L., ed. *Building Peace and Democracy in Post-Conflict Societies*. Halifax: Centre for Foreign Policy Studies, 1998.

Griffiths, Martin, Iain Levine and Mark Weller. "Sovereignty and Suffering." In John Harriss, ed. *The Politics of Humanitarian Intervention*, 33–90. London: Pinter Publishers, 1995.

Grillot, Suzette. "The Emergence and Effectiveness of Transational Advocacy Networks." Paper presented at the International Studies Association-Southern-Region meeting, Florida, 12–14 October 2001.

Grossman, Dave. *On Killing: The Psychological Cost of Learning to Kill in War and Society*. Boston, MA: Little, Brown and Co., 1996.

Guest, Iain. "Misplaced Charity Undermines Kosovo's Self-Reliance." The Overseas Development Council. Washington, DC: The Overseas Development Council, 2000. http://www.odc.org/commentary/vpfeboo.html.

Gurr, Ted Robert. *Minorities at Risk: A Global View of Ethnopolitical Conflicts*. Washington, DC: USIP Press, 1993.

Gutman, Roy. *A Witness to Genocide*. New York: Macmillan, 1993.

Haacke, Jurgen. "The Concept of Flexible Engagement and the Practice of Enhanced Interaction: Intramural Challenges to the 'ASEAN way'." *The Pacific Review* 12, no. 4 (1999): 581–612.

Haas, Ernst B. "Why Collaborate? Issue-Linkage and International Regimes." *World Politics* 32 (1980): 357–405.

Haas, Michael. *Genocide by Proxy: Cambodian Pawn on a Superpower Chessboard*. New York: Praeger, 1991.

Haas, Peter M. "Epistemic Communities and the Dynamics of International Environmental Co-operation." In Volker Rittberger, ed. *Regime Theory and International Relations*, 168–201. Oxford: Clarendon Press, 2002.

——. "Introduction: Epistemic Communities and International Policy Coordination." *International Organization* 46, no. 1 (Winter 1992): 1–36.

Habermas, Jurgen. *The Post-national Constellation*. Cambridge, MA: MIT Press, 2001.

Halpern, Shanna. *The United Nations Conference on Environment and Development: Process and Documentation*. Providence, RI: Academic Council on the United Nations System, 1993.

Hampson, Fen Osler and Maureen Molot, eds. *The Axworthy Legacy: Canada Among Nations 2001*. Toronto: Oxford University Press, 2001.

Harker, John. *Human Security in Sudan: The Report of a Canadian Assessment Mission*. Ottawa: Department of Foreign Affairs and International Trade, January 2000.

Harrell-Bond, Barbara. *Imposing Aid: Emergency Assistance to Refugees*. Oxford: Oxford University Press, 1986.

Hartmann, Florence. "Bosnia." In Roy Gutman and David Rieff, eds. *Crimes of War: What the Public Should Know*. New York: WW Norton and Co., 1999.

Hasenclever, Andreas, Peter Mayer and Volker Rittberger. "Interests, Power, Knowledge: The Study of International Regimes." *Mershon International Studies Review* 40, no. 2 (1996): 177–228.

——. *Theories of International Regimes*. Cambridge: Cambridge University Press, 1997.

Hayes, Bradd C. and Jeffrey I. Sands. "Non-traditional Military Responses to End Wars: Considerations for Policymakers." *Millennium: Journal of International Studies* 26, no. 3 (1997): 819–44.

Hegel, Georg Wilhelm Friedrich. *Phenomenology of Spirit: Selections*. Trans. and annot. Howard P. Kainz. University Park, Pa.: Pennsylvania State University Press, 1994.

Heiberg, Marianne. "Peacekeepers and Local Populations: Some Comments on UNIFIL." In Indar Jit Rikhye and Kjell Skjelsbaek, eds. *The United Nations and Peacekeeping: Results, Limitations and Prospects: The Lessons of 40 Years of Experience*, 147–69. London: Macmillan, 1990.

Heinbecker, Paul. "Human Security: The Hard Edge." *Canadian Military Journal* 1, no. 1 (2000): 11–16.

Held, David. *Democracy and the Global Order: From the Modern State to Cosmopolitan Governance*. Stanford CA: Stanford University Press, 1995.

Henze, Paul. "How Stable Is Siyaad Barre's Regime?" *Africa Report* 27, no. 2 (March–April 1992): 54–58.

Hirsch, John. *Sierra Leone: Diamonds and the Struggle for Democracy*. Boulder, CO: Lynne Reinner, 2001.

Hohe, Tanja. "Clash of Paradigms: International Administration and Local Political Legitimacy in East Timor." *Contemporary Southeast Asia* 24, no. 3 (December 2002): 569–90.

——. "Totem Polls: Indigenous Concepts and 'Free and Fair' Elections in East Timor." *International Peacekeeping* 9, no. 4 (Winter 2002): 69–89.

Hopf, Ted. "The Promise of Constructivism in International Relations Theory." *International Security* 23, no. 1 (Summer 1998): 177–200.

Howe, Herbert. "Lessons of Liberia: ECOMOG and Regional Peacekeeping." *International Security* 21, no. 3 (Winter 1996/1997): 145–76.

Hull, H.F. "Fighting stops for polio immunization." World Health Organisation. http://www.who.int/inf/polio.html.

Human Rights Watch 1992. "Thirst for Justice: A Decade of Impunity in Haiti." http://www.hrw.org.

Human Rights Watch World Report. http://www.hrw.org/wr2k1/americas/haiti.html.

Human Rights Watch. *Civilian Deaths in the NATO Air Campaign*. New York: Human Rights Watch, 8 February 2000.
——. *Haiti Human Rights Developments*. http://hrw.org/wr2k/americas-06.htm.
——. *World Report 1999: Haiti Human Rights Developments*. http://www.hrw.org/hrw/worldreport99/americas/haiti.html.
Human Rights Watch/Africa. "Liberia: Emerging from Destruction." *Human Rights Watch Publications* 9, no. 7 (November 1997). http://www.hrw.org/press97/nov/libngvt.htm.
——. "Waging War to Keep the Peace: The ECOMOG Intervention and Human Rights." *Human Rights Watch Publications* 5, no. 6 (June 1993). http://www.hrw.org/reports/1993/liberia/.
Hunt, Swanee and Cristina Posa. "Women Waging Peace." *Foreign Policy* (May–June 2001): 38–48.
Huntington, Samuel. *The Clash of Civilizations and the Remaking of World Order*. New York: Simon and Schuster, 1996.
Ignatieff, Michael. "Nation-Building Lite." *The New York Times Magazine*. July 28, 2002: 26–35.
——. "Unarmed Warriors." *New Yorker*, March 24, 1997.
——. *The Warrior's Honor*. New York: Henry Holt and Company, 1998.
"Innocents Abroad: Bill Clinton's Commitment to Asia." *Far Eastern Economic Review*, 2 May 1996.
International Action Network on Small Arms. "Founding Document." 11–15 May 1999. http://www.iansa.org/oldsite/mission/nespub/launch/hap.htm.
——. *The Small Arms Survey 2002: Counting the Human Cost*. Oxford: Oxford University Press, 2002. http://www.iansa-org/documents/2002/small_arms_survey.htm.
International Commission on Intervention and State Sovereignty. *The Responsibility to Protect: Report of the International Commission on Intervention and State Sovereignty*. Ottawa: International Development Research Centre, 2001.
——. *The Responsibility to Protect: Research, Bibliography, Background. Supplementary Volume to the Report of the International Commission on Intervention and State Sovereignty*. Ottawa: International Development Research Centre, 2001.
International Crisis Group. *Is Dayton Failing? Bosnia Four Years after the Peace Agreement*. ICG Balkans Report No. 880. Sarajevo, 28 October 1999.
——. *Starting from Scratch in Kosovo, The Honeymoon is Over*. ICG Balkans Report No 83. Pristina, 10 December 1999.
——. *The Loya Jirga: One Small Step Forward?* ICG Asia Briefing Paper. Kabul/Brussels. 16 May 2002. www.crisisweb.org.
——. *The Afghan Transitional Administration: Prospects and Perils*. ICG Asia Briefing Paper. Kabul/Brussels. 30 July 2002. www.crisisweb.org.
"International Federation of Red Cross and Red Crescent Societies." http://www.ifrc.org/; http://www.ifrc.org/pubs/sphere/Index.htm.
International Peace Academy. *Chairmen's Report of Joint OAU/IPA on the OAU and Conflict Management in Africa*. New York: International Peace Academy, 1993.
——. *Humanitarian Action: A Symposium Summary*. New York: International Peace Academy, 2000.
Iriye, Akire. *Cultural Internationalism and World Order*. Baltimore and London: The Johns Hopkins University Press, 2001.

Jackson, Stephen and Peter Walker. "Depolarising the 'Broadened' and 'Back-to-Basics' Relief Models." *Disasters* 23, no. 2 (1999): 93–113.

Jacobson, Ruth. *Gender and Democratization: the Mozambican Election of 1994*. Bradford, UK: University of Bradford, Department of Peace Studies, 1996. www.brad.ac.uk/research/ijas/rjijasel.htm.

Jan, Ameen. "Somalia: Building Sovereignty or Restoring Peace?" In Elizabeth M. Cousens and Chetan Kumar, eds. *Peacebuilding as Politics: Cultivating Peace in Fragile Societies*, 68–69. New York: International Peace Academy, 2001.

Jarquin, Edmundo and Fernando Carrillo. *Justice Delayed*. Washington, DC: Johns Hopkins Univ Press, 1998.

Jentleson, Bruce, ed. *Opportunities Missed, Opportunities Seized: Preventive Diplomacy in the Post-Cold War World*. Lanham, MD: Rowman and Littlefield, 1999.

Johnston, Alistair Iain. "The Myth of the ASEAN Way? Explaining the Evolution of the ASEAN Regional Forum." In Helga Haftendorn, Robert Keohane and Celeste Wallander, eds. *Imperfect Unions*, 287–324. New York: Oxford University Press, 1999.

Jones, Bruce. *Peacemaking in Rwanda: The Dynamics of Failure*. Boulder, CO: Lynne Reinner, 2001.

Jorgenson-Dahl, Arnfinn. *Regional Organisation and Order in Southeast Asia*. London: Macmillan, 1982.

Jusu-Sheriff, Yasmin. "Sierra Leonean Women and the Peace Process." *Accord* 1. http://www.c-r.org/accord/s-leone/accord9/women.shtml.

Kacowitz, Arie M. "Negative International Peace and Domestic Conflict, West Africa, 1957–96." *Journal of Modern African Studies* 35, no. 3 (1997): 367–85.

Karp, Aaron. "Laudable Failure: The UN Small Arms Conference." Paper presented at the International Studies Association-Southern Region, Salem, North Carolina, 12–14 October 2001.

Kartha, Tara. "Controlling the Black and Grey Markets in Small Arms in South Asia." In Jeffrey Boutwell and Michael T. Klare, eds. *Light Weapons and Civil Conflict: Controlling the Tools of Violence*, 49–61. Carnegie Commission on Preventing Deadly Conflict and the American Academy of Arts and Sciences. Lanham, MD: Rowman and Littlefield Publishers, 1999.

Katzenstein, Peter J., ed. *The Culture of National Security: Norms and Identity in World Politics*. New York: Columbia University Press, 1996.

Keating, Tom. "A Symposium on Peacebuilding in Post-Conflict Societies." University of Alberta. 10 March 2000.

Keck, Margaret E. and Kathryn Sikkink. *Activists Beyond Borders: Advocacy Networks in International Politics*. Ithaca, NY: Cornell University Press, 1998.

——. "Transnational Advocacy Networks in International and Regional Politics." *International Social Science Journal* 51, no. 1 (1999): 89–102.

Keen, David. "The Economic Functions of Violence in Civil Wars." *Adelphi Papers* 320 (1998): 1–96.

Kennedy, K.M. "The Relationship between the Military and Humanitarian Organizations in Operation Restore Hope." In W. Clarke and J. Herbst, eds. *Learning from Somalia: The Lessons of Armed Humanitarian Intervention*, 99–117. Oxford: Westview Press, 1997.

Keohane, Robert O. "The Demand for International Regimes." In Stephen Krasner, ed. *International Regimes*, 141–71. Ithaca: Cornell University Press, 1983.

Keohane, Robert O. and Joseph S. Nye. *Power and Interdependence*. Boston: Harper Collins, 1989.

Kilby, Christopher. "Aid and Sovereignty." *Social Theory and Practice* 25, no. 1 (1999): 79–93.

Knight, W. Andy. "Establishing Political Authority in Peace-Maintenance." *Global Governance* 4, no. 1 (January–March, 1998): 19–40.

——. "Soft Power and Moral Suasion in Establishing the International Criminal Court: Canadian Contributions." In Rosalind Irwin, ed. *Ethics and Security in Canadian Foreign Policy*, 113–37. Vancouver: University of British Columbia Press, 2001.

Knight, W. Andy and Annika Björkdahl. "Towards a Culture of Prevention: the Evolution and Influence of Norms." Paper presented at the 1999 ISA Annual Convention, Washington, DC, February 1999.

Krasner, Stephen D. "Sovereignty." *Foreign Policy* 122 (Jananuary–February 2001): 20–27.

——. *Sovereignty: Organized Hypocrisy*. Princeton: Princeton University Press, 1999.

——. "Structural Causes and Regime Consequences: Regimes as Intervening Variables." *International Organization* 36, no. 2 (Spring 1982): 185–206.

Kratochwil, Friedrich and John Gerard Ruggie. "International Organization: A State of the Art on an Art of the State." *International Organization* 40, no. 4 (Autumn 1986): 753–76.

Krause, Keith. "Description of the Annual *Small Arms Survey*." Programme d'Études Stratégiques et de Sécurité Internationale (PESI) and the Institute Universitaire de Hautes Études Internationales (IUHEI), Geneva, October 1999.

——. "Norm-Building in Security Spaces: The Emergence of the Light Weapons Problematic." http://ww2.mcgill.ca/regis/krause.pdf.

——. "Review Essay: Multilateral Diplomacy, Norm Building, and UN Conferences: The Case of Small Arms and Light Weapons." *Global Governance* 8, no. 2 (April–June 2002): 247–63.

Krauthammer, Charles. "The Short, Unhappy Life of Humanitarian War." *The National Interest* 57 (Fall 1999): 5–9.

Kumar, Chetan. *Building Peace in Haiti*. Boulder, CO: Lynne Reinner, 1998.

Kung, Hans. *A Global Ethic for Global Politics and Economics*. New York: Oxford University Press, 1998.

Kung, Hans and Karl-Josef Kuschel. A Global Ethic: *The Declaration of the Parliament of the World's Religions*. New York: Continuum, 1994.

Kuperman, Alan J. "Rwanda in Retrospect." *Foreign Affairs* 79, no. 1 (January/February 2000): 94–118.

Kurth, James. "Lessons from the Past Decade." *Orbis* 45, no. 4 (2001): 569–79.

La'o Hamutuk. "The World Bank in East Timor." *The La'o Hamutuk Bulletin* 1, no. 4 (31 December 2000). www.etan.org/lh/bulletin04.html.

Laitin, David and Said Samatar. *Somalia: Nation in Search of a State*. Boulder, CO: Westview Press, 1987.

Lange, David A. "The Role of the Political Advisor in Peacekeeping Operations." *Parameters* (Spring 1999): 92–109.

Langford, Tonya. "Things Fall Apart: State Failure and the Politics of Intervention." *International Studies Review* 1, no. 1 (Spring 1999): 59–83.

Langley, Norwood. "The National Reconstruction Program in Liberia." In *State Rebuilding after State Collapse: Security, Democracy and Development in Post-War Liberia.* Report of the Strategic Planning Workshop on Liberia. London: Centre for Democracy and Development, 19 June 1998. http://www.cdd.org.uk/.

Laqueur, Walter. "Terror's New Face: The Radicalization and Escalation of Modern Terrorism." In Charles W. Kegley Jr. and Eugene Wittkopf, eds. *The Global Agenda: Issues and Perspectives*, 82–88. 6th ed. New York: McGraw-Hill, 2001.

Large, Judith. "Disintegration conflicts and the restructuring of masculinity." *Gender and Development* 5, no. 2 (June 1997): 23–31.

Lastarria-Cornhiel, Susana. "Privatization of Land Rights and Access to Factor Markets: a Path to Gender Equity?" Paper presented at the Agrarian Reform and Rural Development: Taking Stock Conference sponsored by the Social Research Center, American University, Cairo, October 2001.

Latham, Andrew. "Theorizing the Landmine Campaign: Ethics, Global Cultural Scripts, and the Laws of War." In Rosalind Irwin, ed. *Ethics and Security in Canadian Foreign Policy*, 160–80. Vancouver: University of British Columbia Press, 2001.

Laurance, Edward J. *Light Weapons and Intrastate Conflict: Early Warning Factors and Preventative Action.* A Report to the Carnegie Commission on Preventing Deadly Conflict. July 1998.
http://www.iansaorg/oldsite/documents/research/res_archive/r9.htm.

Lawson, Bob. "Towards a New Multilateralism." *Behind the Headlines* 54, no. 4 (Summer 1997): 18–23.

Lederach, John Paul. *Building Peace: Sustainable Reconciliation in Divided Societies.* Tokyo: United Nations University Press, 1997.

Legum, Colin. *Pan-Africanism: A Short Political Guide.* New York: Praeger, 1962.

Leifer, Michael. *ASEAN and the Security of Southeast Asia.* London: Routledge: 1989.

Levy, Jack S. "Learning and Foreign Policy: Sweeping a Conceptual Minefield." *International Organization* 48, no. 2 (Spring 1994): 279–313.

Lewis, I.M. "The Nation, State, and Politics in Somalia." In David R. Smock and Kevumena Betsi, eds. *The Search for National Integration in East Africa*, 285–306. New York: Collier MacMillan Publishers, 1975.

"Liberia." *The Economist Intelligence Unit.* Fourth Quarter 1997, 1–10.

"Liberia." *The Economist Intelligence Unit.* Third Quarter 1998, 11.

"Liberia." *The Economist Intelligence Unit.* First Quarter 1999, 8.

"Liberia." *The Economist Intelligence Unit.* March 2001, 49.

"Liberia: Problematic Peacekeeping." Special issue, *Africa Confidential*, 2–3. 4 March 1994.

Liu, F.T. "Peacekeeping and humanitarian Assistance." In Leon Gordenker and Thomas G. Weiss, eds. *Soldiers, Peacekeepers and Disasters*, 33–51. London: Palgrave / MacMillan, 1992.

Lloyd, Carolyn. "Small Arms and Light Weapons: Post-Conference Prognosis." In David Mutimer, ed. *Canadian International Security Policy: Reflections for a New Era.* Selected Proceedings of the International Security Research Outreach Program-York Centre for International and Security Studies Symposium, York University, 2001.

Loescher, Gil. Beyond Charity: *International Cooperation and the Global Refugee Crisis.* Oxford: Oxford University Press, 1993.

Lonergan, Bernard. *Method in Theology.* New York: Herder and Herder, 1972.

Lord Robertson of Port Ellen, Secretary of State for Defence. "Kosovo: An Account of the Crisis." United Kingdom Ministry of Defence. http://www.kosovo.mod.uk/account/lessons.htm.

Lovenduski Joni and Azza Karam. "The Effect of Electoral Systems on Women's Representation." *International IDEA Women in Politics: Women in Parliament.* www.idea.int/women/parl/ch3c.htm.

Loyd, Anthony. *My War Gone By, I Miss it So.* London: Doubleday, 1999.

Lumpe, Lora. "U.S. Policy and the Export of Light Weapons." In Jeffrey Boutwell and Michael T. Klare, eds. *Light Weapons and Civil Conflict: Controlling the Tools of Violence,* 65–88. Carnegie Commission on Preventing Deadly Conflict and American Academy of Arts and Sciences. Lanham, MD: Rowman and Littlefield Publishers, 1999.

Lund, Michael S. *Preventing Violent Conflicts: A Strategy for Preventive Diplomacy.* Washington, DC: United States Institute for Peace, 1996.

Luttwak, Edward N. "Give War a Chance." *Foreign Affairs* 78, no. 4 (July–August 1999): 36–45.

——. "Kofi's Rule: Humanitarian Intervention and Neocolonialism." *The National Interest* 58 (Winter 1999/2000): 57–63.

Lyons, Gene M. and Michael Mastanduno, eds. Beyond Westphalia: *State Sovereignty and International Intervention.* Baltimore, MD: Johns Hopkins University Press, 1995.

Lyons, Terrence. "The Role of Postsettlement Elections." In Stephen John Stedman, Donald Rothschild and Elizabeth M. Cousens, eds. *Ending Civil Wars: The Success and Failure of Negotiated Settlements in Civil War,* 215–36. New York: International Peace Academy, September 2002.

——. *Voting For Peace: Post Conflict Elections in Liberia.* Washington DC: The Brookings Institution, 1998.

Maass, Peter. *Love Thy Neighbor: A Story of War.* New York: Vintage Books, 1996.

MacFarlane, S. Neil and Thomas G. Weiss. "Political Interest and Humanitarian Action." *Security Studies* 10, no. 1 (Autumn 2000): 112–42.

——. "Regional Organizations and Regional Security." *Security Studies* 2, no. 1 (Autumn 1992): 6–37.

MacKinlay, John and Jarat Chopra. "Second Generation Multinational Operations." *The Washington Quarterly* 15, no. 3 (Summer 1992): 113–31.

Mackinley, J. "The Role of Military Forces in a Humanitarian Crises." In Leon Gordenker and Thomas G. Weiss, eds. *Soldiers, Peacekeepers and Disasters,* 13–32. London: Macmillan, 1991.

Macrae, Joanna. "Purity or Political Engagement?: Issues in Food and Health Security Interventions in Complex Political Emergencies." *Journal of Humanitarian Assistance* (7 March 1998): 10. http://www.jha.ac/articles/a037.htm.

Macrae, Joanna and Anthony Zwi, eds. *Engaging with Violence: A Reassessment of Relief in Wartime in War and Hunger.* London: Zed Books, 1996.

——, eds. *War and Hunger: Rethinking International Responses to Complex Emergencies.* London: Zed Books, 1994.

Magyar, Karl and Earl Conteh-Morgan, eds. *Peacekeeping in Africa: ECOMOG in Liberia.* London: Macmillan / New York: St. Martin's Press, 1998.

Makinda, Samuel. *Seeking Peace from Chaos: Humanitarian Intervention in Somalia.* International Peace Academy Occasional Paper Series. Boulder, CO: Lynne Reinner, 1993.

Malan, Mark, Phenyo Rakate and Angela McIntyre. *Peacekeeping in Sierra Leone: UNAMSIL Hits the Home Straight*. Pretoria: Institute for Security Studies, 2002.

Mamdani, Mahmood. *When Victims Become Killers: Colonialism, Nativism, and the Genocide in Rwanda*. Princeton, NJ: Princeton University Press, 2001.

Mandelbaum, Michael. "A Perfect Failure, NATO's War Against Yugoslavia." *Foreign Affairs* 78, no. 5 (September–October 1999): 2–9.

Maren, Michael. *The Road to Hell*. New York: Free Press, 1997.

Markakis, John. *National and Class Conflict in the Horn of Africa*. New York: Cambridge University Press, 1987.

Martin, Guy. *Controlling Small Arms Proliferation and Reversing Cultures of Violence in Africa and the Indian Ocean*. Monograph 30. Pretoria, South Africa: Institute for Security Studies, 1998.

Martin, Linda, ed. *The ASEAN Success Story*. Honolulu: University of Hawaii Press, 1997.

Martin, Lisa L. and Liliana Botcheva. "Institutional Effects on State Behavior: Convergence and Divergence." *International Studies Quarterly* 45, no. 1 (2001): 1–26.

Mathews, Jessica. "Power Shift." *Foreign Affairs* 76, no. 1 (1997): 50–67.

Mayor, Federico. "A New Beginning." *UNESCO Courier* 48, no. 11 (1995): 6–8.

McPartland, Thomas. "Lonergan and Cosmopolis." The Lonergan Center, Santa Clara, University of California, 12th Eleanor Giuffre Lonergan Conference, March, 1994.

Médecins sans Frontières. *World in crisis: the Politics of Survival at the End of the Twentieth Century*. London: Routledge, 1997.

Melvern, Linda R. *A People Betrayed: The Role of the West in Rwanda's Genocide*. London: Zed Books, 2000.

Menkhaus, Ken. "International Peacebuilding and the Dynamics of Local and National Reconciliation in Somalia." In Walter Clarke and Jeffrey Herbst, eds. *Learning From Somalia: The Lessons of Armed Humanitarian Intervention*, 42–66. Boulder, CO: Westview Press, 1997.

MICIVIH. "Quarterly Report." *Human Rights Review*. October–December 1998.

——. "Quarterly Report." *Human Rights Review*. April–June 1999.

Middlemiss, Danford W. "Civil-Military Relations and Democracy." In Ann L. Griffiths, ed. *Building Peace and Democracy in Post-Conflict Societies*, 71–82. Halifax: Centre for Foreign Policy Studies, 1998.

Mills, Kurt. "Sovereignty Eclipsed? The Legitimacy of Humanitarian Access and Intervention." *Journal of Humanitarian Assistance* (1997). http://www.jha.ac/articles/a019.htm.

Minear, Larry and Thomas G. Weiss. *Humanitarian Action in Times of War*. Boulder, CO: Lynne Reinner, 1993.

Monteiro, Natalina Teixeira. "The War of Liberation/Frelimo. Mozambique: Women in the Informal Sector." Unpublished Paper presented at Northern Arizona University, 2001. http://www.dana.ucc.nau.edu/~nm5/Independence.html.

Moore, Jonathan, ed. *Hard Choices: Moral Dilemmas in Humanitarian Intervention*. Lanham, MD: Rowman and Littlefield, 1998.

Moore, Scott. "Today It's Gold, Not Purple." *Joint Force Quarterly* (Autumn/Winter 1998–1999): 100–106.

Morphet, Sally. "Current International Civil Administration: The Need for Political Legitimacy." *International Peacekeeping* 9, no. 2 (Summer 2002): 140–63.

Mortimer, Robert. "ECOMOG, Liberia and Regional Security in West Africa." In Edmond Keller and Donald Rothchild, eds. *Africa in the New International Order: Rethinking State Sovereignty*, 149–83. Boulder, CO: Lynne Reinner, 1996.

——. "From ECOMOG to ECOMOG II: Intervention in Sierra Leone." In John W. Harbeson and Donald Rothchild, eds. Africa in *World Politics: The African State System in Flux*, 188–204. 3rd ed. Colorado and Oxford: Westview Press, 2000.

Mousavizadeh, Nader, ed. *The Black Book of Bosnia: The Consequences of Appeasement*. New York: Basic Books, 1996.

Mueller, John. "The Obsolescence of Major War." In Charles W. Kegley, Jr. and Eugene Wittkopf, eds. *The Global Agenda: Issues and Perspectives*, 57–66. 6th ed. New York: McGraw-Hill, 2001.

Muggah, Robert and Eric Berman. *Humanitarianism Under Threat: The Humanitarian Impacts of Small Arms and Light Weapons*. Special Report, Study Commissioned by the Reference Group on Small Arms of the United Nations Inter-Agency Standing Committee. Geneva: Small Arms Survey, 2001.

"Multidisciplinary Peacebuilding: Lessons from Recent Experience." http://www.un.org/Depts/dpko/lessons/PBPUHandbook.htm.

Murden, Simon. "Cultural Conflict in International Relations." In John Baylis and Steve Smith, eds. *The Globalization of World Politics*. 2nd ed. New York: Oxford University Press, 2001.

Naidu, M.V. War, *Security, Peace*. Brandon, Manitoba: M.I.T.A. Press, 1996.

Narine, Shaun. "ASEAN in the Aftermath: The Consequences of the East Asian Economic Crisis." *Global Governance* 8, no. 2 (2002): 179–94.

——. "ASEAN and the ARF: The Limits of the 'ASEAN Way'." *Asian Survey* 37, no. 10 (October 1997): 961–79.

——. "ASEAN and the Management of Regional Security." *Pacific Affairs* 71, no. 2 (Summer 1998): 195–214.

——. "ASEAN into the Twenty-first Century: Problems and Prospects." *The Pacific Review* 12, no. 3 (Summer 1999): 357–80.

——. "Institutional Theory and Southeast Asia: the Case of ASEAN." *World Affairs* 161, no. 1 (Summer 1998): 33–48.

Natsios, Andrew S. "An NGO Perspective." In William Zartman and Lewis Rasmussen, eds. *Peacemaking in International Conflict: Methods and Techniques*, 81–96. Washington, DC: United States Institute of Peace, 1997.

——. "NGOs and the UN System in Complex Emergencies: Conflict or Cooperation?" *Third World Quarterly* 16, no. 3 (1995): 405–21.

——. "NGOs and the UN System in Complex Humanitarian Emergencies: Conflict or Cooperation?" *Third World Quarterly* 16, no. 3 (1995): 405–19.

——. "Nongovernmental Organizations." In Andrew S. Natsios. *U.S. Foreign Policy and the Four Horsemen of the Apocalypse: Humanitarian Relief in Complex Emergencies*, 56–75. Westport, Conn: Praeger, 1997.

——. *U.S. Foreign Policy and the Four Horsemen of the Apocalypse: Humanitarian Relief in Complex Emergencies*. Westport, CT: Praeger, 1997.

Nelson, Daniel N. "Damage Control." *Bulletin of the Atomic Scientists* 55, no. 1 (January–February 1999). http://ploughshares.ca/content/MONITOR/mons98f.html.
Nischalke, Tobias Ingo. "Insights from ASEAN's Foreign Policy Cooperation: The 'ASEAN Way', a Real Spirit or a Phantom?" *Contemporary Southeast Asia* 22, no. 1 (April 2000): 89–112.
"No Exit without Strategy: Security Council Decision-making and the Closure or Transition of United Nations Peacekeeping Operations." Report of the Secretary-General, UN Doc. S/2001/394 of 20 April 2001.
North Atlantic Treaty Organization. "KFOR Objectives." http://www.nato.int/kfor/kfor/objectives.htm.
——. "KFOR Web Page." http://www.kforonline.com.
Nowrojee, Binaifir. "Joining Forces: UN and Regional Peacekeeping, Lessons from Liberia." *Harvard Human Rights Journal* 18 (Spring 1995): 128–52.
Nye, Joseph. "Redefining the National Interest." *Foreign Affairs* 78, no. 4 (July-August 1999): 22–36.
O'Brien, William V. *The Conduct of Just and Limited War*. New York: Praeger, 1991.
Oakley, Robert B., Michael Dziedzic and Eliot M. Goldberg, eds. *Policing the New World Disorder*. Washington, DC: National Defence University Press, 1998.
Obasanjo, Olusegun. *Not My Will*. Ibadan: Ibadan University Press, 1990.
OECD-DAC. *Conflict, Peace and Development Co-operation on the Threshold of the 21st Century*. Development Co-operation Guideline Series. Paris: Organization for Economic Co-operation and Development, 1998.
Olonisakin, Funmi. "UN Co-operation with Regional Organizations in Peacekeeping: the Experience of ECOMOG and UNOMIL in Liberia." *International Peacekeeping* 3, no. 3 (Autumn 1996): 33–51.
Omach, Paul. "The African Crisis Response Initiative: Domestic Politics and Convergence of National Interests." *African Affairs* 99, no. 394 (2000): 73–95.
Orbinski, James. University of Alberta Visiting Lectureship in Human Rights. University of Alberta, Edmonton, Tuesday, March 6, 2001.
Organization of African Unity. *Declaration of the Assembly of Heads of State and Government on the Establishment Within the OAU of a Mechanism for Conflict Prevention, Management and Resolution*. AHG/DECL.3 (29), 1993.
——. *Introductory Note to the Report of the Secretary-General*. CM/1851 (LX1). 23–27 January 1995.
——. *Resolving Conflicts in Africa: Implementation Options*. Addis Ababa: OAU Information Publication, 1993.
Organization for Economic Co-operation and Development. *Helping Prevent Conflict: Orientations for External Partners. Supplement to the DAC Guidelines on Conflict, Peace and Development Co-operation on the Threshold of the 21st Century*. Paris: OECD, 2001. http://www.oecd.org/dac/htm/g-gom.htm.
Orr, Robert. "Governing When Chaos Rules: Enhancing Governance and Participation." *The Washington Quarterly* 25, no. 4 (Autumn 2002): 139–52.
Ospina, Sofi and Tanja Hohe. *Traditional Power Structures and the Community Empowerment Project—Final Report*. Dili: World Bank/UNTAET, 2001.

Padelford, N.J. "The Organization of African Unity." *African Quarterly* 33, no. 1 (1993): 78–87.
Paris, Roland. "Peacebuilding and the Limits of Liberal Internationalism." *International Security* 22, no. 2 (Fall 1997): 54–90.
Patman, Robert. *The Soviet Union in the Horn of Africa: The Diplomacy of Intervention and Disengagement*. Cambridge: Cambridge University Press, 1990.
Pearson, Frederic S. *The Global Spread of Arms: Political Economy of International Security*. Boulder, CO: Westview Press, 1994.
Peck, Connie. *Sustainable Peace: The Role of the UN and Regional Organizations in Preventing Conflict*. Lanham, MD: Rowman and Littlefield, 1998.
Plunkett, Mark, "Reestablishing Law and Order in Peace-Maintenance." *Global Governance* 4, no. 1 (January–March 1998): 61–79.
Powell, Mike and David Seddon. "NGOs and the Development Industry." *Review of African Political Economy* 71 (1997): 3–10.
Power, Samantha. *A Problem from Hell: America and the Age of Genocide*. New York, NY: Basic Books, 2002.
Prendergast, John. *Crisis Response: Humanitarian Band-Aids in Sudan and Somalia*. London: Pluto Press, 1997.
——. *Frontline Diplomacy: Humanitarian Aid and Conflict in Africa*. Boulder, CO: Lynne Reinner, 1996.
President Mengistu Haile Mariam, Secretary-General of the Workers Party of Ethiopia. Address to the National Shengo. *FBIS*, April 26, 1991.
Prunier, Gérard. *The Rwanda Crisis: History of a Genocide*. New York: Columbia University Press, 1997.
Pugh, Michael. *The Challenge of Peacebuilding: The Disaster Relief Model*. Plymouth International Papers No. 3. Halifax: Centre for Foreign Policy Studies, Dalhousie University / Plymouth: University of Plymouth, 1995.
——. "Civil-Military Relations in the Kosovo Crisis: An Emerging Hegemony?" *Security Dialogue* 31, no. 2 (2000): 229–42.
Putnam, Robert D. "Bowling Alone: America's Declining Social Capital." *Journal of Democracy* 6, no. 1 (1995): 65–78.
Ramcharan, Robin. "ASEAN and Non-interference: A Principle Maintained." *Contemporary Southeast Asia* 22, no. 1 (April 2000): 74–76.
Ramsbotham, Oliver and Tom Woodhouse. *Humanitarian Intervention in Contemporary Conflict: a Reconceptualization*. Cambridge, UK: Polity Press, 1996.
Regan, Patrick. *Civil Wars and Foreign Powers: Outside Intervention in Intrastate Conflict*. Ann Arbor: Michigan University Press, 2000.
Regan, Richard J. *Just War: Principles and Cases*. Washington, DC: Catholic University Press of America, 1996.
Renner, Michael. "An Epidemic of Guns." *World Watch Institute* (July–August 1998): 22–29.
——. *Small Arms, Big Impact: The Next Challenge of Disarmament*. Worldwatch Paper 137. Washington, DC: WorldWatch Institute, October 1997.
Reno, William. "The Business of War in Liberia." *Current History* 96, no. 601 (May 1996): 211–15.
——. *Warlord Politics and African States*. Boulder, CO: Lynne Reinner, 1998.
Reychler, Luc and Thanian Paffenholz. *Peacebuilding: A Field Guide*. Boulder, CO: Lynne Reinner, 2000.

Richards, Paul. *Fighting for the Rainforest: War, Youth and Resources in Sierra Leone.* Oxford: James Currey / New Hampshire: Heineman, 1996.
——. "Rebellion in Liberia and Sierra Leone: A Crisis of Youth?" In Oliver Furley, ed. *Conflict in Africa*, 134–70. New York and London: Tauris Academic Studies, 1995.
Richmond, Oliver P. "A Genealogy of Peacemaking: The Creation and Re-creation of Order." *Alternatives* 26, no. 3 (July–September 2001): 317–48.
Rieff, David. "A New Age of Liberal Imperialism." *World Policy Journal* 16, no. 2 (Summer 1999): 1–11.
——. "The Humanitarian Trap." *World Policy Journal* (1995–1996): 1–11.
——. *Slaughterhouse, Bosnia and the Failure of the West.* New York: Touchstone, 1996.
Rigby, Andrew. "Humanitarian Assistance and Conflict Management: the View from the NGO Sector." *International Affairs* 77, no. 4 (2001): 957–66.
Robinson, D., T. Hewitt and J. Harriss, eds. *Managing Development: Understanding Inter-organizational Relationships*. London: Sage, 2000.
Rollins, J.W. "Civil-military Cooperation (CIMIC) in Crisis Response Operations: the Implications for NATO." *International Peacekeeping* 8, no. 1 (2001): 122.
Ronayne, Peter. *Never Again? The United States and the Prevention and Punishment of Genocide since the Holocaust.* Lanham, MD: Rowman and Littlefield Publishers, Inc., 2001.
Rosenau, James N. *Along the Domestic-Foreign Frontier.* Cambridge, England: Cambridge University Press, 1997.
——. *Turbulence in World Politics: A Theory of Change and Continuity.* Princeton: Princeton University Press, 1990.
——. *The United Nations in a Turbulent World.* Boulder, CO: Lynne Reinner, 1992.
Rubinstein, Robert A. "Cross-Cultural Considerations in Complex Peace Operations." *Negotiation Journal* 19, no. 1 (January 2003): 29–49.
Ruggie, John. *Constructing the World Polity.* London: Routledge, 1998.
Ruland, Jurgen. "ASEAN and the Asian Crisis: Theoretical Implications and Practical Consequences for Southeast Asian Regionalism." *The Pacific Review* 13, no. 3 (2000): 421–51.
Rupesinghe, Kumar. *Civil Wars, Civil Peace: An Introduction to Conflict Resolution.* London: Pluto Press, 1998.
Rupesinghe, Kumar and Michiko Kuroda, eds. *Early Warning and Conflict Resolution.* New York: St. Martin's Press, 1992.
Russett, Bruce, Harvey W. Starr and David Kinsella. *World Politics: The Menu for Choice.* 6th ed. Boston: Bedford / St. Martin's Press, 2000.
Rutherford, Ken. "The Hague and Ottawa Conventions: A Model for Future Weapon Ban Regimes?" *The Nonproliferation Review* 6, no. 3 (Spring–Summer 1999): 36–49.
Ryle, John. "Sudan: The Perils of Aid." *New York Review of Books*, 11 June, 1998.
Salim, Ahmed Salim. "The Architecture for Peace and Security in Africa." http://www.uneca.org/eca_resources/speeches/2002_speeches/030603salim.htm.
——. "An Introduction to IGADD." In Lionel Cliffe, Abdel Ghaffar, M. Ahmed, J Markakis, and Matin R. Doornbos, eds. *Beyond Conflict in the Horn: Prospects for Peace, Recovery and Development in Ethiopia, Somalia and Sudan*, 1–5. New Jersey: The Red Sea Press, 1992.
——. "The OAU and the Future." In Tajudeen Abdul-Raheem, ed. *Pan-Africanism: Politics, Economy and Social Change*, 229–36. London: Pluto Press, 1996.

——. "The OAU Role in Conflict Management." In Olara Otunu and Michael W. Doyle, eds. *Peacemaking and Peacekeeping for the New Century*, 47–49. New York: Rowman and Littlefield Publishers, 1998.

——. "Searching Solutions to Internal Conflicts: The Role of the OAU." Address to the Consultation of the International Peace Academy on Internal Conflicts in Africa: In Search of Response, Arusha, 1992.

Sawyer, Amos. "Foundations for Reconstruction in Liberia: Challenges and Responses." In *State Rebuilding after State Collapse: Security, Democracy and Development in Post-War Liberia*, 64–71. Report of the Strategic Planning Workshop on Liberia. London: Centre for Democracy and Development, 19 June 1998.

Scholte, Jan Aart. "Global Civil Society: Changing the World?" Centre for the Study of Globalisation and Regionalisation (CSGR), University of Warwick. Working Paper 31, May 1999, 2. http://www.warwick.ac.uk/fac/soc/CSGR/wpapers/wp3199.PDF.

Schreiber, Shane. "Creating Compliance: Some Lessons in International Cooperation in a Peace Support Operation." *Canadian Military Journal* 1, no. 1 (2001–2002): 11–22.

Scott, James. *Seeing Like a State: How Certain Schemes to Improve the Human Condition have Failed*. New Haven: Yale University Press, 1998.

Shaw, Tim and Clement E. Adibe. "Africa and Global Issues in the Twenty-First Century." *International Journal* 51, no. 1 (Winter 1995–6): 1–26.

Shils, Edward. *Center and Periphery*. Chicago: University of Chicago Press, 1975.

Shiras, Peter. "Humanitarian Emergencies and the Roles of NGOs." In Jim Whitman and David Pocock, eds. *After Rwanda: The Coordination of United Nations Humanitarian Assistance*, 106–17. London: Macmillan Press, 1996.

Sikkink, Kathryn. "Principled-Issue Networks, Human Rights, and Sovereignty in Latin America." *International Organization* 47, no. 3 (1993): 411–42.

Simmel, George. *The Conflict of Modern Culture and Other Essays*. Trans. K. Peter Etzkorn. New York: Teachers College Press, 1968.

Simons, Anna. *Networks of Dissolution: Somalia Undone*. Boulder, CO: Westview Press, 1995.

Simons, Anna and P.H. Liotta. "Thicker than Water? Kin, Religion and Conflict in the Balkans." *Parameters* 28, no. 4 (Winter 1998–99): 11–28.

Slim, Hugo. "The Continuing Metamorphosis of the Humanitarian Practitioner: Some New Colours for an Endangered Chameleon." *Disasters* 19, no. 2 (June 1995): 110–26.

——. "International Humanitarianism's Engagement with Civil War in the 1990s: A Glance at Evolving Practice and Theory." *Journal of Humanitarian Assistance* (19 December 1997). http://www.jha.ac/articles/a033.htm.

——. "Military Humanitarianism and the New Peacekeeping: An Agenda for Peace?" *Journal of Humanitarian Assistance* (22 September 1995). http://www.jha.ac/articles/a003.htm.

——. "The Stretcher and the Drum: Civil-Military Relations in Peace Support Operations." *International Peacekeeping* 3, no. 2 (1996): 123–40.

——. "Violence and humanitarianism: moral paradox and the protection of civilians." *Security Dialogue* 32, no. 3 (2001): 325–39.

Small Arms Survey: Profiling the Problem. Oxford: Oxford University Press, 2001.

Smillie, Ian. "NGOs and Development Assistance: A Change in Mind-Set?" In Thomas G. Weiss, ed. *Beyond UN Subcontracting: Task-Sharing with Regional Organizations and Service-Providing NGOs*, 184–202. London: Macmillan Press, 1998.

Smillie, Ian, Lansana Gberie and Ralph Hazleton. *The Heart of the Matter. Sierra Leone: Diamonds and Human Security.* Ottawa: Partnership Africa Canada, January 2000.

Smith, Donald and John Hay. "Canada and the Crisis in Eastern Zaire." In Chester Crocker, Fen Hampson and Pamela Aall, eds. *Herding Cats*, 85–107. Washington: United States Institute for Peace, 1999.

Smith, Jackie, Charles Chatfield and Ron Pagnucco. *Transnational Social Movements and Global Politics: Solidarity Beyond the State*. Syracuse: Syracuse University Press, 1997.

Smock, David R. "Humanitarian Assistance and Conflict in Africa." *Journal of Humanitarian Assistance* (July 1997). http://www.jha.ac/articles/a014.htm.

Snidal, Duncan. "The Limits of Hegemonic Stability." *International Organization* 39, no. 4 (Autumn 1985): 579–615.

Sollis, Peter. "Partners in Development? The State, NGOs, and the UN in Central America." In Thomas G. Weiss and Leon Gordenker, eds. *NGOs, the UN, and Global Governance*, 189–206. Boulder, CO: Lynne Reinner, 1996.

Somali Government. Northern Frontier District (NFD): *Problem Planted By Britain Between Kenya and the Somali Republic*. Mogadishu: Ministry of Information, 1963.

——. *The Somali Peninsula: A New Light on Imperial Motives*. St. Albans: The Information Services of the Somali Government, 1962.

"Somalia/Ethiopia Hostilities." *AfricaCurrents* 5 (1979): 137.

Somavia, Ambassador Juan, Permanent Representative of Chile to the UN. "The Humanitarian Responsibilities of the United Nations Security Council." Gilbert Murray Memorial Lecture, Oxford, England, 26 June, 1996.

Spraakman, Gary. "Values for peace." In Paris Arnopoulos, ed. *Prospects for Peace*, 44–45. Montreal: Gamma Institute Press, 1986.

Starr, Harvey, ed. *The Understanding and Management of Global Violence:Nnew Approaches to Theory and Research on Protracted Conflict.* New York: St. Martin's Press, 1999.

Statistics Canada. "Crime Statistics." http://www.statcan.ca/Daily/English/020717/d020717b.htm.

Stoessinger, John. *Why Nations Go to War.* New York: Wadsworth, 2001.

Stohl, Rachel. "Post-Sept.11 Arms Sales and Military Aid Demonstrate Dangerous Trend." http://www.cdi.org/terrorism/military-transfers-pr.cfm.

Stotzky, Irwin P. *Transition to Democracy in Latin America and the Role of the Judiciary.* Boulder, CO: Westview Press, 1993.

Stubbs, Paul. "Croatia: NGO Development, Globalism and Conflict." In J. Bennett, ed. *NGOs and Governments: A Review of Current Practice for Southern and Eastern NGOs*, 77–87. Oxford; INTRAC, 1997.

Suh, Sangwoh. "Unease over East Timor." *Asiaweek* 25, no. 41 (1999). http://www.asiaweek.com/asiaweek/magazine/99/1015/easttimor.html.

Suhrke, Astri, Arve Ofstad and Are Knudsen. *A Decade of Peacebuilding: Lessons Learned for Afghanistan*. Oslo: Chr. Michelsen Institute, April 2002.

Sullivan, Michael P. *Power in Contemporary International Relations*. Columbia, SC: University of South Carolina Press, 1990.

Swedberg, Richard. "Socioeconomics and the New 'Battle of Methods': Toward a Paradigm Shift?" *Journal of Behavioral Economics* 19, no. 2 (1990): 381–92.

Talbot, Strobe. "Globalization and Diplomacy: A Practitioner's Perspective." *Foreign Policy* 108 (Fall 1997): 69-85.

Tangermann, R.H., H.F. Hull, H. Jafari, B. Nkowane, H. Everts, and R.B. Aylward. "Eradication of Poliomyelitis in Countries Affected by Conflict." *Bulletin of the World Health Organization* 78, no. 3 (2000): 330–38. http://www.who.int/bulletin/.

Tanner, Victor. "Liberia: Railroading Peace." *Review of African Political Economy* 25, no. 75 (March 1998): 133–47.

Taylor, John. *East Timor: The Price of Freedom.* New York: Zed Books, 1999.

Tessitore, John and Susan Woolfson, eds. *A Global Agenda: Issues Before the 55th General Assembly.* Lanham, MD: Rowman and Littlefield, 2000.

Thayer, Carlyle. "ASEAN and Indochina: the Dialogue." In Alison Broinowski, ed. *ASEAN into the 1990s*, 138–61. London: Macmillan, 1990.

The Commonwealth Secretariat *Gender Management System Handbook.* June 1999. http://www.thecommonwealth.org/gender.

The Proceedings of the Summit of Heads of State and Government of IGAD Member States for the Launching of Revitalized IGAD. Djibouti, 25–26 November 1996. http://www.iss.co.za/AF/RegOrg/unity_to_union/pdfs/igad/5thIGADSUMMIT.pdf.

Thompson, Vincent Bakpetu. *Africa and Unity: The Evolution of Pan-Africanism.* New York: Humanities Press, 1969.

Tilahun, Wondimneh. *Egypt's Imperial Aspirations Over Lake Tana and the Blue Nile.* Addis Ababa: United Printers Ltd, 1979.

Tilman, Robert O. *Southeast Asia and the Enemy Beyond.* Boulder, CO: Westview Press, 1987.

"Tlatelolco Treaty Marks 30th Anniversary." *IAEA Newsbriefs* 12, no. 1 (January–February 1997). http://www.iaea.or.at/worldatom/Press/Newsbriefs/1997/newsv12n1.html#A11.1.

Toure, Augustine. *The Role of Civil Society in National Reconciliation and Peacebuilding in Liberia.* New York: International Peace Academy, 2002.

Traube, Elizabeth G. *Cosmology and Social Life: Ritual Exchange among the Mambai of East Timor.* Chicago: University of Chicago Press, 1986.

Tripodi, Paulo. "Peacekeeping: Let the Conscripts do the Job." *Security Dialogue* 32, no. 2 (2001): 155–68.

Turay, Thomas Mark. "Civil Society and Peacebuilding: The Role of the Inter-Religious Council of Sierra Leone." Special Issue, *Accord* 9 (2000). http://www.c-r.org/accord/s-leone/accord9/society.shtml.

Tvedt, Terje. *Angels of Mercy or Development Diplomats?* NGOs and Foreign Aid. Trenton, NJ: Africa World Press, 1998.

Tylor, Edward. *Primitive Culture.* 1870. New York: Harper, 1958.

United Nations. *Consolidated Inter-Agency Appeal for Somalia 2002.* UN Office for the Coordination of Humanitarian Affairs, 26 November 2001. www.reliefweb.int.

——. *Gender, Women and Human Development: an Agenda for the Future.* United Nations Development Program: National Human Development Report on Mozambique, 2002.

——. *Report of the Independent Inquiry into the Actions of the United Nations During the 1994 Genocide in Rwanda.* New York, 15 December 1999. Section III-2.

——. *Report of the Panel on United Nations Peace Operations.* A/55/305-S/2000/809, 21 August 2000.

——. *Report of the Secretary-General on Sierra Leone.* S/1997/80, 26 January 1997.

——. *Report of the Secretary-General on the work of the Organization to the 55th General Assembly Session, Prevention of Armed Conflict.* A/55/985-S/2001/574, 7 June 2001.
——. *Seventeenth Progress Report of the Secretary-General on the United Nations Observer Mission in Liberia.* S/1996/362, 21 May 1996.
——. *Somalia: IRIN Guide to the Somali National Peace Conference.* UN Office for the Coordination of Humanitarian Affairs: Integrated Regional Information Networks, 2000. http://www.reliefweb.int/IRIN/cea/coutnrystories/somalia/20000630a.phtml.
——. *Third Report of the Secretary-General on the United Nations Mission in Sierra Leone.* S/2000/186, 7 March 2000.
——. Third Session of the Preparatory Committee for the UN 2001 Conference on the Illicit Trade in Small Arms and Light Weapons, 19–30 March 2001. A/conf.192/PC/L.4. Revised Draft Programme of Action to Prevent Combat and Eradicate the Illicit Trade in Small Arms and Light Weapons in all its Aspects.
——. *Thirteenth Report of the Secretary-General on the United Nations Mission in Sierra Leone.* S/2002/267, 14 March 2002.
——. *United Nations Study on Disarmament and Non-proliferation Education.* 2002. http://disarmament.un.org/education/study.html.
——. *War-torn Society Project Report: Women and Post-Conflict Reconstruction: Issues and Sources.* War-torn Society Project Report. Geneva: UN Research Institute for Social Development, 1 June 1998. http://www.unrisd.org/wsp/op3/op3-03.htm.
United Nations Development fund for Women. *Somalia between Peace and War.* Nairobi: UNIFEM, 1998.
——. *A Climate of Fear: Gender in the 1993 Cambodian General Elections.* Bangkok: UNIFEM, October 2000.
——. *A New Gender Sensitive Constitution for Rwanda.* Kigali: UNIFEM, June 2001.
——. *Draft Proposal: Strengthening Gender Justice in Post-Conflict Peace Building.* New York: UNIFEM, July 2001.
United Nations Development Programme. "Decentralized Governance Programme: Strengthening Capacity for People-Centred Development." Management Development and Governance Division, September 1997. www.magnet.undp.org/Docs/dec/DECEN923/Decenpro.htm.
——. *Development Dimensions of Conflict Prevention and Peace Building,* An Independent Study Prepared by Bernard Wood for the Emergency Response Division. New York: United Nations Development Programme, 2001.
——. *Governance Foundations for Post-Conflict Situations: UNDP's Experience.* New York: UNDP, January 2000.
——. *Human Development Report 2002: Deepening Democracy in a Fragmented World.* New York: Oxford University Press, 2002. http://hdr.undp.org/reports/global/2002/en/pdf/complete.pdf.
United Nations Division for the Advancement of Women. "Beijing Declaration and Platform for Action." Strategic Objective E.1. http://www.un.org/womenwatch/daw/beijing/platform.
United Nations Economic and Social Council. "Strengthening the Coordination of Humanitarian and Disaster Relief Assistance of the United Nations, Including Special Economic Assistance." A/50/50/Rev.1.E/1995/100. June 1995.
——. Resolution E.1997.L.10. 17 July 1997.

United Nations High Commissioner for Refugees. "Statistics on Refugees and the Internally Displaced." http://www.unhcr.ch/world/world.htm.

United Nations Security Council. Annual Summit Declaration. New York: UNSC, 31 January 1993.

——. *First Report on the United Nations Mission in Sierra Leone* (UNAMSIL). S/1999/1223, 6 December 1999.

——. *Report of the Secretary-General on the United Nations Interim Administration in Kosovo.* S/2000/177. New York, 3 March 2000.

——. *Report of the Panel of Experts on Violations of Security Council Sanctions Against UNITA.* S/2000/203. New York, 10 March 2000.

——. *Fourth Report on the United Nations Mission in Sierra Leone.* S/2000/455, 19 May 2000.

——. *Fifth Report on the United Nations Mission in Sierra Leone.* S/2000/751, 31 July 2000.

——. Resolution #912. 21 April 1994.

——. Resolution #929. 22 June 1994.

——. Resolution #1291. 24 February 2000.

——. Resolution #1325. 31 October 2000. http://www.un.org/events/res_1325e.pdf.

——. *Twenty-second Progress Report of the Secretary-General on the United Nations Observer Mission in Liberia.* S/1997/237, 19 March 1997.

United States Department of State. "Access Agreement with Somalia." *State Bulletin* 80, no. 2043 (1980): 19.

United States Government. The Mutual Security Act of 1951. 65 Stat. 377. 10 October 1951.

United States House of Senate. *US Policy and Request for Sale of Arms to Ethiopia.* Hearings Before the Subcommittee on International Political and Military Affairs, 94th Congress, 1st Session (Washington, 1975).

——. *US Security Agreements and Commitments Abroad.* Senate Foreign Relations Committee, Subcommittee on US Security Agreements and Commitments Abroad, 2, Part 8, 1935–37 (1971).

UNMIK. Kosovo Consolidated Budget for 2000. www.seerecon.org/Kosovo/UNMIK/Budget2001/index.html.

Uphoff, Norman. "Monitoring and Evaluating Popular Participation in World Bank-Assisted Projects." In Bhuvan Bhatnagar and Aubrey C. Williams, eds. *Participatory Development and the World Bank: Potential Directions for Change,* 135–53. World Bank Discussion Paper 183. Washington: World Bank, 1992.

——. *Learning from Gal Oya: Possibilities for Participatory Development and Post-Newtonian Social Science.* Ithaca: Cornell University Press, 1992.

Uvin, Peter. *Aiding Violence: The Development Enterprise in Rwanda.* West Hartford, CT: Kumarian Press, 1998.

Uvin, Peter and Charles Morenko. "Western and Local Approaches to Justice in Rwanda." *Global Governance* 9, no. 2 (2003): 219–31.

Valente, F., M. Molten, F. Balbina, R. Van de Weerdt, C. Chezzi, P. Eriki, J. Van-Dúnnen, and J.M. Okwo Bele. "Massive Outbreak of Poliomyelitis Caused by Type-3 Wild Polio Virus in Angola in 1999." *Bulletin of the World Health Organization* 78, no. 3 (2000): 339–46. http://www.who.int/bulletin/.

Van Brabant, K. "Understanding, Promoting and Evaluating Coordination: an Outline Framework." In D.S. Gordon and F.H. Toase, eds. *Aspects of Peacekeeping,* 141–62. London: Frank Cass, 2001.

van der Merwe, Deirdre and Mark Malan. "Codes of Conduct and Children in Armed Conflicts." In Andrew Cooper, John English and Ramesh Thakur, eds. *Enhancing Global Governance: Towards a New Diplomacy*, 229–47. Tokyo: United Nations University, 2002.

Van Walraven, Klaas. *The Netherlands and Liberia: Dutch Policies and Interventions with Respect to the Liberian Civil War.* The Hague: Netherlands Institute of International Relations, 1999.

——. *The Pretence of Peace-keeping: ECOMOG, West Africa and Liberia (1990–1998).* The Hague: Netherlands Institute of International Relations, 1999.

Vance, Cyrus and Herbert Okun. "Creating Healthy Alliances: Leadership and Coordination among NGOs, Governments, and the United Nations in Times of Emergency and Conflict." In Kevin M. Cahill, ed. *Preventive Diplomacy—Stopping Wars Before They Start.* New York: Basic Books, 1996.

Väyrynen, Raimo. "More Questions Than Answers: Dilemmas of Humanitarian Action." *Peace and Change* 24, no. 2 (1999): 172–97.

——. *New Directions in Conflict Theory: Conflict Resolution and Conflict Transformation.* Newbury Park, CA: Sage Publications, 1991.

Velkey, Richard L. *Being after Rousseau: Philosophy and Culture in Question.* Chicago: University of Chicago Press, 2002.

Vogt, Margaret, ed. *The Liberian Crisis and ECOMOG: A Bold Attempt at Regional Peacekeeping.* Lagos: Gabumo Press, 1992.

Von Bernuth, R. "The Voluntary Agency Response and the Challenge of Coordination." In "The Rwandan Emergency: Causes, Responses, Solutions." Special issue, *Journal of Refugee Studies* 9, no. 3 (1996): 281–90.

Von Hippel, Karin. "Democracy by Force: A Renewed Commitment to Nation-Building." *Washington Quarterly* 23, no. 1 (2000): 95–113.

Wah, Chin Kin. "Regional Perceptions of China and Japan." In Chandran Jeshurun, ed. *China, India, Japan and the Security of Southeast Asia*, 3–25. Singapore: Institute of Southeast Asian Studies, 1993.

——. "The Long Road to 'One Southeast Asia'." *Asian Journal of Political Science* 5, no. 1 (June 1997): 1–19.

Wahlstrom, Riitta. "The Challenge of Peace Education: Replacing Cultures of Militarism." In Elise Boulding, ed. *New Agendas for Peace Research: Conflict and Security Reexamined*, 171–83. Boulder, CO: Lynne Reinner, 1993.

Wallensteen, Peter. "Global Development Strategies for Conflict Prevention." Report to the Parliamentary Committee on Swedish Politics for Global Development (Globkom). August 2001.

Wallensteen, Peter and Margareta Sollenberg. "Armed Conflict, 1989–98." *Journal of Peace Research* 36, no. 5 (1999): 593–606.

Walt, Stephen M. "Building Up a New Bogeyman: Review of Huntington's *The Clash of Civilizations and the Remaking of World Order.*" *Foreign Affairs* 76, no. 3 (1998): 132–39.

——. "International Relations: One World, Many Theories." *Foreign Policy* 110 (1998): 29–46.

Walta Information Center. "Declaration of the 7th IGAD Summit of Heads of State and Governments." Djibouti, 26 November 1999. www.waltainfo.com/conflict/basicfacts/1999/december/fact1.htm.

Waltz, Kenneth N., ed. *The Use of Force: Military Power and International Politics*. 3rd ed. Lanham, MD: Rowman and Littlefield, 1999.

Walzer, Michael. "Can There Be a Decent Left?" *Dissent* 49, no. 2 (Spring 2002): 19–24.

———. "Five Questions About Terrorism." *Dissent* 49, no. 1 (Winter 2002): 5–11.

———. "Governing the Globe: What is the Best We Can Do?" *Dissent* 47, no. 4 (Fall 2000): 44–52.

———. *Just and Unjust Wars*. 2nd ed. New York: Basic Books, 1992.

———. *Just and Unjust Wars: A Moral Argument with Historical Illustrations*. New York: Basic Books, 1997.

———. *Thick And Thin: Moral Argument at Home and Abroad*. Notre Dame, Indiana: University of Notre Dame Press, 1994.

Wapner, Paul. *Environmental Activism and World Civic Politics*. Albany: State University of New York Press, 1996.

Wapner, Paul and Lester Edwin J. Ruiz, eds. *Principled World Politics: The Challenge of Normative International Relations*. Lanham, MD: Rowman and Littlefield, 2000.

Warah, Rasna. "Afghanistan's Silent Revolution." *HABITAT Debate* 8, no. 1 (March 2002): 19–20.

Ward, Michael, Ed Gallagher, Doug Delaney and Hugh Ferguson. "Task Force Kosovo: Adapting Operations to a Changing Security Environment." *Canadian Military Journal* 1, no. 1 (2000): 67–74.

Waterhouse, Rachel. "Women's Land Rights in Post-war Mozambique." Paper presented at the Inter-Regional Consultation in Kigali, Rwanda, February 1998.

Weber, Janet M. "Demands of OOTW on Ground Forces: Implications for Recruiting and Training." National War College Student Paper (1997). http://www.ndu.edu/ndu/library/n1/97-E-61.pdf.

Weber, Max. *Economy and Society, An Outline of Interpretive Sociology*. Guenther Roth and Claus Wittich, eds. Berkeley: University of California Press, 1978.

Weiss, Thomas G., ed. *Beyond UN Subcontracting: Task-Sharing with Regional Security Arrangements and Service-Providing NGOs*. London: Macmillan Press, 1998.

———. *Military-Civilian Interactions: Intervening in Humanitarian Crises*. Oxford: Rowman and Littlefield, 1999.

———. "Triage: Humanitarian Interventions in a New Era." *World Policy Journal* 11, no. 1 (Spring 1994): 59–69.

Weiss, Thomas and Leon Gordenker, eds. *NGOs, the UN, and Global Governance*. Boulder, CO: Lynne Reinner Publisher, 1996.

Wendt, Alexander. "Anarchy Is What States Make of It: The Social Construction of Power Politics." *International Organization* 46, no. 2 (Spring 1992): 391–426.

———. "Collective Identity Formation and the International State." *American Political Science Review* 88 (June 1994): 384–97.

———. "Constructing International Politics." *International Security* 20, no. 1 (Summer 1995): 71–81.

———. *Social Theory of International Politics*. Cambridge: Cambridge University Press, 1999.

Wesley, Michael. "The Asian Crisis and the Adequacy of Regional Institutions." *Contemporary Southeast Asia* 21, no. 1 (April 1999): 54–73.

West, Katrina. *Agents of Altruism: The Expansion of Humanitarian NGOs in Rwanda and Afghanistan*. Aldershot, UK: Ashgate, 2001.

Whitman, Jim. "Those That Have the Power to Hurt but Would Do None': The Military and Humanitarianism." *Journal of Humanitarian Assistance* (2001). http://www.jha.ac.uk/articles/a012.htm.

Whittaker, David J. *United Nations in the Contemporary World*. New York: Routledge, 1997.

Willetts, Peter. "From 'Consultative Arrangements' to 'Partnership': The Changing Status of NGOs in Diplomacy at the UN." *Global Governance* 6, no. 2 (2000): 191–212.

Williams, Michael C. "Civil-Military Relations and Peacekeeping." *Adelphi Papers* 321 (August 1998): 1–93.

Wilton Park. "Strengthening the United Nations in Conflict Prevention and Peace-Building." Wilton Park Conference WP667, Wilton Park, UK, 2002.

"Women and the Reconstruction of East Timor." *The La'o Hamutuk Bulletin* 2, no. 5 (August 2001). The East Timor Institute for Reconstruction Monitoring and Analysis. http://www.etan.org/lh/bulletins/bulletinv2n5.html.

Women at the Peace Table: Making a Difference, New York: UNIFEM, March 2000.

Woods, Samuel Kofi. "Civic Initiatives in the Peace Process." *Accord* 1 (2003). http://www.c-r.org/accord/lib/accord1/woods.shtml.

World Bank Group, Public Sector Governance. "Institutional and Governance Reviews (IGRs)." http://www1.worldbank.org/publicsector/igrs.htm.

World Bank. *Annual Report*. Washington, DC: World Bank, 1998.

——. *Annual Report*. Washington, DC: World Bank, 1999.

——. East Timor: Community Empowerment and Local Governance Project. Project Information Document. 27 December 1999. www.worldbank.org.

——. *Post-Conflict Reconstruction: The Role of the World Bank*. Washington, DC: The World Bank, 1998.

——. Rwanda: Community Reintegration and Development Project. Report No. PID6101. 23 November 1998. www.worldbank.org.

World Health Organization. *World Report on Violence and Health*. Geneva: World Health Organization, 2002. http://www5.who.int/violence_injury_prevention/download.cfm?id=0000000582.

Wright, Jared. "Conclusions: Problems and Prospects in Peace building." In Ann L. Griffiths, ed. *Building Peace and Democracy in Post Conflict Societies*, 163–71. Dalhousie University: Centre for Foreign Policy Studies, 1998.

Young, Oran. "International Regimes: Toward a New Theory of Institutions." *World Politics* 39, no. 1 (October 1986): 104–22.

"Youth Culture and Political Violence: The Sierra Leone Civil War." Special issue, *African Development* 22, nos. 2 and 3 (1997).

Zack-Williams, A.B. and Steve Riley. "Sierra Leone: the Coup and its Consequences." *Review of African Political Economy* 20, no. 56 (1993): 91–98.

Zartman, I. William. *Collapsed States: The Disintegration and Restoration of Legitimate Authority*. Boulder, CO: Lynne Reinner, 1995.

——, ed. *Governance as Conflict Management: Politics and Violence in West Africa*. Washington, DC: Brookings Institution Press, 1997.

——. "Inter-African Negotiation and State Renewal." In John W. Harbeson and Donald Rotchild, eds. *Africa in World Politics: Post–Cold War Challenges*, 142. 2nd ed. Boulder, CO: Westview Press, 1995.

——, ed. *Preventive Negotiation: Avoiding Conflict Escalation*. Lanham, MD: Rowman and Littlefield, 2000.

——. "Putting Things Back Together." In William I. Zartman, ed. *Collapsed States: The Disintegration and Restoration of Legitimate Authority*, 267–73. Boulder, CO: Lynne Reinner, 1995.

——. *Ripe for Resolution: Conflict and Intervention in Africa*. New York: Oxford University Press, 1995.

Zartman, I. William and J. Lewis Rasmussen, eds. *Peacemaking in International Conflict: Methods and Techniques*. Washington, DC: USIP Press, 1997.

Index